# Export Credit Insurance
## *(Opportunities & Challenges)*

# Export Credit Insurance

## *(Opportunities & Challenges)*


Edited by

**VELMURUGAN PS**
**P. PALANICHAMY**

Pondicherry University
Puducherry, India



**SERIALS PUBLICATIONS**
NEW DELHI (INDIA)

First Published – 2009

ISBN: 978-81-8387-254-6



*Published by*

**SERIALS PUBLICATIONS**
4800/24, 1st Floor, Ansari Road
Darya Ganj, New Delhi-110002 (India)
Phone : 23245225. Fax : 91-11-23272135
E-mail: serials@satyam.net.in

# CONTENTS

# ACKNOWLEDGEMENTS

We humbly thank our Vice- Chancellor Professor J.A.K. Tareen for his support and encouragement in taking up this volume. Thanks are also due to Prof. A. Balasubramanian (Director, culture and cultural Relations), Shri. S. Loganathan (Registrar), Dr. R. Pannerselvam (Dean), and the Department colleagues Prof. Malabika Deo, Prof.P. Natarajan, Dr. D. Lazar, Shri S. Aravanan, Shri. K.B. Nideesh. We are also grateful to Shri V. Viswanathan General Manager (ECGC) and Shri. Samuel Jesurathnam (Coface India), Shri. Suresh Johnson (SBI), Shri. Kumar (Director of Industries, Govt of Pondicherry) for all their help in bringing out this book including financial support.

January 2009
Pondicherry, India

**P. Palanichamy**
**Velmurugan PS**

# LIST OF CONTRIBUTORS

**Shri Viswanathen V.,** General Manager, Export Credit Guarantee Corporation of India, Mumbai.

**Dr. Velmurugan PS,** Lecturer, Department of Commerce, Pondicherry University.

**Dr. P. Palanichamy,** Professor, Department of Commerce, Pondicherry University.

**Ashok Phadtare,** Deputy General Manager, Export Credit Guarantee Corporation of India, Mumbai.

**Rohit Pandya,** Deputy General Manager, Export Credit Guarantee Corporation of India, Mumbai

**R. Mohan,** Deputy General Manager, Export Credit Guarantee Corporation of India, Mumbai.

**Dr. P. Natarajan,** Professor, Department of Commerce, Pondicherry University.

**V. Vijayakumar,** Research Scholar, Department of Commerce, Pondicherry University.

**Dr. T. Mallikarjunappa,** Professor, Department of Business Administration, Mangalore University.

**Dr. Malabika Deo,** Professor, Department of Commerce, Pondicherry University

**G. Saravanan,** Research Scholar, Department of Commerce, Pondicherry University.

**A. Mahalakshmi,** Lecturer, Department of Management Studies, M.S. Ramaiah Institute of Technology, Bangalore.

**Dr. R. Shanmugham,** Reader, Bharathiar School of Management & Entrepreneur Development, Bharathiar University, Coimbatore.

**Dr. K. Jeyachandran,** Reader in Commerce, Sourashtra College, Madurai.

**Dr. N. Sundaram,** Assistant Professor Vellore Institute of Technology VIT University, Vellore.

**Dr. K. Mohan,** Professor & Head Department of International Business, Pondicherry University.

**M. Suresh,** Research Scholar Department of International Studies Pondicherry University.

T. L. Prabhu, Final Year MBA Student Department of International Business, Pondicherry University.

**Rizwana,** Lecturer, Department of Management, M.S Ramaiah Institute of Technology, Bangalore.

**Dr. A. Kumudha,** Reader, Department of Business Management, P.S.G.R. Krishnammal College for Women, Coimbatore.

**S. Senthilkumar,** Research Scholar in the department of Management Studies, Annai Mathammal Sheela Engineering College, Namakkal.

**N. Priya,** Research Scholar Department of Commerce, Sri Ganesh College of Arts & Science, Salem

**Dr. J. Srinivasan,** Selection Grate Lecturer in Commerce Arignar Anna Govt. Arts College Cheyyar. Tiruvanamalai District.

**MS. Shanmugha Priya,** Research Scholar, Department of Commerce, PSG Colloge of Arts & Science, Coimbatore.

**Dr. K. M. Chinnadorai,** Head of the Department, Department of Commerce, PSG Colloge of Arts & Science, Coimbatore.

**Ms. M. Divya,** Research Scholar, Department of Commerce, PSG Colloge of Arts & Science, Coimbatore.

**Dr. N. Thangavel,** Principal (PG) Jeppiar Engineering College, Chennai.

**Mrs. R. Akila,** Senior Lecturer in Management, Jeppiar Engineering College, Chennai.

**Mr. R. Mahaprabhu,** Lecturer in Management, Jeppiar Engineering College, Chennai.

**Dr. Arati Basu,** Senior Faculty New Delhi Institute of Management, New Delhi

**Dr. Gajendra Singh,** Associate Professor Department of Business Management H.N.B Garhwal University, Uttarkhand.

**Charu Singhal,** Research Scholar Department of Business Management H.N.B Garhwal University, Uttarkhand.

**Dr. K. Krishnakumar,** Dean, Faculty of Management Studies VMKN Engineering Division, Vinayaga Mission University, Salem.

B. Nirmala Devi, Faculty of Management Studies VMKN Engineering Vinayaga Mission University, Salem.

S. Muruganandan, Research Scholar Department of Commerce Pondicherry University

**E. P. Sengottuvel,** Research Scholar Department of Commerce Pondicherry University.

P. Velmurugan, MBA Student, KSR-B-School, KSRCAS-Tiruchengode.

N. Chakravarthy, MBA Student, KSR-B-School, KSRCAS-Tiruchengode.

## HISTORY OF CREDIT INSURANCE

- Origins in the insurance of domestic credit risks in a number of European countries especially France, the UK, Germany and Switzerland, commencing in the middle of the 19th century.
- In Britain in the latter part of that century British merchants shipping goods to Australia created one of the first recorded demands for export credit insurance. After the First World War, the perceived need of many European countries to protect and expand their external reserves and to stimulate employment through the promotion of export activity added a new dimension to the concept of export credit insurance. This was clearly illustrated in 1919 when the British government launched the original official export credit scheme with the object of encouraging exports to eastern Europe where credit risks were considered to be a serious deterrent to the development of British exports.
- Since then a steadily increasing number of countries in both the developed and developing world have seen in the establishment and development of an export credit insurance scheme an important tool for promoting their export trade, increasing employment opportunities, and improving the credit side of their balance of payments. There has also been the growing incidence of risk in international trading arising from political unrest, trade embargos and the restrictions imposed by importing countries in balance of payments difficulties on the transfer of foreign exchange required to make payment to foreign suppliers. These factors have boosted the demand from exporters and their financiers for the protection of export credits.

## THE NEED FOR EXPORT CREDIT INSURANCE

- Imperfect information in banks, trading companies and exporter firms on overseas buyers and their economies.
- Today, credit in world trade is in greater demand than ever before. Due to the efforts that have been and are progressively

being made in various countries to develop and expand industries, competition has become increasingly intense in recent years. For most commodities, the seller's market has given place to buyer's market. This is creating demand for goods being sold on credit terms i.e. where payment is due to be made in the buyer's country after shipment. If goods are sold on credit terms, there will be a need for protecting oneself against bad debts just as there is need for protecting oneself against fire, theft, loss in transit etc.

- When goods are sold on credit and the buyer and seller are in the same country, the main risk involved is on the buyer, that is, the refusal or inability of the buyer to pay for the goods purchased by him. But, if the buyer and seller are in two different countries, then apart from the risk on the buyer, there are other risks which are created by the political, financial and economic situation in the buyer's country. Protection for such export credit risks world over can be provided by export credit insurance schemes.

## BENEFITS OF EXPORT CREDIT INSURANCE

- Export credit insurance reduces the risk involved in export related transactions.
- Export credit insurance is an effective marketing and sales tool. A policy enables to increase presence in new markets, be more competitive by extending higher and longer credit terms with buyers.
- Export credit insurance is a smart financial tool because it serves as collateral. Banks view insured clients as competent clients.
- Export credit insurance reduces the need for Letters of Credit. If an exporter has a policy, there is no need for his client to issue a Letter of Credit before buying his products or services. Most of the paperwork is done when the buyer is being approved for insurance. This reduces the amount of paperwork for both parties, and the expense that the buyer endures with every Letter of Credit.

## BASIC PRINCIPLES OF CREDIT INSURANCE

- The whole turnover principle followed by all export credit insurers is one of the main factors which have made it possible for them to achieve the results that they have in fact achieved.
- Co-insurance principle is another factor. By making the insured participate in the risk to a certain extent, they seek to achieve improvement in the quality of risks that they cover. It is an offence for the banks or the exporters to circumvent the co-insurance principle. Such offences would negate the principle of utmost good faith and attract the penalty of non-payment of claims. The percentage of cover provided differs with the nature of contract and the risks covered. The percentage of cover is some times varied for difficult markets.
- Credit appraisal: The basic responsibility for credit appraisal is that of the insured (exporter or banker). Carelessness in credit appraisal on the part of the insured is at his own peril. The insured is obliged to conduct his business with normal care and prudence. The credit insurer does not appraise proposals on behalf of the insured. He only examines to see whether it is a risk acceptable to him or not. But the credit insurer has certain advantages over the others in the matter of country risk analysis and appraisal of buyer risks. What distinguishes the credit insurer from others is (a) the insight that is gained by them over years of experience with a wide range of markets and (b) his access to the other Berne Union members (union of credit insurers) for information and experience. Through the Berne Union, he also brings pressure on International Credit Information Agencies for improvement in the quality of reports.
- Risks covered and not covered: Like most other insurers, the credit insurer also specifies the risks that he covers as well as the risks not covered. The cause of loss is thus of critical importance for the purpose of claim.
- Amount covered: The insurance covers loss of principal and not loss of interest. Further, the inability of the insured

to recover from the buyer/exporter has to be reasonably proved. The mere filing of a suit is not adequate; the credit insurer should also be satisfied that the insured has done his best and is yet unable to make good his loss. The principle followed in this regard is that the insured should conduct his business with normal care and prudence and act as if he is uninsured.

- Rights of subrogation: Credit insurers do not exercise the right of subrogation, although the documents may provide for it. In practice, the insured is expected to take effective steps for recovery after payment of claim. The principle of coinsurance spoken of earlier ensures that the insured involves himself actively in the recovery process.
- Existence of debt: Existence of a clear debt is a necessary condition. If there are disputes, the credit insurer will act only after it is settled and the debt is clearly established. In other words, normal trade risks are not covered.
- Utmost good faith: The principle of utmost good faith underlines export credit insurance as well. At the time of effecting the insurance, the insured should declare to the insurer all material facts affecting the risk. The principle holds good not only during the currency of the insurance contract but even after the payment of claim when recoveries are made.
- Indemnity: An insurance contract is a contract of indemnity. This means that it should not be entered for the purpose of speculation. The amount of compensation shall not exceed the actual amount of loss sustained and the loss shall be shared on the basis of contract entered into.

## THE BERNE UNION

- The Berne Union is an unique organization of 53 members from 42 countries. The union works for international acceptance of sound principles of export credit insurance and foreign investment insurance.
- It also provides a vital forum for the exchange of information, experience, and expertise between Members.

- The Berne Union and its members play a role of central importance in world trade, both as regards exports and foreign direct investments.
- Without the active involvement of Berne Union members, it will often not be possible to organize the financing and credits required for projects on any scale, especially in developing countries.
- Currently, Berne Union members cover 7% of global trade.
- In the period 1982-2003, Berne Union members supported trade exports world wide to the tune of USD 8452 billion, investment to the tune of USD 167 billion. Total claims paid are USD 184 billion.
- Combined outstanding commitments of Berne Union members as at 31st December 2002 was USD 550 billion out of which USD 485 billion was in respect of export credit insurance and USD 65 billion was in respect of investment insurance
- Members of the Berne Union meet together at least twice a year and there are Workshops and one special Seminar each year covering various technical business topics

## RECENT DEVELOPMENTS IN EXPORT CREDIT INSURANCE

- There is considerable growth in private market capacity and internationalization of the industry. There has been a significant growth in international private sector insurance as many ECAs have privatized their Short Term business supported by an increasing reinsurance capacity from the private reinsurance market, both for commercial and political export credit risks.
- The growth strategies of the larger insurers have led to a high degree of market consolidation. Three European based insurers (Coface, Euler Hermes, Atradius) now dominate the world market. Further globalisation will be driven by a need for a geographic spread of risk and large opportunities for growth in North America and East Asia.

- Market consolidation is intensifying competition and strengthening market capacity and appetite for risk. It is also resulting in products not traditionally provided by credit insurers, such as credit information and debt management services that take advantage of the enormous data bases of the large insurers.
- The market is now dominated by a small number of large international companies that are investing heavily in IT databases and e-commerce products for deeper, faster market penetration, including for smaller exporters.
- Another emerging feature is a range of financial instruments in the private sector that are providing some competition to traditional credit insurance as a means of risk management. These include securitisation, factoring and forfaiting.
- Most credit insurers are now opting for tailor-made policies to suit exporters' requirements in addition to the traditional wholeturnover schemes.
- Another development is the blurring of the distinction between commercial and political risks, leading to what is generally known as the grey area, such as a series of claims stemming from the Argentinean crisis that were due to host Government's actions. The increased demand for Political Risk Insurance coverage of transactions that involve the government in some commercial relationship to the project has blurred the distinction further, especially in the Medium and Long Term sector.

## CO-OPERATION WITH OTHER ECA

- Co-operation Agreements/MoU, may be entered into with counterparts and other export promotional agencies to:
  - support trade between the two countries by provision of full range of facilities to exporters and banks in the respective countries;
  - consult and identify any obstacles to trade and seek solutions;
  - identify projects in mutually acceptable third countries in which goods and services of both the countries may be involved;

- exchange information on buyers/banks;
- exchange information on legal and regulatory framework and economic situation in the two countries;
- co-operate in respect of recovery of dues on the claims paid;
- work out specific co-operation arrangement for joint insurance or parallel insurance or re-insurance arrangements with the expansion of trade between the two countries and the opportunities that would emerge; and to organise training for officials.

# 2

# ELEMENT OF RISK IN INTERNATIONAL TRADE AND THE ROLE OF EXPORT CREDIT AGENCIES IN MITIGATING THE RISK–AN OVERVIEW

**Velmurugan PS. & P. Palanichamy**

## INTRODUCTION

It is believed that insurance is one of those subjects around which it is almost impossible to generate passion. It has a dry, boring image, which is perhaps justified when one consider that he/she uses it only in an emergency. However, credit insurance is somewhat different, and it is exciting. Insurance emerged from dramatic events or series of events which illustrated people its usefulness. Fire insurance emerged following the Great fire of London. Marine insurance grew from the growth in merchant traders in the 19$^{th}$ century. Likewise credit insurance has a history.

The World War–I, gave birth to organized credit insurance movement. It is better to cast ones mind back to what history tells of those days. Germany was defeated. Britain and its allies, and France, were victorious but exhausted. Even the mighty USA had enough. Europe's economies were on their knees, manpower depleted, infrastructure damaged, trading relationships destroyed, shortage of materials were felt and so on. The result was inflation and stagnation and then depression. Millions became unemployed and the fabric of society was threatened. Faced with this scenario, the Western Governments had to try to kick-start their economies. Many initiatives were aired and quite a few became reality. In Germany, National Socialism became established and formed the bedrock for the next conflict. In Britain, socialism prospered and nationalization of the mines and railways was under consideration. Any initiative with half a chance was also considered. It was in this fevered atmosphere that credit insurance was delivered.

To see the relevance of credit insurance, it is necessary to view the contrast as to what has happened up to that time in the orderly conduct of trade with what was to follow. Most trade in Western economies was within each countries' borders and export and import trade was whether with a countries' colonies or conducted by specialist import/export merchants on the back of long-standing relationships. Trust and integrity were vital factors in facilitating the free trade and the unsecured credit was not very common unless there was a strong relationship.

All these arrangements became strained by economic or national pressure and as trade became more international, the old networks became less reliable. At the same time, to expand trade, companies had to take more risks. Against this background, Western Governments fostered private insurance companies to develop credit insurance within their own country and the Governments themselves underwrote export credit insurance. The growth of credit insurance was particularly strong in Western Europe and most of the world supply until the late 20$^{th}$ century was concentrated in Britain, France, Germany, Holland, Belgium and Italy. The credit insurers prospered as, they were often, monopolies or duopolies. Commonly, there would be one insurer for domestic trade and another for export trade within each country.

So far as the user of credit insurance was concerned, this situation had two major effects. Firstly, the product and price of it were dictated by the insurer and the insured had to buy it as offered or do without it. Secondly, it gave the insurer enormous amount of power to influence the conduct of trade, where the insurer was covering a domestic trade which was a heavy user of credit insurance, such as the UK timber industry, the insurer could literally determine the survival or otherwise of a trader. Where the insurer was a Government covering export trade, credit insurance was a significant tool in the conduct of foreign policy with favorable credit terms and subsidized finance being key elements of the insurance package.

Such power created both friends and enemies for the credit insurers and credit insurance business. They were often either loved or hated. The end of this unhealthy situation was brought about by three changes to the world economy. Firstly, monetarism triumphed over centralized controlled economies such as Russia's and the world economy moved in this direction. Secondly, the developing countries, such as China, started industrialization and now supply manufactured goods at a much lower cost. Finally, the principal countries with significant credit insurance business became one economy in 1992 and, for the first time in its history, credit insurance became subject to market pressures. These pressures have resulted in benefits for the consumer in so far as the cover available has become more driven by demand and supply, the price is keener and the service which banks upon the product is more responsive to user's needs.

Credit insurance provides companies with coverage for outstanding commercial receivables, protecting against risk of buyer default or insolvency. In addition to managing credit risk, credit insurance supports financing needs by reducing the risk of non-payment of trade receivables, whereby firms can borrow at lower interest rates.

Historically, credit insurance has been more popular in Europe than elsewhere. Private trade credit insurance premiums amount to US $ 4.2 billion worldwide, with 84 per cent of that in Europe (i.e., US $ 3.5 billion). The annual premium growth in Europe has been on an average of about 5 per cent over the last 10 years, keeping pace with economic growth. In the United States, premium growth has been more rapid, about 10 per cent per year, but from a smaller base, US premiums are only about US$ 0.5 billion or 12 per cent of worldwide premiums. Given the low penetration of premium growth in the US market, the premium growth is expected to remain strong.

The market for credit insurers is changing rapidly. In the past decade, a consolidated market share total has increased the share of European premiums of the five leading companies– Euler, Coface, Hermes, Gerling and NCM (NCM is 90 per cent

**Figure 1**
**Flow of Transaction under Credit Insurance Cover**

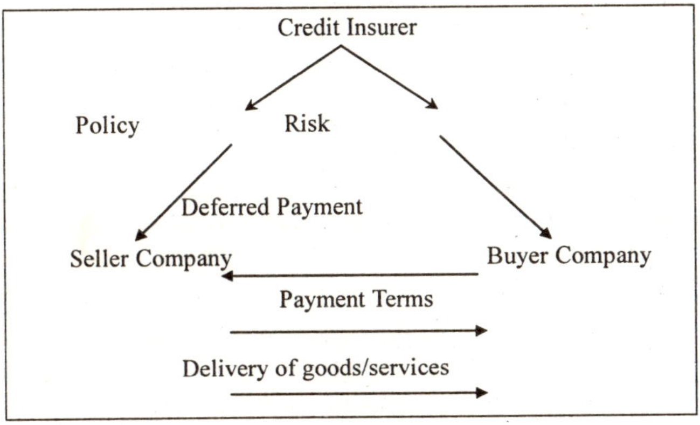


owned by Swiss Re) from 50 per cent to 80 per cent. Competition has pushed credit insurers to enter new markets and to provide new products and unbundled services such as credit information, debt collection, lines of credit for commercial purchases etc.

The outlook of the credit insurers is promising. Credit insurers enjoy a significant competitive advantage due to their vast experience in credit risk management and their proprietary databases on millions of companies worldwide. This expertise and information on trade receivables is the basis for underwriting credit risk. It can be used to provide new services to credit departments, in addition to credit insurance. The market for credit insurance is expected to grow by about 5 per cent to 7 per cent a year in Europe over the next five years, as the export growth accelerates. North American premium growth is estimated to be about 10 per cent per year.

Credit insurers are beginning to provide new products and to un bundle existing products by separately providing information and risk coverage. Related services, such as invoicing and debt collection, are providing additional sources of earnings. The internet is facilitating these developments by providing a less expensive distribution channel and high-speed communication to support services such as claims adjustment etc. The explosive growth of business-to-business internet transactions is providing an opportunity for credit insurers and the credit insurers are enhancing their fee-based revenues by leveraging their proprietary information on the credit worthiness of buyers. Finally, the growing market for derivatives and asset backed securities presents opportunities and challenges for credit insurers. Credit insurers can provide asset specific credit enhancement, particularly for the underlying assets of the asset backed commercial paper of trade receivables.

There have been three stages in the internationalization of credit insurance. In the first stage, credit insurers were mono liners, focusing almost exclusively on domestic policy holders. There was generally one domestic and one (often state owned) export credit insurer in each country. A characteristic feature of credit insurance is that the risk is not often the insured (the seller) but the insured's customer (the buyer). Hence, the local credit insurers mainly monitored the domestic risks and exchanged information with the other foreign credit insurers when insuring exports.

In the second stage, credit insurers insured the foreign companies selling to buyers located in the credit insurer's home country. The insurer served foreign clients, but dealt with domestic risks. In the third stage, credit insurers sell insurance in several countries, which requires local expertise in these countries to monitor trade credit risk. This is very challenging for credit insurers since they are all small compared to a typical global company. To control monitoring costs, credit insurers have entered into local joint ventures with each other and have become closely aligned with or integrated by multi line insurers with foreign affiliates.

The need for credit insurance arises from two simple facts. First, buying on credit from suppliers is the single largest source of short-term debt for the companies. Accounts receivable or trade credit account for up to 50 per cent of total assets of a typical non-financial corporation. Second, when goods are sold on credit, there is a risk to the sellers that their customers may default or pay later. Sellers often use credit insurance, factoring, letters of credit and other financial instruments to reduce the volatility in the earnings by the defaults of their customers.

## THE RISK IN EXPORT TRADE

The growth of national economies depends to a large extent on the development of international trade. All countries must export and import products, whether primary commodities or manufactured commodities or services. However, credit is needed to bridge the time gap and physical distance between production, distribution and consumption of goods. Credit insurance, therefore promotes trade and in turn trade promotes economic development.

One has to notice that once the credit terms are extended by the exporter, he/she faces the risk of non-payment. Export credit insurance is an integral part of the export financing process. Export credit insurance institutions perform the following functions for the exporters and the exporting country.

(1) Credit insurance institutions' main function is to protect against the risk of non-payment. The exporter is protected against losses or protracted failure to pay on the part of the buyer or buyer's country, which of course gives the exporter an instrument to protect his own financial position.

(2). By protecting the exporter's assets through credit insurance, the insurance policy helps a lot in facilitating the mobilization of working capital to finance transactions. Obtaining sufficient working capital is a crucial factor for exporters to take full advantage of the opportunities in the international market. Lack of information and lack of collateral cause banks to refuse financial assistance to the exporters, or alternatively charge higher interest rates, thus increasing export prices, and hampering exporters' competitiveness.

(3) In order to expand or even to maintain existing business, companies are forced to grant export credit. Capital is scarce commodity and many a companies are only willing to buy when offered financial assistance. Exporters can safely offer credit lines and thus increase sales volumes by securing the credit risks involved. This may also create a competitive advantage towards other suppliers of the exporter's products or services, as the insured exporter may, because of his credit insurance cover, be in a position to grant credit to supplier credit, while other exporters may not have this possibility.

(4) Many firms lose more money from delayed payments than bad debts. Credit insurers offer collection services and can use the economies of scale in this respect to their advantage. The accumulation of claims with an insurer, through the insurer's international standing and contacts, places it in a stronger position to collect overdue debts than any of the individual creditors separately. Exporters can file claim if he does not receive the payment within the so-called waiting period. Many export credit agencies allow a waiting period of six months after the due date of the invoice.

(5) Credit insurance companies also play an important role with respect to developments in the exporter's buyer portfolio. Potential clients can be checked at any time by the credit insurer with regard to their creditworthiness, as a consequence of which the exporter will be in a position to be more proactive towards new clients and/or potential business partners. Since the credit insurance company constantly monitors the risks in its portfolio, the

exporter may be informed immediately of the financial situation.

(6) Compared to domestic trade, additional uncertainties in international trade bring additional risks and grater transaction costs than the domestic trade. If exports to markets with excessive credit risks can be prevented, the country benefits. If better information makes exports possible to buyers in countries with a sound credit risk, the country gains in terms of production capacity, employment and foreign-exchange earnings.

(7) Credit insurance guarantees the continuity of industry and protects against hazards from external factors.

Though, there are no set rules, regulations and standards and link between Export volumes and Export credit insurance, it is clear that export credit insurance provides exporters with an instrument to facilitate their international business.

The export trade normally has three types of risk associated with it viz., Credit Risk, Exchange Rate Risk and Transfer Risk. The risk of insolvency, default, fraud or unwillingness to accept the goods by the buyer, country risk etc., are termed as 'Credit Risk'. Exchange rate risk arises because of the fluctuations in the rate of exchange between the currencies between the time of entering into commercial contract and the settlement of trade i.e., actual payment is made. The possibility of exchange rate movement is referred as 'Exchange Risk'. 'Transfer risk' exists when there is a balance of payment crisis arises and exchange or trade controls are introduced in the Buyer's country which prevents payment in a currency other than the Buyer's domestic currency.

The exporters' finance department must evaluate the buyer's creditworthiness or purchase credit services such as credit insurance. The finance department adds value to its company by providing information to the marketing department on the credit quality of targeted clients. In addition, the finance department can establish the maximum line of credit to be extended to a buyer.

External agencies–including credit insurers can provide country, sector and company specific information. The credit insurer has an information advantage over a single company since it has more information on company specific behavior on payments for receivables. The information base covers more products over a longer time horizon than the single company information base of the finance. At least one company, COFACE has begun to market its information database as stand-alone product. Exporters can purchase credit information from credit insurers or other firms with company credit history databases.

Exporters must decide whether or not to self insure or transfer some of the trade credit risk. It provides value by managing the risk associated with the company's accounts receivable. Part of the trade credit risk can be transferred to a credit insurer or to the capital market, via a credit derivative. Credit insurers are now beginning to provide non-traditional risk transfer products such as derivatives.

Once the goods or services are delivered, the accounts receivable need to be converted into cash on a timely basis. This requires collection management and in case of non-payment, legal actions or other types of collection activities should be initiated. Many of these functions can be "outsourced" from external specialist companies, although certain credit insurers have also begun to provide these services. Companies can contract to have collection of receivables done by an external firm. This could include dealings with debt collectors and credit insurers if there is a problem of collecting the payments. NCM, for example, has decided to purchase collection agencies to provide an extra service to its clients and additional revenue for itself.

Exploring viable export credit management alternatives can be time consuming but it can have significant rewards.

The five *key export management areas* in which exporters should concentrate are:

- *Payment terms:* The payments may be through the Bill of Exchange, or Letter of Credit (LC) or through Cash against Documents etc., If it is under LC, ensure whether the terms comply with it. Unable to comply with the terms may lead to withhold the payments by the establishing bank. The LC is as goods as that of the issuing bank. If the issuing bank is in financial difficulty or if the market is experiencing economic problems, then the bank may not be able to honor the LC. So, when exporting to a new buyer or new market, *more secure payment terms must be used.*

- *Credit information:* Set and agree credit limit with insurer. Review credit limits on a regular basis and share information with credit insurer since external factors outside the control of the buyer can affect their ability to pay.
- *Assessment of the buyer:* It is important to have good relationship with the buyer. By understanding how well they are performing, one can make better decisions and manage issues that may arise before they become a problem. Understand the legal, cultural and economic elements of the buyer market. Visit the buyers place if possible and ask for information like financial statements and company brochure etc. Exporting to diversified buyers in various countries may be less vulnerable to uncertainties affecting one industry or market. If any problem is encountered with a buyer it is better to stop exporting to that particular buyer and ask for modified payment terms.
- *Monitoring Payment:* It is better to train employees to be familiar with the buyer, his requirements, and how to deal with payment problems etc., Ensure that all the documents are prepared correctly as per contract or as per LC. Formulate a plan in the event of payment dispute.
- *Risk management:* The exporter has to decide whether to accept the risk of possible non-payment or sell down the risk. Export credit insurance agencies are the most logical acceptors or purchasers of the risk. Export credit insurance can help companies to leverage a

competitive advantage, minimize credit risk and negotiate trade finance.

Gary Mendell in his article states that the normal payment terms of cash in advance and letters of credit are no longer competitive in the international marketplace. World merchandise trade is experiencing trading on open account credit terms. The exporters are supposed to extend competitive terms in order to grow. In such a situation the exporter can protect the foreign receivables against non-payment losses with an export credit insurance policy. Export credit insurance is not only a viable means of securing payment but also an effective sales tool to help increase order quantities by allowing the buyers to economically stock more products. He further states that Export credit insurance can also be an effective sales tool for acquiring new overseas customers. It allows the exporter to extend competitive credit terms to new buyers, to enter new risky markets and the emerging economies.

Insured foreign receivables are an attractive base for raising funds from bankers. Export credit insurance protects the exporter against commercial and political risk like buyers insolvency, protracted non payment, fluctuations in demand, natural disasters, poor economic conditions, war, revolution, currency inconvertibility, changes and import and export regulations etc., When cash in advance and letters of credit aren't feasible or desirable, exporter can extend competitive credit terms overseas, and be confident of getting paid, with export credit insurance. When a buyer fails to pay, exporter can file an insurance claim with the export credit insurer and payment will be pursued through international channels and claims will be settled pending recovery efforts.

Export credit insurance is available from Government and private agencies. They are referred in international trade as *"Export Credit Agencies"*. Geetha Muralidhar, states that several types of policies are available with credit insurers that may suit to the need of the exporter. The cost of export credit insurance is cheaper when compared to the risk associated with the international trade. It is predicted that the export credit insurance will grow at a faster rate in the future owing to the increased competition in international trade and the subsequent demand for longer credit period. Export credit insurance is growing annually at the rate of 20 per cent in Asia.

ECA is an institution with a vested interest in promoting its country's exports through various programs of export financing such as loans, guarantees and insurance. Many of the ECAs perform the dual role of export financing and credit insurance (ECGC of UK, EXIM Bank of China & EXIM Bank of Thailand). Some countries have separate agencies for providing this services (EXIM Bank and ECGC of India).Every member of OECD except Iceland has an agency that extends official support to export credit by one means or another. Some ECA's are Governmental agencies while others are private companies.

With the backing of their respective Governments, ECA's are able to take on longer terms and higher risks. Large scale projects that need sufficient credit and carry high investment risk would simply not be viable without the involvement of ECAs. ECAs have often been compared with multinational organizations such as the World Bank, the International Finance Corporation (IFC) and those established on a regional basis such as the Asian Development Bank (ADB) in terms of support they provide to the development of International trade. Japan's Bank for International Cooperation, established in 1950, is the oldest ECA in Asia. A number of ECAs were created during the course of economic development of many Asian Countries in line with their Government's export oriented strategy.

ECA's are classified into four categories. Namely, Multilateral ECA's, Official ECA's, Private Credit Insurers and Oversight Groups:

**Multilateral Export Credit Agencies**

- African Export-Import Bank (Afreximbank, Africa).
- Corporacion Andina de Fomento (CAF, Andean Countries)
- European Bank for Reconstruction and Development (EBRD, Central & Eastern Europe).

- Inter-American Development Bank (IADB, Latin America).
- Islamic Corporation for the Insurance of Investment and Export Credit (ICIEC, part of the Islamic Development Bank).
- Multilateral Investment Guarantee Agency (MIGA, part of World Bank).

**Official Export Credit Agencies**

Asuransi Ekspor Indonesia (ASEI, Indonesia)

Banco de Inversion y Comercia Exterior (BICE, Argentina)

Banco Nacional de Comercio Exterior SNC (Bancomext, Mexico)

BNDES-EXIM (Ex-Finamex, Brazil)

Compagnie Francise d Assuracne pour le Commerce Exterieur (COFACE, France)

Companhia de Seguro de Creditos S.A (COSEC, Portugal)

Compania Espanola de Seguros de Credito a la Exportacion, S.A (CESCE, Spain)

Corporacion Financiera Nacional Fondo de Promocion de Exportaciones (CFN Fopex, Ecuador)

Credit Guarantee Insurance Corporaion of Africa Limited (CGIC, South Africa)

Credit Insurance Zimbabwe (Credsure, Zimbabwe)

Croatian Bank for Reconsruction and Development (HBOR, Croatia)

ECICS Credit Insurance Lts., (ECICS, Singapore)

EXGO (a division of State Insurance, New Zealand)

Export Credit Bank of Turkey (Turk Eximbank, Turkey)

Export Credit Guarantee Agency (ECGA, Oman)

Export Credit Insurance Corporation (Kuke, Poland)

Export Credits Guarantee Department (ECGD, UK)

Export Development Canada (EDC, Canada)

Export Finance and Insurance Corporation (EFIC, Australia)

Export Guarantee and Insurance Corporation (Egap, Czech republik)

Export-Import Bank of India (EXIM Bank, India)

Export-Import Bank of Korea (Keximbank, South Korea)

Export-import Bank of the Russian Federation (Eximbank, Russia)

Export-import Bank of Thailand (Thai Exim, Thailand)

Export-import Bank of Trinidad & Tobago (Eximbank, Trinidad & Tobago)

Export-import Bank of the United States (EXIM, US)

Export Credit Insurance Organisation (ECIO, Greece)

Export Kredit Fonden (EFS, Denmark)

Export Risk Guarantee Agency (ERG, Switzerland)

Exportkreditnamnden (EKN, Sweden)

Finnvera plc (Finnvera, Finland)

Guarantee Institute for Export Credits (GIEK, Norway)

Hermes Kreditversicherungs-AG (Hermes, Germany)

Hong Kong Export Credit Insurance Corporation (HKEC, Hong Kong)

Hungarian Export Credit Insurance Ltd., (MEHIB, Hungary)

Israel Foreign Trade Risks Insuance Corporation (Iftric, Israel)

Istituto per I Servizi Assicurativi ecl Creito all'Espotazione (Sace,Italy)

Japan Bank for Interntaional Cooperation (formerly JExim)

Korea Export Insurance Corporation (KEIC, South Korea)

Malaysia Export Credit Insurance Berhad (MECIB, Malaysia)

Nederlandsche Credietverzkering Maatschappij NV (NCM,Netherlands)

Norwegian Guarantee Institute for Export Credits (Giek, Norway)

Office Natioanl du Ducroire (OND, Belgium)

Oesterreichische Kontrollbank Aktiergesellschaft (OeKB, Austria)

Overseas Private Investment Corporation (OPIC, United States)

Segurexpo de Columbia (Segurexpo, Columbia)

Slovene Export Credit Insurance Corporation (SLECIC, Sri Lanka)

Svensk Esportkredit (SEK, Sweden)

Uzbekinvest National Export-Import Insurance Company (Unic, Uzbekistan)

**Private Export Credit Insurance**

CAN Insurance (CNA, USA)

Cox Insurance Political Risk Unit (CPRU, UK)

Credito y Caucion (Spain)

EULER Group (France)

Eurofactor (France)

Exporters Insurance Company (Bermuda)

Hiscox Trade Credit Insurance (UK)

Seguradora Brasileira de Credito a Exportacao (SBCE, Brazil)

**Organizations to Over See the Functioning of ECA's**

*ECA Watch:* Runs a reform campaign hoping to get ECAs to adopt and upgrade environment and social policies.

*Berne Union:* This union works for international acceptance of sound principles of export credit insurance and foreign investment insurance. The Berne Union (International Union of Credit and Investment Insurers) was founded in 1934 by four members (France, Italy, Spain and U.K) and now has 52 members from 43 countries.

Drawing on 69 years of experience, the Berne Union plays an important role in acting as a facilitator for cross-border trade and investments by providing its members with a forum for cooperation and professional interaction. The Berne Union has extensive international contacts and speaks for its members both with the international financial institutions and with individual buyer countries.

The union works for international acceptance of sound principles of export insurance and foreign investment insurance. It also provides a vital forum for exchange of information, experience, and expertise between members.

The purpose of the Berne Union is to work for:

- The international acceptance of sound principles of export insurance and the establishment and maintenance of discipline in the terms of credit for international trade.
- International cooperation in encouraging a favorable investment *climate* and in developing and maintaining sound principles of foreign investment insurance; and
- The exchange of information, assistance, expertise and advice in relation both to the commercial and political risks involved in export credit insurance, to the political risks involved in foreign investment insurance and to the range of associated matters arising thereto.

To achieve these aims the members have agreed that they will:

- Exchange information and furnish the Union with the information necessary for the accomplishment of its tasks;
- Maintain and adhere to the maximum credit terms and starting points for credit etc., set out in a series of Agreements and Understandings;
- Consult together on a continuing basis, carry out studies and participate in agreed projects; and
- Cooperate closely and, where ever appropriate take coordinated action; and cooperate with other international institutions concerned with these matters;

There are three *specialist committees* within the Berne Union;

- Short-term Export Credit Insurance Committee (Supported by Technical sub-committee)
- Medium and Long Term Export Credit Insurance Committee (Supported by Technical sub-committee)

- Investment Insurance Committee (Supported by a Technical Panel)

  Both the state-linked organizations and private insurance companies make up the membership. Members meet every year in the form of an Annual General Meeting, and on other occasions for specialist committee meetings, workshops and seminars.

**Table 1**
**Important ECA's in Asia Pacific Region**

| *Country* | *Institution* | *Year of Establish-ment* | *Major Services* |
|---|---|---|---|
| Australia | Export Finance & Insurance Corporation | 1956 | Short, Medium and long term Guarantees, Insurance and finance |
| China | The Export-Import Bank of China | 1994 | Medium and long term guarantees, short and medium term insurance and medium and long term finance |
| India | Export Import Bank of India | 1982 | Medium and Long term financing |
| Indonesia | PT Bank Export Indonesia | 1999 | Short term Guarantees and Refinancing facility |
| Japan | Japan bank for International Cooperation | 1950 | Medium and Long term finance, guarantee and overseas investment insurance |
| Korea | Export-Import Bank of Korea | 1976 | Medium and long term finance, guarantee, trade refinancing and overseas investment credit |
| Malaysia | Export-Import Bank of Malaysia Berhad | 1995 | Guarantees and medium and long range finance |
| New Zealand | HIH Casualty and General Insurance | 1997 | Short and medium term insurance |
| Philippines | Trade and Investment corporation of Philippines | 1977 | Short, medium and long term guarantees and short term insurance |
| Thailand | Export-Import Bank of Thailand | 1993 | Short, medium and long term guarantee and finance |

## Top Export Credit Agencies in the World and their Aims

### *CESCE, Spain*

CESCE is a Spanish export credit insurance organization which is governed by a law which regulates its activities and is considered as a part of the Spanish scheme to promote exports financing administered by the Ministry of Economy and in particular by the state trade department.

*COFACE, France*

The COFACE group's mission is to help businesses to limit their political and commercial risks by providing business information and credit insurance. Its products and services cover not only the risks associated with trading activities and the related financial transactions, but also those attached to overseas investments.

**ECGD, United Kingdom**

To benefit the economy of United Kingdom by helping exporters of UK's goods and services and UK's firms to invest overseas by providing guarantees, insurance and reinsurance against loss, taking into account the Government's international policies.

*EDC, Canada*

Being a recognized leader in providing ground-breaking commercial and financial solutions for companies of all sizes, helping them to succeed in the global marketplace and create enduring prosperity for Canada.

*EKN, Sweden*

To promote Swedish exports by issuing guarantees. EKN shall offer the Swedish export companies support which corresponds to the supports available for their competitors in other countries. EKN's activities shall be financially self supportive.

*Exim Bank, USA*

Exim Bank's mission is to support US exports and sustain US jobs through exports. It provides financing, guarantees and insurance.

*GERLING NCM, Netherlands*

To create the conditions for Dutch exporters to enable them to compete on equal terms with their foreign competitors, by providing credit-insurance and guarantees complementary to the market.

### *HERMES, Germany*

HERMES primary objective as stated in its official export credit guarantee scheme is the promotion of exports. Those eligible for promotion contain aspects such as job security, structural consideration, defense of traditional markets as well as the importance of a project in terms of foreign policy and development aid.

### *NEXI, Japan*

NEXI was established in order to provide administrative services efficient enough to address the globalization of financing and the diversifying needs of Japanese companies.

### *SACE, Italy*

No specific goals other than to grant insurance and reinsurance cover against payment default connected to political, economic, commercial and exchange risks or natural disaster risk faced by Italian exporters having trade relations with foreign buyers.

### *Atradius*

Atradius, a multinational insurer, is the world's second largest credit insurance and credit Management Company with a global presence with global market share of 25 per cent and more than 1.3 billion EUR premium incomes. Atradius operates in 43 countries and insures trade worth over 300 billion EUR against the risk of non-payment.

To sum up, countries around the world have realized the importance of helping their exporting community by making available the equal support enjoyed by their competitors in other countries.

## Selected Asian Export Credit Guarantee Agencies

### *Hong Kong Export Credit Insurance Corporation (HKECIC)*

HKECIC was created by a statute in 1966 to encourage and support expansion of foreign trade and its commitments are fully guaranteed by the government. HKECIC's capital is fully subscribed by the government. HKECIC operates without any subsidy from the government and is autonomous in its day to day operations. It has a 12 member advisory board consisting of representatives from the finance, insurance, legal, trade, and industrial sectors and government officials.

HKECIC's facilities include insurance cover for short term consumer goods and services and medium and long term credit and export guarantees (one to five years). HKECIC provides export guarantees directly to exporter's banks in respect of export of capital goods and projects on medium and long term credit. Such guarantees are available only to an exporter who has been issued a specific policy and guarantees are generally provided only after the goods have been shipped.

100% indemnity is provided to the bank for the amount financed with a 10% recourse to the exporter. Guarantees can be issued in all major currencies with the exchange rate to be fixed at the time of issuance of guarantee.

### *Malaysian Export Credit Insurance Berhad (MECIB)*

MECIB which was established in 1977 offers a range of export insurance and guarantee facilities to Malaysian exporters. Its facilities include comprehensive short-term insurance cover, specific policies for capital goods and bankers' export finance insurance policies. Export Credit Guarantee facilities include both short term bank guarantees (Banker's Export Finance Insurance Policy–BEFIP) and medium and long term bank guarantees (Buyer credit and bond indemnity support facility).

The BEFIP indemnifies commercial banks against loss arising from failure of an exporter/supplier (indirect exporter) to repay export loans/advances and/or protracted default. The policy is available for both pre-shipment and post-shipment financing by commercial banks. BEFIP covers 75% of loss for pre-shipment loans/advances and 85% for post-shipment loans/advances. Only the principal sum is covered and the maximum repayment term is 180 days.

Medium and long term guarantees applies to loans given by a lender in Malaysia to an overseas buyer or bank for purchase of Malaysian goods and services. MECIB also provides guarantees to banks to encourage issue of bonds as required by overseas buyers/principals of capital goods/projects.

**Pakistan Insurance Corporation (PIC)–Export Credit Guarantee Scheme (ECGS)**

ECGS was established in 1962 and is wholly funded by the government through PIC. Two types of guarantees are available–for pre-shipment risks and post shipment risks. Export Finance Guarantee covers risks of banks on the pre-shipment side in respect of losses sustained in connection with loans granted to exporters. The policy requires all banks to insure all loans made by them for exports during the12 month period of the policy. Cover is available for manufacturing, processing or purchasing of goods for export under firm agreement/contract of sale.

EGCS pays two-thirds of the amount of loss within a maximum of 6 months after due date of payment and also it (ECGS) had established that the amount cannot be recovered from the customer. On the post-shipment side, two types of policies are available-Comprehensive Post-Shipment Guarantee and Selected Markets Guarantee. Under both the policies, all goods except raw cotton, raw jute, perishables and bulk food grains are covered against

(i) Insolvency of buyer abroad or his failure to pay within 6 months from due date for goods of which he has accepted delivery.

(ii) Political and economic risks inherent in trading overseas

(iii) Risks of repudiation or refusal of the foreign buyer to take delivery of goods ; and

(iv) Any other cause of loss occurring outside Pakistan or not within the control of the exporter or buyer.

***Export Credit Insurance Corporation of Singapore (ECICS)***

ECICS Credit Insurance, formerly known as the Export Credit Insurance Corporation of Singapore was incorporated in June 1991 to take over the business of credit insurance of ECICS

Holdings. A member of the Berne Union, ECICS provides insurance services and guarantees banks directly in respect of advances made to exporters

There are two basic policies–Letter of Assignment and Bonds. Letter of Assignment enables the policy holder to assign to the bank his rights to claim proceeds. All risks related to the buyer under the comprehensive policy such as insolvency and transfer delay are covered. The issue of performance advance payment and bid bonds are also available.

### *Sri Lanka Export Credit Insurance Corporation (SLECIC)*

SLECIC was established in 1978 under a separate Act for the purpose of export credit guarantee and insurance facilities to exporters. SLECIC provides pre-shipment and post-shipment guarantees. Pre-shipment guarantees are provided to commercial banks which grant credit facilities to exporters for the purchase, manufacture and packing of goods for export against confirmed orders or in connection with the execution of an export order. Guarantee coverage is 66% which protects commercial banks against non-payment by exporters. Post-shipment guarantees supplement pre-shipment guarantees as it is designed to cover commercial banks from losses in respect of advances made to exporters by way of discount, purchase or negotiation of export bills

SLECIC has an export performance guarantee scheme which is designed to assist exporter's secure Bank guarantees that may be called upon to furnish to either Government Authorities in Sri Lanka or to parties awarding contracts of construction works or services in the course of their export business. Other guarantee schemes include Export Production Credit Guarantee, Guarantees to gem exporters and guarantee schemes for small and medium scale exporters. The latter guarantees up to 75% and 85% against advances to exporters who have a turnover of Rs. 50,00,000.

### *Korea Export Insurance Corporation (KEIC)*

KEIC was established in July 1992 and took over the KEXIM's export insurance and guarantee business. Under the Export

Credit Bank Guarantee Scheme, KEIC provides repayment guarantees to banks, which extend credits to exporters for contracts insured under Export Bill Insurance (EBI) programme. EBI terms are upto 360 days, in the form of discounting bills of exchange or negotiating L/Cs in post shipment, by way of paying claims within one month after filing a claim, even if exporters' claim under Export Bill Insurance is negated by KEIC i.e. irrespective of whether or not the responsibility for failing to execute the sales contract falls on exporters. Only where the responsibility for failing to execute the export contract falls on exporters can KEIC take recourse to the exporters for the amount paid to the bank. Thus the scheme covers banks' loss from default by both exporters and buyers and also covers the exporter against the buyers' default.

**Leading Players in the World Credit Insurance Market**

***COFACE***

COFACE, one of the world's leading credit insurance and credit management service providers, has nearly 60 years experience of facilitating global trade. COFACE is currently a limited company. In 2002, its turnover reached Euro 973 million.

COFACE serves companies of all sizes and nationalities, operating in all sectors of the economy. Its global credit risk rating, management, insurance and financing services allows companies to tap the myriad opportunities created by globalization, armed with first rate information and protection.

COFACE presently meets the credit insurance and credit management needs of 83,000 clients worldwide as well as providing various add-on services. The Group's expertise in credit insurance covers both domestic and export credit. The credit management services encompass credit information, credit rating (the world's first credit risk information and rating system), receivables collection and management. Additional services included guarantee insurance, B to B marketing and receivables financing.

COFACE has international presence with subsidiaries and branches in 56 countries and offers local services in 91 countries through its partners in the 'Credit Alliance', the credit insurance network and 'Info Alliance', credit information network. The backbone for the company is its strong database that enables the Group's employees and clients to track 44 million companies throughout the world on real-time basis,

COFACE, in France, manages to cover risks that are not insurable by other private sector, on behalf of the state. Its German, Austrian and Italian subsidiaries are all rated 'AA' by Fitch ratings and 'Aa3' by Moody's.

**COFACE's Major Facilities**

Lines of service offered are built around two core businesses ie., Domestic credit insurance and export credit insurance, under which the major facilities are;

- Credit Management Services (Credit information, Ratings, Recovery and Trade Receivables Management)
- Guarantee insurance, B to B marketing services and Receivables Financing

  In addition to the above, COFACE covers the risks that are not insurable in the private sector, on behalf of the state;
- Export credit insurance
- Project Finance
- Investment insurance (conversion/transfer cover, war and civil war cover, expropriation/confiscation cover, cover against non honoring of sovereign debt and breach of contract)
- Bonds and Guarantees.

***Atradius***

ATRADIUS–formerly GERLING NCM, is recognized internationally for its expertise in credit management. It has an unrivalled wealth of knowledge in underwriting and debt recovery, world market intelligence, and tailored credit insurance. ATADIUS can also provide additional credit management services that enable trade–including debt collections, outsourced credit management, factoring, guarantees, credit process review and other financial solutions.

Having its Headquarters at Amsterdam, the company was formed in August 2003 when the shareholding restructure of GERLING NCM was completed. GERLING NCM itself, formed from a combination of the German Gerling Credit Insurance Group and credit insurer NCM, boasting with over 75 years of experience in credit management business and this experience has been passed to the new company, ATRADIUS.

ATRADIUS, which is currently number two in the world credit insurance market, protects EURO 350 billion of world trade, and has a total income of about EURO 1.3 billion. Its total market share is 25 per cent of world trade. It has been rated as 'A' by Standard & Poor's and 'A2' by Moody's. Its main shareholders are Duetsche Bank and Swiss Re. ATRADIUS, with staff of 3,700, has operations in over 40 countries in all the five continents. It has access to credit information on 45 million companies worldwide and makes 12,000 credit limit decisions daily.

The major facilities of ATRADIUS are:

- Domestic credit insurance.
- Credit/international credit insurance (including commercial and political risks).
- Medium and long term credit insurance & investment insurance.
- Special project financial facilities
- Investment insurance. Conversion/transfer cover; war and civil war cover; expropriation/confiscation cover; cover against breach of contract by government/public entities.
- Bonds and Guarantees. Customs, tax and/or similar bonds; bonds concerning purchases of goods and/or services; bonds concerning constructions and/or supply contracts; other bonds;
- Other services like interim credit management services; software for credit management; financial solutions/securitizations; factoring/forfeiting etc.,

### *Euler Hermes UK PLC (EH UK)*

The Trade Indemnity Company Limited was established in 1918. In 1996 Trade Indemnity became a wholly owned subsidiary of Euler, subsequently changing its name to Euler Trade Indemnity in March 1998. In 2002, after completion of merger between Euler and Hermes, both members of the Allianz Group, Euler Trade Indemnity became part of the enlarged Euler Hermes Group and in 2002 changed its name to Euler Hermes UK.

The company offers a full range of credit insurance services, covering GBP 88 billion of trade (domestic and export) in 60 countries. It has developed value added services in the credit management field and many of its services are now available online to its customers.

Major facilities of EULER HERMES are:

- Export credit insurance
- Short-term (up to one year) cover;
- Commercial and Political risk cover
- Pre-shipment cover
- Credit facilities and domestic cover
- Medium and long term (over one year) cover;
- Supplier credit facilities
- Investment insurance
- Expropriation/Confiscation cover
- Bonds and Guarantees
- Cover against unfair calling

### *Export Finance and Insurance Corporation (EFIC)*

The Export Finance and Insurance Corporation (EFIC) is a self-funding statutory Corporation, wholly owned and guaranteed by the Commonwealth of Australia. Its charter is to encourage and facilitate Australia's export trade and to work with financial institutions to enhance their capacity to support Australian exporters.

On 3rd September 2003, EFIC divested its short-term export insurance business to GERLING NCM. EFIC continued to provide medium to long term export finance facilities under its on going mandate from the Australian Government. Specifically, EFIC provides finance and insurance facilities to Australian exporters of capital goods and services and Australian companies investing in overseas markets and sectors where there is limited or no commercial market capacity. EFIC also manages the Australian Governments National Interest Account. This includes the 'Safety net' facility to private market insurers who provide short-term export credit insurance but, in extreme circumstances, are unwilling or unable to provide such insurance.

Major facilities of EFIC are:

- Export Finance: Direct loans (buyer and supplier credit); Medium term insurance and guarantees covering commercial and political risks; Pre-shipment finance; Lines of Credit;
- Project Financing: Project financing (pre and post completion) through Export Finance products.
- Investment Insurance: Cover offered to investors and financiers; Currency inconvertibility and exchange transfer blockage; war damage and political violence cover; expropriation/confiscation cover; breach of contract and arbitration award default cover;
- Bonds and Guarantees: Cover against unfair calling of bonds;

## SUMMARY

Credit insurance provides companies with coverage for outstanding commercial receivables, protecting against risk of buyer default or insolvency. In addition to managing credit risk, credit insurance supports financing needs by reducing the risk of non-payment of trade receivables, whereby firms can borrow at lower interest rates.

ECA is an institution with a vested interest in promoting its country's exports through various programs of export financing such as loans, guarantees and insurance. All relevant information on various Export Credit Agencies functioning around the world especially the Multilateral ECA's, Official ECA's, Private sector ECA's, Top ECA's around the world, Leading ECA's in Asia and the overseeing organizations such as Berne union has been presented, which gives a bird's eye view on the entire frame work of the export credit insurance and guaranteeing set-up functioning throughout the world.

## REFERENCE

Gary Mendell (1997), 'Export Credit Insurance: An effective marketing and financing tool', Business America–October.

Geetha Muralidhar (2004), General Manager-Marketing and Personnel Relations, ECGC, 'Exports on a higher trajectory', Industrial Economist Economic Awareness Series–June.

*www.wto.org*

*www.irdaindia.org*

*www.berneunion.org*

*www.ecgcindia.com*

Export-Import Bank of India–Occasional Paper No. 41–Regional Co-operation in Export Credit and Export Credit Guarantees (1995), New Delhi.

Export-Import Bank of India–Occasional Paper No. 38 – Export Credit Agencies Arround The World : A Comparative Analysis (1995), India Book House Private Limited, New Delhi.

Exim Banks in Asia: A Comparative Analysis, 1996.

Exports in India's Growth Process, 1999.

# 3

# PROJECT EXPORTS–THE INSTITUTIONAL MECHANISM AND CREDIT INSURANCE

**Viswanathan V.**

## WHAT IS PROJECT EXPORTS?

Export of engineering goods on deferred payment terms and execution of turnkey projects and civil construction contracts abroad are collectively referred to as 'Project Exports'. Project export contracts are generally of high value and exporters undertaking them are required to offer competitive credit terms to be able to secure orders from foreign buyers in the face of stiff international competition. Indian exporters offering deferred payment terms to overseas buyers in respect of export of goods and those who have been awarded turnkey, civil construction contracts by overseas parties have to secure prior approval at post award stage from various institutions such as Authorised Dealer /Exim Bank / Working Group/Reserve Bank of India as the case may be for credit terms to be offered, third country imports etc.

## WORKING GROUP AND CLEARANCE OF PROJECTS

(i) Exporters who have secured orders for undertaking supply contracts on deferred payment terms or those who have secured turnkey/civil construction contracts abroad require approval/assistance of different institutions like Reserve Bank (ECD), Exim Bank and ECGC besides their own bankers. With a view to obviating the need for exporters to approach each institution separately for such approvals and to avoid delays, a Working Group has been constituted with representation from Reserve Bank (ECD), Exim Bank and ECGC for the purpose of giving package approval for proposals submitted by exporters who have secured orders for execution of overseas contracts. In case of contracts of high value, representatives of Government of India are also invited to participate in the meetings of the Working Group. In order to obtain immediate clarifications for speedy clearance of proposals by the Working Group, the concerned exporters and their bankers are also associated with the meetings. With the same objective, participation of the main sub-suppliers, sub-contractors or other associates and their bankers in such meetings is also encouraged, particularly in respect of proposals for high value contracts.

(ii) The Working Group also considers proposals for export of services in the area of management, technical consultancy, etc. where execution of the contracts involves grant of fund-based and/or non-fund-based facilities from the Indian banking system or where deferred payment terms are to be offered.

## CRITERIA FOR CONSIDERATION OF PROPOSALS BY WORKING GROUP

(i) The Working Group will mainly examine, among others, the following aspects while considering grant of package approval for proposals for export of engineering goods on deferred payment terms or for undertaking turnkey/ construction contracts abroad:

(a) Period of deferred credit offered vis-a-vis foreign competition, moratorium, rate of interest, adequacy of advance and down payment provided for as well as requirement of foreign exchange for execution of contract (viz. imports from third countries, agency commission, freight, etc.) and overall economics of the proposal.

(b) Nature of security obtainable from the foreign buyers against payments due and nature and extent of various bonds/guarantees required to be offered by the exporter (including those for procuring third country supplies).

(c) Nature of escalation, force majeure and arbitration clauses provided in the contract and penalty/damages payment provisions.

(d) Extent of fund-based and non-fund-based facilities required in India including pre-shipment and post-shipment credit and/or bridge finance requirement.

(e) In case of turnkey contracts, economic and technical viability thereof as well as special features relating to erection, supervision and commissioning of the contract.

(ii) As regards civil construction contracts, the Working Group will consider proposals only from contractors who are on the approved list of Ministry of Commerce and Industry, Government of India. This is to ensure that only contractors having the necessary competence and capability undertake overseas construction contracts. While considering proposals, the Working Group will endeavour to promote, wherever possible, the idea of high value construction contracts being undertaken on a consortium basis. Apart from examination of special features relevant to the proposal under consideration and the factors enumerated in sub-paragraph (i) above, the Working Group will also take into account the following aspects while considering grant of package approval for construction contracts abroad:

(a) Availability of infrastructural facilities in the importer country like transport, water, construction material, skilled/unskilled labour, etc. and nature of laws governing civil matters, labour usages, etc.

(b) Estimated monthly/quarterly cash flows for the entire duration of the contract and arrangements between prime contractor and associate/sub-contractors for timely execution of the contract in case of consortium arrangement.

(c) Whether the contract would need any bridge finance facility abroad to meet temporary cash flow deficits in working capital, if so, the manner of raising the bridge finance and its full repayment with interest.

(iii) In regard to service contracts, the Working Group will, inter alia, take into account relevant factors like size of the contract, nature of services to be rendered, overall economic condition of the importer country, extent of international competition and potential and prospects for further export of services, goods or turnkey projects from India.

(iv) The Working Group may suitably relax the above criteria at its discretion where warranted by merits of the proposal. While considering proposals, the Working Group may also make such suggestions or tender such advice as may be necessary to avoid inter se competition and to promote, as far as possible, exports in such a way that the foreign exchange benefit for the country is maximised.

## PROCEDURE FOR CLEARANCE OF PROPOSALS

(i) All applications to the Working Group are required to be submitted by the exporters through their bankers (who must be authorised dealers in foreign exchange) in the prescribed form in the required number of copies sufficiently in advance to enable the Working Group to hold a meeting of its members for consideration of the proposal. When a proposal is approved by the Working Group, a package clearance is granted by Exim Bank, on behalf of all the members of the Working Group and conveyed to the exporters' bankers through whom the proposal was received. The Working Group's clearance will ordinarily be given within a period of seven days from the date of receipt of the application, provided it is complete in all respects.

(ii) Exporters desiring to submit bids for execution of projects abroad including service contracts will not be required to obtain clearance for submission of bids from the authorised dealer/Exim Bank/Working Group. However, exporters in such cases are required to ensure that the conditions as laid down in the Memo PEM are complied with.

(iii) On the basis of experience gained over the years and in order to enable the exporters to expediticusly obtain clearance for contracts for supply of engineering goods on deferred payment terms, turnkey contracts and civil construction contracts, powers have been delegated to authorised dealers and Exim Bank to grant post-award clearances in cases where the contract value does not exceed U.S. Dollar 100 Million. Proposals for undertaking such export contracts up to the value of U.S. Dollar 100 Million will, therefore, be cleared by authorised dealers / Exim Bank. Proposals for undertaking such contracts exceeding U.S. Dollar 100 Million in value will need to be cleared by the Working Group.

(iv) In the case of contracts for export of services on cash payment terms requiring fund-based and/or non-fund based facilities, as also those involving deferred payment terms, authorised dealers and Exim Bank have been empowered to grant clearance upto the value of U.S. Dollar 100 Million. Proposals for undertaking such export contracts will, therefore, be cleared by authorised dealers/ Exim Bank upto the value of U.S. Dollar 100 Million. Proposals for undertaking such contracts exceeding U.S. Dollar 100 Million in value will need to be cleared by the Working Group.

(v) Proposals for deferred payment export or turnkey projects against Buyers' Credits as well as for export of managerial/ technical consultancy services on deferred payment terms as also those on cash payment terms involving grant of any fund-based and/or non-fund based facilities in excess of the monetary limits mentioned in sub-paragraph (iv) above will need the prior approval of the Working Group.

## CONDITIONS NECESSARY FOR CLEARANCE OF PROPOSALS BY AUTHORISED DEALERS/ EXIM BANK

While it is not necessary for exporters to obtain prior approval for submission of bid/offers for execution of contracts, authorised dealer/Exim Bank should, while granting post-award clearance, ensure that the export proposals satisfy, inter-alia, the following conditions:

(a) Moratorium or grace period applicable to repayment of principal (and not to payment of interest) should not exceed one year in respect of export of capital or producer goods. In the case of turnkey contracts, the moratorium should not exceed two years. No moratorium should be permitted in respect of export of consumer durables. Interest should be payable even during the period of moratorium.

(b) In case of supply contracts, deferred receivables should be received in equal half-yearly instalments over the agreed period with relation to mean date of shipment (i.e. the date by which 50 per cent supplies in terms of value will be completed) or the date of respective shipment. In case of turnkey projects, instalments should be related to either date of contract or the mean date of shipment or commissioning as agreed upon between the parties.

(c) The rate of interest on deferred receivables should be such that taking into account the cost of deferred credit in India the overall profitability is ensured.

(d) Ordinarily, down payment together with advance payment or mobilisation advance should not be less than 15 per cent of the contract value. In exceptional cases, this may be reduced to 5 per cent of the contract value. In the case of civil construction contracts, it should not ordinarily be less than 5 per cent.

(e) Down payments and deferred instalments receivable should be secured by a letter of credit/acceptable bank guarantee. In case the overseas importer/project authority is a Government department or a public sector undertaking, a guarantee from the foreign Government and/or a promissory note from the foreign Government/public sector undertaking will suffice.

(f) As far as possible, turnkey projects and civil construction contracts should be self-financing. However, bridge finance required for meeting temporary shortfalls in working capital should not normally exceed 25 per cent of the contract value. However, authorised dealer/Exim Bank/Working Group may clear proposals involving bridge finance in excess of 25% of contract value also wherever they are satisfied that such finance is necessary.

(g) Ordinarily, deferred payment terms in respect of the services segment of a turnkey contract may be offered only if the competitors of the exporter from other countries are known to have offered similar terms. In such cases, other terms for the deferred receivables towards services like period of credit, rate of interest and security should be the same as offered for the supply portion of the contract.

*Note: Authorised dealer / Exim Bank may relax conditions at (d) and (e) above, if necessary, based on their commercial judgement.*

Cases where exporters desire to offer, due to local conditions, commercial credit not exceeding one year in respect of goods specified in Annexure I may be considered by the authorised dealers / Exim Bank as per powers delegated.

## ECGC'S SCHEMES FOR PROJECT EXPORTS

Export of capital goods on deferred payment terms and execution of turnkey projects, construction works contracts as also rendering of services abroad are collectively referred to as project exports. As these transaction are not of repetitive nature and they involve medium/long terms credit, ECGC's insurance cover for such transactions are provided on a case to case basis under Specific Policies. Normally these contracts are of very high value and involve longer credit period. The country/political risks involved in such transactions are unpredictable in view of long credit period involved. Although in most cases the overseas buyers are the government or semi government organisations, there is a need to safeguard the payment risks. In many cases these contracts are funded by International Financial Institutions and payments are secured under L/C or Bank Guarantee. There are cases where even government or central bank guarantees are available safeguarding payments. However, the elements of *political risk* such as *war, civil disturbances, exchange transfer delay, imposition of sanctions* etc. are existent in all these cases despite having payment security as stated above. Due to the high value and specific nature of the contracts, a frustration of contract at the *pre shipment stage* due to any of the political risks would result in considerable loss to the exporter. In addition to the political risks as mentioned above, *commercial risks* i.e. the risk of non payment by the buyer or the L/C opening bank exists both when the buyer is a govt/semi govt or a private entity.

**Credit Insurance Policies to Exporters**

In order to protect such exporters from the risk of non payment due to *political* risks or *commercial* risks, ECGC has the following types of covers.

(1) For covering Supply Contracts and Turnkey Projects, Specific Shipments/Contract Policy can be taken. This Policy can be for covering.

(a) only political risks or

(b) comprehensive risks i.e. both commercial and political risks.

The *Political Risks Policy* provides protection against country related events i.e war, civil war, new import restrictions, imposition of sanctions, cancellation of existing import or export licenses, exchange transfer blockages as a result of which money cannot be repatriated out of the country.

The *Comprehensive Risks Policy* provides protection against commercial risks such as Insolvency of Buyer, protracted default of the buyer, non-acceptance of goods shipped, in addition to covering political risks as mentioned above.

Coverage can also be provided for *pre shipment risks* i.e frustration of contract due to any of the political risks as mentioned above, as an Add On cover.

2. For covering construction contract, a Construction Works Policy can be obtained. This policy can be for either political risks alone or for comprehensive risks.
3. For covering services contract, which involves only technical and/or professional services, a Services Policy can be obtained. This also can be either for political or comprehensive risks.
4. If the contracts provide for payment against Letter of Credit, an L/C comprehensive risks policy would provide protection against default/insolvency of the L/C opening bank and also against political risks.
5. The covers are given on a case by case basis, with loss coverage generally at 90% but may be reduced if necessary.

### Credit Insurance Covers to Banks

In addition to the policy covers, which are issued to exporters, ECGC also extends its *Export Credit Insurance for Banks-ECIB (guarantee)* support to banks in India against both funded and non-funded facilities extended to Project Exporters. The types of ECIB covers issued by Indian bank are:

***Funded***

(a) Pre Shipment

(b) Post Shipment

(c) Overseas Lending Finance

(d) Rupee Loan

***Non Funded- Bank guarantees issued as follows***

(a) Bid Bond

(b) Advance Payment

(c) Performance Guarantee

(d) Retention Money Guarantee

(e) Overdraft (Overseas Borrowing)

(f) Visa Guarantee etc.

ECIB covers can be obtained by banks in India to protect them against any loss that they may sustain owing to failure of the exporter to repay on invocation of the above Bank Guarantees.

| | | |
|---|---|---|
| Risk Covered | : | insolvency of the exporter/ protracted default of the exporter |
| Percentage of Loss Covered | : | 75% or 90% |
| Rate of Premium | : | 0.70 Paise per Rs. 100/- p.a. for 75% cover & 0.84 paise per Rs.100/- p.a. for 90% cover |

As per RBI's recent directive, no pre-bid approval from authorised dealer, Exim Bank or Working Group is required to be taken by project exporters. Only post-award approval is required to be taken. However, it would be in the interest of project exporters to obtain 'In - Principle' clearance from their bankers and ECGC assuring them of support in the event of their securing the contracts.

ECGC's approval of project exports and services contracts is based on the following aspects:

(i) The capacity of the project exporter to carry out large value contracts-technical, professional and managerial, and their past experience in the line of business.

(ii) Country to which the exports are to be made- stability of political set-up/government, soundness of economy, payment records, relations with IMF, World Bank & other International Financial Institutions & Donor countries.

(iii) Overseas contract/project-value, type of project, whether cleared by local authorities, profitability.

(iv) Buyer/employer-private/government.

(v) Payment terms & security, rate of interest for deferred receivables.

(vi) ECGC's underwriting policy on the country and its experience, whether any transfer delay experienced.

(vii) Berne Union experience-whether the credit period offered is in line with Berne union understanding.

(viii) Reinsurance back-up available or not.

(ix) Whether need for covering the contract under National Export Insurance Account set-up by Government of India.

## BUYER'S CREDIT/ LINE OF CREDIT COVER

Financial institutions in India extend Buyer's Credit/Lines of Credit to overseas buyers/institutions to facilitate export of goods & services from India. Institutions like Exim Bank, SIDBI etc. often seek ECGC cover for Buyers Credit/Line of Credit cover to protect them against non payment by the borrower due to Political or Commercial risks. Buyers Credit/Line of Credit cover can be obtained either for covering political risks or for comprehensive risks.

Factors weighing approval of Buyers Credit proposals are:

(a) Competence and capacity of exporter in executing the contract.

(b) Commercial justification of the contract.

(c) Economic viability of the overseas project for which credit is required to be offered.

(d) Credit worthiness, standing and financial position of foreign buyers and general economic conditions of the Buyers country.

Lines of Credit are generally extended by Exim Bank of India to Financial Institutions/Governments in Overseas Countries facilitating export of consumer goods and capital goods.

## OVERSEAS INVESTMENT INSURANCE (OII) COVER

OII provides cover for the investments made by Indian corporates abroad in Joint Venture or their wholly owned subsidiary (WOS) either in the form of equity or loan. Government of India or RBI should approve the Joint Venture. The basic principle is that the investment should emanate from India and benefit of dividend/interest therefrom should accrue to India. The investment should not in any way conflict with the policy of both our government and the overseas government. Normally, there should be a bilateral agreement between India and the host country for promotion and protection of Indian Investment. In case there is no such agreement the Corporation should be satisfied that the existing laws of the host country adequately safeguard Indian Investment.

### Types of Investment

The overseas investment may be made either by way of equity or by way of loans

#### *Equity*

Any contribution made to the enterprise in return for shares either by cash remittances or by way of export of capital goods or services can be covered. Any fees payable towards technical know-how, consultancy or management services etc. and agreed to be converted into capital will be considered for cover at the discretion of the Corporation.

#### *Loans*

Loans advanced by way of a formal agreement but not tied to export of goods and supplies are eligible for cover. Any 'suppliers/buyers' credits and lines of credit extended to support sale of goods or services from India may be covered under the appropriate insurance schemes of the Corporation and not under investment insurance.

#### *Dividend and Profit*

In case of equity the investor can choose to cover the original investment as well as his share of retained earnings and dividends declared, to the extent they are eligible for repatriation. Cover on account of original investment, retained earnings, dividend receivable and any additional investment will be subject a ceiling of 150% of the original investment calculated as in the proceeding paragraphs. In case of loan, the insurance will cover the principal as well as interest actually earned.

*Portfolio Investment*

Any investment in shares of overseas concerns not related to setting up, development and expansion of overseas projects will not be eligible for cover under the investment insurance.

*Additional Investment*

Additional investment can be covered subject to a ceiling of 50% of the original investment. Any additional investment out of retained earnings should have been made by formal capitalization and for the purpose of expansion for development of the enterprise. If the additional investment is made out of retained profits, which are not eligible for repatriation such as investment will not be eligible for cover. Initially cover is issued for 3 years. On expiry of the 3 years it is at the option of the exporter to renew the cover / review of the JV / WOS by ECGC. The duration of insurance cover shall not normally exceed 15 year but extension can be given upto 20 years for longer projects. The amount of investment eligible for cover shall be to the full extent during the first 10 years of cover. Percentage of cover is 90 - can be reduced. The amount of investment eligible for cover will be reduced to 90%, 80%, 70%, 60% and 50% respectively of the original investment during the $11^{th}$, $12^{th}$, $13^{th}$, $14^{th}$ and $15^{th}$ years of insurance. OII provides cover for original investment retained earning, dividend receivables and additional investment upto 50% of the original investment.

OII covers only political risks of war, expropriation and restrictions on remittances. As the investor has a hand in running the overseas enterprise, commercial risks associated with the investment are not covered.

### *Premium Rate*

Base rate 2.5% of the investment value. Actual premium rate will be depend on size of Investment, country of the investment, previous experience of the Importer etc. Premium rate varies from 1% to 2.5% p.a.

The exporter has to furnish proposal form alongwith fee of Rs. 01% of the investment amount subject to ceiling of Rs. 25,000/- if cover is agreed application fee paid shall be adjusted towards premium payable. In case, the application for insurance is rejected, half the fee paid shall be refunded. Premium is taken up front. Income from the premium is allocated over the tenor of the cover extended. Installment facility is provided by ECGC for collecting premium after analyzing and approving the proposal.

ECGC enters into agreement with the exporters for providing cover mentioning the terms and conditions alongwith the maximum liability. The exporters have to submit annual report about the progress and working of the project.

## NEW INITIATIVES

ECGC has since revised its premium structure providing substantial reduction in the rates both for short term as well as for medium and long term contracts. This will go a long way in providing cost effective credit insurance support to project exporters which in turn will enable them to compete effectively for international tenders. Installment facility in payment of premium without charging interest is being extended to exporters in case the premium incidence is large.

In order to increase project exports and to encourage project exporters Govt. of India have initiated various steps. Institutions like ECGC and Exim Bank are being strengthened to provide adequate support to project exporters. The *National Export Insurance Account (NEIA)* has been set up by the Government of India to provide credit insurance support to exporters where ECGC is not in a position to do so due to its own underwriting constraints and where the export is strategically important in the long term interests of the country.

# 4

# CHALLENGES FACED BY ECAs IN MARKETING CREDIT INSURANCE PRODUCTS–AN INDIAN EXPERIENCE

**Ashok Phadtare**

## BACKGROUND

The origin and evolution of Credit insurance can be better understood by knowing the history of global trade and its evolution to the present status. Except in the beginning era of human civilization, trade has been part and parcel of our life. In the earlier era of the human specie, the dependence was purely on nature available in the raw form. Man's needs were very limited and they were met from the surroundings. However, with the change of time, and development, his requirements for survival started increasing and were not met by his own supply. He started looking outwards for his requirement and started procuring it by exchanging his surpluses with others who were ready to exchange their surpluses. And with this was born 'barter-trade'. But barter trade was free from 'credit' which is the mother of 'credit insurance, which came into existence at a later stage.

## BIRTH OF "CREDIT INSURANCE"

As the barter trade was unable to meet the requirements of mankind, he started trading the produce with far of places, beyond a limited border. Initially trade was facilitated by exchange of commodities and later on accepted forms of precious metals and later on developed exchange through currencies. There were times when he was unable to sell his produce on 'cash' basis due to various constraints. This lead to credit dominated trade.

Whenever he started extending credit in trade activities, he started facing new challenges in form of credit risk–a risk of non-payment. He started looking for a remedy to mitigate this risk and thus was born credit insurance. In reality credit is beginning of credit insurance. Historical evidences indicate that the process of providing credit insurance started evolving in present state in the early $13^{th}/14^{th}$ century. However, it developed to the present state and started growing rapidly at the onset of industrialization in Europe.

Before focussing our attention on credit insurance itself, we must understand that credit risk is part and parcel of one of the major contingencies threatening social security. Among the various ways in which the member of a community may be disappointed in his reliance upon another member, the credit risk is the most probable one as the creditor will not be able to recover a debt.

The international economic disintegration which set in with the First World War had created obstacles to many international transactions which had hitherto been regarded as vital for the economy of many countries.

On the basis of available records, a British Commercial Insurance Company wrote credit insurance in the UK from 1820 onwards for a certain time. After the 1847, crisis no less than seven other companies or so were known to have made short lived attempts in this field in England upto 1885, about the same number in Germany upto 1890, about ten in France upto 1890 and a few more upto the First World War, two in Sweden and two in Belgium upto that same time. Nevertheless, a continuous development began, in several countries, well before the First World War. In all of them, the priority was with private enterprise.

After post war inflation, the governments organized extensive export credit insurance facilities, whilst the pressure of repatriations and of foreign debts made it necessary to maintain and expand exports. Most of the leading export credit insurance agencies were formed in and around early 20$^{th}$ century.

As we are specifically dealing with 'export credit insurance' it will be worthwhile to understand what exactly is meant by 'export credit'. The term export credit describes a range of facilities or schemes and can mean different things in different contexts. Strictly speaking, export credit refers to (i) credit extended by exporters to importers (i.e. supplier credit) or (ii) short-term/medium and long term loans made by banks, used for financing working capital for export of goods and services/ projects and capital goods exports (i.e. buyer credit). It includes both at pre-shipment as well as post-shipment stage.

## ROLE OF AN ECA AND POLITICAL/ COMMERCIAL RISKS

The traditional role of an ECA is to support and encourage exports and outward investment by insuring international trade and investment transactions. At the very basic level, the common function of an ECA is to provide cover to exporters, banks or investors for political and commercial risks causing loss over a short, medium or long term.

For export credit transactions, political risks are the risks of non-payment under an export contract or project due to an action or failure by an importer's host government. Such action may include intervention to prevent the transfer of payments, cancellation of a licence or acts of war or civil war. Commercial risks arise primarily as a result of non-payment by a private buyer, commercial bank or a public buyer, due to default, insolvency or bankruptcy, or failure or willingness to take delivery of the goods.

## NECESSITY OF ECA

We have seen here above how trade has evolved to the present state, predominantly dominated by 'credit'. We have also seen the risks involved in the trade carried with credit and to mitigate these risks, the role played by an ECA. We have seen that the long credit cycle, starting with the Latin American debt crisis in the early 1980s, the collapse of the Soviet Union and the Asian financial crisis through to the later economic boom and substantial liquidity worldwide. During the difficult times, ECAs played a key role in helping sustain global trade and investment flows and they have benefited from the financial boom of the past few years, evidenced by the positive impact on business results.

With the development of the sub-prime loan issue in mid 2007, the world was re-awakened to new risks created by new financial technologies. In addition to this market turmoil there is further uncertainty resulting from the global imbalances of savings and investments, a shifting geopolitical equilibrium and the increasing constraints on natural resources.

As the world economy enters into these uncharted waters, we are finding renewed interest in the services offered by the ECAs to help to mitigate risks involved in cross border transactions.

**CREDIT INSURANCE PRODUCTS:**

Insurance industry was not only growing but developing rapidly. The insurance companies were looking for opportunities for growing rapidly and capturing bigger markets. Insurance industry started developing, based on the experiences in the past, and evolving products based on basic principles of 'wholeturnover', 'spread' and law of average or probability.

Initial products were based on demand. The industry had always to struggle to strike a balance between more spread and right cost related to these insurances. There is always a conflict between 'wholeturnover' based policies to a single transaction based policies.

Evolvement of credit insurance products is normally depending upon (i) demand/supply (ii) presence of competition. In most of the countries, ECAs are predominantly owned by the Government. Initially these organizations were very conservative in offering export credit insurance products. They were basically governed by the principle of 'whole turnover'; it means the exporter has to give entire business, which goes on credit. No exclusions (except few agreed) will be permitted. However, with the change of time and changing trading practices world-wide and with the onset of competition from private credit insurance companies, there has been attitudinal change in the mindset of ECA while offering or designing products.

Every industry has changed with the changing times and ECA cannot be exception to this rule. ECAs all over the world have changed their product portfolios over the period. There has been a drastic shift from products based on 'whole turnover' to 'single transaction'. Broadly speaking today's products range is as under:

(i) Policy which covers all the shipments;
(ii) Policy specifically designed for a particular class of exporters;
(iii) Policy for a single transaction;
(iv) Policy to cover transactions with a specific buyer;
(v) Exposure based policies;

## MARKETING OF CREDIT INSURANCE

Marketing has always remained one of the main functions of every industry. Normally, it is believed that marketing is always related to an industry involved in goods and commodities only. To certain extent, it was true as historically trading activities were related only to the trading of goods and commodity. However, from the 18$^{th}$ century onwards, 'service' sector started assuming an important role in trade.

It is not always the case that competition based industries alone have to struggle in marketing their products. History provides evidence in companies enjoying 'monopolistic' status having faced problem in selling their products to the customers. The problem of marketing these products, like any other products, mainly can be attributed to (a) suitability, (b) right costing and (c) acceptability.

Export Credit Insurance sector, being a service sector, faces many unique challenges while marketing its products. Basically, insurance industry has always been facing these challenges historically. However, Export Credit Insurance, being an unique section of the general insurance industry, faces tougher times. The basic reasons for these marketing challenges can be summarized as under:

(a) Exporters thinking 'nothing will happen to me' as nothing happened in the past;

(b) Having insurance protection is not a 'must';

(c) How to reduce transaction cost is the main guiding principle;

(d) Lack of awareness of the Credit Insurance;

(e) Limited scope for Export credit insurance;

(f) Wholeturnover principle is one of the main obstacles;

(g) Availing finance assumes main focus of exporting industry;

(h) Negative publicity;

(i) Non-availability of variety of products;

(j) Traditional belief of 'must' expecting in return against premium paid;

(k) Natural conflict of interest between the parties, each under the temptation of giving too little and asking too much;

(l) Exporter's thinking that the insurance policies bring more restrictions than benefits;

(m) Averse to the multiple procedures;

(n) Competition;

These issues can be discussed as under:

*Exporters thinking 'nothing will happen to me' as nothing happened in the past:* Many a time, a section of exporting community, dealing with certain commodities and specific market does not feel need for credit insurance. The basic reason for this can be attributed to their dealing in these commodities and markets traditionally. Most of the times, they have been dealing with their buyers/market for a considerably longer time and have developed a mutual trust. They never had any problem in realizing their payments. Besides, the commodities they have been dealing, were always in demand and it has been predominantly a seller's market. However, with the change of time, presence of new suppliers from different countries and competition, perception of risks has changed. Due to availability of supply from different sources, buyers are more demanding. This change enhances different risks.

*Having insurance protection is not 'must':* Unless and until a customer perceives risks, he will not think of availing insurance to protect himself. In the competitive world, it has become necessary for the customers especially the exporters to look out for more and more business, irrespective of the destinations. Most of the times, an exporter is focussed on expansion of his business and does not give any attention to the dangers lurking at the corner. Non-availability of authentic information on a particular market/buyer may be one of the reasons for not perceiving the probable risks. Exporters fail to appreciate that prompt payment by a buyer need not necessarily mean that he is credit worthy and will keep honoring his commitments at all the times. It must be understood by them that the past experience does not guarantee future payment and often the buyers' ability to pay depends not only on his credit worthiness and financial capacity but also host of other factors like local business environment, commodity behaviour and most of the time, government restrictions. The exporter needs to understand and appreciate these factors and there is a need to take care of the payments through a suitable insurance.

*How to reduce transaction cost is the main guiding principle:* Traditionally Indian society is very cost conscious. To maximize returns, a businessman is always on the lookout for reduction in transaction costs. And as the Indian society is normally low on insurance consciousness, first victim of transaction cost reduction exercise is always the premium payable for insurance. Unfortunately, export credit insurance is not mandatory like marine insurance sector. Society which is highly insurance conscious, normally looks insurance buying is an investment rather than expenditure. It is a very common experience of the marketing team of ECAs to face stiff resistance from the exporting community on account of 'costly insurance'. They always have ready-made answer that they have been operating on 'thin' margins and with high input cost they will not be competitive in the global market. It is true that in order to remain competitive, the input cost has to be reduced. However, one must identify right areas. While remaining competitive, one should not loose sight of risks in the competitive market. Higher the competition, the magnitude of payment related risks will always be higher.

*Lack of awareness of Credit Insurance:* One of the reasons for low insurance consciousness in the developing market is lack of awareness of availability of insurance products. In Indian society 'insurance' means normally 'life insurance'. General Insurance section of the total insurance society comes later and very insignificantly unless and until it is mandatory like Motor Vehicle Insurance or Marine Insurance for export transaction. Or it has to be stipulated mandatory by somebody like bank insisting for house insurance while granting housing loan. Export Credit Insurance comes last on the insurance list and therefore it has always been challenging for an ECA to create awareness not only on the availability of different products but many a time on its own existence itself. Publicity is one of the predominant tools in the hands of insurance companies to increase awareness among the prospective customers. Insurance sector like Life Insurance and other General Insurance Sector have large probable customer base and hence can be targeted in general. However, export credit insurance sector has a very limited market and therefore it is always not possible to take the mass publicity route. At ECGC, we have been selling our products mainly through direct selling though in-house marketing team and with the help of commercial banks. Indian economy is doing very well and exports in particularly been growing at the on and average rate of 20%. However, Credit insurance companies like ECGC have been struggling to penetrate beyond 10% of total exports, mainly due to lack of awareness of the concept of credit insurance. Setting up of the regulatory authority (IRDA), opening of the insurance sector and creating competition have helped to increase the insurance awareness greatly.

*Limited scope for Export credit insurance:* Though Indian economy is doing well and is second fastest growing, after China, Indian exports form a small portion of the entire economic activity. It accounts for just above 10% of the GDP. Thus, the business available to the ECA is very limited. The Indian exports during 2007-08 amounted to approximately US$160 bn. However, out of this there were several segments which fall outside the insurable exports viz. Govt to Govt transactions, export of petroleum and petroleum products, exports against advance payment, exports against confirmed Letter of Credit, exports to/through associates etc. Though the authentic data is not available, it is estimated that insurable export is only in the range of 30% of the total Indian exports. Further, Indian Software Export industry is doing exceptionally well but due to its peculiarity, they do not feel need to have credit insurance protection or the credit insurer is not able to address the specific risks related to software exports like omission and commission, cost escalation and time escalation leading to losses not recoverable from the buyer. Thus, there is a need to expand the base of credit insurance to address the varying needs of the Indian exporting community and find credit insurance solutions in order to increase the scope of credit insurance.

*Wholeturnover principle is one of the main obstacles:* Like any other insurance sector, export credit insurance also looks for a larger spread. Traditionally, most of the ECAs have been offering products based on the principle of 'wholeturnover', where exporter is supposed to offer his entire business which goes on credit and no exclusions are permitted (except certain sections such as exports against L/cs or exports to the Associates). This has been one of the main obstacles in expanding export credit insurance business as most of the exporters are not willing to give their 'secured' business. Most of the times they may be dealing with certain buyers/markets traditionally and for reasonably a longer period. In the process, they would have developed mutual trust and thus don't perceive any risks and therefore the need for insurance. Moreover, compulsion of giving comprehensive risks (Commercial Risks and Political Risks) is also one of the reasons as to why exporters avoid export credit insurance products since they do not perceive political risks in certain market such as Europe, USA etc. Any insurance cost for such transactions, according to the exporter is avoidable and unnecessary. The whole turnover policy has strongly gained ground in the countries where it has always been the only form of policy which credit insurers dared to offer. However, with the changing times and market practices and onset of competition from private insurer, customers are demanding change and wish to have policies of their choice.

*Availing finance assumes main focus of exporting industry:* Traditionally, attention of Indian exporters is always focussed around finance, either at pre-shipment or post-shipment stage. 'Money' is always the centre of any business activity and export can not be an exception to this. However, exporters lose sight of very significant trade risks which can jeopardize the entire business activity. While organizing finances, exporters must also insulate themselves from the probable risks factors. With the availement of export credit insurance they can save themselves from the likely losses. Traditionally, ECGC has been selling export credit insurance products, most of the times, with the help of Indian commercial banks as till recently while granting export finances banks used to make export credit insurance policies mandatory. However, with a change of times and intense competition in the banking sector, bankers can hardly offer to make ECGC policies compulsory. While choosing between retention of a customer and safeguarding the customer's as well as banker's interest, the retention of a customer weighs far more in the minds of the bankers, even at the cost of the attendant credit risks.

*Negative publicity:* Compared to any other sector, services sector is more prone to negative publicity, normally spread by existing dissatisfied customers. This comes as a stumbling block in the business expansion. It is always experienced that negative message spreads very fast. 10 positive facts can be overshadowed by one negative fact. Insurance sector is always seen with a lot of disbelief as to whether they will be with the insured in the needy hour. It is most unfortunate but common belief that *"insurance company is like an umbrella which never opens when it starts raining"*. If a claim of exporter is rejected due to certain non-compliance, the exporter will never appreciate the lapses or his failures; instead he expects that the insurance company is just finding excuses to say no. An aggrieved customer would not only spread adverse news in the market but would also drag the insurer to a court of law. To avoid this type of negative publicity, the ECA should always take positive approach while dealing with claims of the exporters. To avoid procedural lapses the ECA should initiate pro-active steps in educating customers.

*Non-availability of variety of products;* Non-availability of the variety of products is one of the marketing challenges generally faced by ECAs. Traditionally, ECAs have been offering products based on 'wholeturnover' (WT) and rarely single transaction based products. However, due to changing business practices all over the world and strong competition, the requirements of the customers are changing fast and they are hardly identical or similar to the past. ECA has to be pro-active and responsive to address these changing expectations from their customers. At ECGC we have been operating Standard Policy, for more than four decades, which is based on 'wholeturnover'. However, we have brought suitable changes not only in our approach but in product port-folios and now have more than 25 different products to meet varied requirements of exporters as well as banks.

*Traditional belief of 'must' expecting in return against premium paid:* Traditionally, in India when somebody buys insurance, he expects more than the premium paid in return. He fails to understand that he is buying pure insurance (buying peace!) which will protect them in case of crises. One of the readymade argument the marketing team of an ECA faces is that we have been paying premium for years and have not received anything in return. He fails to understand that even if nothing went wrong in the past, there is no guarantee that nothing will happen in future. A customer buying credit insurance shall have to look at it as a tool which insulates him from risks of non-payment. The assured must realize that what he buys for his premium is security. He must not expect always to get the whole of the premium, or even more, back in cash through the payment of indemnities.

*Natural conflict of interest between the parties, each under the temptation of giving too little and asking too much:* A balance between the sacrifices of the one and the advantages of the other party must rest on some considerations derived from the general principles of insurance. Nevertheless, credit insurance policies stipulate a number of obligations on the part of the assured designed to enforce a diligent management of the insured debt. Provided that these requirements do not go too far, they are also in the interest of the assured. In most of the cases, the creditors are neither usually apt to act rashly, upsetting the financial position of their customer by too brutal a recovery of the debt, nor are they inclined to accede too easily to a demand for too long an extension of credit. Further, as and when payments had fallen overdue, the credit insurer may expect the assured of not making further shipments. However, the assured feels this condition of the insurer is too harsh as it comes in the way of continuing business relationship with the buyer.

*Exporter's thinking that the insurance policies bring more restrictions than benefits:* As explained at 6.13 above, most of the times exporter feels that terms and conditions of the insurance policies to be observed are very restrictive and instead of helping him to expand his business, come in the way of his growth. There are more Don'ts than Do's. Slightest delay in receipt of payment, which, he feels is common practice in the particular business/market, the insurance company insisting on reporting a default, insurer's advice to exporter not to have further business dealings until the payments are realized are all viewed as impediments resulting in strained relations between the buyer and the exporter leading to loss of future business. He always feels that policies should be more flexible. He fails to understand that the terms and conditions stipulated are evolved only to protect his interest.

*Averse to the multiple procedures:* It is a very common perception amongst exporting community that the conditions of the insurance policies are always difficult to observe and also are cumbersome. Preparation of different statements, submission of reports is time consuming and enhances the administrative cost. Apart from this, they have to submit these statements/reports 'in time'. Most of the times, exporters feel that the insurance companies use these technical non-compliances as an excuse to avoid their liability.

*Competition:* Since the late 90s, Indian Insurance industry has been opened up for private players and Credit Insurance is not an exception. Virtual monopolistic status of ECGC for more than 4 decades is a thing of the past. There are about six to seven players in credit insurance market today in India. Most of the competitors are on a highly sophisticated technology platform and are supported by overseas ECAs in terms of technical knowledge. Besides, their concentration is on the high end customers. Thus, there is an intense competition today in this field and the best of the companies in every aspect, technology, flexibility, affordability and simplicity etc.,alone will survive.

## RESISTANCE

It is not only the credit insurance industry that has been facing resistance but in general, all types of insurance businesses have faced resistance in one form or the other. Some of the resistances are based on attitudinal characteristics of a community, industry and trade practices. With regard to the export market, strong resistance comes not only from exporters dealing with traditional commodities but also in form of self insurance. Cost of insurance is another deterrent. There has always been a tussle between the insurer and the customer on this front.

## INDIAN EXPERIENCE

Indian society is known for its cost consciousness. Moreover, in Indian scenario 'insurance consciousness' level is very low.

People in general do not feel the necessity for insurance. This has been one of the major reasons for non-development of a matured insurance market as in case of developed countries. However, times have been changing and Indians are also waking up to the changes taking place, nationally and internationally. Competition has helped in creating awareness in the Indian society in general. Time is changing for good.

**HOW ECGC HAS RESPONDED TO THE CHALLENGES?**

Export Credit Guarantee Corporation of India Ltd (ECGC) has been in this field for last more than five decades and the organization has faced similar problems as the ones faced by other Export Credit Agencies around the world, while doing business. However, as a responsive organization, it has changed from a product oriented organization to a customer focused organization. The drastic changes brought into effect by the Corporation as far as the product portfolio is concerned are evident of these changes. The Corporation has also started using different marketing channels instead of traditional direct selling. ECGC is a case study to know how an ECA can effectively tackle the marketing challenges. It is not out of context to mention that the competition which has arisen in Indian market as far as Credit Insurance is concerned has spurred the organisation to bring about these developments.

When Export Credit Insurance is not mandatory, the job of ECGC becomes more difficult to impress upon the prospective client the necessity of having export credit insurance protection. ECGC has been conducting various meetings, addressing specific segments of export community and in general creating awareness of Export Credit Insurance. During the course of such meetings/conferences, emphasis is given not only on different products but primarily to create awareness of the insurance and why it is necessary for them. Unless and until the need is felt, a customer will not think of insurance. Many a times it is a very tactful job. To awaken the prospective client to the perception of his danger is probably the daunting task an insurer will face. Even the suspicion of any blame of incompetence or recklessness on the part of the client will offend the latter's self esteem and provoke his spirited resistance. It is therefore, always felt that selling insurance needs greater skills over and above the normal marketing skills. During the course of such meetings, we do share, many a times, success stories/catastrophic situations which were encountered by us. Further, ECGC has been spending considerable amount on print/electronic media publicity apart from sponsoring events of different Export Promotion Councils and Commodity Board, to create awareness on export credit insurance products.

How to reduce transaction cost is the main guiding principle–At ECGC we are very conscious of this issue. Like any other ECA, we have to strike a balance between right price and right cover so that we can successfully provide the needed protection to the client and also remain in the business. ECGC, as a responsive organization has reduced premium rates upto 40% a couple of years back and a further reduction of upto 10% last year. Besides, the No Claim Bonus rates have also been increased to as much as 70% in certain cases. A further reduction of 5% is available for upfront payment of full premium. Besides, customized solutions to meet the credit insurance requirements of exporters within their budgetary allocations have assumed greater role in the recent times. In a novel way, ECGC has also addressed the 'cost' concerns of exporters by facilitating marine insurance covers along with its own credit insurance covers through a tie up with one of the public sector general insurance companies. ECGC would meet the cost of such 'add on' marine cover to its customers.

Limited scope for Export credit insurance: ECGC is aware of these stark realities and developed different products for different segments of the export industry e.g. some of the risks covered under software export policies. These risks cannot be treated strictly as credit risks but could result in the risk of non-payment as consequential risks. Further, when you have very limited business opportunities available, it should be your endeavor to ensure that you capture maximum share of available pie. Flexible approach helps you to do this many times. ECGC is not only having off-the-self readymade products which can meet standard requirements of different sections of exporting community but have shown enough flexibility to design customer specific products.

Wholeturnover principle is one of the main obstacles– While addressing this world-wide constrain of every ECA, the ECGC has, at the beginning of 21st century, changed its products port-folio considerably. Today ECGC is in position to offer more than 15 products to exporters and an equal number of products to banking sector, apart from customized covers that can be designed on the basis of specific requirements of a customer.

Negative Publicity: No insurance company can avoid this most unwanted aspect of business. However, they will always try to minimize the same. On the basis of past experience ECGC has decided to tackle the main route cause of this negative publicity. Some of the major exercises undertaken by the ECGC to bring down claim rejection ratio were simplification of different procedures and educating customers so that they can keep their policies in order. Further, when your customer is likely to face a problem, initiate pro-active steps and enhance confidence level amongst your clienteles. Advise them the steps to be taken to minimize the losses and also get ready to help them in time. This has always helped ECGC to create positive image and the recent brochures on Dos and Don'ts is a step in that direction.

Averse to the multiple procedures – This issue, as discussed earlier in this paper, has been addressed by bringing in more simplification of the procedural aspects. Some of the newer products designed recently like exposure based policies, do not require the client to apply for credit limits, submit monthly/quarterly statements. This has helped the client not only to save administrative cost of complying with these procedures but also eliminated lapses related to them thereby resulting in enhanced prospects of getting claims. More and more Discretionary Powers have been given to the clients, not only in deciding the buyer exposures but deciding timely actions such as in case of re-sale, re-import etc.

Competition–As stated earlier, ECGC was enjoying virtually a monopolistic status till late 1990s, when the Indian insurance market was not opened to private Sector. Though this sense of Monopolistic status never cultivated a sense of arrogance nor increased the comfort levels while providing services to the customer, at ECGC we have always been more willing to listen to the customers and respond accordingly. However, in the post-competitive era the process of change has definitely fastened up. We have changed our image from 'product oriented organization 'to a 'customer focused' organization. At ECGC, we have successfully addressed the 'competition' not only by changing our product port-folio but diversifying into newer areas such as Full Fledged Factoring and Domestic Credit Insurance. ECGC has been constantly reviewing its schemes and making changes to meet the requirements of the customers and at the same time coming out with new schemes.

## CONCLUSION

The speed at which the world is changing, more so the developing economies, calls for sophistication and efficiency. It calls for new models. As a responsive organization ECGC is constantly refining its approach to devise solutions that will meet the needs of the market place. ECAs will continue to be relevant players in the international trade. It has been our experience in ECGC to keep a constant watch on the developments in the international trade for the past 50 years. And as we face the future, we will just keep looking at our products constantly and bring out the changes in tune with the need of the hours. In fact that is what we had been doing all these years and the changes have kept us on course and that's what will keep us from foundering as the journey continues. For us, changes are permanent.

## REFERENCE

T. C. Kapur (1956), Committee Reports on Export Credit Insurance & Export Finance.

Elements of Credit Insurance–By Hans Karrer, Switzerland;

Berne Union Annual Publications.

Personal guidance by Shri V. Viswanathan, GM, ECGC.

5

# NATIONAL EXPORT INSURANCE ACCOUNT AS A FACILITATOR FOR INCREASING PROJECT EXPORTS FROM INDIA

**Rohit Pandya**

## INTRODUCTION

The purpose of this paper is threefold. First to provide to all the project exporters and institutions involved in facilitation of the project exports from the country a detailed understanding of the National Export Insurance Account (NEIA) administered by the Export Credit Guarantee Corporation Of India Limited on behalf of the Government of India. Secondly, to review the challenges and gaps posed in implementing the NEIA scheme in India since 2006. Thirdly, to draw conclusions and make recommendations for appropriate responses to meet the challenges and gaps as well as propose some initiatives to ensure that the scheme fulfils the mandate for which it has been evolved.

## PREFACE

A Task Force which was set up in June 2002 to look into the various issues related to turnkey and other project exports from India and to make appropriate recommendations, had submitted its report in January 2003. On examination of various issues on the subject, it had found that in order to promote project exports in the national interest, in many of the countries, the host governments extended support to the export credit insurance schemes for project exports in one form or the other.

The rationale was that the Export Credit Agencies (ECAs) were unable to assume huge exposures under project exports because of their sheer size and the ECAs' inability to underwrite such exports because of commercial considerations or for nonavailability of reinsurance arrangements for such transactions. Keeping in view the national interests the governments had created a "dedicated" fund to underwrite the export credit risks associated with such transactions. On a similar footing, the Government of India, in January 2006, set up a National Export Insurance Account (NEIA) to ensure availability of credit risk cover for projects and other high value exports which are desirable from the point of view of national interest, which ECGC was unable to underwrite at terms which will not affect the competitiveness of exports. It was envisaged that this would ensure along with the other measures to augment the project exports and lead to a quantum jump of this category of exports linearly and to also to more diversified destinations.

## RECOMMENDATIONS OF TASK FORCE ON PROJECT EXPORTS

The Task Force on Project exports had recommended inter-alia, that the following actions be taken to give an impetus to project exports from India:

- Constitution of high level standing committee on project exports
- Country programming missions to target countries
- Harmonisation of policies having direct bearing on project exports
- Establishment of coordinating agency–projects export promotion council
- Improvement of India's performance in projects funded by multilateral funding agencies

- Capacity building of Indian missions
- Strengthening of EXIM bank of India
- Strengthening of ECGC.
  - Government should extend support to ECGC to provide service in the same manner as a project exporter in a competing country would be getting from his export credit insurance provider (counterpart of ECGC in competitor's country).
  - ECGC should be reimbursed the losses on account of political risks by Government of India by taking over the debts of Iraq. It has been done so in other countries in similar situations where the national governments have paid out compensations out of their budgets without affecting the financial position of credit risk insurer.
  - Strengthening of equity base of ECGC to ensure capital adequacy as per accepted norms of credit insurance business
  - Wherever reinsurance is possible to arrange, if the costs are prohibitive, consideration of governmental support in the pricing to ensure smooth cash flow and lesser financial burden for exporter.
    (a) Government Guarantees to enable ECGC to cover high value project risks without the need of reinsurance, which will make them competitive and also provide cover in some countries in emerging markets like Africa & Latin America.
    (b) In the absence of reinsurance, ECGC should be in a position to draw support from the Government National Interest Account, or even to operate the cover on behalf of the Government.
    (c) The underwriting of risks may be done on behalf of and to the account of Government.
  - Yearly allocation currently to equity takes care of only short term underwriting capacity. A quantum jump in contribution to the equity of ECGC will enable

ECGC to undertake higher exposures based on the increased equity.

- The proposal regarding National Interest Account as is prevalent in other countries like UK, Australia, and Republic of Korea should be implemented. This enables cover for project exports which otherwise do not meet the normal commercial underwriting criteria.
- ECGC, as an institution, must evolve and gear itself to function as a significant credit insurance agency to support project exports from India.

## EXPORT CREDIT INSURANCE IN INDIA

Export Credit Insurer's involvement in the Project Exports business is very different from that of the Short Term business. Foremost, is the horizon of risk which is much longer. Risks are not only high but also difficult to predict. The gross uncertainties faced do not get solved even by host country's guarantees. The absence of reinsurance market means, each case is considered as a large block of exposure on the insurer's books for a long drawn period of many years.

It has been observed lately that Project Term export flows from international financial institutions are declining. With the official aid reducing, ECAs are more involved in project financing. There are instances of not only Underwriting risks of sovereign governments but also that of states, countries and cities. The demand for investment insurance is also going up on ECAs.

Project & Term Exports underwriting is done on a case by case basis and an individual policy is issued either as a Buyer's credit or a Line of Credit. This results in high premium rates, sometimes as high as even 10% of project cost. The claim incidence has been very high in the past and huge compensations made by ECAs have led to a greater interest being evinced by Ministry of Finance of governments in various countries who go in detail into the rationale, underwriting, cost of cover and even accounting procedures.

The reasons for political risk underwriting, particularly for project export business being done by Public Sector and that too with the backing of Government in most of the countries are:

(i) Risks to be covered are unpredictable and cannot be subject to commercial actuarial analysis and consequent pricing.

(ii) Risks come in large lumps in the form of high value contracts, projects or investments.

(iii) Risks are required to be covered for long periods inclusive of manufacturing, construction, maintenance, credit periods, etc.

(iv) In the case of high risk markets or emerging markets or economies undergoing reform in difficult circumstances, private insurers will have no experience and little appetite for risks.

(v) Another inhibiting factor is the unacceptable level of risk aggregation i.e. overall exposure to a country builds up quickly and takes too long to run off.

(vi) In the case of loss situation, recovery is possible either bilaterally or on a government to government basis or under the auspices of multinational forums like Paris Club.

(vii) The governments are forced to involve themselves due to absence of reinsurance.

(viii) The role of creditor governments in exporting or investing countries have gained importance. This is to ensure matching the credit terms more closely to the actual cash flow needs of project.

## EXPORT CREDIT GUARANTEE CORPORATION INDIA LIMITED (ECGC)

Export Credit guarantee Corporation of India Limited (ECGC), a company wholly owned by the Government, was set up in 1957 with the objective of supporting and strengthening the country's export promotion efforts. The present paid up capital of ECGC is Rs. 900 crores out of authorized share capital of Rs. 1000 crores. ECGC provides credit insurance covers to Indian exporters for both short term and project exports against loss in export of goods and services due to non-payment arising out of commercial and political risks and also catalyses the availability of adequate finance for exporting activity through export credit insurance covers provided to the commercial banks.

ECGC has been extending cover for exports from India since its inception. Such covers have been instrumental in promoting exports from India. These Exports have been effected by exporters under the Suppliers credit extended to them as well as under the Lines of Credit and or/Buyer's credit granted by Exim bank of India from time to time. This has enabled the Indian exporters to expand their exports to new markets.

ECGC has been operating various schemes under Project exports business through the following types of covers:

(i) Supply contracts and turnkey projects: For covering supply contracts and turnkey projects, Specific Contract/Shipments policy can be taken. This policy can be issued for covering only political risks or for covering comprehensive risks i.e. both commercial and political risks.

(ii) Construction contract: For covering a construction contract, a Construction Works policy can be obtained. This policy can be issued for covering either political risks alone or for comprehensive risks. The Comprehensive Risks Policy provides protection against commercial risks such as insolvency protracted default, nonacceptance of goods by buyer, in addition to covering political risks of war, civil war, exchange transfer delay etc. The political risks policy, on the other hand, provides protection against the political risks.

(iii) Services Contract: For covering services contract, which involves only technical and/or professional services, a Services policy can be obtained. This also can be either for political or comprehensive risks.

In addition to the policy covers, which are issued to exporters, ECGC also extends its export credit insurance support to banks in India against both funded and nonfunded facilities extended to project exporters. The types of export credit insurance for banks are as under:

**Funded**

- Packing Credit
- Post Shipment
- Overdraft
- Rupee Loan

**Non-Funded**

- Bid Bond
- Advance payment
- Performance guarantee
- Retention Money guarantee
- Overseas Lending Finance guarantee

ECGC's cover can be obtained by banks in India to protect them against any loss that they may sustain owing to the risks of non-payment by the exporter due to insolvency or default.

ECGC's approval of project exports and services contracts is based on the following aspects:

(i) The capacity of the project exporter to carry out large value contracts-technical, professional and managerial, and their past experience in the line of business.

(ii) Country to which the exports are to be made-stability of political setup/government, soundness of economy, payment records, relations with IMF, World Bank and other international FIs and donor countries.

(iii) Overseas contract/project-value, type of project, whether cleared by local authorities, profitability.

(iv) Buyer/employer-private/government.

(v) Payment terms and security, rate of interest for deferred receivables.

(vi) ECGC's underwriting policy on the country and its experience, whether any transfer delay experienced.

(vii) Berne Union experience-whether the credit period offered is in line with Berne Union understanding.

(viii) Reinsurance back-up available or not.

(ix) Whether cover can be extended for the contract under National Export Insurance Account set-up by Government of India.

**Line of Credit/ Buyer's Credit**

Financial institutions in India extend Buyer's Credit/Line of Credit to overseas buyers/institutions to facilitate export of goods and services from India. Institutions like Exim Bank as also commercial banks often seek ECGC cover for Buyer's.

Credit/LOC. Buyer's Credit/LOC cover can be obtained either for covering political risks or for comprehensive risks.

Factors weighing approval of Buyer's Credit proposals are: Competence and capacity of exporter in executing the contract; commercial justification of the contract; economic and financial viability of the overseas project for which credit is required to be offered; credit worthiness, standing and financial position of foreign buyers, and general economic conditions of the buyer's country.

Lines of Credit are generally extended by Exim Bank of India to financial institutions and governments in overseas countries facilitating export of consumer goods and capital goods.

**Overseas Investment Insurance**

Overseas Investment Insurance provides cover for the investments made by Indian corporates abroad in a joint venture or their wholly owned subsidiary (WOS) either in the form of equity or loan. The Government of India/RBI should approve the Joint Venture. The basic principle is that the investment should emanate from India and benefit of dividend/interest there-from should accrue to India. The investment should not in any way conflict with the policy of both our government and the overseas government. Normally, there should be a bilateral agreement between India and the host country for promotion and protection of Indian investment. In case there is no such agreement, the Corporation should be satisfied that the existing laws of the host country adequately safeguard Indian investment.

## TRENDS IN ECGC COVERS FOR PROJECT EXPORTS

The trends in ECGC coverage for the nineties and subsequent decade are highlighted below:

**Medium and Long Term Exports-Policy to Exporters (1993 to 1999)**

| | *1993* | *1994* | *1995* | *1996* | *1997* | *1998* | *1999* |
|---|---|---|---|---|---|---|---|
| Value Covered *(Rs crores)* | 651 | 1107 | 789 | 882 | 1014 | 1184 | 1551 |
| Premium Income *(Rs crores)* | 7.37 | 11.87 | 8.60 | 9.76 | 11.10 | 12.50 | 11.89 |
| No. of covers issued *(Numbers)* | 52 | 44 | 49 | 40 | 64 | 60 | 39 |
| Claims Paid *(Rs crores)* | 41.13 | 66.79 | 148.76 | 106.97 | 75.14 | 30.39 | 17.49 |
| Recovery made *(Rs crores)* | 15.55 | 9.96 | 16.52 | 5.80 | 0.16 | 1.12 | 0.54 |

*Source*: ECGC

**MLT Policy (2000–2006)**

| | *2000* | *2001* | *2002* | *2003* | *2004* | *2005* | *2006* |
|---|---|---|---|---|---|---|---|
| Value Covered *(Rs crores)* | 1815 | 574 | 360 | 737 | 1720 | 1436 | 1510 |
| Premium Income *(Rs crores)* | 12.70 | 8.70 | 5.77 | 8.62 | 10.62 | 12.83 | 16.00 |
| No. of covers issued *(Numbers)* | 47 | 25 | 37 | 48 | 42 | 44 | 35 |
| Claims Paid *(Rs crores)* | 0.71 | 5.62 | 0.00 | 0.28 | 4.14 | 1.98 | 10.42 |
| Recovery made *(Rs Crores)* | 0.00 | 2.78 | 0.00 | 0.53 | 0.09 | 0.00 | 13.45 |

*Source*: ECGC

**Medium and Long Term Exports-ECIB to Banks (1993 to 1999)**

| | *1993* | *1994* | *1995* | *1996* | *1997* | *1998* | *1999* |
|---|---|---|---|---|---|---|---|
| Value Covered *(Rs crores)* | 366 | 766 | 490 | 640 | 345 | 327 | 843 |
| Premium Income *(Rs crores)* | 3.82 | 5.13 | 6.34 | 5.06 | 5.61 | 5.49 | 6.01 |
| No. of covers issued *(Numbers)* | NA | NA | NA | NA | NA | NA | NA |
| Claims Paid *(Rs crores)* | 19.35 | 49.20 | 49.82 | 70.52 | 44.47 | 84.86 | 0.00 |
| Recovery made *(Rs crores)* | 0.00 | 24.95 | 29.25 | 36.77 | 22.35 | 11.14 | 0.00 |

*Source*: ECGC.

**MLT ECIB (2000–2006)**

| | 2000 | 2001 | 2002 | 2003 | 2004 | 2005 | 2006 |
|---|---|---|---|---|---|---|---|
| Value Covered *(Rs crores)* | 493 | 323 | 744 | 699 | 1088 | 1048 | 1917 |
| Premium Income *(Rs crores)* | 5.41 | 6.36 | 5.77 | 8.62 | 10.62 | 12.83 | 16.00 |
| No. of covers issued *(Numbers)* | NA | NA | NA | NA | NA | NA | 253 |
| Claims Paid *(Rs crores)* | 0.00 | 34.05 | 12.93 | 0.00 | 0.00 | 1.80 | 0.00 |
| Recovery made *(Rs Crores)* | 0.08 | 0.00 | 0.60 | 23.54 | 0.60 | 14.46 | 0.45 |

*Source:* ECGC.

### Details of OII Covered by ECGC Since Inception (The Scheme was Introduced during the Year 1980)

Since inception ECGC has issued 55 numbers of OII covers totalling a value of Rs. 619.60 crores. Of which 6 agreements are in force amounting to Rs. 194.14 crores, mainly equity investments. The countries included Nepal, Sri Lanka, Ethiopia, Canada, and China.

One Claim in Yugoslavia has been paid on account of War Risk amounting to Rs. 110.75 lacs.

## NATIONAL EXPORT INSURANCE ACCOUNT

### Definition of Neia

The National Export Insurance account is the account set up by the Government of India (GOI) and operated by ECGC to provide adequate credit insurance cover to project and term exports and overseas investment insurance covers.

### Setting up of Neia

The Task Force on Project Exports considered the matter of strengthening of ECGC.ECGC needs to strengthen its financial position which should result in providing cost–effective credit insurance schemes to the exporters in India. After 9/11, the reinsurance market had almost dried up. If there is a reinsurance market for project exports, ECGC can off load a part of its exposure in the reinsurance market. In its absence, it will have to bear the entire risk. ECGC has been adopting a cautious approach while considering proposals for large value projects and/or projects involving longer credit periods, in the aftermath of the gulf war. The claim payments have been made out of its own resources unlike the treasury support from the national governments to ECGC's counterparts like UK, Germany and France. In a calamitous situation like that of Iraq, the national governments have paid out of their budgets without affecting the financial position of credit risks insurers. ECGC had suggested that in the case of large projects, government should bear the risks.

Increasing the equity base of ECGC was considered as an alternate to provision of a NEIA facility. However, NEIA is to cater to project exports where as ECGC's capital base enables it too primarily to cover short term exports, which is the core, segment of its business. Further since ECC services more than 13000 policy holders and 23000 exporters thorough the ECIB covers, it would be conceptually sound to segregate risk exposure in terms short term exports and project term exports. If additional equity is provided to ECGC, it would be in a position to cover more exports, including project exports. However, for purposes of settlement of claims, it would be difficult to segregate premium earned and claim settled on short term and project exports. High value claim settlement in the project exports may also adversely impact the interest of small and medium exporters. Therefore, the handling of project exports under the NEIA is a more viable option. Yearly allocation currently to equity takes care of only short term underwriting capacity. . It was therefore decided to set up a National Export Insurance Account (NEIA) to ensure the availability of credit risk cover for project and deferred payment exports, which are considered commercially viable and which are desirable from the point of view of national interests, but which ECGC is unable to underwrite at its own terms. This will enable ECGC to evolve and grow itself to function as a significant credit insurance agency to support project exports from India.

**NEED FOR NEIA**

Indian companies secure overseas projects against stiff international competition. Adequate credit insurance that covers the political as well as the commercial risks of the country and the buyer involved enables the Indian companies to compete effectively with their competitors abroad and provides a level playing field. These projects are of crucial importance to the growth of the Indian economy due to the long term economic interests and political relationship with importing country. Indian companies , both in the public and private sector , are able to secure orders for overseas projects and ECGC is being called upon to provide underwriting support to an increasing number of such project exports and deferred payment exports , but its resources do not permit it to underwrite such high value project and deferred payment exports , as the organization underwriting exports has to be in a position to fully honour its commitments as and when the risk against which it has provided insurance materializes. ECGC would have been in a position to underwrite high value project and deferred payment exports if reinsurance was available at commercially acceptable terms. However, reinsurance is not available from even the General Insurance

Corporation of India, which is the national re-insurer or from international reinsurers. The objective of setting up NEIA is to provide insurance cover to project and term exports of high value, but beyond the underwriting capability of ECGC to underwrite and for which reinsurance is either not available or is available at a very high cost.

The initiative to enhance the equity base of ECGC every year is to meet its existing level of business. However since large value projects with medium and long term credit are being proposed to ECGC for coverage, the proposed NEIA would facilitate the required cover. Further though there are 13 private insurers in the market, after liberalization of the insurance sector, practically none of them is underwriting project exports even though some of these private insurance companies have tied up with global reinsurers. Most exporting countries have created National Interest Account or provide government guarantee or reinsurance because of nonavailability of privates the insurance/reinsurance in the global market. Thus the NEIA fund will facilitate a quantum jump in project exports while providing a level playing field to India exporters in the global project export market.

## PURPOSE OF NEIA

The purpose of NEIA is to promote exports from India and to protect the payment risks for commercially acceptable high value projects which are in national interest but beyond ECGC's underwriting capacity. Further, it purports to meet the cost of credit insurance (including reinsurance charges payable by ECGC) which ECGC would levy for project exports in circumstances where competitiveness of the Indian project exporters is affected.

## OBJECTIVES OF NEIA

The objectives of the NEIA are:

(i) To provide credit insurance risk covers for projects of high value which are of national interest but beyond the underwriting capacity of ECGC, without affecting the competitiveness of Indian exporters

(ii) Projects to be promoted will be those for which reinsurance is not available or the cost of such reinsurance is high.

(iii) To meet part of the cost of credit insurance where ECGC can provide cover with or without reinsurance at premium rates higher than those available in competing countries.

(iv) To provide cover to project exports to countries which are of strategic importance to India even though:

(a) the countries are temporarily experiencing economic and political difficulties

(b) the cover sought is beyond the country exposure limit of ECGC

(c) the countries are having non-marketable risks.

## BENEFITS TO EXPORTERS FROM NEIA

Exporters need to be assisted in undertaking projects overseas with help of credit insurance covers similar to those available to their competitors abroad. International Governments of all major exporting countries facilitate project exports through support for political risks cover. NEIA similarly helps Indian companies' secure insurance cover on international lines to ensure their competitiveness. The ability of Indian project exporters will not be hampered by non-availability of insurance cover. The NEIA will provide a level playing field to Indian exporters by providing insurance covers comparable with that provided by international organizations to their competitor's at rates and having features of schemes prevailing abroad.

## NEIA TRUST

The NEIA Trust, a public trust set up by the government will manage the funds provided by the government. The total corpus is Rs. 2000 crores to be funded during the tenth and eleventh plan period and currently the Fund has a corpus of Rs. 546 crores. Resources of the trust are the corpus and the premium income, interest income, and recovery of claims paid. ECGC will deduct a small amount from the premium towards administrative expenses.

## MECHANISM

The methodology for approvals of the NEIA scheme is as follows:

(i) The scheme is operated by ECGC, which receives the proposal, examines them as per guidelines approved by the Committee set up by GOI to examine the proposals and submits it to them for approval.

(ii) Approval for cover is given by the Committee set up by the government of India for approval viz. the Committee of Directions (COD).

(iii) The approved transactions are underwritten on NEIA account.

(iv) Premiums are received by ECGC and are credited to the NEIA trust after deducting the administrative expenses. Claims are paid by the NEIA trust.

## CRITERA TO BE TAKEN INTO ACCOUNT FOR SUPPORT TO PROJECT AND TERM EXPORT PROPOSLAS UNDER NEIA

NEIA is set up to consider only genuinely viable proposals and that supporting them will be in the national interest and must meet the following criteria:

(i) The project should be commercially viable and the risk should be acceptable.

(ii) The extent of International competition in the selection of the project exporter for executing the project.

(iii) Trade and political relationship with the country of the overseas buyer where the project is to be executed; the project should be strategically important for India, with regards to the economic and political relationship of India with the project country.

(iv) Proposal should conform to the guidelines issued by Reserve Bank of India, Director General of Foreign Trade and Financial institutions.

(v) The standing of the Indian project and his experience in execution of similar and other projects within and outside India; the exporter should be capable of executing the contract, as shall be evident from the previous track record.

(vi) Availability/Non-availability of reinsurance and the price.

(vii) Risks covered under the project.

(viii) ECGC is not able to cover the project on its own, due to its underwriting constraints.

## TYPE OF PROJECTS AND TRANSACTIONS FOR NEIA SUPPORT

The NEIA support is available for medium and long term project exports involving civil construction, turnkey projects , supply of equipment ands services and overseas investments provided they are viable and for which reinsurance is not available or the cost is high.

The transactions in the nature of a Buyer's credit, Line of credit, Supplier's credit and those involving project exports are considered for assistance under NEIA. This apart, investments involving Indian companies in overseas market can be covered for protection of their investments against expropriation risks and limited recourse covers (insolvency risks) against such joint ventures entities in favour of banks when they seek funding of international banks.

## NEIA ROLE

The average size of individual projects is not less than Rs. 100 crores. Countries in which project export opportunities have been occurring include countries like Iraq, Afghanistan, Libya, Sudan and Syria involving credit terms ranging from cash terms to deferred credit up to 5 years or even more.

Both in respect of new project exporters and well established companies, the banks are seeking ECGC's ECIB covers for the guarantees executed by them. In addition many project exporters also seek credit insurance protection from

ECGC.ECGC has had requests to cover projects in Libya, Iraq and Qatar of total value of Rs. 1200 crores. Moreover, some of the projects which have been bid for by Indian exporters are of a very high value, and in some cases exceeding Rs. 1000 crores. Some such projects are supply of railway wagons to South Africa, construction of railway lines in Malaysia, oil exploration in Sudan and power projects in Libya. Though exposures on such projects are justified, ECGC increasingly found it beyond its risk bearing capacity to underwrite the projects.

Setting up of National Export Insurance Account (NEIA) has enabled ECGC to provide underwriting support to more project exports. This ensures that more and more projects can be taken up for implementation. A corpus of Rs. 2000 crores on a conservative basis permits underwriting projects of a value of Rs. 15000 crores to Rs. 20000 crores. Assuming that on an average project has to be underwritten for a period 5 to 7 years; this would mean that project value of Rs. 3000 crores to Rs. 4000 crores can be provided underwriting support every year.

The NEIA can play major role in pushing projects and joint ventures in Africa. The mutual trade enhancement and synergy between India and Africa is enormous. Africa, despite many challenges it faced, has made considerable progress through astute macro-economic management and continued structural progress in a number of countries. Africa presents an ideal opportunity for export of projects in a variety of sectors. The credit insurance support through NEIA can establish and foster the presence of Indian exporters in a number of African countries. ECGC can support the efforts of Indian companies in their endeavours in seeking to contribute to the development of the emerging economic powerhouse–Africa.

## PROPOSALS COVERED UNDER NEIA:

The following Proposals were referred for NEIA cover:

The total number of projects considered under the NEIA were 6 . The project value of these contracts were USD 592 mn and the nature of projects were Development of Postal, Telecom

& IT sectors, Setting up of "Sudan Electronic city, Laying of multiproduct gas pipeline, Equity investment for setting up a fertiliser plant, Setting up 2X250 MW thermal power plant, Supply of aluminium conductors. The countries were Angola, Sudan, Iran, Indonesia and Ethopia. Two projects amounting to USD 60 mn are presently covered under NEIA.

The proposals in the pipeline are 5 in number of project value amounting to Rs. USD 303.05 mn The include contracts amounting to USD 303.05 mn. They included supply of aluminium, errection of MTPA gas plant, supply of helicopters, construction contracts. The countries are Ethopia, Iran, Bolivia, Namibia and Sri Lanka.

**DEMAND CONSTRAINTS FOR NEIA COVER:**

The demand for NEIA cover is driven by the defining trend in project exports, some of them are as under:

(i) Indian Contractors are not venturing abroad unlike their counterparts in the other countries because the infrastructure as well as demand for domestic projects in India more or less exhausts their capacity and unless the projects have an attractive element of higher profits, favourable terms, earning foreign exchange etc.

(ii) After the fallout of the Iraq war and consequent losses, Indian contractors are entering into cash contracts where payment is being made on progressive bills rather than equi-monthly instalments on a deferred terms basis. Thus, at the most one month's bills will be outstanding and therefore the payment risks are reduced to that extent. Further, unlike commodity supplies, the overseas clients are more interested in seeing that the project is complete in all respects as a semi-finished contract is of no use to them and therefore will be less inclined to terminate the contract mid-way. Also, with current scenario of banks hesitating to provide finance at competitive terms for such long duration projects, contractors can overcome their cash flow problems only by insisting on cash contracts.

(iii) Many of the projects offered internationally are funded by Multi-Lateral agencies and for which payment is secured which obviates the need for insurance cover.

(iv) Further, Indian contractors are employing sub-contractors for doing various portions of their contracts and who are to be paid immediately, whereas the main Indian contractor has to wait for payment from overseas client. Therefore, Indian contractors have to insist on cash contracts to overcome cash flow problems. In addition, the contractors are entering into consortium arrangements with local partners and therefore the risks are shared.

(v) Many Indian contractors are setting up their own companies abroad via investment route or outright buy out of foreign companies and these companies bid for contracts abroad and all insurance covers are availed of in overseas markets where the companies are located.

(vi) Another feature is that the contractors are insisting on Letters of Credit on practically majority of the contracts and the Indian contractors perceive the political risks as low even if they are executing contracts in the Middle East, Africa or South East Asia or South Asia as they have securities such as Central Bank LCs or LCs opened by Banks located in Free Foreign Currency areas. Also after the Iraq debacle, losses on account of Political Risks have come down significantly and therefore contractors are less inclined to cover their contracts on account of political risks.

(vii) Another notable feature is that many of the eligible contracts under deferred terms especially to emerging markets are covered by Lines of credit backed by the Government of India and therefore no demand for insurance cover is made to ECGC for such projects.

(viii) Many Indian contractors such as Larsen Toubro, KEC International, Punj Lloyd, Voltas, and BHEL, RITES etc have over the years with ECGC support and other factors grown in size and have with strong balance sheets. Also they have developed expertise in the field of executing contracts abroad and have become internationally reputed and they know the country well and their clients, Laws etc. They have expanded their basket of countries, the type and size of contracts and therefore believe that they have a sufficient pool of risks to hedge the payment risks on their own.

(ix) Contractors are also hesitant to approach the insurers for cover because of some features of the insurance products such as the pricing, the risk coverage, foreign exchange coverage, and procedural formalities at the time of claim and the responsibility of follow up of recovery.

(x) Many of the contractors and banks have a knowledge gap in the area of ECGC covers , NEIA etc. While some of the big players may be aware, the vast community of contractors are still to be educated on the availability of insurance cover under the umbrella of ECGC or the NEIA. It is not as if there is no appetite to cover political risks, many companies are approaching MIGA as well as Private Markets, Private Banks/Foreign Banks who have strong presence in the project countries.

## STEPS TO ENHANCE THE UTILISATION OF THE NEIA

The demand for Insurance covers and NEIA is likely develop over a period of time because of the following:

(i) The average size of contracts is now in the region of Rs. 1000 crores and large value contracts amounting to couple of thousand crores are more the rule rather than the exception. The contractors are therefore likely to seek risk mitigation techniques to offload the liability from their balance sheets.

(ii) The contractors are entering Africa in a big way and some of the political events in East, West and North Africa are likely to impinge on their ability to withstand losses on account of war, civil strife, unstable governments and political turmoil on their own without suitable Political Insurance cover.

(iii) Notwithstanding the existing financial turmoil in US, the oil and commodity shock, the inflation in most markets and consequent slowdown, India is poised to continue to develop its industrial prowess and it appears that Indian contractors will continue to seek contracts abroad. There will be a tremendous opportunity for ECAs in India and particularly ECGC and NEIA cover to support their efforts by taking care of their political risks and permit them to bid at competitive rates and secure contracts.

(iv) The pricing of ECGC products is done in a more transparent manner and in an aggressive manner in view of the fact that but for the large value claims paid on account of projects undertaken in Iraq during the 1st Gulf war, ECGC's claim: Premium ratio is favourable under medium and long term exports. Also, some features of pricing based on types of customer (volume discounts) will attract the contractors.

(v) Where Reinsurance is not available or highly priced, NEIA cover could be an enabling mechanism to support the contractors.

(vi) As Indian companies have developed the critical size and are venturing abroad by setting up joint ventures through equity or loan route or outright purchase, the demand for Overseas Insurance Cover is bound to increase with restructuring of the present Insurance cover in the form of wider scope and risks covered both political and commercial.

(vii) The Indian contractors are dispersed geographically within India and the marketing effort has to be re-galvanised to the contractors/banks through workshops/seminars/one to one meetings to educate them of the availability of NEIA facilities and request them to come forward and avail of these facilities which is remarkable for a country like India to have established, given the stage of economic development that it is presently placed..

## CONCLUSION

India's total merchandise trade (both exports and imports) is approximately US $ 400 billion during 2007-08, accounting for nearly 1.5% of world trade. If trade in services is added, India's commercial engagement with the world would be to the tune of US $ 525 billion. India is expected to achieve 5% share of world trade by 2020. If this were to happen, project exports would have a significant role to play.

Role of exports in economic growth has been increasing in recent years .Share of exports in GDP has increased from 3.4 % in 1970-71 to 4.7% in 1980-81 and further to 5.7% in 1990-91 and in 2000-2001 it was 9.9%. Subsequently, the contribution of exports to country's GDP has been significant accounting for as much as13% in 2005-06 and 14% in 2006-07. Export Growth leads to GDP growth and a 10% growth in exports would lead to an estimated 1% per cent growth in GDP.

An increased funds flow to export sector would enable project exports to be executed, which would be possible with highly competitive financial packages from the institutional set up. To enhance capacity utilisation and to create fresh capacity in many industries in India, availability of additional export credit would drive growth in exports thus enhancing India's economic growth and attendant multiplier effects.

Though the value of project exports of US$ 4.4 bn currently appears impressive, the potential is enormous. India's export basket has been dominated with performance of the software exports and gems and jewellery exports. But in the years to come, as India improves its industrial and technological capability and acquires expertise in power, refinery, construction, utilities, etc., it will be an industrial force to reckon with in the world. In the forthcoming decade as Asia, Africa start the process of accelerated development, China, South Korea, India etc will be in the fore front of leading the economic transformation of large parts of the globe. India and project exports will be the harbinger of the outward investment and exports to the emerging markets. Project exports and overseas investment will not only lead India's exports but also give a fillip to India foreign trade, overseas investment and economy. In this scenario, financial institutions, export promotion councils, Indian missions, Reserve bank of India, Government of India and not the least the national export credit insurer viz., ECGC will have to play a vital role in facilitating the emergence of India as a exporter of projects and setting up joint ventures companies overseas.

The National Export Insurance Account will be called upon increasingly to shoulder the burden of this responsibility of putting India on the global map of the super power in Turnkey contracts and project exports.

Clearly, Indian companies have demonstrated capabilities to secure contracts in India under stiff international competitive bidding conditions. This, however, does not get reflected into contracts overseas although the nature of such projects, the sectors to which these pertain and the skills and expertise required are well within the capabilities of Indian project exporters.

However, Indian companies are handicapped in terms of offering competitive credit and insurance package involving foreign currency, long repayment periods, and fine pricing. There is tremendous potential to boost the project exports from the current level of US $ 4 bn( cumulative value of contracts secured in the past few years and which are currently under different stages of execution) to US$ 10 bn in a very short period of time through institutional support , which may be achieved through GOI's steps to strengthen the ECGC's capacity and capability to support large project export contracts in line with international practices followed by other host governments for their officially supported export credit insurance organizations.

The major initiative taken in January 2006 of establishing the National Export Insurance Account (NEIA) is a step in this direction and will go a long way in giving an impetus to India's Project exports and to the advantage of the emerging opportunities around the world. It has enabled the ECGC to provide internationally competitive insurance packages at low premiums to project exporters in order to enable them to offer competitive bids in the face of stiff international competition and ensure success. The NEIA poses to be the harbinger of growth for the India's project exports and it is necessary that ECGC advertises this facility amongst the project exporters and they come forward to avail of the scheme which offers export credit insurance packages comparable to those available world over.

## REFERENCES

Report on the Task Force on Project Exports, January 2003.

Web–site of Department of Commerce, Ministry of Commerce and Industry, Government of India.

Web-site of Export Credit Corporation of India Limited.

Web-site of EXIM Bank of India.

Web-site of Reserve Bank of India.

Web-site of Projects Export Promotion Council.

Annual Reports of Export Credit Guarantee Corporation of India Ltd.

Annual Report of Department of Commerce, Government of India.

Annual Report of EXIM Bank of India.

Publications of Export Credit Guarantee Corporation of India Limited.

Press Release dated 24 March 2006 by Department of Commerce, Ministry of Commerce and Industry.

Smt. Tapasi Sen De, Deputy General Manager ,Project Exports Branch, Export Credit Guarantee Corporation of India Limited

Shri V.C.Kothari, Deputy General Manager, Larson & Toubro Limited.

Shri Sachin Raole, Deputy General Manager – Finance, KEC International Ltd.

Shri Pankaj Kumar, Assistant General Manager, State Bank of India, International Division, Mumbai.

# 6

# CHALLENGES FACED BY ECAs IN PROVIDING EXPORT CREDIT INSURANCE AND THE SOLUTIONS–AN INDIAN EXPERIENCE!

**V. Viswanathan**

## EXPORT CREDIT

The term "export credit" describes a range of facilities or schemes, and can mean different things in different contexts. Strictly speaking, export credit refers to (i) credit extended by exporters to importers (i.e. supplier credit), or (ii) Short Term/ Medium and Long Term loans made by banks (or EXIM Banks), used to finance working capital for export of goods and services/projects and capital goods exports (i.e. buyer credit). It includes credit extended both during the period before goods are shipped or projects completed (often referred to as the pre-shipment period or pre-credit period) and the period after delivery or acceptance of the goods or completion of the project (often referred to as the post-shipment period or credit period). Export credit and export credit insurance are the main types of facilities offered by an ECA. In India, the ECGC offers only the export credit insurance and commercial banks as well as Exim Bank of India provide export finance.

## ROLE OF AN ECA AND POLITICAL/ COMMERCIAL RISKS

The traditional role of an ECA is to support and encourage exports and outward investment by insuring international trade and investment transactions. While no two ECA are identical, they do share some common characteristics and mandates. At the very basic level, the common function of an ECA is to provide cover to exporters, banks, or investors for political and commercial risks causing loss over a short, medium, or long term.

For export credit transactions, political risks are the risks of non-payment under an export contract or project due to an action or failure by an importer's host government. Such action may include intervention to prevent the transfer of payments, cancellation of a licence or acts of war or civil war. Commercial risks arise primarily as a result of non-payment by a private buyer, commercial bank or a public buyer, due to default, insolvency or bankruptcy, or failure or willingness to take delivery of the goods (i.e. repudiation).

For foreign direct investments, ECAs (through Investment Insurance or Political Risk Insurance) can also cover political risks associated with expropriation, confiscation and nationalization without compensation, inability to convert and transfer profits and dividends and the effects of war and civil war.

Most ECA export credit support is provided via insurance or guarantees, and there is little practical difference between these instruments. ECA guarantees are more similar to insurance than typical financial guarantees. Typically, an insurance or guarantee policy embraces commercial and political causes of loss against specified risks or classes of risks and is therefore conditional. Insurance is normally available for less than 100%. Most of the ECAs like ECGC provide a maximum of 90% risk protection.

## EXPORT TRADE IS MUCH MORE COMPLEX

The modern picture of international trade is much more complex and much more dynamic. Businesses are investing in new markets to not only facilitate foreign sales, but to build global supply chains that will help them stay competitive. They are not only exporting goods, but services and technology –all of which still call for risk management expertise. And the unique market knowledge and skills that ECAs have cultivated for decades should make them more relevant than ever to businesses facing the pressures and realities of today's global marketplace.

## CHANGING EXPORT CREDIT BUSINESS AND CHALLENGES FOR ECAs

There have been profound changes in the export credit business across all market segments. Parallel to these changes are trade and investment liberalization, privatization and deregulation in emerging markets, launching of the HIPC (Highly Indebted and Poor Countries) Initiatives, and structural and institutional changes in the ECA sector. In addition, in many countries, the Government involvement is on the decline and the Credit Insurance is now mostly provided by the private sector. Credit insurers have globalized and in the recent times, there has been a significant consolidation within the industry.

Since their beginning, ECAs have had the ability to overcome obstacles to business transactions. But today, they have to remove obstacles to their very existence. The role that ECAs assume–the way they choose to shape themselves in the future—will determine their future viability. In that regard, they need to dispel the conventional role of a pure export credit and insurance provider and adopt a mandate framed in today's and tomorrow's terms–a mandate that responds to today's trade dynamics. They need to take a broader look at the market they serve, yet employ more dexterity in delivering support to their customers. Unlike the past, the ECAs face greater challenges today and they need to respond a lot more quicker.

## ECGC, THE NATIONAL CREDIT INSURER IN INDIA

Export Credit Insurance is the youngest in the branch of Insurance and in India the concept is just 50 years old. Export Credit Guarantee Corporation of India (ECGC) is the national credit insurer established in 1957 and has completed 50 years of its existence. Credit insurance as it exists to day in most of the countries including India is purely optional. In other words, there is no statutory backing as is available for the other general insurance business. In India, General Insurance business viz., insurance for property, safe custody of goods and also marine insurance have, to some extent, the regulatory backing. For instance, the Indian Customs authorities will not allow an export consignment to leave the shores of India unless the goods are adequately insured for marine risks. No such support is available for the Credit Insurance business. In addition, the concept of insurance be it Life Insurance or any other type of Insurance including credit insurance is yet to gain full acceptability. Thus, selling of insurance is a very challenging job. It is necessary for the Insurer to create a need in the customer before he can be successful. In practical terms, every customer would think of Insurance either after facing a catastrope or anticipates one.

## CHALLENGES FACED BY AN ECA IN PROVIDING EXPORT CREDIT INSURANCE

From the Indian experience, the following are some of the challenges faced by the ECAs in providing credit insurance covers for exports.

(i) Insensitivity of customers to Credit Risks.

(ii) Years of experience with buyers and countries with no major losses.

(iii) Willingness of banks to finance export receivables with out a credit Insurance backing.

(iv) Reduction in 'transaction cost' and the first cut will be in cost of Insurance covers that are not mandatorily required.

(v) Lack of awareness of the Credit insurance products.

(vi) Lack of credible information on buyers/ banks and the complex legal systems in certain countries.

(vii) The basket of business available for cover being very limited, as exports form a small portion of the entire economic activity in india

(viii) Competition due to opening of Insurance sector for private players.

(ix) Past unsatisfactory experience with the insurer in after sales service including claim settlements which spreads like a wild fire amongst the business community.

(x) Out dated principles still in place in the Credit insurance business like, the Principle of Whole turnover which requires an Insured to offer all his business for cover and insistence of covering Political risks automatically for any country etc.,

(xi) Lack of variety of products to suit the customers' requirements.

(xii) Alternate products like Factoring, Forfaiting available to exporters.

(xiii)Non availability of suitable reinsurance arrangements for ECAs especially under the Medium and Long term exports.

Let us discuss the issues now!

**Insensitivity of Customers to Credit Risks**

Insurance is nothing but a perception and therefore requires that the customers feel the need for the same. In the competitive world, it has become necessary for the customers especially the exporters to look out for more and more business irrespective of the destinations. More often, the exporters do not even look at the attendant risks relating to the buyers or the importing countries but only look at the business opportunities. In India, till recently, even the commercial banks were not country risk sensitive and had only a few countries in the negative list. Thus, the customers do not feel that they need to take insurance for the eventuality of the buyer or the importing country not paying in time for the goods. The exporters are often guided by general market information and unchecked credit information on the buyers. As regards importing countries, they hardly have any information. Exporters fail to appreciate that prompt payment by a buyer need not necessarily mean that he is credit worthy and will keep honouring his commitments at all times. It must be understood by them that the past experience does not guarantee future payments and often the buyers' ability to pay depends not only on his credit worthiness and financial capacity but also a host of other factors like the trade/business environment, behaviour of the commodity in the market and Government dictums. The exporter needs to understand and appreciate that he is dealing with buyers who are not governed by the same laws and regulations as those of his own country and there is a need to take care of the payments through a suitable insurance programme.

### Years of Experience with Buyers and Countries with No Major Losses

This is one of the major factors that contributes to the resistance of exporters in seeking insurance. Indian exporters feel that their buyers are good and the markets are safe purely from their own past experience and do not envisage any problem in future. They also hold the view that if a buyer is from a developed market, non payment risks may not exist at all. It is also seen that most of the export trade to these countries is done on 'open account' basis and Letters of Credit are a rarity. Our own experience in ECGC is that out of the commercial claims paid on account of buyer risks, developed countries account for more than 80%. In the recent times, due to recession in certain industries as also the economic slow down, default and insolvency claims in such countries have arisen and in most of the cases the buyers were very old. In a few of the recent cases, claims had arisen on account of insolvency of buyers who were in business for more than 7 to 8 decades.

### Willingness of Banks to Finance Export Receivables with Out a Credit Insurance Backing

Commercial banks in India consider post shipment finance to exporters against the export receivables. Normally, the banks look for tangible collateral securities for such credit facilities.

Intense competition and inability of the borrowers to provide matching collaterals are the major reasons for the banks to relax the conditions relating to collateral requirements. In most of the cases, the banks used to insist on the credit insurance covers to be obtained by their exporter customers. Such insurance provides the much needed collateral as, in case a claim is to be paid on a shipment that had resulted in default, the payment is usually made to the bank that handled the export bills, thereby enabling the bank to adjust the amount against the outstanding dues. In today's environment, customers are reluctant to obtain such covers and in the process, the banks too dispense with the credit insurance covers as a condition of sanction. Banks have to choose between the credit insurance cover and retention of customers. Thus, where the banks are not in a position to persuade a borrower to go for credit insurance cover, they have to look to the customer alone, in case any of the bills on overseas buyers is dishonoured. Credit insurers have to work overtime to convince exporters on the benefits of the covers and should also innovate a product that is not only reasonably priced but will meet the exporters' and their bankers' requirements. Export Factoring is one such product which will address the twin concerns of finance and credit insurance without recourse but alas, it is too expensive! Innovations are required to increase the business with the partnership of banks. In India, ECGC has introduced the concept of Bancassurance whereby banks are the Corporate agents to market the credit insurance covers and get paid for such selling! Hitherto, banks were helping ECGC without a return and now the arrangement is formalized. As on date 26 leading commercial banks in India both in the private sector and public sector are the Corporate agents of ECGC. In addition, insurance brokers, not known in credit insurance market have become very active in recent times and ECGC has empanelled about 100 of them to market its products. The Corporate agents and brokers are paid attractive commission of 10% for new business and this has made them take increased interest in selling ECGC's credit insurance products.

### Reduction of Transaction Cost and the First Cut will be in Insurance Covers that are not Mandatorily Required

Indian exporters are highly cost conscious. Often, when confronted with the Credit insurance proposal, one will not be surprised to find a ready made answer that the profit margin in exports is wafer thin and they can ill afford to take a cover. Exporters need to understand that where the margins are significantly high, the attendant credit risks will also be comparatively high. Where the margins are very low, the exporter will be under pressure to protect his principal against payment defaults! However, the whole of the exporting community today talks of reducing the 'transaction cost' to make exports competitive in the international market, totally ignoring the payment risks attendant to the cross border trade. In doing so, profits rather than prudence scores and the first victim will be the credit insurer. Besides, as already said, credit insurance for exports is not mandatory and exporter can choose to cover at his will. Credit insurers are, therefore, under pressure to substantially reduce the costs and make the covers attractive. ECGC had brought about a reduction of upto 40% in the premium rates a couple of years back and a further reduction of upto 10% last year. Besides, the No Claim Bonus rates have also been increased to as much as 70% in certain cases. A further reduction of 5% is available for upfront payment of full premium. Besides, customized solutions to meet the credit insurance requirements of exporters within their budgetary allocations have assumed greater role in the recent times. In a novel way, ECGC has also addressed the 'cost' concerns of exporters by facilitating marine insurance covers along with its own credit insurance covers through a tie up with one of the public sector general insurance companies. ECGC would meet the cost of such 'add on' marine cover to its customers which will be available on 'warehouse to warehouse' basis.

### Lack of Awareness of the Credit Insurance Products

Lack of awareness of the credit insurance services and the attendant risks in export trade is a major challenge that the credit insurers have been facing though the situation is fast changing now. In India, the credit insurance schemes are in place for more than 5 decades now but the awareness has not set in fully. The Indian economy has been booming in the recent years and the exports have been growing at a faster pace of more than 20% on an annual basis. Software and services exports have shown exponential growth. Indian exports go to as many as 200 and odd markets in the world. Indian exporters have accessed unchartered territories now and have become successful. The potential for Indian exports lies everywhere today. 'India everywhere' is the slogan adopted by the business community. However, Indian exporters do not have a sound knowledge of the credit risks in these markets as also the available insurance support. Till recently, the credit insurance products were sold with the assistance of the commercial banks and by personal selling. The information gap continued to remain till the late 90s when the Indian Insurance industry was opened up and the competition had set in. Per force, the Insurance companies had to spend substantially on advertisement and publicity. Credit Insurance industry in India continues to be dominated by ECGC even today but the need to publicise its products and services has become very important not only for increasing the business but even to retain the existing clients. Because of continuous efforts, the level of awareness has significantly risen but a lot more needs to be done in this direction. In addition, in India, the Insurance Regulatory and Development Authority (IRDA) has been set up as the nodal authority to regulate insurance business including the Credit insurance. The association with the IRDA has enabled the insurers including ECGC to spread the message to the customers in an effective manner.

### Lack of Credible Information on Buyers/ Banks and Complex Legal Systems in Certain Countries

Yet another challenge faced by an ECA is the problem of getting credit information on buyers and banks in some countries. Exporters are now going to unchartered territories and invariably look to the ECA to support them as they are new to the buyers as well as the importing countries. In many such situations, though the ECA will be more than willing to support the trade, the problem of getting proper buyer/bank information comes as a cropper. In addition, the complex legal systems in certain countries which result in delayed decisions also pose a challenge to the ECAs in looking at such markets more favourably. Thus, the need of the hour is the availability of data and information on buyers, banks and countries, their political and legal systems. One possible solution is a better cooperation among the ECAs operating in such countries or having a fair amount of experience in insuring exports to these countries. ECGC has been endeavouring to get into cooperation alliances and as on date about 20 such arrangements are in place. The other solution is the tie up with credit information agencies of repute which the channel normally used by most of the ECAs. ECGC has arrangement with more than 15 credit information agencies as on date. The third option is the credit information/report on the buyers from the buyers' banks, which is very rare to come and is more often not available due to the confidentiality issues between the banks and their borrowers. However, there have been cases where buyers have willingly agreed for parting with the credit information for furthering their business.

**The Basket of Business Available for Cover being Very Limited**

Indian exports form a small portion of the entire economic activity. It accounts for just above 10% of the GDP. Thus, the business available to the ECA is very limited. The Indian exports in 2007-08 amounted to approximately USD160 bn. There are several components of the export trade viz., Government to Government exports, export of petroleum and petroleum products, exports against advance payment terms, exports backed by Letters of Credit which are confirmed by local banks, certain commodities like exports of gem & jewellery where a significant portion of exports take place to the overseas associates, which are not amenable to credit insurance. Therefore, a major portion of exports out of India will be outside the ambit of credit insurance. On a rough estimate, the available credit insurance market is estimated to be around 30% to 40%. This figure could be much lower as no authentic data is available and the same is based on past estimates and figures. Even in this limited market, there could be transactions like exports against Letters of Credit or other services exports like software or ITES exports that may not need the credit insurance support or the type of risks attendant to these trade (risk of non payment due to commission and omission, cost and time escalation not secured under the contract etc.,) may not come under the ambit of covers offered by an ECA. The answer to this is innovation. ECAs have to think out of the box and consider covers for risks which will not be strictly credit risks but could be ancillary risks.

Some such risks that may arise are as under:

(a) Risks of rejection/penalties due to Governmental action like anti dumping duty.

(b) Under software exports, sudden cancellation of visas for the personnel undertaking a project.

(c) Illegal detention of personnel in the country where services are rendered by an exporter.

(d) Rejection of consignments due to certain antibiotic or other chemical contents that could not be detected even after very rigorous inspection procedures due to lack of advanced inspection techniques.

These risks cannot be treated strictly as credit risks but could result in the risk of non payment as a consequential risk. ECAs have to innovate and find answers for these risks. ECGC has come out with special 'add on' covers for these types of risks. In respect of software exports, covers for software exports and ITES have been devised and some of the above risks have been brought under special risks. However, it may have to be mentioned that there are still certain risks which will still remain outside the domain of credit insurance and a constant interaction with other general insurers is the only way to find answers. As has always been the case, ECGC endeavours to facilitate coverage of export risks either under its own schemes or in partnership with other insurers. In addition to the credit insurance covers, a vast market exists for insuring commercial banks against the non payment risks of exporters who avail 'working capital finance' from the banks. ECGC has in place credit insurance schemes to banks protecting them against the non payment risks of Indian exporters. What is protected in the lending risk of a banker! The schemes are in place for well over 4 decades and have immensely contributed to the growth of exports and export financing in India. The credit insurance covers to banks are in the nature of sureties.

**Competition Due to Opening of Insurance Sector for Private Players**

Since the late 90s, Indian Insurance industry has been opened up for private players and Credit insurance is not an exception. There are about six to seven players in credit insurance market today in India. Most of the competitors are on a highly sophisticated technology platform and are supported by overseas ECAs in terms of technical knowledge. Besides, their concentration is on the high end customers. Thus, there is a real threat for the ECAs to sustain the existing level of business. ECGC, being a pioneer in this field and having time tested schemes well suited to local conditions, is able to ward off the threat and increase its coverage substantially over the years. By operating the credit insurance schemes to banks, ECGC is in an advantageous position to target customers better than the competitors. In addition, constant churning of the schemes and carrying out changes and improvements in the schemes which are very essential for procuring new business and also for retention of existing customers is a regular activity in ECGC. ECGC has been constantly reviewing its schemes and making changes to meet the requirements of the customers and at the same time coming out with new schemes. As on date, there are in all about 15 covers available to an Indian exporter to choose from and this apart a customized cover can also be designed to suit any exporter's requirements. In the ever growing market like India, exporters seek solution for insuring not only their export receivables but also their domestic sales. Competitor are able to offer risk insurance solutions to address the concerns of exporters in respect of their overseas as well as local sales. ECGC is geared up to offer such domestic credit insurance covers not only to the exporters but also to their banks who will finance the receivables. The Corporation is awaiting regulatory approvals and the products will hit the markets shortly. Thus, change and innovation are keys to beat the competition!

**Past Unsatisfactory Experience with the Insurer in Claim Settlements which Spreads Like a wild Fire amongst the Business Community**

Nothing works against an insurer than an adverse publicity. Normally, insurers are not liked because they are seemed to be wiser at the time of crisis. It is not uncommon for an insurer to disown liability in a catastropic situation. The problems faced by insurers, more so ECAs, is the non compliance of the terms and conditions of the insurance cover by the exporters. Problems become acute in case of whole turn over covers, wherein the exporter would not have kept the covers in good order, would not have declared all the shipments or remitted premium in due time. While exporters would deem it their right to get a claim when the insurer accepts premium, the insurer would argue that mere payment of premium in itself is not sufficient. An aggrieved customer would not only spread adverse news in the market but would also drag the insurer to a court of law. In many situations, the courts have also given their verdict against the insurer thereby giving an impression that the insurers have a general attitude to repudiate the liabilities. Thus, an ECA needs to be careful before taking a negative view of a claim. There is a need for a very positive approach. Here again, there are certain steps that the insurer can take to avoid facing the criticism. Proper customer education and claim workshops to explain the details to the exporters will go a long way in building a lasting relationship. Besides, the insurer should constantly evaluate the impediments in the operation of the schemes and make changes. In India, it was found that the declaration policies where the exporters are to pay premium in the succeeding month of shipment is a serious impediment in administering the schemes. On the one hand, exporters did not declare shipments and pay premium if the payments for shipments were already received by the time they are to report to ECGC and on the other, they would rush up and pay premium in and around the due dates of the shipments, if they remained unpaid as on those dates. It is not uncommon for an exporter to claim ignorance of the procedural requirements and claim immunity. The insurer is placed in a piquant situation. While he would deem it a requirement on the part of the exporter to pay the premium, when it is the question of assuming a liability, he would hesitate to take a positive view. There could be many such procedural bottlenecks. On the basis of the experience gained over the years, ECGC brought about procedural simplifications. The exporters are now required to pay advance premium and ECGC encourages them to avail of instalment facility, if for any reason the exporter cannot pay the annual premium in full in one stroke. This measure is also in compliance with the Section 64 VB of the Insurance Act 1938, which warrants that the insurer shall have the premium in advance in his kitty before he assumes the attendant risks. In addition, the returns are collected on a consolidated basis either on a monthly basis (one consolidated turnover figure per buyer) or on a quarterly basis depending on the status of the buyer. It was also observed that proper customer education is the key to success of insurance products. ECGC has come out with detailed brochures on its schemes and a scheme wise Dos and Donts. These requirements are explained in customer meets organized at various centres. These measures have not only helped exporters understand the covers better but has also enabled ECGC to bring down the rejection ratio of the claims. Lower rejections have lead to higher customer satisfaction and retention.

**Out Dated Principles Still in Place in the Credit Insurance Business Like, the Principle of Whole Turnover which Requires an Insured to Offer all his Business for Cover; the Principle of Covering Political Risks Automatically for any Country etc.,**

Traditionally, the credit insurance principles postulate as under:

- Exporter shall offer for cover all his shipments during a specified period of one or two years of cover (Whole turnover principle).
- Political risks are automatically covered irrespective of the country of destination and the exporter will have no choice to exclude the risks.
- Commercial risks or Political risks are available only as a bouquet and the exporter will have no freedom to choose among the risks in that category; in otherwords, if exporter chooses to cover commercial risks on a buyer, he has to necessarily cover the risks of insolvency, default and repudiation , even if any of the risks is not perceived by the exporter.
- Insurer has to be consulted at every stage with very little discretion to the exporter.
- While the insurer will have an option to cover or not to cover a particular shipment, no such option will be available for the exporter. The exporter will have an option to exclude a shipment only if the insurer has refused cover. Even in such cases, the exporter would be required to pay premium for Political risks.

These principles have lost their significance in Indian context today. In a competitive environment where the exporter can have a choice and would also choose to cover transactions selectively, these stipulations have lost their importance. Where such covers are sold, invariably there would be non compliance by exporters. Here again, ECAs have to rethink of alternate strategies and relaxations in procedures. In ECGC while we have retained the traditional principles under certain covers, there are new innovations which an exporter can examine. The

Whole turnover principle has been diluted giving the option to exporters to selectively cover shipments at a reciprocal cost, increased discretionary powers at the time of coverage and at the claim settlement stage. Now, an exporter can choose to cover all or any of the credit risks under the Commercial/Political risks category under a customized solution. In respect of a shipment under cover, there are automatic provisions like no requirement of a drawee-wise limit upto a certain amount depending on the size of exports and credit insurance availed. In addition, the exporter is not required to obtain the prior approval, if the losses in respect of a shipment due to resale, re-import etc. do not exceed 25% of the Gross Invoice Value etc., Further, commodity, country, LC and buyer exclusions are also available. ECGC is also currently providing on a selective basis, as a customized solution, cover for buyer risks alone keeping the political risks outside the purview.

**Lack of Variety of Products to Suit the Customers' Requirements**

Lack of a choice of products from an ECA makes the selling of covers very difficult. Most of the ECAs have a very limited number of products. There could be a Whole turnover product (WT) or a single transaction cover. These do not meet the requirements of exporters. While the WT product requires insuring all the shipments, opting for covers on shipment basis will increase the administrative work of an exporter and the cover will also be priced relatively higher. The WT policies are based on turnover coverage and an exporter would not like to cover the entire turnover. Based on past experience in bad debts, exporters look for cover options based on outstanding at any given point of time, known as exposure covers. In addition, where an exporter is dealing with more than one buyer, country or commodity, he would choose to cover or exclude credit risks/buyers/countries/commodities as per his own risk perception. The limited covers available with ECAs do not address the requirements in today's changed environment. ECGC in anticipation of the customer needs and also to keep itself updated with the market requirements has evolved several covers. An exporter can have any or a combination of the following:

- Wholeturnover cover for all his shipments.
- Small exporters covers for exporters with annual exports not exceeding IRS5mn.
- Specific shipment covers for each export transaction.
- Annual turnover covers where a lot of procedural simplifications are available for large exporters paying an annual premium of not less than IRS1mn.
- Buyerwise turnover covers where an exporter can selectively cover his exports to a specified buyer.
- Buyerwise exposure covers where the exporter can have a cover on anticipated outstanding or exposure basis on a specified buyer.
- Multi buyer covers where an exporter can choose to cover more than one buyer on exposure basis.
- Covers for MSME exporters on exposure basis
- Consignment exports covers (Stock holding agent/ Global entity) where goods are sold on consignment basis.
- Software exports cover for exporters dealing in software exports (on site or off site or both).
- IT enabled services ( Single buyer) cover for a specified buyer for a defined period.
- IT enabled services (Multi buyer) cover for more than one buyer for a defined period.
- In addition, if the exporter desires to have a combination of any of these covers or desires cover for select risks, ECGC can customize a cover for him. Thus, it is very necessary for the ECAs to keep adding products to meet the growing needs of the exporters. This is very much possible!

**Alternate Products Like Factoring, Forfaiting Available to Exporters**

One of the recent developments in Indian financial system is the emergence of Factoring/Forfaiting as an alternate tool for financing and credit insurance. The receivables financing by commercial banks as well as the insurance provided by ECAs are with recourse. In case of non payment of the bills, the bank will look to the exporter to repay the advances availed. In case of an ECA, the exporter is required to initiate recovery action against the buyer at his own cost and share the recoveries with the insurer. Thus, an exporter in India has a choice to look to a Factor from whom he can avail both finance and credit protection without recourse. However, Export Factoring is in the nascent stages in India and is not seen as a threat for the reason that the cost of factoring service is prohibitively high and the bank's do not agree to the request of exporters for purchase of debts by a Factoring company. However, Factors in course of time, with increased volumes and reduced costs can be a big challenge to the ECAs. Sensing the potential problems that may arise, ECGC has already introduced factoring services by tying up with a commercial bank for finance. The scheme has an added benefit of providing the credit protection to the bank if the payment by overseas buyer is refused due to trade disputes.

**Non Availability of Suitable Reinsurance Arrangements for ECAs Especially Under the Medium and Long term Exports**

It is learnt that there are very few re-insurers who are willing to support ECAs with a suitable reinsurance programme. Non availability of reinsurance arrangements restrict the ability of ECAs to underwrite liberally. It is our experience in ECGC that wherever we have floated the queries, the re-insurers looking for utmost safety have provided unattractive offers. The target markets for countries like India and the related export potential are some of the factors that need to be seriously considered by the reinsurance market. Even with an enviable past track record, obtaining a reinsurance cover on attractive terms is becoming very difficult. The problems worsen if we are to seek reinsurance covers for Medium and long term exports. Indian contractors are going in a big way to secure contracts overseas. The contracts are secured in countries in Africa and South East Asia. In most of the cases, the project period is not less than 5 to 7 years. Thus, credits of not less than 10 to 13 years with initial moratorium of 3 to 4 years are sought. Re-insurers are not willing to look at such long horizons! Thus, for a healthy growth of credit insurance, availability of reinsurance covers at affordable rates is very necessary. With sustained efforts both in India and overseas, ECGC could secure reinsurance covers now for its short term business. This is made possible through a reinsurance programme with the General Insurance Corporation of India, the national reinsurer and some of the public sector general insurance companies. Further efforts are on to secure reinsurance for the medium and long term export covers as well.

## CONCLUSION

The speed at which the world is changing, more so the developing economies, calls for sophistication and efficiency. It calls for new models. In response, ECGC is constantly refining its approach to devise solutions that will meet the needs of the market place and other ECAs are doing the same. ECAs will continue to be relevant players in the international trade. It has been our experience in ECGC to keep a constant watch on the developments in the international trade for the past 50 years. And as we face the future, we'll just keep looking at our products constantly and bring out the changes in tune with the need of the hours! In fact that is what we had been doing all these years and the changes have kept us on course and that's what will keep us from foundering as the journey continues. For us, changes are permanent!

# 7

# ALTERNATE CHANNELS FOR MARKETING CREDIT INSURANCE PRODUCTS

**R. Mohan**

## BIRTH OF CREDIT INSURANCE IN INDIA

After independence, India had to evolve the system of five year plan to take care of the economic, fiscal and trade policies. After the five year plan in 1955-56, the planners raised the slogan Export or Perish. This slogan is relevant even today. It is expected that any country has to be self reliant in both agriculture and industry. The imports for both these sectors would have to be paid for by the exports and foreign aid playing the part of only a catalytic agent.

The export promotion drive started immediately after independence even though India had some sterling balances built up by exports to Britain during the World War II. The leaders knew that these balances would not last long after the initiation of massive development projects. This resulted in the formation of Export Promotion committee by the Government of India in 1949. The purpose of this committee was to recommend measures for accelerating exports. It was felt that there will not be that amount of business which would allow such a scheme to be worked successfully in all the circumstances. Therefore, it took a lot of time for the Government of India in setting up the scheme. In 1955 it was realized the importance of export promotion and a special committee was appointed under the chairmanship of Mr. T. C. Kapur retired General Manager of Bombay Mutual Life Assurance Society Limited to examine the feasibility of setting up an effective organization to provide insurance against exports.

It is indeed a risky operation to export goods to other countries. Though general insurance companies were underwriting risks relating to fire, plunder, riots, loss in accidents etc, no company in India was willing to underwrite a risk involving bankruptcy of the importer or due to changes caused by political upheavals. The Kapur committee built up a formidable case for the establishment of an organization for export credit insurance. By opting for the credit insurance, the insured is enabled to sell on credit terms and thereby successfully compete with exporters from other countries and increase the volume of his business. In the 1950s when traditional items like jute fabrics, tea, cotton textiles were exported no attempt was made to venture into new countries. Young companies could discover new markets only if export credit insurance could be readily made available to them. The recommendations of the committee were accepted and thus the export credit insurance business took birth in India in the name of Export Risks Insurance Corportation (ERIC) on July 30, 1957. Statistics show that though it was a monopoly business for ERIC, it successfully carried forward the role for which it was set up. ERIC was renamed as Export Credit Guarantee Corporation and it is now known as Export Credit Guarantee Corporation of India Limited (ECGC).

## ROLE OF ECGC IN THE ECONOMY

The role of ECGC is to promote exports from India. The main goal of ECGC is to excel in providing cost effective credit insurance products to the customers. The ECGC aims at providing world class service at the lowest cost that can be borne by the exporting community.

## NECESSITY OF ALTERNATE CHANNELS

It is acknowledged fact that Insurance, especially in India, is more sold than bought. The complexities involved in export credit insurance are difficult to explain and understand. There is always a tendency to postpone or avoid taking an insurance product. The low awareness levels in the society further add to the difficulty in selling credit insurance products. Distribution channels, therefore, becomes the key link in the chain of activities in the business of insurance. In India, distribution, which essentially means carrying the message of insurance through the last but toughest mile, acquires even greater pre-eminence. The expectation of the prospect is that after obtaining insurance, the claim should not be repudiated and therefore, the insurance company is expected to be transparent not only in providing all the details of the scheme but also periodically check and advise measure of mitigation of losses, if any. It requires constant touch with the policyholder in order to understand the business transacted and examination of the risks involved. Thus alternate channel provides the opportunity to the insurer to be present everywhere through agency arrangements for marketing and servicing of the insurance products. The innovate method of alternate channels paved the way for the insurance companies to penetrate the potentially untouched markets.

## PROVISIONS IN INSURANCE ACT 1938

In India, the Insurance Act 1938 has laid out clear cut provisions on the following issues pertaining to distribution of insurance.

(1) Licensing of Insurance Agents

(2) Conditions/ceilings on payment of commission

(3) Privileges of Agents

(4) Code of conduct for agents

Since the insurance industry was run by the state owned companies, the distribution of insurance was largely confined to the agency channel. The credit insurance business was exclusively conducted by ECGC with the monopoly status. Certain provisions of the insurance act 1938 was waived for

ECGC keeping in mind the promotion of exports from India. ECGC did not resort to any distribution channel for credit insurance and therefore was managing the entire distribution and servicing by its own personnel.

### IRDA

Following the privatisation of the insurance industry in 1999, the Insurance Regulatory and Development Authority (IRDA) was set up to regulate, promote and ensure orderly growth of the insurance industry. It became mandatory for all insurance and reinsurance companies operating in India to register with this body.

IRDA has brought modifications to the distribution channels by way of regulations. The following were the changes made by IRDA pertaining to distribution channels.

(1) Specification of minimum educational qualification for agents and intermediaries;

(2) Mandatory pre-license training and examination;

(3) Issue of License by IRDA

(4) Code of conduct for all intermediaries;

(5) Issue of regulations allowing/regulating corporate agencies, brokers and referrals.

The changes that were brought in by IRDA have contributed to improvement in the quality of distribution in the insurance sector.

### EXPORT CREDIT INSURANCE – GENERAL INSURANCE PRODUCT

The export credit insurance is categorized as 'miscellaneous' category of insurance under general insurance by the IRDA. Since ECGC is dealing only with Export Credit Insurance, the details of the business done by ECGC are shown as 'specialised companies' by IRDA. Several steps are taken to increase the penetration level but the statistics show that general insurance penetration in India is the lowest at 0.60% of the GDP. Talking on the export credit insurance, ECGC has been covering around 10% of India's exports. The reason for the low penetration was that the insurable exports such as petroleum products, government to government trade, exports covered by line of credit by Exim Bank of India and soft ware exports are not generally insured with ECGC. Of the insurable exports, ECGC is covering a sizeable portion of the exports made. The trend in International trade is changing with the buyers not willing to send advance payment, open letters of credit and opting for more and more credit and open account transactions. Thus, the future of export credit insurance in the years to come seems to be quite bright. It is gathered that more than 60% of the business is coming from the agency channel, around 17% through brokers, about 15% from the Corporate Agencies and referrals constitute only 6.4% of the general insurance business India. The ratio for credit insurance is very less compared to other general insurance business.

### Guiding Principles for Alternate Channels

As explained above, it is necessary to keep the following principles so that the insurance industry can provide economic growth and employment opportunities too.

- Bring credit insurance to the doorstep of the customer;
- Expand distribution–In addition to developing existing insurance channels, get other existing retail distribution infrastructure to sell credit insurance;
- Encourage virtual channels and direct customer interaction;
- Unlike life and other general insurance products, export credit insurance needs frequent interactions with the insured by the intermediary to ensure proper compliance of the policy conditions, to notify any loss situation and to take prompt steps for mitigating the loss.

## CORPORATE AGENCY/ REFERRAL AND BANCASSURANCE MODELS

Export credit insurance is protecting the foreign currency receivables of the exporter. It becomes necessary for the exporter who is the beneficiary under the export contracts, to ensure that the rules of Foreign Exchange Management Act are complied with properly. In India, Reserve Bank of India has authorized the commercial banks to handle foreign exchange. Hence, it is necessary for the exporters to receive the payments from the overseas buyers only through the authorized channels i.e. the commercial banks. The commercial banks lend money to their exporter customers in the form of export packing credit, bill discounting and bank guarantees etc. The commercial banks have a large data base of the active exporters. Therefore, this is one of the important models especially for distribution of export credit insurance.

## REFERRAL MODEL

The data base available with the commercial banks is used by the credit insurer for expanding the clientele and business. However, this model does not seem to have made an impact as the data does not give full details of the exporter such as the terms of payment on which the exports are made, commodity dealt, countries to which the exports are made etc. (Refer to the IRDA site for referral arrangements and add). In addition to the commercial banks, there could be various other entities which could act as a referral provider due to the large data base of members such as export promotion councils, commodity boards, Federation of Indian Exporters Organisation etc. These organizations may not be a licensed intermediary but can be regulated by the Insurance regulator.

## CORPORATE AGENCY/ BANCASSURANCE MODEL

Bancassurance in India is developing as an important channel for distribution to a growing class of customers. The persistency rate in Bancassurance due to the continuing contact of the bank with its customers, the ease of payment of premium and the facility of maturity/claim payments to the Bank account make it a very customer friendly channel. Bancassurance in India has been a recent phenomenon. In the past seven years it has emerged as a rapidly growing distribution channel. The banks, for the purpose of increasing the fee based in income, started entering into Corporate Agency agreements with the insurance companies. This facilitates the exporter customer of the bank to seek proper financial and insurance solutions from the counters of the banks. As per the current regulations, Banks can either opt to become a corporate agent or act as a referral provider to an insurance company. However they are permitted to act for only one life and one non life company in India. In the current regulatory provisions, the basic difference between a corporate agent and a referral provider is that of licensing–Corporate agent is a licensed intermediary while referrals need not be licensed.

The salient features of the Corporate Agency regulation dated 16th October, 2002 are as under:

(1) Corporate Agent can hold license to act for one general insurance or one life insurance company;

(2) Composite Corporate Agent means a Corporate Agent who holds a license to act as an insurance agent for a life insurer and a general insurer;

(3) Any of the following entity can become a Corporate Agency:

   (i) A firm;

   (ii) A company formed under the Companies Act, 1956

   (iii) A banking company as defined in Clause (4A) of section 2 of the act; or

   (iv) A corresponding new bank as defined under clause (d(a)) of sub-section (1) of section 5 of the Banking Companies Act, 1949 (10 of 1949); or

   (v) A regional rural bank established under section 3 of the Regional Rural Banks Act, 1976;

   (vi) A co-operative society including a co-operative bank, registered under the Co-operative Societies Act 1912 or under any law for the registration of co-operative societies;

   (vii) A panchayat or a local authority;

   (viii) A NGO or a micro lending finance organisation covered under the Co-operative Societies Act or a

Non Banking Financial Company registered with the Reserve Bank of India; or

(ix) Any other institution or organisation which is specifically approved by the IRDA.

(4) An application has to be made to the Insurance company's designated person and on scrutiny and satisfaction, such designated person shall grant or renew the licence with in a period of 3 months from the date of application. The requisite fee is to be remitted to IRDA.

(5) The applicant shall ensure that the constitution of the entity shall contain as one of its main objects soliciting or procuring insurance business as a Corporate Agent.

(6) The Corporate insurance executive and a specified person shall possess the minimum qualification of a pass in 12th Standard or equivalent examination.

(7) The Corporate insurance executive and specified person shall have completed from an approved institution, at least, one hundred hours practical training and if the executive is professionally qualified then he needs to undergo fifty hours of practical training;

(8) Every Corporate Agent shall abide by the code of conduct by ensuring that the corporate insurance executive and specified person

(i) is responsible for all acts of omission and commission;

(ii) is properly trained, skilled and knowledgeable in the product;

(iii) does not misrepresent on policy benefits;

(iv) does not force any prospect to by an insurance product;

(v) gives adequate pre and post sales advice;

(vi) extends all co-operation in the event of a claim;

(vii) does not underwrite the risks or act as an insurer.

## LIMITATIONS

While in the developed countries it is said that the corporate agents' route is very successful and up to 25% of the total premium is secured by the corporate agents, in India, the credit insurance through bancassurance model is yet to be successful and suffers due to the following:

(a) Post VRS arena, the bank officials do not find time to concentrate on the marketing or sale of the insurance products;

(b) The commission does not attract the specified persons as the commission is paid to the corporate agent and no incentives are passed on to the specified person or the executive depending on the sales;

(c) It is comparatively easier to sell the general insurance products and life insurance than the credit insurance product;

(d) The after sales service is looked up on as a cumbersome procedure;

(e) The lack of knowledge on the credit insurance products from the sales personnel make it more difficult;

(f) Fear of loss of business prospects for the bank.

With the introduction of core banking solutions, creation of new generation banks and the adoption of software technologies adopted by the insurance companies, synergy will pave way for adequate business solutions for the customers. It is expected that in India, bancassurance model will play an important role in developing both financial and insurance markets in future by the technologies adopted. During 2006-07 Corporate Agents had procured 7.3% of the total new business premium mobilized, two-thirds of which had come from the bancassurances.

## AGENCY MODEL

Insurance agent means an agent who holds a license to act as an insurance agent for a life or a general insurance company. As stated else where, 60% of the general insurance business is secured through this model. The agency system is predominant in India as historically face to face contact was considered essential in selling an insurance product. Despite the emergence of new channels of distribution, agency channel remains the mainstay of the insurance sector. However, in the general insurance industry around 40,000 agents were enrolled by the general insurance companies in the year 2005-06 as against 7 lakhs intermediaries licensed by the life insurance companies. This is due to the fact that general insurance is not being considered an attractive career option as it is perceived to be difficult for the agent to make a livelihood from sales of only general insurance products. Taking credit insurance agency is all the more complex as the products can be sold only to the exporting community which is very limited in number. The limitations faced by the agents are the fixed commission, alternative lucrative distribution opportunities and restriction of selling products of more than one insurance company. IRDA has specified the obligations of the agent as the ones that are stipulated for the Corporate Agency. The life insurance agents are more in numbers as the commission is attractive. Compared to this, General Insurance products commission is not remunerative and is also difficult to sell. The agents do not choose to sell the credit insurance products as the product is to be focussed to the exporters and necessary post sales service is to be provided in case a claim arises. As per the IRDA regulations in vogue, if the agent opts to sell the credit insurance products he will not be allowed to sell any other general insurance product.

As regards training of the agents, credit insurance organisation has no recognition to train and issue the license and depend mostly on the general insurance companies for the mandatory training though expertise lies with the credit insurance company. This leads to lack of knowledge on the credit insurance products and ultimately the agents are not successful.

The Insurance regulatory and Development Authority has constituted a committee under the Chairmanship of Shri Govardhan Ex Chairman of the LIC of India to examine the existing channels of distribution of insurance products and suggest ways and means to strengthen the same for an effective development of the Insurance industry in India. The

Committee, in its report submitted to the Authority, has suggested the following steps to be taken in order to develop agents in the general insurance market:

- The cap on commission be removed;
- Insurance company would extend training and financial support. The trainee will be attached with an existing agent of the company. The trainee would acquire knowledge of and practice in general insurance soliciting;

There is enough potential available in India to develop the agency route and create awareness on the credit insurance products. Innovation is the key word for success. The agents by their virtue of knowledge on the market requirement, may be able to suggest the insurance companies to introduce new products and make suitable changes in the existing products to meet the requirement of the customers. If the recommendations of the Govardhan Committee are accepted, the agency model will pave way for more awareness and expansion of the credit insurance market in India.

## INSURANCE BROKERS

Insurance broker means a person for the time-being licensed by the IRDA, who for remuneration, arranges insurance contracts with insurance companies on behalf of his clients. The term insurance broker can be a direct broker, a reinsurance broker or a composite broker.

The basic functions of a direct broker are:

(1) obtaining detailed information of the client's business and risk management philosophy;

(2) familiarizing himself with the client's business and underwriting information so that this can be explained to the insurer;

(3) Advice the client on appropriate insurance cover and the terms;

(4) Maintaining detailed knowledge on the insurance products available;

(5) Obtain and submit the quotation of the insurance company to the client;

(6) Provide all the requisite information to the insurance company in assessing the risk and pricing the terms and conditions of cover;

(7) Acting on the instructions of the client in obtaining insurance;

(8) Assisting the client in payment of premium in accordance with the insurance act;

(9) Assisting in the negotiation of claims and maintaining proper records of claims.

A composite broker who is licensed to act for remuneration arranges insurance for his clients with insurance companies and/or reinsurance for his clients. A composite broker shall carry out any one or more of the functions or a direct broker or reinsurance broker.

This model is utilized only by the corporate companies who engage the broker to find out the different products available on the credit insurance besides looking for all the general insurance products. The general insurance companies who also provide credit insurance products offer all the insurance requirements of the client as a package. Since the general insurance rates are in the post de tariff arena, the competition is acute and the general insurance companies are able to sell bundled insurance products. However, in case of an insurance company whose core business is export credit insurance, the company is not able to offer the other products along with credit insurance product. At present, due to synergy among the general insurance companies, it is possible to offer general insurance products by the credit insurance company and vise versa.

## OTHER ALTERNATE CHANNELS

In addition to the above three models, the other channels which can be utilized by the credit insurance agencies are:

### Small Scale Exporters Insurance Through NSIC

SMEs play an important role in the growth of our economy. It is necessary to nurture this sector in the national interest.

Frequent interactions with them to understand the need and provide the adequate and simple insurance will pave a long way in promoting this sector. The National Small Industries Corporation acts a Corporate Agency in bringing awareness to the industry on various credit insurance products and marketing them for the Export Credit Agency. This arrangement works on the similar lines of a Corporate Agency.

### Export Promotion Councils (EPC)

The role of Export Promotion Councils is to facilitate expansion of trade from India. EPCs organize buyer seller meets, arrange for participation in exhibitions, maintain statistics of exports of various products from India besides taking up policy matters with the Ministry of Commerce and Trade. EPCs enroll the exporters as members for various benefits and information on exports. The EPCs may be recognized as a Corporate Agency by the Export Credit insurance agency for distributing the insurance products. The commission structure may be the same as that of Corporate Agency. Similarly the Commodity Boards can be empanelled to become the Corporate Agency on the same lines of EPC.

### Others

The developments in internet, web based selling, e-marketing, telecalling, SMS in mobile etc have brought in revolutionary changes and made insurance easy to reach out to the customers. This is an emerging channel which may contribute to the insurance industry in the years to come.

### Basics of Export Credit Insurance

The export credit insurance covers the risks of non payment by the overseas buyer or insolvency of the buyer and the political risks such as war, civil war and delay in transfer of funds in foreign currency, diversion in voyage etc which are connected to the countries. These risks are known as commercial and political risks by the credit insurers. Thus, the credit insurance will be available after scrutiny of the financial capacity of the overseas buyer and the importing country's political and economic conditions. The pricing is done based on the standing of the country and the terms of payment on which the payments are to be made by the buyer. Insurance companies innovate new products to suit the requirements of the exporter. The covers are now offered as declaration policies and exposure based policies.

## POINTS TO BE NOTED BY THE INTERMEDIARIES

- The nitty-gritty of the products has to be explained to the intermediaries by the insurance companies before they start selling the products.
- The profile of the prospect has to be studied before the suitable product is sold, as insurance is looked upon as a long standing business relationship.
- The policyholder has to be advised to comply with the terms and conditions of the policy in order to keep the insurance in force.
- Periodical interaction with the policyholders is necessary to understand the transactions of the policyholder in order to suggest the ways of mitigating risks during the currency of the policy.
- Warning signals with regard to the developments of the financial position of the buyer are to be sent to the policyholders at different points of time in order to arrest their losses.
- In case of claim, educating the policyholders to take prompt and suitable action against the overseas buyer is necessary to preserve recourse for recovery.
- Since subrogation right is not directly available to the credit insurance company in India, it becomes necessary that the policyholder is advised to take steps to recover the dues from the overseas buyer and on recovery share the same with the insurance company.

## DIFFICULTIES OF MARKETING CREDIT INSURANCE THROUGH INTERMEDIARIES

As indicated, the commission paid under credit insurance for the services to be rendered is not felt adequate. Therefore, the intermediaries do not show much of interest in selling the credit insurance products. The commercial banks, who act as Corporate Agents, faces problems in the post VRS time and the officials are hard pressed for time to complete the banking operations. The identified person is given additional charge of the banking operations in addition to selling of credit insurance and therefore is unable to do his role as intermediary on full time. There is no incentive for the specified person for achieving or exceeding the target set for selling such policies. There is fear that if the claim under the policy marketed by the corporate agency gets rejected by the insurance company for non compliance of the terms of insurance, the reputation of the corporate agency is at stake. Thus, there is a necessity for the insurance company to keep in close contact with the intermediaries at frequent intervals to ensure that the intermediaries are motivated with prompt payment of commission as prescribed by the authority and also provide sufficient technical inputs and professional training to the intermediaries on credit insurance to update the knowledge level.

## CONCLUSION

In my view, there is enough potential available in the market and to develop the alternate channel method. By doing this, the insurance company would not only help employment opportunities to the needy but also create awareness on credit insurance in India.

I thank the Management of ECGC of India Limited for having given me the opportunity to write on the subject for the National Conference on Export Credi Insurance organized by the Pondicherry University.

## REFERENCE

Govardhan Committee Report.

IRDA regulations.

Internet on Bancassurance and agents.

8

# CONTRIBUTIONS OF ECGC IN FACILITATING PROJECT EXPORTS

**P. Natarajan, V. Vijayakumar**

## INTRODUCTION

Project exports from India commenced its modest beginning in the late 1970s. Since then, project exports evolved over the years, with companies demonstrating capabilities and expertise spanning a wide range of sectors. The nature of project exports being undertaken reflects the technological maturity and industrial capabilities in the country. The export of capital or engineering goods/services on deferred payment terms and execution of turnkey projects and civil construction contracts abroad are collectively referred to as "Project Exports".

Our total exports constitute just 0.7 per cent of the world trade. The government aims to increase India's share in world trade to 1 per cent by 2007. This means that our exports have to grow at the rate of 12-13 per cent every year. Increasing project exports is an important means to meet the targeted growth rate. In case of project exports, the number of transactions might be less, but each transaction is of a higher value than, say, short-term exports. Therefore, even if there is one default, our loss will be huge. It has been suggested that in the case of large projects, government should bear the risks.

An attempt has been made in this article to describe the role of ECGC in promoting project exports from India.

**WHAT ECGC DOES?**

ECGC has been extending cover for exports from India since its inception. Such covers have been instrumental in promoting exports from India. This has enabled the Indian exporters to expand their exports to new markets.

ECGC has been adopting a cautious approach while considering proposals for large value projects and/or projects involving longer credit periods involved. When reinsurance is available, ECGC considers proposals in case of large value projects and/or projects with longer period. The claims payments have been made out of its own resources.

ECGC has been operating various schemes under Medium & Long Term Business through various types of covers:

(i) Specific Shipment Policies where only supplies of heavy machinery or equipment are involved and where payments start forthcoming after 2 or 3 years.

(ii) Specific Services Policies for covering services exports on deferred payment basis.

(iii) Specific Contract Policies for covering transaction from the date of contract i.e., inclusive of pre-shipment risks.

(iv) Construction Work Policies are offered to cover turnkey projects from the pre-shipment stage to the end of the maintenance period.

Apart from the above types of policy covers, ECGC also issues counter-guarantees to Indian Banks who issue guarantees to overseas entities on behalf of Project exporters. ECGC covers even the pre-shipment finance extended to exporters and sometimes issues Overseas Lending Guarantees to enable exporter to avail finance abroad.

In addition to the policy covers, which are issued to the exporters, ECGC also extends its guarantee support to banks in India against both funded and non-funded facilities extended to project exporters. The types of guarantees issued by Indian banks are:

**Funded**

- Packing Credit
- Post Shipment
- Overdraft
- Rupee Loan

**Non-Funded**

- Bid Bond
- Advance payment
- Performance guarantee
- Retention Money guarantee
- Overseas Lending Finance guarantee

ECGC's counter-guarantee can be obtained by banks in India to protect them against any loss that they may sustain owing to invocation of the above guarantees.

*Risk covered:* Insolvency of the exporter/protracted default of the exporter

*Percentage of loss:* 75 per cent to 90 per cent covered

*Rate of premium:* 0.80 paise per Rs. 100 p.a. & 0.95 paise per Rs. 100 p.a.

As per RBI's recent directive, no pre-bid approval from authorised dealer, Exim Bank or Working Group is required to be taken by project exporters. Only post-award approval is required to be taken. However, it would be in the interest of project exporters to obtain 'in-principle' clearance from their bankers and ECGC assuring them of support in the event of their securing the contracts.

ECGC Premium for Project exports are around 1.7% and in case of deferred payments, these are quoted as high as 9%. ECGC does not cover the loss even when the clients become defaulters.

- ECGC has paid gross claim of Rs. 1104 crores as against a premium of Rs. 271 crores under the covers extended for medium and long term exports (project exports, lines of credit and buyers credit extended by Exim India).

- While the share of premium earned under Project Exports is about 11% of the total premium income, the claims payment in respect of project exports constitute about 49% of the total claims.
- The claims in respect of project exports constitute a major part of the aggregate claims.

ECGC has set up National Interest Account (NIA) which provides cover for project exports of those who are not able to meet the normal commercial underwriting criteria. Consortia approach is essential to take up large project exports contract. The government is giving a major thrust to project exports

## ECGC'S GUIDELINES FOR PROJECT EXPORTERS

(i) The capacity of the project exporter to carry out large value contracts-technical, professional and managerial, and their past experience in the line of business.

(ii) Country to which the exports are to be made-stability of political set-up/government, soundness of economy, payment records, relations with IMF, World Bank and other international FIs and donor countries.

(iii) Buyer/employer-private/government.

(iv) Payment terms and security, rate of interest for deferred receivables.

(v) ECGC's underwriting policy on the country and its experience, whether any transfer delay experienced.

(vi) Berne union experience-whether the credit period offered is in line with Berne union understanding.

(vii) Reinsurance back-up available or not.

(viii) Whether need for covering the contract under National Export Insurance Account set-up by Government of India.

## MAJOR MARKETS COVERED BY ECGC

West Asia is a major market for Indian project exports followed by South-East Asia, Pacific and South Asia. An important aspect of Indian project exports is that it is concentrated in certain pockets of the world and there is need to increase its geographical spread. Currently, the market revolves around only 40 countries indicating scope for expansion is rich. Despite this, Indian project exporters have executed a variety of projects in diverse sectors.

There is good scope for Project exports to Africa, the Middle East and South-East Asia. Indians have already taken up several projects in Saudi Arabia. Currently, opportunities of project exports to Iraq are few. Africa is a good destination for project exports

## WHAT ECGC REQUIRES?

- Government should extend support to ECGC to provide service in the same manner as a project exporter in a competing country would be getting from his export credit insurance provider (counterpart of ECGC in competitor's country).
- ECGC should be reimbursed the losses on account of political risks by Government of India It has been done so in other countries in similar situations where the national governments have paid out compensations out of their budgets without affecting the financial position of credit risk insurer. CYMK.
- Strengthening of equity base of ECGC to ensure capital adequacy as per accepted norms of credit of credit insurance business.
- Wherever reinsurance is possible to arrange, if the costs are prohibitive, governmental support in the pricing to ensure smooth cash flow and lesser financial burden for exporter should be considered.
- *(a)* Government Guarantees to enable them to cover high value project risks without the need of reinsurance, which will make them competitive and also provide cover in countries of emerging markets like Africa & Latin America.

  *(b)* In the absence of reinsurance, ECGC should be in a position to draw support from the Government National Interest Account etc., or even to operate the cover on behalf of the government.

*(c)* The underwriting of risks may be done on behalf of and to the account of government.

Correspondingly, ECGC, as an institution, must evolve and grow itself to function as a significant credit insurance agency to support project exports from India.

## CONCLUSION

Project exports evolved over the years, with companies demonstrating capabilities and expertise spanning a wide range of sectors. There has been robust export growth on both merchandise and invisibles performing well. ECGC issues counter-guarantees to Indian Banks who issue guarantees to overseas entities on behalf of Project exporters. Currently, the market revolves around only 40 countries indicating scope for expansion is reachable. Despite this, Indian project exporters have executed a variety of projects in diverse sectors. ECGC covers even the pre-shipment finance extended to exporters and sometimes issues Overseas Lending Guarantees to enable exporter to avail finance abroad technology-intensive products, the export structure has not shown any significant change. ECGC, as an institution, must evolve and grow itself to function as a significant credit insurance agency to support project exports from India.

There is sometimes a complaint that ECGC's premium rates are high when compared to others. Countering this, Hakeem says, "After 9/11, the reinsurance market has almost dried up. If there is a reinsurance market we can share part of the risk. In its absence we will have to bear the entire risk. Though our premium rates are high, they have come down over the years. Our premium rate is high because of higher claim-premium ratio, which is around 4.5 times. There is no general norm for permissible claim-premium ratio. In case of insurance companies, 0.6 is considered as normal. In our case 0.8 is acceptable as our manpower cost is not much and also profit is not main motive. Because of huge loss incurred by ECGC during the first Gulf War, its claim-premium ratio is high. Otherwise it is well within the normal limits."

## REFERENCES

Goel B. B., Project Management-Principles and Techniques, Deep & Deep Publications, New Delhi.

Chandra Prasanna, Projects–Planning, Analysis, Selection, Implementation and Review, Tata Mc Graw-Hill Publishing Co. Ltd, New Delhi.

PEPC Website, *www.projectexports.com*

Government of India, Economic Survey (Various issues), Ministry of Finance and Company Affairs.

Exim Bank of India Website, *www.eximbankindia.in*

Dutt, G.S., I.A.S (Jan 2003), "Report of Task Force on Project Exports", Foreign Trade and Investment, Department of Economic Affairs, Ministry of Finance, Government of India.

# 9

# SENSITIVITY OF FIRMS' PERFORMANCE TO EXCHANGE RATE MOVEMENTS: A STUDY OF INDIAN COMPANIES

**T. Mallikarjunappa**

## INTRODUCTION

The export and imports of the firms have attracted researcher's attention at conceptual as well as empirical levels. This is partly because the world is becoming an open world where the nations freely import and export goods and services under the WTO regime. The global economies today are dependent on one another for different needs. The open economies have caused intense world-wide competition in many industries. Many times openess of the economy is associated with the efficieny of the economy. At the same time this open market economic system also poses the problmes which some of the countries in the world have experienced. Therefore, every nation would like to export as much as possible to build a health position of balance of trade and payments. Exports play a dominant role in this regard. The increasing exports can substantially benefit economy of that country. It would also benefit the companies that are involved in exports.

A nation's exports provides resources that can be increase social prosperity and development, generate foreign exchange needed for economic activities, creates backward and forward linkages in the economy, and increases employment opportunities. Companies involved in exports also benefit from improved innovation and performance, enhanced managerial skills and capabilities, diversified business risks accruing from operating in domestic market and foreing markets, intensified utilization of organizational resources, and increased company's financial position.

The above discussion shows that a study of export oriented companies is important from the point of view of the economy. The performance of export oriented companies is a direct results of the currency movements in the foregin exchage market. An export oriented company will gain by depreciating home currency if the exports are denominated in the foreign currency. Similarly a company which imports more that it exports would gain by the appreciating domestic currency when the imports are denominated in the foreign currency. If a company is both an exporter and importer, it would benefit from home currency depreciation if it is net exporter and vicee-versa.

The most important aspect of foreign exchange risk management is to incorporate expectations of currency rate changes into corporate decisions. No company can afford to neglect this as its survival may be dependent on the currency movements. The movements in exchange rates can impact company costs and revenues and therefore, profits. The degree to which a firm is affcted by the currency movements would depend on the exposure a company routienly has in the foreign exchange market. As a change in exchange rate can change the volume of trade, the firms can be adversely affected by such changes. The impact of exchange rate changes on the realizations or costs in the company is direct and immediate.

**Foreign Exchange Market**

The primary function of foreign exchange market is to transfer purchasing power dominated in one currency to another and facilitate international trade and investment. The foreign exchange market consists of the interbank market, which is a dominant whole sale market in which major banks trade with each other and; the retail market in which banks deal with their commercial customers. The exchange rate movements are the results of the relative demands for two currencies, usually home currency and foreign currency. If the demand for home currency increases vis-à-vis the demand for a foreign currency, it results in increase the price of home currency on the foreign exchange market. Many factors that affect a currency's value are: currency's usefulness as a store of value, countries economic conditions, countries balance of payments, trade balance, resource base, future plans, GDP growth etc. Foreign exchange performs the function of converting one nation's currency into another, and of transferring money from one country to anther.

**Exchange Rate**

The exchange rate is the value of one nations currency that can be exchanged of a unit of foreign currency. Thus, exchange rate is a conversion factor one nation's currency vis-à-vis another nations currency. Therefore, exchange rate can be defined as a price of home currency for unit of foreign currency. The exchange rate can be freely determined by the market forces of demand and supply or they can be managed exchange rates by the central banks of the countries. Exchange rate lot of significance in the international trade as they determine the health of the nation's economy. Historically there are many examples of economies experiencing unprecedented problems because of adverse movements of their currencies *vis-à-vis* hard currencies. The examples of south east Asian nations, mexico, the USSR, are of recent ones. As the nations are affected so also the companies by the adverse movement in the exchange rates. Therefore, the study of the impact of exchange rates on the companies performance is an important topic.

Exports oriented companies earn valuable foreign exchange for the country. Therefore, every nation gives importance to export oriented companies. A nations balance of trade and balance of payments positions would depend on the total exports and imports of different sectors of the economy. Manufacturing and serivice sectors are the important contributors to the exports of India. The imports and exports of these sectors of the economy significantly determine influence the nations foregin exchange reserves. These, in turn, influence the exchane rates of the countries currencies. These exchange rates determine the competitiveness of the export oriented companies. Exchange rate changes also significantly influence the company profitability. This is because as the exchange rates change, the rates at which the foreign currency denominated export proceeds are converted would also change. The foreign exchange rates can significantly impact the company profitability. Therefore, it is important that a study of the impact of exchange rates on the export oriented companies is made. This study is undertaken to study the sensitivity of company performance variables for changes in exchange rates.

## Objectives

The study is conducted with following objectives:

(1) To study the impact of foreign exchange rate on export/import oriented units.

(2) To conduct sensitivity analysis of the company profit taking the different exchange rate scenarios.

## Nature and Scope of Study

The study covers the companies in manufacturing sector, financial service sector, and service sector which are dealing with exports of goods and services. For the purpose of this study financial data of 18 years from March 1989 to March 2007 is used. The exchange rates of Indian rupees against other currencies are available for only 10 years from 1998 to 2007 and therefore, these rates have been used. Since the exports are denominated in US dollars, the exchange rate used is US dollar versus Indian rupee.

The discussion in the paper reveals that companies are affected by the ER changes and the magnitude of the effect increases with increasing/decreasing ERs. The analysis also showed that the companies which are net exporters are worst affected when the rupee appreciates and companies which net importers are worst affected when the rupee appreciates. To mitigate the losses in the foreign currency, some of the techniques are advocated.

This paper is organized in six sections. Part one deals with the introduction, part 2 reviews the relevant literature, part 3 discusses the data, sample and methodology; part 4 presents the analysis of the company variables for different exchange rate scenarios, part 5 focuses on some the techniques that can be used for managing the foreign exchange risks to which companies are exposed to and part 6 summarises the paper and presents the conclusion. Tables are given after part 6 and references are given after the tables.

## LITERATURE REVIEW

De Jong et al (2006) (1) examine the relationship between exchange-rate changes and stock returns for a sample of Dutch firms over 1994â€" 1998. They find that over 50 per cent of the firms are significantly exposed to exchange-rate risk. Furthermore, all firms with significant exchange-rate exposure benefit from a depreciation of the Dutch guilder relative to a trade-weighted currency index. This result confirms that firms in open economies, such as the Netherlands, exhibit significant exchange-rate exposure. They collect unique information on the most relevant individual currencies for each firm with respect to their influence on firm value. The results of the study indicate that the use of a trade-weighted currency index and the use of individual exchange rates are complements. They also measure the determinants of exchange-rate exposure. As expected, it was found that firm size and the foreign sales ratio are significantly and positively related to exchange-rate exposure. In contrast with their hypothesis, they found that off-balance hedging using derivatives has no significant effects. Finally, in line with theory, they find that exposure is significantly reduced through on-balance sheet hedging, i.e., through foreign loans and by producing in factories abroad.

Cerf and Elmy (1998) (2), provide an analysis necessary to prepare and evaluate accounting for a derivative transaction used by Atlantic Richfield Company (Arco) to hedge foreign exchange rate exposure.

The study analyses (1) the international interest rate environment which motivated Arco to borrow in yen; (2) foreign exchange rate risk, including the effective dollar cost of the yen debt if Arco did not hedge this exposure; (3) how the cash flows of the currency swap interact with the cash flows of the debt to hedge the foreign exchange risk, (4)how entering into the currency swap mitigates currency risk, but exposes Arco to counterpary credit risk and legal risk; (5) the attributes of accounting and reporting for the debt and currency swap as separate instruments or as a combined synthetic instrument; and (6) accounting for the currency swap at fair value.

Chang *et al* (2005) (3), suggest a model to develop an intertemporal international asset pricing model (IAPM). They show that the expected international asset return is determined by a weighted average of market risk, market hedging risk, exchange rate risk and exchange rate hedging risk. The total of these weights is one. Their model explicitly separates hedging against changes in the investment opportunity set from hedging against exchange rate changes as well as exchange rate risk from intertemporal hedging risk. A test of the conditional version of their intertemporal IAPM using a multivariate GARCH process supports the asset pricing model. They find that the exchange rate risk is important for pricing international equity returns and it is much more important than intertemporal hedging risk. Schwah and Lusztig (1972) (4), present information on apportioning foreign exchange risk through the use of third currencies. The existence of currency borders and international exchange risks may represent not simply a burden on contracting parties but may even prevent otherwise profitable transactions. Many international transactions are denominated in third currencies. Also, when various mixed currency instruments and units have been introduced to the market, many have found ready acceptance. Third currencies including units will not aid in apportioning foreign exchange risk but that they may serve as a convenient way of stabilizing real returns and costs as perceived by the transacting parties. Longer-term international contracts involving natural resources such as coal are quite common today. Pricing is one important aspect of such agreements, and it is clear that the choice of currency could be critical.

Lewis (1995) (5), The relationship between foreign exchange intervention and monetary policy underlies the question of whether sterilized interventions can affect the exchange rate In this article, the author examine this relationship using data on U S foreign exchange interventions from 1985 to 1990, recently made publicly available. He examines whether interventions could be viewed as "signaling" changes in future monetary policy variables. He also consider whether changes in monetary policy may induce inter- ventions in an effort by central bankers to "lean against the wind" of exchange rate movements. The author find evidence both that interventions help predict monetary policy variables and that monetary variables help predict interventions

Samuel(1996) (6), presents a question and answer segment on international trading; Paying in local currency the equivalent dollar value for purchases; Definition of free zone; Exporting through a third country. Hertzell and Caspar (1988) (7), discuss how international companies are affected by currency rate changes, giving the example of the money that Sony lost when the value of the American dollar dropped against the Japanese yen. They state that the three dimensions of risk that companies face with foreign exchange rate changes are contractual exposure, portfolio exposure, and competitive exposure. The authors present an example of the impact of foreign exchange rates on the price to U.S. consumers of imported cars.

Kit Pong Wong and Ho Yin Yick (2004) (8), examine the production and hedging decisions of a globally competitive firm under exchange rate uncertainty. The firm is risk averse and possesses export flexibility in that it can distribute its output to either the domestic market or a foreign market after observing the realized spot exchange rate. To hedge against its exchange rate risk exposure, the firm can trade fairly priced currency call options of an arbitrary strike price. The authors show that both the separation and the full-hedging results hold if the strike price of the currency call options is set equal to the ratio of the domestic and foreign selling prices. Otherwise, neither result holds. Specifically, they show that the optimal level of output is always less than that of an otherwise identical firm that is risk neutral. Furthermore, an under-hedge (over-hedge) is optimal whenever the strike price of the currency call options is below (above) the ratio of the domestic and foreign selling prices.

Shapiro (1985) (9), discusses on the conditions under which banks are subject to currency and country risks on their dollar-denominated loans to foreign firms and governments. We conclude that currency risk is a function of the rates of domestic and foreign inflation, deviations from purchasing power parity, and the effect of these deviations on the firm's and the nation's dollar-equivalent cash flows. Country risk is largely determined by the variability of the nation's terms of trade and the government's willingness to allow the national economy to adjust rapidly to changing economic fortunes.

Thomas III (1988) (10), discusses the exchange rate risk associated with foreign stocks. The most basic measure of risk is volatility of return measured by the annualized standard deviation of monthly foreign stock returns. He points out that equity prices are much more volatile than their associated exchange rates. The sensitivity of the stock to changes in the value of the market portfolio, which is a measure of the stock's systematic risk is called its beta. The average beta for the 15 foreign equity markets examined is 0.62. It implies that a 1 per cent change in the U.S. stock price is associated with a change of about two thirds of 1 per cent in the average foreign market index. The article points out that investors should always hedge if they believe that foreign currencies are likely to be worth less than the value indicated by the forward exchange rate. Investors should also hedge if they believe that forward rates fairly value foreign currencies. The hedge leaves the expected return to the portfolio unchanged but reduces the portfolio's risk.

Campa (1993) (11), tests the effects that real exchange rate fluctuations had on foreign direct investment into the United States during the1980s. Using a sample of foreign investments in 61 four-digit SIC US wholesale industries, the author finds out the exchange rate volatility to be negatively correlated with the number of foreign investments that occur in these industries This negative effect is most pronounced for industries where sunk investments in physical and intangible assets are relatively high Although exchange rate volatility deters investment from all countries, its effect was most significant for investments by Japanese companies.

Peijie and Ping (2001) (12), investigate the risk transmission between the spot and forward foreign exchange markets. In particular, the effect of innovation basis and signs of shocks in both markets are assessed. The market is less predictable when the spot and forward market shave experienced shocks of opposite signs. The spot market and the forward market are less predictable when both the spot and forward markets have experienced higher uncertainty in the previous periods, but the forward market is influenced more by the uncertainty of its own.

WenShwo and Miller (2007)(13), examine the weak relationship between exchange rate depreciation and exports for Singapore, using a bivariate generalized autoregressive conditional heteroscedasticity in mean model that simultaneously estimates time-varying risk. The evidence shows that depreciation does not significantly improve exports, but that exchange rate risk significantly impedes exports. The authors conclude that Singaporean policy makers can better promote export growth by stabilizing the exchange rate rather than generating its depreciation.

Levy and Sarnat (1978) (14), present an exploration into optimal portfolio selection theory as applied to the diversification of non-interest foreign currency holdings, exchange rate fluctuations, and the economic changes made manifest in the 1970s. They discuss the rise in foreign exchange divergences in the late 1960s and their consequences on the portfolio theories of economists Harry Markowitz and James Tobin. The optimal portfolio theory is applied to create diversified combinations of currencies and address issues of demand for money in view of Tobin's theory of riskless lending. Moon (1982) (15), asserts that the two central tenets of dependency theory are supported by the analysis of the causes and consequences of the exchange rate policies of less developed countries (LDCs). First, one critical component-high partner trade concentrations-is recreated by the choice of exchange arrangements. Specifically, nations that have maintained a dollar peg have significantly increased their concentration of trade with the United States since 1973. This occurs because of the exchange rate risk present in any transaction that involves a dollar-pegged currency and any other major currency against which it floats. Second, such an effect produces incentives for internal and external actors with an interest in the partner composition of future trade to influence the exchange rate policy of LDCs. Various components of the dependence situation that strengthen the role of such actors-partner trade concentrations, treaty arrangements, foreign aid, etc.-are significantly correlated with actual exchange rate practice. Thus, exchange rate policy is a linchpin mechanism, in that it both manifests distortions produced by dependency and further acts to recreate a vital aspect of the situation that gave rise to the distortions.

Wai-Ching Poon, Chee-Keong Choong and Habibullah (2005) (16), examine the relationship between exchange rate volatility and exports of the five selected East Asian economies. A measure of the quantitative proxy of the exchange rate risk is constructed, focusing on the role of moving-average in smoothing the persistence of the risk measure. Vector autoregressive (VAR) model, error correction modelling (ECM), and variance decomposition (VD) are applied to characterize the joint dynamics of variables in both the short and long run. The Johansen results indicate a stable long-run relation between exports and exchange rate. Results show that a great fluctuation of exchange rate volatility has significantly impacted the volume of exports for the economies concerned. To this end, the forecast error VD shows that the innovations of exchange rate volatility have minor impact on export patterns in the study.

Doyle, (2001) (17), examines how exchange-rate volatility affected Ireland's exports to its most important trading partner, the United Kingdom, from 1979 to 1992. To ensure reliable inferences regarding income and price elasticities and the impact of exchange rate volatility on exports, the time series properties of the series used are investigated. The analysis here is conducted at both aggregate and2-digit SITC Division levels since exchange rate volatility can reasonably be presumed to affect sectors differently. Since expectations matter for exchange rate determination real volatility was generated according to a first-order GARCH process. Both real and nominal volatility were important determinants for over 35% of Irish-UK trade, with positive effects predominating. This may be due to the nature of Irish firms operating in a small open economy where they have little option in dealing with increased exchange rate risk except to 'weather the storm' for fear of losing market share or facing costs of either exit, re-entry, or both.

Carriero, (2006) (18), tests the uncovered interest rate parity (UIRP), allowing for transitory deviations from it. These deviations may arise from variations in risk premia, errors in expectations and linearization errors, and are modelled as a zero-mean noise around the restrictions implied by the UIRP on a vector autoregression (VAR) in the interest rate differential and the spot exchange rate. This approach includes the traditional one as a special case, which is derived by simply setting the noise to zero. When the noise is set to zero the UIRP is rejected, but if some degree of noise is allowed the UIRP is strongly supported by the data. Thus the UIRP relation does not hold exactly, but on average, with a stationary risk premium as opposed to a constant one. This result implies that analysing the effects of policy experiments under the null of the UIRP may be both safe and useful.

Wong (2003) (19), studies the behavior of an export-flexible firm under exchange rate uncertainty. It shows that the separation theorem holds if selling exclusively in the domestic market is suboptimal even under the most unfavorable spot exchange rate. Otherwise, the firm's optimal output depends on its preferences and on the underlying uncertainty. The study further shows that the full-hedging theorem holds only when the firm always finds it optimal to sell its entire output in the foreign market. Otherwise, export flexibility introduces a convexity into the firm's foreign exchange risk exposure, which calls for the use of currency options for hedging purposes.

The review of the studies above reveal that the firms are affected by the exchange rate changes and therefore, there is a need to understand how firms are affected by these. Further, there is also a need to understand how firms can manage these risks. The discussion to follow focuses on these issues.

## DATA, SAMPLE AND METHODOLOGY

### Data and Sample

The study is focussed on the export oriented units of India. There are different ways in which sample companies can be chosen. One way is to choose companies from different industry groups and select top companies from each of these sectors. The other way is to use top companies based on some criteria for manufacturing sector, services and financial services. If we select all top companies from each industry group, there is a problem of selecting insignificant company. Therefore, we use the second method and select top companies from these three groups. Further, we use a criteria to select these companies based on the ratio of total exports to total sales of the companies. The sample companies are chosen by applying the export to sales ratio for the financial year 2006-2007. The companies which have more than or equal to 0.5 ratio of export/total sales is included for samples. There are 475 manufacturing companies, 293 service companies and 20 financial service companies that satisfy the criteria. For the purpose of analysis 19 companies from financial sector, 25 top export companies from service and manufacturing sector are taken. Source of data is prowess, a database maintained by Centre For Monitoring Indian Economy (CMIE). Exchange rate of rupee and dollars has been taken from the Reserve Bank of India.

## Methodology

Different methodologies can be used for studying the impact of the exchange ratee on companies performance. We can take the total exports and assess the impact of the exchange rates on the companies profitability. Similarly we assess the influence of the exchange rate changes on the imports and its impact on the profitability of companies. We can also chose some financial parameter and assess the sensitivity of this for given exchange rate changes. We use the sensitivity analysis to assess the impact of changes in exchanges rates on company performances. For this purpose we chose exports, imports, operating profits, net profit, profit before tax as some of the variables and conduct sensitivity analysis. For the purpose of conducting the sensitivity analysis, we use the exchanges rates for the 10 year period and take the average exchange rates for each year. Further, the values of exports, imports, operating profit, net profit and profit before taxes are collected for the 18 year period and average of these values are taken as of March 2007. If a company does not have data for all the 18 years, the available data for the available period is collected used. The average values of the selected variables are taken as the actual values for the average exchange rates for the selected periods. The average exchange rates are worked out the years for the company data is available. However, the exchange rates for the companies which have data for the entire period is the average exchange rates for the 10 year period. Taking different exchange rates as Rs. 40, 41, 42, 44, 45, 46, 47, 48, 50 per US dollar, the changes in the company values are worked and these are interpreted. We assess the impact of the changes in exchange rates on company variables and also suggest some of the strategies which companies can use to hedge foreign exchange risk.

## THE SENSITIVITY ANALAYSIS OF COMPANY VARIABLES FOR DIFFERENT EXCHANGE RATES

The selected companies have been subjected to sensitivity analysis of net profit, operating profit, exports, imports, net benefits (exports-imports) taking the different exchange rates (ERs) scenarios. The existing values of the variable taken for analysis are taken at the average exchange values and the values of these variables for different ERs have been computed. The negative numbers indicate the possible losses which these companies can incur if the ERs turn out to be lower than the existing ER and the positive numbers indicate the possible profits which these companies could have derived if the ER turns out to be higher than the existing number. Since the companies chosen are the export oriented companies this argument holds. For a net importing company exactly opposite holds. The numbers in the Table 1 show that Infosys would have derived additional net profits of Rs. 1.63, 18.77, 35.92, 53.07, crores if ERs were to be Rs. 45, 46, 47, and 48 respectively, instead of the existing Rs. 44.9051. The numbers in the table 3.1 also show that Infosys would have incurred losses of Rs 15.52, 32.67, 49.81, 66.96, and 84.11 crores if ERs were to be Rs. 44, 43, 42, 41and 40 respectively, instead of the existing Rs. 44.9051. The numbers in the table show that TCS would have derived additional profits of Rs 16.60186, 53.95644, 91.31101, and 128.6656 crores if ERs were to be Rs. 45, 46, 47, and 48 respectively, instead of the existing Rs 44.55556. The numbers in this table also show that TCS would have incurred losses of Rs. 20.7527, 58.1073, 95.4619, 132.816, and 170.171 crores if ERs were to be Rs. 44, 43, 42, 41 and 40 respectively, instead of the existing Rs. 44.55556. The numbers in the table show that Wipro would have derived additional profits of Rs 1.135694, 13.10674, 25.07779, and 37.04885 crores if ERs were to be Rs. 45, 46, 47, and 48 respectively, instead of the existing Rs 44.90513. The numbers in this table also show that Wipro would have incurred losses of Rs.10.8354, 22.8064, 34.7775, 46.7485, and 58.7196 crores if ERs were to be Rs. 44, 43, 42, 41 and 40 respectively, instead of the existing Rs 44.90513. Similar analysis holds for all the companies that have positive net benefit as shown in the table.

The companies shown in serial numbers 61 to 68 starting from Gitanjali Exports have negative net benefit ratio but positive net profits. The negative net benefit ratio indicates that as the ERs decrease below the existing levels, these companies will start earning more profits and if the ERs rise above the existing levels, these companies would incur losses. The numbers in the table 1 show that Gitanjali Exports would have derived additional profits of Rs 0.121823 and 0.271543 crores if ERs were to be Rs. 47 and 48 respectively, instead of the existing Rs. 46.18633. The numbers in the table 1 also show that Gitanjali Exports would have incurred losses of Rs 0.0279, 0.17762, 0.32734, 0.47706, 0.62678, 0.77649, and 0.92621 crores if ERs were to be Rs. 46, 45, 44, 43, 42, 41and 40 respectively, instead of the existing ER. Similar analysis for Sterliteshows that it would have derived additional profits of Rs 0.32905, 3.797485, 7.265921, 10.73436 crores if ERs were to be Rs. 45, 46, 47, and 48 respectively, instead of the existing Rs 44.90513. The numbers in this table also show that this company would have incurred losses of Rs. 3.13938, 6.60782, 10.0763, 13.5447 and 17.0131 crores if ERs were to be Rs. 44, 43, 42, 41 and 40 respectively, instead of the existing Rs 44.90513. The analysis for these companies show that the results are similar to that of the companies with positive net benefits. This is because the net profit values are positive and therefore are higher at higher ER as per the cacluation procedure used. Similar analysis holds for the companies like Sundaram Fasteners, Moser Baer,Gitanjali Gems, Rajesh Exports, Jindal Saw, Essar Oil, ONGC Videsh that have net benefit negative as shown in the table. This result is not in the expected lines. This is because these companies have net benefit negative but sources of profits may be domestic market or their expenses in the export- import trade are incurred in the domestic currency. Therefore, it is important for us to understand how the companies whose net benefits are positive(negative) are affected by the changes in ERs. The next paragraph deals with the analysis of the net benefit of the companies.

Companies in serial numbers 1 to 60 have net benefit ratio positive and 61 to 69 have net benefit ratio negative. The

**Table 1**
**Different Exchange Rate Scenarios — Effects on Net Profits (Scenario Profits - Existing profits)**

| | *40* | *41* | *42* | *43* | *44* | *45* | *46* | *47* | *48* |
|---|---|---|---|---|---|---|---|---|---|
| Infosys | -84.1059 | -66.9594 | -49.8129 | -32.6664 | -15.5198 | 1.626691 | 18.77321 | 35.91974 | 53.06626 |
| Tata Consultancy | -170.171 | -132.816 | -95.4619 | -58.1073 | -20.7527 | 16.60186 | 53.95644 | 91.31101 | 128.6656 |
| Tata International | -1.34807 | -1.07324 | -0.79841 | -0.52358 | -0.24875 | 0.026073 | 0.300901 | 0.575729 | 0.850556 |
| Wipro Ltd. | -58.7196 | -46.7485 | -34.7775 | -22.8064 | -10.8354 | 1.135694 | 13.10674 | 25.07779 | 37.04885 |
| H C L Tech. | -40.9413 | -33.4166 | -25.8918 | -18.3671 | -10.8423 | -3.31759 | 4.207157 | 11.73191 | 19.25665 |
| Wall Street Fin | -0.10752 | -0.0856 | -0.06368 | -0.04176 | -0.01984 | 0.002079 | 0.023999 | 0.045918 | 0.067837 |
| Patni Comps. | -19.6498 | -15.3364 | -11.023 | -6.70968 | -2.39633 | 1.917028 | 6.230384 | 10.54374 | 14.8571 |
| Satyam Comps. | -42.7412 | -34.0276 | -25.314 | -16.6005 | -7.88691 | 0.826656 | 9.540217 | 18.25378 | 26.96734 |
| Surya Vinayak | -0.23677 | -0.07344 | 0.089891 | 0.253221 | 0.416552 | 0.579883 | 0.743214 | 0.906544 | 1.069875 |
| Siva Ventures . | -93.1824 | -75.7065 | -58.2305 | -40.7546 | -23.2786 | -5.80269 | 11.67325 | 29.14919 | 46.62513 |
| Ranbaxy Labs | -22.286 | -17.7426 | -13.1992 | -8.6558 | -4.11238 | 0.431034 | 4.974449 | 9.517863 | 14.06128 |
| Mindtree Consult. | -5.64048 | -3.97824 | -2.31601 | -0.65377 | 1.00847 | 2.670708 | 4.332946 | 5.995184 | 7.657422 |
| Wipro B P O | -10.7277 | -8.71517 | -6.70261 | -4.69006 | -2.6775 | -0.66494 | 1.347616 | 3.360172 | 5.372729 |
| Kudremukh | -2.023 | -1.61057 | -1.19815 | -0.78572 | -0.3733 | 0.039127 | 0.451552 | 0.863977 | 1.276402 |
| Gokaldas Exports | -3.99716 | -3.01159 | -2.02602 | -1.04045 | -0.05488 | 0.930695 | 1.916266 | 2.901837 | 3.887408 |
| Dr. Reddy'S Labs. | -18.6715 | -14.865 | -11.0584 | -7.25191 | -3.44539 | 0.361124 | 4.167643 | 7.974162 | 11.78068 |
| K E C Inter. | -6.01896 | -4.24519 | -2.47141 | -0.69764 | 1.076139 | 2.849915 | 4.623691 | 6.397467 | 8.171243 |
| P K S Ltd. | -0.19466 | -0.1632 | -0.13173 | -0.10026 | -0.0688 | -0.03733 | -0.00586 | 0.025604 | 0.05707 |
| I-Flex Solutions | -12.2131 | -9.72326 | -7.23339 | -4.74352 | -2.25365 | 0.236214 | 2.726082 | 5.21595 | 7.705819 |
| GE Shipping | -28.2592 | -22.498 | -16.7369 | -10.9757 | -5.21459 | 0.546561 | 6.307713 | 12.06887 | 17.83002 |
| Karp Impex | -2.37386 | -1.8899 | -1.40595 | -0.92199 | -0.43804 | 0.045913 | 0.529866 | 1.01382 | 1.497774 |
| Take Solutions | -0.33615 | -0.26789 | -0.19963 | -0.13136 | -0.0631 | 0.005164 | 0.073426 | 0.141689 | 0.209952 |
| L K P Forex | -0.13566 | -0.11162 | -0.08758 | -0.06354 | -0.03951 | -0.01547 | 0.008568 | 0.032605 | 0.056642 |
| Essar Ship | -10.4208 | -8.29632 | -6.17185 | -4.04738 | -1.92292 | 0.201548 | 2.326014 | 4.45048 | 6.574945 |
| Orient Craft | -2.39657 | -1.94345 | -1.49033 | -1.03722 | -0.5841 | -0.13098 | 0.322134 | 0.775251 | 1.228368 |

*Contd...*

| | 40 | 41 | 42 | 43 | 44 | 45 | 46 | 47 | 48 |
|---|---|---|---|---|---|---|---|---|---|
| Tech Mahindra | -6.72645 | -5.35514 | -3.98383 | -2.61252 | -1.24121 | 0.130096 | 1.501405 | 2.872715 | 4.244024 |
| Orchid Chemicals | -10.5552 | -8.40333 | -6.25146 | -4.09959 | -1.94772 | 0.204148 | 2.356018 | 4.507888 | 6.659758 |
| Sakuma Exports | -0.25923 | -0.18283 | -0.10644 | -0.03005 | 0.046348 | 0.122742 | 0.199137 | 0.275531 | 0.351925 |
| Cipla Ltd. | -18.0645 | -14.3817 | -10.699 | -7.01618 | -3.3334 | 0.349385 | 4.032167 | 7.714949 | 11.39773 |
| Firstsource Solu. | -2.69093 | -2.13889 | -1.58685 | -1.03481 | -0.48278 | 0.069264 | 0.621303 | 1.173342 | 1.725382 |
| Sesa Goa Ltd. | -11.4031 | -9.0784 | -6.75366 | -4.42893 | -2.10419 | 0.220548 | 2.545285 | 4.870022 | 7.19476 |
| E I H Ltd. | -7.43803 | -5.92165 | -4.40528 | -2.8889 | -1.37252 | 0.143859 | 1.660237 | 3.176615 | 4.692993 |
| Flextronics Soft | -6.54914 | -5.21398 | -3.87882 | -2.54365 | -1.20849 | 0.126667 | 1.461827 | 2.796988 | 4.132148 |
| L&T Infotech | -4.72117 | -3.75867 | -2.79618 | -1.83368 | -0.87118 | 0.091312 | 1.053808 | 2.016304 | 2.978799 |
| Asian Star Co | -2.2739 | -1.81032 | -1.34675 | -0.88317 | -0.4196 | 0.043979 | 0.507555 | 0.971131 | 1.434706 |
| Jindal Iron | -3.47095 | -2.76334 | -2.05572 | -1.3481 | -0.64049 | 0.067132 | 0.774748 | 1.482365 | 2.189982 |
| Magnanimous Trade | 0.012674 | 0.009991 | 0.007308 | 0.004624 | 0.001941 | -0.00074 | -0.00342 | -0.00611 | -0.00879 |
| Su-Raj Diamonds | -2.6557 | -2.11429 | -1.57288 | -1.03146 | -0.49005 | 0.051364 | 0.592777 | 1.13419 | 1.675603 |
| Syntel Ltd. | -12.9856 | -10.8253 | -8.66506 | -6.50477 | -4.34449 | -2.1842 | -0.02391 | 2.136376 | 4.296664 |
| HP Globalsoft | -4.57526 | -3.64251 | -2.70976 | -1.77701 | -0.84426 | 0.08849 | 1.021241 | 1.953992 | 2.886742 |
| Aurobindo Pharma | -7.5786 | -6.03356 | -4.48853 | -2.94349 | -1.39846 | 0.146577 | 1.691613 | 3.236648 | 4.781683 |
| South Asian Petro | -1.44985 | -1.1867 | -0.92355 | -0.66041 | -0.39726 | -0.13411 | 0.129032 | 0.392179 | 0.655326 |
| Uttam Galva | -1.90336 | -1.51532 | -1.12729 | -0.73926 | -0.35122 | 0.036813 | 0.424847 | 0.812882 | 1.200916 |
| Telecom Consultants | -3.59104 | -2.85894 | -2.12684 | -1.39474 | -0.66264 | 0.069454 | 0.801553 | 1.533652 | 2.265751 |
| Tashi India Ltd. | -0.05931 | -0.04722 | -0.03513 | -0.02304 | -0.01094 | 0.001147 | 0.013239 | 0.025332 | 0.037424 |
| Tata Industries Ltd. | -1.02646 | -0.8172 | -0.60794 | -0.39867 | -0.18941 | 0.019853 | 0.229116 | 0.43838 | 0.647643 |
| Welspun Trading | -0.22583 | -0.18826 | -0.15069 | -0.11312 | -0.07555 | -0.03798 | -0.00042 | 0.037153 | 0.074721 |
| Transcorp International | -0.029 | -0.02309 | -0.01717 | -0.01126 | -0.00535 | 0.000561 | 0.006472 | 0.012384 | 0.018295 |
| Vyapar Industries | -0.56947 | -0.46058 | -0.35169 | -0.24281 | -0.13392 | -0.02503 | 0.083858 | 0.192746 | 0.301635 |
| Shaw Wallace Fina | -14.2703 | -11.2457 | -8.22106 | -5.19644 | -2.17183 | 0.852791 | 3.877409 | 6.902026 | 9.926644 |
| Qpro Infotech | -0.0301 | -0.02396 | -0.01783 | -0.01169 | -0.00555 | 0.000582 | 0.006719 | 0.012855 | 0.018991 |
| Bodhtree Consult. | -0.04816 | -0.04012 | -0.03207 | -0.02402 | -0.01598 | -0.00793 | 0.000113 | 0.008159 | 0.016205 |
| Nucleus Netsoft G I S | -0.04549 | -0.03621 | -0.02694 | -0.01767 | -0.00839 | 0.00088 | 0.010153 | 0.019427 | 0.0287 |

*Contd...*

| | *40* | *41* | *42* | *43* | *44* | *45* | *46* | *47* | *48* |
|---|---|---|---|---|---|---|---|---|---|
| Greycells Entertain. | 0.00284 | 0.002261 | 0.001682 | 0.001103 | 0.000524 | -5.5E-05 | -0.00063 | -0.00121 | -0.00179 |
| Marvel Capital & Finance | -0.02075 | -0.01652 | -0.01229 | -0.00806 | -0.00383 | 0.000401 | 0.004633 | 0.008864 | 0.013095 |
| Serveall Enterprise | 0.003034 | 0.002416 | 0.001797 | 0.001179 | 0.00056 | -5.9E-05 | -0.00068 | -0.0013 | -0.00191 |
| Data Quest | 0.137361 | 0.109357 | 0.081354 | 0.05335 | 0.025347 | -0.00266 | -0.03066 | -0.05866 | -0.08667 |
| K C P Biotech Ltd. | -0.00196 | -0.00159 | -0.00122 | -0.00086 | -0.00049 | -0.00012 | 0.000246 | 0.000614 | 0.000982 |
| Thakral Services | 0.033442 | 0.026624 | 0.019806 | 0.012989 | 0.006171 | -0.00065 | -0.00746 | -0.01428 | -0.0211 |
| Gitanjali Exports | -0.92621 | -0.77649 | -0.62678 | -0.47706 | -0.32734 | -0.17762 | -0.0279 | 0.121823 | 0.271543 |
| Sundram Fast Invst. | -0.02661 | -0.02119 | -0.01576 | -0.01034 | -0.00491 | 0.000515 | 0.00594 | 0.011366 | 0.016791 |
| Moser Baer | -9.5597 | -7.61078 | -5.66186 | -3.71294 | -1.76402 | 0.184894 | 2.133812 | 4.08273 | 6.031649 |
| Gitanjali Gems | -2.85945 | -2.27607 | -1.69269 | -1.10931 | -0.52593 | 0.057445 | 0.640824 | 1.224204 | 1.807583 |
| Rajesh Exports | -2.6237 | -2.08881 | -1.55392 | -1.01903 | -0.48414 | 0.050745 | 0.585633 | 1.120522 | 1.65541 |
| Jindal Saw | -4.5685 | -3.63712 | -2.70575 | -1.77438 | -0.84301 | 0.088359 | 1.01973 | 1.951101 | 2.882472 |
| Essar Oil | -1.12649 | -0.89683 | -0.66718 | -0.43752 | -0.20787 | 0.021787 | 0.251442 | 0.481096 | 0.710751 |
| ONGC Videsh | -9.16185 | -7.29404 | -5.42623 | -3.55842 | -1.69061 | 0.177199 | 2.04501 | 3.912821 | 5.780632 |
| Sterlite Indust | -17.0131 | -13.5447 | -10.0763 | -6.60782 | -3.13938 | 0.32905 | 3.797485 | 7.265921 | 10.73436 |

*Different Exchange Rate Scenarios — Effects on Net Profits (Scenario Profits - Existing profits)*

| *Descriptive Stat* | *40* | *41* | *42* | *43* | *44* | *45* | *46* | *47* | *48* |
|---|---|---|---|---|---|---|---|---|---|
| Total | -809.794 | -643.386 | -476.979 | -310.572 | -144.165 | 22.24184 | 188.6489 | 355.056 | 521.4631 |
| Maximum | 0.137361 | 0.109357 | 0.089891 | 0.253221 | 1.076139 | 16.60186 | 53.95644 | 91.31101 | 128.6656 |
| Minimum | -170.171 | -132.816 | -95.4619 | -58.1073 | -23.2786 | -5.80269 | -0.03066 | -0.05866 | -0.08667 |
| Range | 170.3084 | 132.9258 | 95.55175 | 58.36051 | 24.35477 | 22.40456 | 53.9871 | 91.36968 | 128.7523 |
| Mean | -11.9087 | -9.46157 | -7.0144 | -4.56724 | -2.12008 | 0.327086 | 2.774249 | 5.221412 | 7.668575 |
| Median | -2.77519 | -2.20748 | -1.63977 | -1.03314 | -0.48346 | 0.051054 | 0.631064 | 1.198773 | 1.766482 |
| SD | 26.27789 | 20.77174 | 15.27732 | 9.814326 | 4.498746 | 2.269294 | 7.145203 | 12.56787 | 18.0511 |
| Q1 | -10.5983 | -8.48129 | -6.36425 | -4.18193 | -1.98684 | -5.6E-05 | 0.012468 | 0.102847 | 0.176145 |
| Q3 | -0.23403 | -0.17793 | -0.12541 | -0.09108 | -0.01887 | 0.208248 | 2.403335 | 4.598421 | 6.793508 |
| CV | -220.661 | -219.538 | -217.799 | -214.885 | -212.197 | 693.7913 | 257.5545 | 240.6987 | 235.3905 |

numbers in the Table 2 show that Infosys would have derived additional net benefits of Rs 13.34155, 153.9714, 294.6012, 294.6012 and 435.231 crores if ERs were to be Rs. 45, 46, 47, and 48 respectively, instead of the existing Rs. 44.9051. The numbers in the Table 2 also show that Infosys would have incurred net benefits losses of Rs 127.288, 267.918, 408.548, 549.178 and 689.808 crores if ERs were to be Rs. 44, 43, 42, 41and 40 respectively, instead of the existing Rs. 44.9051. The numbers in the table show that TCS would have derived additional net benefits of Rs. 33.88951, 110.1417, 186.3938 and 262.646 crores if ERs were to be Rs. 45, 46, 47, and 48 respectively, instead of the existing Rs 44.55556. The numbers in this table also show that TCS would have incurred net benefits losses of Rs. 42.3627, 118.615, 194.867, 271.119 and 347.371 crores if ERs were to be Rs. 44, 43, 42, 41 and 40 respectively, instead of the existing Rs. 44.55556. The numbers in the table show that Wipro would have derived additional net benefits of Rs 1.873031, 21.61616, 41.35929 and 61.10243 crores if ERs were to be Rs. 45, 46, 47, and 48 respectively, instead of the existing Rs. 44.90513. The numbers in this table also show that Wipro would have incurred net benefits losses of Rs. 17.8701, 37.6132, 57.3564, 77.0995 and 96.8426 crores if ERs were to be Rs. 44, 43, 42, 41 and 40 respectively, instead of the existing Rs. 44.90513. The numbers in the table show that Surya Vinayak Industries would have derived additional net benefits of Rs. 0.089891, 0.253221, 0.416552, 0.579883, 0.743214, 0.906544 and 1.069875 crores if ERs were to be Rs. 42, 43, 44, 45, 46, 47, and 48 respectively, instead of the existing Rs 41.44964. The numbers in this table also show that this company would have incurred net benefits losses of Rs. 0.07344 and 0.23677 crores if ERs were to be Rs. 41 and 40 respectively, instead of the existing Rs 41.44964. Similar analysis holds for all the companies that have net benefit positive as shown in the table.

The companies shown in numbers 61 to 69 starting from Gitanjali Exports and ending with Sterlite Industries have negative net benefit ratio but positive net profit. The negative net benefit ratio indicates that as the ERs decrease below the existing levels, these companies will start earning more profits and if the ERs rise above the existing levels, these companies would incur losses. The numbers in the Table 1 show that Gitanjali Exports would have incurred losses of Rs 0.04953 and 0.11041 crores if ERs were to be Rs. 47 and 48 respectively, instead of the existing Rs. 46.18633. The numbers in the table 1 also show that Gitanjali Exports would have of derived additional net benefits profits Rs. 0.011343, 0.072219, 0.133096, 0.193973, 0.254849, 0.315726, and 0.376602 crores if ERs were to be Rs. 46, 45, 44, 43, 42, 41and 40 respectively, instead of the existing ER. Similar analysis for Sterliteshows that it would have incurred net benefits losses of Rs. 1.47735, 17.0497, 32.622 and 48.1944 crores if ERs were to be Rs. 45, 46, 47, and 48 respectively, instead of the existing Rs. 44.90513. The numbers in this table also show that this company would have derived additional profits of Rs. 14.095, 29.66735, 45.2397, 60.81205 and 76.3844 crores if ERs were to be Rs. 44, 43, 42, 41 and 40 respectively, instead of the existing Rs. 44.90513. The analysis for Rajesh Exports shows that it would have incurred net benefits losses of Rs. 0.04879, 0.56309, 1.07739, and 1.59169 crores if ERs were to be Rs. 45, 46, 47, and 48 respectively, instead of the existing Rs. 44.90513. The numbers in this table also show that this company would have derived additional net benefits profits of Rs. 0.465506, 0.979804, 1.494102, 2.0084 and 2.522698 crores if ERs were to be Rs. 44, 43, 42, 41 and 40 respectively, instead of the existing Rs 44.90513. Similar analysis holds for the companies like Sundaram Fasteners, Moser Baer, Gitanjali Gems, Jindal Saw, Essar Oil, ONGC Videsh and Sterlite that have net benefit negative as shown in the table. This result is in the expected lines. This is because these companies have net benefits negative and as argued the net exporters have gained by rupee depreciation and net importers have gained by rupee appreciation. The next paragraphs deal with the analysis of the imports, exports, operating profits and profit before taxes ( PBT).

Ideally one should analyse the imports, exports, operating profits and profit before taxes of individual companies as was done for net profit and net benefits. But the presentations of long tables become unwieldy and therefore, the researcher has calculated the summary measures of these variables relating

**Table 2**
**Different Exchange Rate Scenarios — Effects on Net Benefits (Scenario Net Benefits - Existing Net Benefits )**

| | 40 | 41 | 42 | 43 | 44 | 45 | 46 | 47 | 48 |
|---|---|---|---|---|---|---|---|---|---|
| Infosys | -689.808 | -549.178 | -408.548 | -267.918 | -127.288 | 13.34155 | 153.9714 | 294.6012 | 435.231 |
| Tata Consultancy . | -347.371 | -271.119 | -194.867 | -118.615 | -42.3627 | 33.88951 | 110.1417 | 186.3938 | 262.646 |
| Tata International | -158.322 | -126.045 | -93.7683 | -61.4915 | -29.2147 | 3.062099 | 35.33889 | 67.61569 | 99.89248 |
| Wipro Ltd. | -96.8426 | -77.0995 | -57.3564 | -37.6132 | -17.8701 | 1.873031 | 21.61616 | 41.35929 | 61.10243 |
| H C L Tech. | -87.3451 | -71.2917 | -55.2382 | -39.1848 | -23.1313 | -7.07782 | 8.975643 | 25.02911 | 41.08257 |
| Wall Street Fin | -78.7294 | -62.679 | -46.6285 | -30.5781 | -14.5277 | 1.522703 | 17.57312 | 33.62353 | 49.67395 |
| Patni Comps. | -64.476 | -50.3227 | -36.1695 | -22.0162 | -7.86298 | 6.290269 | 20.44352 | 34.59677 | 48.75002 |
| Satyam Comps. | -65.4381 | -52.0974 | -38.7566 | -25.4159 | -12.0751 | 1.265637 | 14.60639 | 27.94714 | 41.28789 |
| Surya Vinayak | -17.9575 | -5.56994 | 6.817619 | 19.20518 | 31.59274 | 43.98031 | 56.36787 | 68.75543 | 81.14299 |
| Siva Ventures . | -55.3123 | -44.9387 | -34.5651 | -24.1916 | -13.818 | -3.44443 | 6.929139 | 17.30271 | 27.67628 |
| Ranbaxy Labs | -50.4117 | -40.1343 | -29.857 | -19.5797 | -9.30233 | 0.975011 | 11.25235 | 21.52969 | 31.80703 |
| Mindtree Consult. | -34.3371 | -24.218 | -14.099 | -3.97989 | 6.139182 | 16.25825 | 26.37733 | 36.4964 | 46.61547 |
| Wipro B P O | -42.2747 | -34.3439 | -26.413 | -18.4821 | -10.5512 | -2.62033 | 5.310548 | 13.24143 | 21.17231 |
| Kudremukh | -39.135 | -31.1566 | -23.1782 | -15.1998 | -7.22147 | 0.756909 | 8.735284 | 16.71366 | 24.69204 |
| Gokaldas Exports | -32.5057 | -24.4908 | -16.476 | -8.46112 | -0.44626 | 7.568593 | 15.58345 | 23.59831 | 31.61317 |
| Dr. Reddy'S Labs. | -36.9815 | -29.4421 | -21.9028 | -14.3634 | -6.82409 | 0.715258 | 8.25461 | 15.79396 | 23.33331 |
| K E C Inter. | -23.5347 | -16.5991 | -9.66346 | -2.72782 | 4.207808 | 11.14344 | 18.07907 | 25.0147 | 31.95034 |
| P K S Ltd. | -40.0721 | -33.5946 | -27.1171 | -20.6395 | -14.162 | -7.68446 | -1.20693 | 5.270602 | 11.74813 |
| I-Flex Solutions | -32.6586 | -26.0006 | -19.3425 | -12.6845 | -6.0264 | 0.631649 | 7.289702 | 13.94775 | 20.60581 |
| GE Shipping | -31.4016 | -24.9998 | -18.598 | -12.1962 | -5.79445 | 0.607338 | 7.009128 | 13.41092 | 19.81271 |
| Karp Impex | -29.7823 | -23.7106 | -17.639 | -11.5673 | -5.49565 | 0.576019 | 6.647686 | 12.71935 | 18.79102 |
| Take Solutions | -26.6805 | -21.2624 | -15.8444 | -10.4263 | -5.00824 | 0.409833 | 5.827903 | 11.24597 | 16.66404 |
| L K P Forex | -28.6081 | -23.5389 | -18.4698 | -13.4006 | -8.3315 | -3.26235 | 1.806796 | 6.875944 | 11.94509 |
| Essar Ship | -24.4742 | -19.4847 | -14.4952 | -9.50567 | -4.51616 | 0.473355 | 5.462868 | 10.45238 | 15.44189 |
| Orient Craft | -25.8061 | -20.9269 | -16.0478 | -11.1687 | -6.28955 | -1.41042 | 3.468709 | 8.347839 | 13.22697 |

*Contd...*

| | *40* | *41* | *42* | *43* | *44* | *45* | *46* | *47* | *48* |
|---|---|---|---|---|---|---|---|---|---|
| Tech Mahindra | -24.0217 | -19.1245 | -14.2272 | -9.32993 | -4.43266 | 0.464604 | 5.36187 | 10.25914 | 15.1564 |
| Orchid Chemicals | -23.9778 | -19.0895 | -14.2012 | -9.31286 | -4.42455 | 0.463754 | 5.352059 | 10.24036 | 15.12867 |
| Sakuma Exports | -17.0294 | -12.0108 | -6.99233 | -1.97381 | 3.044704 | 8.06322 | 13.08174 | 18.10025 | 23.11877 |
| Cipla Ltd. | -22.8733 | -18.2102 | -13.547 | -8.88389 | -4.22075 | 0.442392 | 5.105533 | 9.768674 | 14.43181 |
| Firstsource Solu. | -22.0095 | -17.4943 | -12.9791 | -8.46388 | -3.94868 | 0.566519 | 5.08172 | 9.59692 | 14.11212 |
| Sesa Goa Ltd. | -21.3428 | -16.9917 | -12.6406 | -8.28944 | -3.93832 | 0.41279 | 4.763905 | 9.11502 | 13.46613 |
| E I H Ltd. | -21.1931 | -16.8725 | -12.5519 | -8.23132 | -3.91071 | 0.409896 | 4.730502 | 9.051109 | 13.37171 |
| Flextronics Soft | -20.6133 | -16.4109 | -12.2085 | -8.0061 | -3.80371 | 0.398681 | 4.601072 | 8.803463 | 13.00585 |
| L&T Infotech | -20.578 | -16.3828 | -12.1876 | -7.9924 | -3.7972 | 0.397999 | 4.593199 | 8.788399 | 12.9836 |
| Asian Star Co | -20.4221 | -16.2587 | -12.0952 | -7.93184 | -3.76843 | 0.394983 | 4.558393 | 8.721802 | 12.88521 |
| Jindal Iron | -15.772 | -12.5566 | -9.34117 | -6.12576 | -2.91036 | 0.305045 | 3.520449 | 6.735853 | 9.951257 |
| Magnanimous Trade | -13.9074 | -10.9631 | -8.01883 | -5.07455 | -2.13027 | 0.814005 | 3.758282 | 6.70256 | 9.646838 |
| Su-Raj Diamonds | -13.363 | -10.6387 | -7.91444 | -5.19014 | -2.46584 | 0.258454 | 2.982753 | 5.707052 | 8.431351 |
| Syntel Ltd. | -15.5926 | -12.9986 | -10.4046 | -7.81063 | -5.21666 | -2.62269 | -0.02871 | 2.565262 | 5.159236 |
| HP Globalsoft | -11.75 | -9.35456 | -6.95911 | -4.56365 | -2.1682 | 0.227257 | 2.622712 | 5.018168 | 7.413623 |
| Aurobindo Pharma | -11.4018 | -9.0773 | -6.75285 | -4.42839 | -2.10393 | 0.220521 | 2.544977 | 4.869433 | 7.193889 |
| South Asian Petro | -9.58546 | -7.8457 | -6.10595 | -4.36619 | -2.62643 | -0.88668 | 0.853078 | 2.592834 | 4.33259 |
| Uttam Galva | -7.04146 | -5.60593 | -4.1704 | -2.73487 | -1.29934 | 0.136189 | 1.571718 | 3.007247 | 4.442777 |
| Telecom Consultants | -4.74173 | -3.77505 | -2.80836 | -1.84167 | -0.87498 | 0.09171 | 1.058399 | 2.025087 | 2.991776 |
| Tashi India Ltd. | -3.14002 | -2.49987 | -1.85972 | -1.21957 | -0.57942 | 0.060731 | 0.700881 | 1.34103 | 1.98118 |
| Tata Industries Ltd. | -2.47064 | -1.96695 | -1.46327 | -0.95958 | -0.4559 | 0.047785 | 0.551469 | 1.055153 | 1.558837 |
| Welspun Trading | -2.60687 | -2.17319 | -1.73951 | -1.30584 | -0.87216 | -0.43848 | -0.0048 | 0.428877 | 0.862556 |
| Transcorp International | -0.62001 | -0.49361 | -0.36721 | -0.24081 | -0.11441 | 0.011992 | 0.138391 | 0.264791 | 0.391191 |
| Vyapar Industries | -0.35799 | -0.28954 | -0.22109 | -0.15264 | -0.08419 | -0.01573 | 0.052716 | 0.121166 | 0.189616 |
| Shaw Wallace Fina | -0.31341 | -0.24698 | -0.18055 | -0.11413 | -0.0477 | 0.018729 | 0.085156 | 0.151584 | 0.218011 |
| Qpro Infotech | -0.28728 | -0.22872 | -0.17015 | -0.11158 | -0.05301 | 0 005556 | 0.064124 | 0.122692 | 0.18126 |
| Bodhtree Consult. | -0.29783 | -0.24807 | -0.19832 | -0.14856 | -0.09881 | -0.04905 | 0.000701 | 0.050455 | 0.100209 |

*Contd...*

| | *40* | *41* | *42* | *43* | *44* | *45* | *46* | *47* | *48* |
|---|---|---|---|---|---|---|---|---|---|
| Nucleus Netsoft G I S | -0.18329 | -0.14593 | -0.10856 | -0.07119 | -0.03382 | 0.003545 | 0.040913 | 0.07828 | 0.115648 |
| Greycells Entertain. | -0.0426 | -0.03392 | -0.02523 | -0.01655 | -0.00786 | 0.000824 | 0.009509 | 0.018194 | 0.026879 |
| Marvel Capital & Finance | -0.03823 | -0.03044 | -0.02264 | -0.01485 | -0.00705 | 0.000739 | 0.008534 | 0.016328 | 0.024122 |
| Serveall Enterprise | -0.0308 | -0.02452 | -0.01824 | -0.01196 | -0.00568 | 0.000596 | 0.006876 | 0.013156 | 0.019435 |
| Data Quest | -0.02032 | -0.01618 | -0.01203 | -0.00789 | -0.00375 | 0.000393 | 0.004535 | 0.008677 | 0.012819 |
| K C P Biotech Ltd. | -0.01323 | -0.01075 | -0.00827 | -0.00578 | -0.0033 | -0.00082 | 0.001662 | 0.004144 | 0.006625 |
| Thakral Services | -0.00218 | -0.00174 | -0.00129 | -0.00085 | -0.0004 | 4.23E-05 | 0.000488 | 0.000933 | 0.001378 |
| Gitanjali Exports | 0.376602 | 0.315726 | 0.254849 | 0.193973 | 0.133096 | 0.072219 | 0.011343 | -0.04953 | -0.11041 |
| Sundram Fast Invst. | 0.600346 | 0.477954 | 0.355563 | 0.233171 | 0.11078 | -0.01161 | -0.134 | -0.25639 | -0.37879 |
| Moser Baer | 0.836414 | 0.665896 | 0.495378 | 0.324859 | 0.154341 | -0.01618 | -0.1867 | -0.35721 | -0.52773 |
| Gitanjali Gems | 0.900165 | 0.716515 | 0.532865 | 0.349215 | 0.165566 | -0.01808 | -0.20173 | -0.38538 | -0.56903 |
| Rajesh Exports | 2.522698 | 2.0084 | 1.494102 | 0.979804 | 0.465506 | -0.04879 | -0.56309 | -1.07739 | -1.59169 |
| Jindal Saw | 4.720815 | 3.758391 | 2.795967 | 1.833543 | 0.871119 | -0.09131 | -1.05373 | -2.01615 | -2.97858 |
| Essar Oil | 60.87725 | 48.46632 | 36.05538 | 23.64445 | 11.23351 | -1.17743 | -13.5884 | -25.9993 | -38.4102 |
| ONGC Videsh | 70.80807 | 56.37255 | 41.93704 | 27.50153 | 13.06602 | -1.3695 | -15.805 | -30.2405 | -44.676 |
| Sterlite Indust | 76.3844 | 60.81205 | 45.2397 | 29.66735 | 14.095 | -1.47735 | -17.0497 | -32.622 | -48.1944 |

*Different Exchange Rate Scenarios — Effects on Net Benefits (Scenario Net benefit - Existing Net Benefits )*

| | *40* | *41* | *42* | *43* | *44* | *45* | *46* | *47* | *48* |
|---|---|---|---|---|---|---|---|---|---|
| Total | -2269.88 | -1790.72 | -1311.56 | -832.407 | -353.249 | 125.9084 | 605.0661 | 1084.224 | 1563.381 |
| Maximum | 76.3844 | 60.81205 | 45.2397 | 29.66735 | 31.59274 | 43.98031 | 153.9714 | 294.6012 | 435.231 |
| Minimum | -689.808 | -549.178 | -408.548 | -267.918 | -127.288 | -7.68446 | -17.0497 | -32.622 | -48.1944 |
| Range | 766.1919 | 609.9898 | 453.7876 | 297.5854 | 158.881 | 51.66477 | 171.0211 | 327.2232 | 483.4254 |
| Mean | -33.3806 | -26.3342 | -19.2877 | -12.2413 | -5.19484 | 1.851594 | 8.898031 | 15.94447 | 22.9909 |
| Median | -17.4934 | -12.7776 | -9.50231 | -5.13235 | -2.31702 | 0.178355 | 3.494579 | 6.805899 | 11.84661 |
| SD | 96.09591 | 76.29227 | 56.53066 | 36.87871 | 17.70542 | 7.486189 | 24.243 | 43.68663 | 63.39115 |
| Q1 | -31.6776 | -24.2862 | -17.8467 | -11.7245 | -5.85244 | -0.01585 | 0.009265 | 0.110445 | 0.164857 |
| Q3 | -0.29519 | -0.24241 | -0.15475 | -0.10148 | -0.00671 | 0.613416 | 7.079271 | 14.40931 | 21.65893 |
| CV | -287.88 | -289.708 | -293.092 | -301.265 | -340.827 | 404.3104 | 272.4535 | 273.9924 | 275.7228 |

to all the companies and presented the analysis for these measures for all the companies together instead of for the individual companies. Table 3 contains these summary measures. The numbers in this table show that the companies would have derived additional operating profits of Rs. 57.20191, 362.6697, 668.1374 and 973.6052 crores if ERs were to be Rs. 45, 46, 47, and 48 respectively, instead of the existing average rate for the companies. These companies would have incurred additional operating losses of Rs. 248.266, 553.734, 859.201, 1164.67, and 1470.14 crores if ERs were to be Rs. 44, 43, 42, 41and 40 respectively, instead of the existing exchange rates applicable to the companies. The maximum additional operating profit that an individual company would have earned is Rs. 220.5389 crores at an ER of Rs. 48. The maximum additional operating profit that an individual company would have earned is Rs. 1.716641crores at an ER of Rs. 40. The maximum row shows that all the numbers in this row are positive. Therefore, it may seem like there are some companies which earn additional profit at any ER. This result goes against our argument that at lower ER the companies would incur losses because they are export oriented companies. We get this result because there are some companies in our analysis which are net importers. For these companies, the lower ER would augur well. The analysis for these companies which are in serial numbers 61 to 68 was presented in the above paragraphs by taking the individual companies and analysing the net profit and net benefit. The minimum number shows that the maximum possible loss that a company would have incurred is Rs. 291.681 at an ER of Rs.40. The number in the minimum row at an ER of Rs. 48 is -5.74287. This shows that an individual company would have incurred a loss of Rs. 5.74287 crores. This results does not follow our argument. This is because there are companies which are net importers and these companies would incur losses if the ER rises above the existing number. Alternatively if the existing operating profit is negative the scenario operating profits at the higher levels ER is also negative but a higher loss than the exisiting loss and therefore, the resultant number would be a negative number. This is the case in this variable as the company, Surya Vinayak, has an existing operating loss. In such cases the analysis of imports and exports are more reliable as these are directly affected by the ER changes.

On average companies would have earned more operating profit of Rs. 14.31772 crores at an ER of Rs. 48 and would have incurred an additional loss of Rs. 21.6197 at an ER of Rs .40. The range number shows the difference between maximum and minimum number and is given to know on average how far the extreme numbers of the companies differ for the respective variables being studied. For example, the number 226.2818 shows that the variation between the maximum additional operating profit and the minimum additional operating profit is Rs. 226.2818 crores at an ER of Rs. 48. The value of the range is more than the maximum number because the minimum number is negative. Similar analysis holds for all the summary measures for profit before taxes and therefore, no separate analysis is given for this variable.

The numbers in this table show that the companies would have derived additional export proceeds of Rs. 216.7106, 1258.868, 2301.026, and 3343.184 crores if ERs were to be Rs. 45, 46, 47, and 48 respectively, instead of the existing average rate for the companies. These companies would have incurred additional operating losses due to export proceeds being less to the extent of Rs. 825.447, 1867.6, 2909.76, 3951.92, and 4994.08 crores if ERs were to be Rs. 44, 43, 42, 41and 40 respectively, instead of the existing exchange rates applicable to the companies. The maximum additional export proceeds that an individual company would have earned is Rs. 837.7938 crores at an ER of Rs. 48. The minimum number shows that the maximum possible loss that a company would have incurred because of exports alone is Rs.1327.84 at an ER of Rs.40. On average companies would have earned more exports sales of Rs. 49.16446 crores at an ER of Rs. 48 and would have incurred an additional loss of Rs. 73.4423 crores at an ER of Rs 40. The range number 837.793 at an ER of Rs.48 shows the difference between maximum and minimum export proceeds of the companies studied. The value of range at an ER of Rs. 40 is

**Table 3**
**Different Exchange Rate Scenarios**

| *Variables and the Descriptive Stat* | | | | | | | | | |
|---|---|---|---|---|---|---|---|---|---|
| *Operating Profits* | *40* | *41* | *42* | *43* | *44* | *45* | *46* | *47* | *48* |
| Total | -1470.14 | -1164.67 | -859.201 | -553.734 | -248.266 | 57.20191 | 362.6697 | 668.1374 | 973.6052 |
| Maximum | 1.716641 | 1.366673 | 1.016704 | 0.666736 | 4.290367 | 28.45638 | 92.4839 | 156.5114 | 220.5389 |
| Minimum | -291.681 | -227.654 | -163.626 | -99.5987 | -35.5711 | -4.51443 | -3.98942 | -4.86615 | -5.74287 |
| Range | 293.3979 | 229.0204 | 164.6429 | 100.2654 | 39.8615 | 32.97082 | 96.47333 | 161.3776 | 226.2818 |
| Mean | -21.6197 | -17.1275 | -12.6353 | -8.14314 | -3.65097 | 0.841205 | 5.333377 | 9.82555 | 14.31772 |
| *Profit Before Taxes* | | | | | | | | | |
| Total | -928.38 | -737.206 | -546.032 | -354.857 | -163.683 | 27.49129 | 218.6656 | 409.8399 | 601.0143 |
| Maximum | 0.134447 | 0.107038 | 0.142736 | 0.402087 | 1.652029 | 18.80771 | 61.12548 | 103.4432 | 145.761 |
| Minimum | -192.781 | -150.463 | -108.146 | -65.8278 | -25.42 | -6.33647 | -0.03374 | -0.05742 | -0.08483 |
| Range | 192.9156 | 150.5704 | 108.2883 | 66.22992 | 27.07203 | 25.14418 | 61.15922 | 103.5007 | 145.8458 |
| Mean | -13.6527 | -10.8413 | -8.02988 | -5.21849 | -2.4071 | 0.404284 | 3.215671 | 6.027058 | 8.838445 |
| *Exports* | | | | | | | | | |
| Total | -4994.08 | -3951.92 | -2909.76 | -1867.6 | -825.447 | 216.7106 | 1258.868 | 2301.026 | 3343.184 |
| Maximum | -0.00131 | -0.00104 | 6.819743 | 19.21117 | 31.60259 | 62.67227 | 296.3857 | 567.0898 | 837.7938 |
| Minimum | -1327.84 | -1057.13 | -786.43 | -515.726 | -245.022 | -10.4472 | -1.4323 | 0.00056 | 0.000827 |
| Range | 1327.837 | 1057.133 | 793.2502 | 534.9375 | 276.6249 | 73.11951 | 297.818 | 567.0892 | 837.793 |
| Mean | -73.4423 | -58.1165 | -42.7906 | -27.4648 | -12.1389 | 3.186921 | 18.51277 | 33.83862 | 49.16446 |
| *Imports* | | | | | | | | | |
| Total | -2724.2 | -2161.2 | -1598.2 | -1035.2 | -472.198 | 90.80223 | 653.8022 | 1216.802 | 1779.802 |
| Maximum | -0.00109 | -0.00087 | 0.002124 | 0.005985 | 11.0585 | 29.28596 | 142.4144 | 272.4886 | 402.5628 |
| Minimum | -638.031 | -507.957 | -377.883 | -247.808 | -117.734 | -9.19161 | -1.44364 | 0.000467 | 0.000689 |
| Range | 638.0299 | 507.9559 | 377.8847 | 247.8143 | 128.7926 | 38.47757 | 143.858 | 272.4881 | 402.5621 |
| Mean | -42.5656 | -33.7687 | -24.9718 | -16.175 | -7.37809 | 1.418785 | 10.21566 | 19.01253 | 27.80941 |

1327.837 and this number is higher than the number at ER Rs.48 because both the maximum and minimum numbers are negative and therefore, the resultant number is greater than the maximum number.

In all the above analysis the positive numbers at ERs of Rs.45, 46, 47 and 48 showed that the companies would have derived additional profits to that extent shown in the respective rows if the rupee were to depreciate. The negative numbers showed the losses that these companies would have incurred. The values for imports show the opposite for those of the exports. This is because, as the exchange rates increase to higher rates the companies would have to pay more in rupee terms and vice-versa. The numbers in the table show that companies would have paid additional Rs. 90.80223, 653.8022, 1216.802, and 1779.802 crores if ERs were to be Rs. 45, 46, 47, and 48 respectively, instead of the existing average rate for the companies. These companies would have saved to the extent of Rs.472.198, 1035.2, 1598.2, 2161.2 and 2724.2 crores if ERs were to be Rs. 44, 43, 42, 41and 40 respectively, instead of the existing exchange rates applicable to the companies. The maximum additional amount that an individual company would have paid for the imports is Rs. 402.5628 crores at an ER of Rs. 48. The maximum savings in costs that a company could have made is Rs. 638.031 crores and the minimum savings a company would have effected because of imports is Rs. 0.00109 at an ER of Rs. 40.

The minimum number further shows that the manimum possible additional costs that a company would have incurred because of imports is Rs. 0.000689 crores at an ER of Rs.48. On average companies would have paid more to the extent of Rs 27.80941 crores for imports at an ER of Rs. 48 and would have saved an additional amount of Rs.42.5656 crores at an ER of Rs. 40. The range value of 402.5621 at an ER of Rs.48 shows the difference between maximum and minimum additional imports costs that companies would have paid. The value of range at an ER of Rs. 40 is 638.0299 and it shows the difference between the savings that the companies with maximum and minimum savings would have effected.

The analysis above has shown that different companies get affected in different ways as the ERs change. The effect of ERs would depend on whether the companies are predominantly exporters or importers. While exporters would suffer as the home currency appreciates, the importers would gain for the same reason and vice-versa. Therefore, whether companies are net exporters or importers they are affected by the ER changes and there is a need to manage these ER risks. The discussion in the next section focuses on some of the techniques that can be used in managing ER risks.

## MANAGING EXCHANGE RATE RISKS

Exchange risk can be defined as the risk of loss because of the fluctuations in the values of one currency vis-à-vis other currency. The currencies of importance for the companies are those in which the company deals either because it is importing, exporting, borrowing, repaying, has assets and liabilities denominated in foreign currency. The companies are said to have ER risk exposure if they have any of the above denominated in foreign currency and are receivable or payable at future period. During the time the above values are created and the time when they are converted into home currency, the ERs may change and as a result of this companies may either gain or lose. Every company would be happy if they are gaining because of the ER changes. The problem arises when the companies start losing because of the ER changes. This is precisely what is happening to the IT/ITES companies in India ever since the rupee starting appreciating against dollars continuosly although the scenario is changing in the most recent time. These companies incurred losses because of rupee appreciation from 2003 to 2007. This is partly reflected in the analysis of the variables presented above for the selected companies. The analysis of the companies showed companies can gain or lose by huge amounts (by hundreds or thousands of crores of rupees) for different scenarios of ERs. Therefore, it is necessary to know the various techniques that can be used for managing the ER risk. The following discussion focuses on these techniques.

Managing exchange rate risk involves managing trasaction exposure, transaltion exposure and economi exposures. Shapiro (1996) (20) has advocated many techniques for managing the risk arising out of foreign currency transactions. These management techniques and other techniques are briefly discussed below.

**Transaction Exposoure**

Transaction exposoure arises from the possibility of incuring future exchange gains or losses on the transaction already entered into and denominated in a foreign currency. In simple a transaction exposure arises whenever a company is committed to a foreign currency denominated transaction. It is measured currency by currency and equals to the difference between contractually fixed future cash inflow and outflows in each currency.

*Managing Transaction Exposoure:* The following techniques are used to managing transaction exposure.

*Forward Market Hedge:* To avoide exchange rate risk a company that is long on a currency will sell the foreign curreny forward, whereas a company that is short on a foreign currency will buy the cuurency forward.

*Money Market Hedge:* It involvles simultaneous borrow and lend in two different currencies to lock in the home currency values of a future foreign currency cash flow.

*Risk Shifting:* It is possible only when the company price the sale in home currency. In this case the risk is not eliminated, it is shifted to the other company ( Importing company).

*Pricing Decision:* Fixing the price after considering the possible future movement of exchange rates. The forward rate in the foreign exchange market can be used as a possible future spot price.

*Exposure Netting:* It involves offsetting exposure in one currency with the exposure in the same or anthor currency, where exchange rates are expected to move in such a way that losses (gains) on the first exposed position should be offset by the gain (losses) on the second currency exposure.

*Currency Risk Sharing:* Currency risk sharing is possible only when the base price is adjusted to reflect certain exchange rate change. The parties would share the currency risk beyond a neutral zone. The neutral zone represents the currency range in which risk is not shared.

*Foreign Currency Options:* Company can enter into an option contract depending on the sitution (call or put option on foreign currency) to avoid the foreign exchange risk.

### Managing Translation Exposure

The following techniques are used for managing the translation exposure:

- Adjusting fund flows
- Entering into forward contract
- Exposure netting

### Foreign Exchange Risk and Economic Exposure

Exchange risk management incorportaes currency change expectation into all basic corporate decisions.

***Real Exchange Rate:*** Change in the ratio of domestic goods prices to prices of foreign goods. In other words changes in the purchasing power of one currency relative to another.

### Inflation and Exchange Rate

The exchange rate also depends on the diffrence between the foreign and domestic rate of inflation.

### The Economic Consequences of Exchange Rate Changes

*Transaction Exposure:* It arises out of the various types of transaction that require settlemnt in a foreign currency.

*Operating Exposure:* It arises out of the basic opertions of the company.

### Managing Economic Exposure

*Marketing Management of Exchange Risk*

- Market selection: Selecting a market for the export of Product and market segmentation within individual countries.

- Pricing Strategy.
- Promotional strategy.
- Product Strategy.

*Production Management of Exchange Risk*

- Input mix.
- Shifting production among Plants
- Plant location.
- Raising production.

**Planning for Exchange Rate Changes**

Planning involves developing several plausible currency scenarios, analysing the effects of each scenario on the firms competitive position, and deciding on strategies to deal with these possibilities.

*Financial Management of Exchange Risk:* This involves financing, investment and dividend decisions.

*Materials Management of Exchange Risk:* This involves purchasing and inventory decisions.

*HR Management of Exchange Risk:* This involves decisions regarding recruitment, selection and training programmes. This also involves outsourcing the services of professionals.

The above techniques can be used any company. The detailed explanation of these techniques is not attempted here for want of space. However, they can be elaborated.

**SUMMARY AND CONCLUSIONS**

This paper attempted to understand the effects of different exchange rates on profitability of companies. To understand the magnitude of the effects, some of the important financial variables were chosen for study. The sample for the study consist of the top 25 companies each from manufacturing and service sector and 18 companies from the financial services. The criteria used for selecting the companies is the ratio of exports to total sales. For the selected companies, the possible effects were computed for net profit, profit before taxes, operating profits, imports and exports using the different exchange rate scenarios. The sensitivity of analysis for individual companies was presented for net profit and net benefits (exports less imports). The sensitivity analysis for other financial variables for all the companies was presented using some of the descriptive statistics. The analysis revealed that the profits of the companies are affected on average to the extent of hundreds and thousands of crores of rupees for different exchange rate scenarios. The direct indication of the profits being affected was given by the exports and imports of companies. The analysis shows that ER can substantially influence the profitability of the companies. Therefore, there is a need to understand the techniques that can be used for managing the risks to which export/import oriented companies are exposed to. In the light of this realization some of the techniques that can be used for managing the trasaction risk and economic risks were discussed. The discussion shows that although there are a lot of techaniques that can be used, there are costs associated with each of these techniques and therefore, one need to make careful analysis before chosing a techniques that best suits a company. There are no short cuts to any of these techniques. Companies need to be dynamic in understanding the movements in the world economy and foreign exchange market to make best use of the available opportunity and chose a technique to manage the risks. One need to understand that no technique can be best technique for all companies for all time to come. As the economy evolves the companies also undergo changes, and therefore, the techniques also need to be updated. No financial manager, however efficient he is, can guarantee a company that the technique he is using will give best result at all times. Therefore, companies must be prepared to incur loss on these transactions and they want to profit from the favourable movements of the exchange rates. It is only the dynamism of the financial managers and companies willingness to incur losses on these transaction that can ensure that make the former to scout for the best possible technique to manage the foreign exchange risk that arises in the usual course of the operation of the business.

## REFERENCES

De Jong, Abe, Ligterink, Jeroen, and Macrae,Victor (2006), "A Firm-Specific Analysis of the Exchange-Rate Exposure of Dutch Firms",

*Journal of International Financial Management & Accounting,* Spring 2006, Vol. 17, Issue 1, p. 1-28

Cerf, Douglas, and Elmy, Frederick J. (1998)", Accounting for Derivatives: The Case of a Currency Rate Swap Used to Hedge Foreign Exchange Bate Exposure", Issues in Accounting Education, Nov., Vol. 13, Issue 4, p. 931-955.

Chang, Jow-ran, Errunza,Vihang, Hogan, Ked and Hung, Mao-wei (2005), "An Empirical Evidence", *European Financial Management,* March, Vol. 11, Issue 2, p. 173-194.

Schwab, Bernhard, and Lusztig, Peter, "Apportioning Foreign Exchange Risk Through the Use of Third Currencies: Some Questions on Efficiency", *Financial Management* (1972), Autumn 78, Vol. 7, Issue 3, p. 25-30

Lewis, Karen K. (1995), "Are Foreign Exchange Intervention and Monetary Policy Related, and Does it Really Matter?" *Journal of Business,* April, Vol. 68, Issue 2, p. 185-214

Samuel, Henry, "Buyers Should Assume Exchange-rate Risk", Crain's Detroit Business; 9/23/96, Vol. 12, Issue 39, p. 1-7.

Hertzell, Staffan, and Caspar, Christian (188), "Coping with Unpredictable Currencies", McKinsey Quarterly; Summer, 88 Issue 3, p. 12-24,

Kit Pong Wong, and Ho Yin Yick (2004), "Currency Options and Export-Flexible Firms", *Bulletin of Economic Research,* Oct., Vol. 56, Issue 4, p. 379-394.

Shapiro, Alan C. (1985), "Currency Risk and Country Risk in International Banking", *Journal of Finance,* July 85, Vol. 40, Issue 3, p. 881-891.

Thomas III, Lee R. (1988), "Currency Risks in International Equity Portfolios", *Financial Analysts Journal,* Mar/Apr. 88, Vol. 44, Issue 2. p68-71

Campa, Josa Manuel (1993), "Entry by Foreign Firms in the United States Under Exchange Rate Uncertainty", *Review of Economics & Statistics,* November, Vol. 75, Issue 4, p. 614-622.

Peijie Wang and Ping Wang (2001), "Equilibrium Adjustment, Basis Risk and Risk Transmission in Spot and Forward Foreign Exchange Markets", *Applied Financial Economics,* April, Vol. 11, Issue 2, p. 127-136.

WenShwo Fang and Miller, Stephen M. (2007), "Exchange Rate Depreciation and Exports: The Case of Singapore Revisited." *Applied Economics,* Vol. 39, Issue 3, p. 273-277.

Levy,Haim and Sarnat, Marshall (1978), "Exchange Rate Risk and the Optimal Diversification of Foreign Currency Holdings", *Journal of Money, Credit & Banking*, November, Vol. 10, Issue 4, p. 453-463.

Moon, Bruce E. (1982), "Exchange Rate System, Policy Distortions, and the Maintenance of Trade Dependence", *International Organization; Autumn*, Vol. 36, Issue 4, p. 715-729.

Wai-Ching Poon, Chee-Keong Choong, and Habibullah, Muzafar Shah (2005), "Exchange Rate Volatility and Exports for Selected East Asian Countries", *ASEAN Economic Bulletin*, Aug, Vol. 22, Issue 2, p. 144-159.

Doyle, Eleanor (2001), "Exchange Rate Volatility and Irish-UK Trade, 1979-1992, *Applied Economics*, Feb., Vol. 33, Issue 2, p. 249-265.

Carriero, Andrea (2006), "Explaining USâ€ "UK Interest Rate Differentials: A Reassessment of the Uncovered Interest Rate Parity in a Bayesian Framework", *Oxford Bulletin of Economics and Statistics*, November, Supplement, Vol. 68, p. 879-899.

Wong, Kit Pong (2003), "Export Flexibility and Currency Hedging", *International Economic Review*, November, Vol. 44, Issue 4, p. 1295-1306

Shapiro Allan C. (1996), Multinational Financial Management, Prentice Hall of India Pvt Ltd, New Delhi.

# 10

# DOES EXCHANGE RATE FLUCTUATION MATTER FOR FOREIGN TRADE–THE CASE OF INDIA

**G. Saravanan & Malabika Deo**

## INTRODUCTION

In this globalised world, countries depend on each other for a variety of economic transactions, i.e., transactions in goods, services and capital, that is, financial transactions. We live and work in national economy, i.e., the economy within the borders of the country. But we also live and work in an international economy or world economy, being a part of the world. No country can therefore live in economic isolation or afford to keep out of the global economy except at its own risk. The risk arises because no country is self-sufficient with regard to its needs or requirements; nor can it consume or use up all that it produces; nor can the country remain a closed economy, insulating itself from external influences. In other words, interdependence of countries is reflected in a whole range of economic relations consisting of exchange of goods, exchange of services, inter country flow of capital funds, financial arrangements and inter-country movement of skills and labour.

India's foreign trade has some special features which are the commodity pattern of imports and exports indicate that India's trade conforms to the theory of comparative. The country's comparative advantage still lies in labour intensive products like agro-products, garments, diamond cutting, information technology and jewelry-making, etc,. In India's foreign trade, imports of India are majorly contributed by petroleum and oil products, capital goods, pearls and precious stones, chemicals, fertilizers, iron and steel, and non ferrous metals, and in export side is contributed by agricultural and allied products, minerals and ores, manufactured goods, IT services, and crude and petroleum products. To understand the importance of foreign trade in India, foreign trade trends have been analyzed and it reveals that the increasing trends in foreign trade, in the year 2002-03, the exports in goods and services are 52.7 and 20.8 US billion dollar respectively (service exports include software exports), and imports in goods and services are 61.4 and 17.1 US billion dollar respectively. In the year 2007-08, the exports in goods and services are 155.5 and 87.7 US billion dollar respectively (service exports include software exports), and imports in goods and services are 235.9 and 50.1 US billion dollar respectively. A foreign trade trend shows that the proportion of foreign trade and growth of foreign trade is higher in import than export in goods and which is vice versa in the foreign trade of services. The growing importance of foreign trade can be identified through the total foreign trade constituents grow to 45% of GDP of India on 2007-08.

Foreign trade being the more important component of economic relations between countries, some specific aspects of interdependence in foreign trade in the form of import and export dependence of the country. This interdependence or foreign trade among countries is varying in degree, in response to variation of many macroeconomic factors. Among many factors, variation in currency exchange rate plays a vital role as a foreign trade determinant. The arrival of the flexible exchange rate system in 1973 produced a significant volatility and uncertainty in exchange rates. This started a debate among policy makers and researchers about the impact of exchange rate volatility on trade flows. However, both the theoretical and empirical studies yielded conflicting results about the relationship between exchange rate variability and international trade flows. Instability in exchange rate can influence longer-term decisions by affecting the volume of exports and imports, the allocation of investment and government sales and procurement policies. In medium term, it can affect the balance of payments and the level of economic activity, while in the short run local consumers and the local trader can be affected. Exchange rate instability gives chances to investors to invest in foreign currency (dollars) to get higher returns and thus resulting in the strengthening the dollar against the home currency, which directly impacts the prices of exports and imports and their growth rates. Risk averter traders and investors always favour the system where the variance of the difference between actual and expected value of exchange rate is minimised, while risk lover traders and investors prefer volatile exchange rate so that they can maximise their profits because of high risk premium. Therefore, exchange rate instability can have positive impact on exports and imports for risk lover traders and *vice versa* for risk averter traders.

Although most of the previous studies argue that exchange rate volatility increases uncertainty and risk and therefore hinders the trade flows, some other studies suggest otherwise. In addition, this issue is mostly examined for developed countries. In developing countries, there are few studies that investigated the relationship due to mainly the lack of sufficient time series data. The main objectives of the study are as follows:

(1) To examine whether exchange rate instability affects trade or not,

(2) How instability of the exchange rate affects exports and imports, if instability is caused by an appreciation of the exchange rate, and

(3) How instability of the exchange rate affects exports and imports, if instability is caused by a depreciation of the exchange rate.

## DATA AND METHODOLOGY

### Data

To study the impact of exchange rate instability on foreign trade, namely export and import of India. Data on exchange rate against dollar, exports and imports have been taken from RBI. Data have been collected at monthly interval from April, 2004 to August, 2008.

### Model

To capture the relationship between exchange rate instability of rupee against dollar and foreign trade movement of India, we have used log-linear regression model. Regressing variables in a raw data form can have problems of spurious regression, to avoid the problem of spurious regression, it is better not to estimate equation in the raw data form. Therefore, variables are converted to log form, and then the log variables are used in the model for estimation. In our model, to capture response of export and import against movement of exchange rate of rupee, exchange rate of rupee against dollar, lagged value of dependent variable and volatility of exchange rate have been used, volatility is calculated using squared residual of AR(2) model of exchange rate. Moreover, in our model we have used dummy variables to capture the impact of appreciation and depreciation of rupee against dollar on export and import, appreciation dummy takes the value of '1' if rupee gets appreciation otherwise '0' likewise, vice versa for depreciation dummy. The Model can be mathematically represented as the following equation

***Exports Equation***

$$X_t = \alpha_0 + \alpha_1 X_{t-1} + \alpha_2 ER_t + \alpha_3 SD_t + \alpha_4 DD_t + \varepsilon_{1t}$$

***Imports Equation***

$$M_t = \beta_0 + \beta_1 M_{t-1} + \beta_2 ER_t + \beta_3 SD_t + \beta_4 AD_t + \varepsilon_{2t}$$

Where, in both equation $X_t$ *and* $M_t$ represents exports and imports of india respectively, $X_{t-1}$ *and* $M_{t-1}$ represents lagged dependent variables of exports and imports respectively, and $ER_t$, $SD_t$, $DD_t$ and $AD_t$ represent the exchange rate of rupee against dollar, volatility of exchange rate, depreciation and appreciation dummy respectively.

If exchange rate instability is caused by an appreciation of the exchange rate then it will affect exports negatively and imports positively, conversely, if instability is caused by depreciation in the exchange rate then it will affect exports positively and imports negatively. In the above export equation, we expect positive relationship between exports and exchange rate if it is depreciation and vice versa for appreciation, and likewise for depreciation and appreciation dummy.

In the above import equation, we expect negative relationship between imports and exchange rate if it is depreciation and vice versa for appreciation, and likewise for depreciation and appreciation dummy. As far as volatility concern we expect either negative or positive relationship between export and volatility of exchange rate, and likewise for import and volatility of exchange rate, as risk averter traders always favour the system where the variance of the difference between actual and expected value of exchange rate is minimised, while risk lover traders and investors prefer volatile exchange rate so that they can maximise their profits because of high risk premium. Therefore, exchange rate instability can have positive impact on exports and imports for risk lover traders and *vice versa* for risk averter traders.

## EMPIRICAL FINDINGS AND RESULTS

To capture the relationship between exchange rate instability of rupee against dollar and foreign trade movement of India we have used log-linear regression model along with descriptive statistics and graphs. Table 1, presents the descriptive statistics of export, import and exchange rate of rupee against US dollar over the observation period from April, 2004 to August, 2008. Average export, import and exchange rate per month are 10151.46 (million $), 14925.85 (million $) and 43.437 (Rs.) respectively. In case of co-efficient of variation, export, import and exchange rate are 28.29, 33.66 and 5.06 respectively. Among these co-efficient of variation, import has higher value as measure for more variation in import than export and exchange rate.

**Table 1**
**Descriptive Statistics**

| *Particular* | *Export Mill $* | *Import Mill $* | *Exchange Rate, Rs/ $* |
|---|---|---|---|
| Mean | 10151.46 | 14925.84 | 43.43713 |
| Median | 10100.35 | 14095.67 | 43.84657 |
| Maximum | 16345.00 | 27143.00 | 46.44609 |
| Minimum | 5603.960 | 6900.150 | 39.26762 |
| Std. Dev. | 2872.277 | 5024.470 | 2.204168 |
| Co-eff variation | 28.29 | 33.66 | 5.06 |
| Skewness | 0.260814 | 0.526746 | -0.609924 |
| Kurtosis | 2.125522 | 2.509286 | 2.161062 |
| Observations | 52 | 52 | 52 |

On an average export grows at the rate of 1.8% per month which is equal to 182.27 mill $, and import grows at the rate of 2.1% per month which is equal to 317.13 mill $. On an average exchange rate appreciate at the rate of 0.23% per month and which is equal to Rs. 0.099. Among these, growth rate of import is higher than growth rate of export as response to rupee gets appreciation, and irrespective of appreciation of rupee, exports also grows but not equal magnitude of import.

Chart 1 and 2, portray the movement of export and import with response movement of exchange rate, on an average export shows growth over period but in short term it shows fluctuation in export. Export is growing over the period irrespective of rupee appreciation from 2007 to 2008, which is against the exchange rate appreciation, would be detrimental to exports. Likewise, import also shows growth over the period with short term fluctuation. From 2004 to 2007, import has increased irrespective of rupee depreciation, which is against that exchange rate depreciation would curtail imports.

This behavior of export and import against the common phenomena might be reasons of many factors. In case of exports, this may be reason of as India is a developing country and most of export in the form of agriculture, marine and services in software and lack of competitiveness of domestic product when compare to product from other competing country. And this is also possible if the existence of the import content of exports, as well as the dynamic effects of productivity improvements. In case of imports, this may be because of as a developing country like India the imports might be constitutes major part in form of import of essential and import of foreign technology etc.

**Chart 1: Export and Exchange Rate**

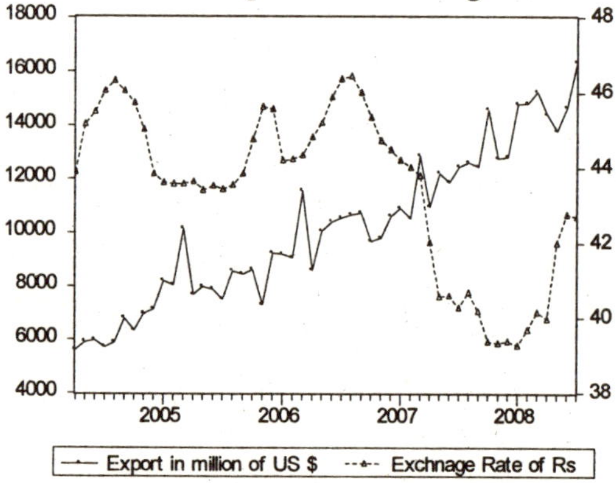


**Chart 2: Import and Exchange Rate**

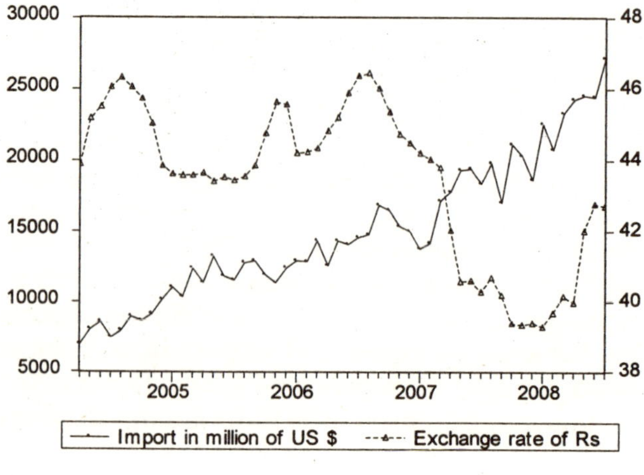

## Results of Export Equation

Table 2 presents the results of regression equation of export and presents separate equation for appreciation and depreciation dummy of exchange rate in panel-A and panel-B respectively. In panel-A, shows negative exchange rate co-efficient as -0.60, which is significant and represents increase in exports even though rupee gets appreciation and vice versa. Co-efficient of appreciation dummy shows 0.025(insignificant) and which supports the coefficient of exchange rate of panel-A. Co-efficient of volatility shows -0.57 (significant) and this supports the increase in volatility affects the exports negatively and gives the proof for presence of risk averter exporter in Indian foreign trade. Panel-B results support the earlier conclusion in panel-A, and with negative insignificant co-efficient of depreciation dummy as -0.03.

**Table 2**
**Export Equation, Dependent: Export**

| *Particular/ Independent Variable* | *Panel-A Appreciation Dummy* | *Panel-B Depreciation Dummy* |
|---|---|---|
| | *Co-efficient* | *Co-efficient* |
| $\alpha_0$ (Constant) | 3.70(1.68)[10] | 3.72(1.72)[10] |
| $\alpha_1$ (Lagged dependent) | 0.85(10.57)[1] | 0.85(10.57)[1] |
| $\alpha_2$ (Exchange rate) | -0.60(1.42)[15] | -0.60(-1.42)[15] |
| $\alpha_3$ (App/Dep dummy) | 0.025(0.80) | -0.03(-0.80) |
| $\alpha_4$ (Std. deviation) | -0.57(1.46)[15] | -0.57(-1.46)[15] |
| R-squared | 0.85 | 0.85 |
| Adjusted R-squared | 0.84 | 0.84 |
| F-statistic | 65.90 | 65.90 |

Results in parentheses are t-Statistics.
1, 10 and 15 represents significance at 1, 10 and 15 percents respectively.

## Results of Import Equation

Table 3 presents the results of regression equation of import and presents separate equation for appreciation and depreciation dummy of exchange rate in panel-A and panel-B respectively. Co-efficient of exchange rate is -0.64 in both panel, which is significant and support the common phenomena, that exchange rate appreciation which stimulates imports and vice versa. As a support for exchange rate co-efficient, appreciation dummy and depreciation dummy show insignificant co-efficient as 0.03 and -0.03 respectively. As for as volatility concern, it show negative insignificant co-efficient as -0.01 for both the panel, which support the increase in volatility affects the imports negatively and presence of risk averter importer in Indian foreign trade.

**Table 3**
**Import Equation**
**Dependent: Import**

| *Particular/ Independentvariable* | *Panel-A Appreciation Dummy* | *Panel-B Depreciation Dummy* |
|---|---|---|
| | *Co-efficient* | *Co-efficient* |
| $\beta_0$(Constant) | 2.81(1.24) | 2.84(1.26) |
| $\beta_1$(Lagged dependent) | 1.00(12.00)[1] | 1.00(12.00)[1] |
| $\beta_2$(Exchange rate) | -0.64(1.46)[15] | -0.64(1.46)[15] |
| $\beta_3$(App/Dep dummy) | 0.03(0.92) | -0.03(0.92) |
| $\beta_4$(Std. deviation) | -0.01(0.03) | -0.01(0.03) |
| R-squared | 0.85 | 0.88 |
| Adjusted R-squared | 0.84 | 0.87 |
| F-statistic | 65.90 | 86.67 |

Results in parentheses are t-Statistics.
1, 10 and 15 represents significance at 1, 10 and 15 percents respectively.

Overall the results suggest that exchange instability affects the trader in both the sides, and appreciation of rupee value against dollar does not affect the export and vice versa. This contrary behavior of export in India, might have been resulted in lack of competitiveness of domestic product when compare to product from other competing country and this is also possible if the existence of the import content of exports, as well as the dynamic effects of productivity improvements. Appreciation of rupee value against dollar supports the common phenomena, as exchange rate appreciation which stimulates imports and vice versa.

## SUMMARY AND CONCLUSION

Foreign trade being the more important component of economic relations between countries, some specific aspects of interdependence in foreign trade, in the form of import and export dependence of the country. This interdependence or foreign trade among countries is varying in degree, in response to variation of many macroeconomic factors. Among many factors, variation in currency exchange rate plays a vital role as a foreign trade determinant. Main objectives of the study are to examine whether exchange rate instability affects foreign trade or not, and how appreciation and depreciation of the exchange rate affects foreign trade. For this study monthly data from April 2004 to August 2008, on exports, imports and exchange rate against dollar have been used. Log-linear model of regression, charts and descriptive statistics have been used for empirical analysis, overall the result reveals that exchange instability affects the trader in both the sides, and appreciation of rupee value against dollar does not affect the export and vice versa. Appreciation of rupee value against dollar supports the common phenomena, as exchange rate appreciation which stimulates imports and vice versa. This contrary behavior of export in India, might have been resulted in lack of competitiveness of domestic product when compare to product from other competing country and this is also possible if the existence of the import content of exports, as well as the dynamic effects of productivity improvements.

## REFERENCES

Akhtar, M. A. and R. S. Hilton (1984), Effects of Exchange Rate Uncertainty on U.S. and German Trade. Federal Reserve Bank of New York, *Quarterly Review*, 9:1, 7–15.

Anderson, T. G., T. Bollerslev, F. X. Diebold and P. Labys (2000), Exchange Rate Returns Standardised by Realised Volatility are (Nearly) Gaussian. National Bureau of Economic Research. (Working Papers No. W7488.)

Arize, A. C. (1996), The Effect of Exchange Rate Uncertainty on Export Growth Evidence from Korean Data, *International Economic Journal*, 10:3, 49–60.

Arize, A. C. (1998), The of Exchange Rate Volatility on U.S. Imports: An Empirical Investigation, *International Economic Journal*, 12:3, 31–40.

Bacchettaa, P. and E. V. Wincoop (1998), Does Exchange Rate Stability Increase Trade and Capital Flows. National Bureau of Economic Research. (Working Papers No. W6704.)

Baldwin, R. and P. Krugman (1989), Persistent Trade Effects of Large Exchange Rate Shocks, *Quarterly Journal of Economics*, 104:4, 635–654.

Bayoumi, T. (1996), International Trade and Real Exchange Rates. Exchange Rate Movements and Their Impact on Trade and Investment in APEC Region. (IMF Occasional Paper 145).

Athukorala, P. (1991), Exchange Rate Pass-through: The Case of Korean Exports of Manufactures, *Economic Letters*, 35, 79Ð 84.

Athukorala, P. and Menon, J. (1994), Pricing to Market Behavior and Exchange Rate Pass-through in Japanese Exports, *Economic Journal*, 104, 271Ð 81.

M. Ali Kemal (2005), Exchange Rate Instability and Trade:The Case of Pakistan, Pakistan Institute of Development Economics, Islamabad.

Tilak Abeysinghe and Tan Lin Yeok (1998), Exchange Rate Appreciation and Export Competitiveness. The Case of Singapore, *Applied Economics*, 30, 51- 55.

T.K. Velayudham (2000), Foreign Trade Theory and Practice, Wheeler Puplishing.

Economic Survey (2007-08), Union Budget 2008-09, RBI Monthly Bulletin, Annual Report & Weekly Statistical Supplement; Ministry of Finance; Ministry of Commerce & Industry; CSO; Institute of International Finance (IIF); EIU; NASSCOM.

Reserve Bank of India, *www.rbi.org*.

EXIM Bank, Annual Report, Mumbai.

# 11

# A STUDY ON CREDIT INSURANCE AND ITS IMPACT ON FIRM'S VALUE WITH SPECIAL REFERENCE TO EXPORTERS IN BANGALORE CITY

**A. Mahalakshmi & R. Shanmugham**

## INTRODUCTION

Credit sales of companies can be divided into the following broad categories:

- Exports Sales
- Domestic Sales

*Export Credit*: The risks associated with Export Sale can be classified in following two categories:

- *Commercial Risk*: These can be in the nature of:
  (1) Protracted default or delayed payments by debtors-the failure of the importer to pay an undisputed debt within six months of the payment due date.
  (2) Insolvency of the buyer-sequestration, liquidation or judicial management of the importer.
  (3) Repudiation-the refusal of the importer to take delivery of the goods, without any apparently valid reason.

(4) Trade disputes

Credit insurance covers the risk at item 1 and 2 above, while other risks are not of insurable nature.

- *Political Risk:* can be any activity- political or economic difficulty preventing or delaying payment of a transaction and can be in the nature of:
  (1) Natural disasters
  (2) Cancellation of import license of the buyer
  (3) Protracted default on state owned entities
  (4) Measures taken by host country to prevent payment of transaction
  (5) Political events, e.g. wars, revolutions or uprisings
  (6) Economic difficulties, such as a currency shortage

  These risks are subject matter of insurance and are considered for risk evaluation and coverage.

## CREDIT INSURANCE

Credit Insurance insures against the risk that a buyer does not pay. It can also cover the risk that a buyer pays very late. Credit insurance policies can include a wider range of cover, depending on the circumstances. If a buyer does not pay, the credit insurance policy will pay out a percentage of the outstanding debt. This percentage usually ranges from 75% to 95% of the invoice amount, but may be higher or lower depending on the type of cover that was purchased. The purpose of a credit insurance policy is to compensate the policyholder for the ascertained financial losses sustained as a result of the above risks.

### Risks Not Covered

The policy does not cover losses due to the following risks:

- Commercial disputes including quality disputes raised by the buyer, unless the exporter obtains a decree from a competent court of law in the buyer's country in his favour.

- Causes inherent in the nature of the goods.
- Buyer's failure to obtain necessary import or exchange authorisation from authorities in his country.
- Insolvency or default of any agent of the exporter or of the collecting bank.
- Loss or damage to goods which can be covered by general insurers.
- Exchange rate fluctuation.
- Failure of the exporter to fulfill the terms of the export contract or negligence on his part.

**Insurance Covers for Exporters**

Export Credit Guarantee Corporation provides insurance covers for exporters that may be broadly divided into the following four groups:

(1) *Standard policies or SCR:* issued to exporters to protect them against payment risks involved in exports on short-term credit, i.e. credit not exceeding 180 days. It is also known as shipments (comprehensive risks) policy. It is issued to exporters whose anticipated export turnover for the next 12 months is more than Rs.50 lacs. It covers both commercial and political risks from the date of shipment.

(2) *Specific Shipment Policy-Short Term(SSP-ST)*: It provides cover to Indian exporters against commercial and political risks involved in export of goods on short-term credit not exceeding 180 days. Exporters can take cover under these policies for either a shipment or a few shipments to a buyer under a contract. These policies can be availed of by: (i) exporters who do not hold SCR Policy and(ii) by exporters having SCR Policy, in respect of shipments permitted to be excluded from the preview of the SCR Policy.

(3) *Construction Works Policy:* It is designed to provide cover to an Indian contractor who executes a civil construction job abroad. The distinguishing features

of a construction contract are that: (i) the contractor keeps raising bills periodically throughout the contract period for the value of work done between one billing period and another; (ii) to be eligible for payment, the bills have to be certified by a consultant or supervisor engaged by the employer for the purpose.

(4) *Specific Policy for Supply Contract:* Contracts for export of capital goods or turnkey projects or construction works or rendering services abroad involve medium/long-term credits. Such transactions are, therefore, insured by ECGC on a case-to-case basis under specific policies.

*This paper contain 2 parts namely*

I. Survey details

II. Insurance covers that protect working capital finance granted by banks against receivables

## SURVEY DETAILS

### Importance of this Study

India's exports of engineering goods are valued at US$ 27 billion during 2006-07 which represents a 6 per cent growth over the exports for 2005-06 (US$ 20 billion). The engineering sector accounted for 14 per cent of the country's total exports. It is also noteworthy that 40 per cent of India's engineering export is from the small and medium enterprises (SME) sector. According to Engineering Exports Promotion Council (EEPC), engineering exports could touch US$ 30 billion by 2008-09. In such a scenario, India, driven by the engineering sector, will emerge as a key global manufacturing hub.

In this context, it is necessary to look into the financing abilities of these exporters to meet export order. *Therefore it is felt important that a study must be carried out to assess their awareness and preference of collection management of foreign and domestic receivables and its relevance to the financial health of the firms.*

## Objectives of the Study

The objectives of the study are:

(1) To locate the reasons why companies prefer/does not prefer credit insurance

(2) To describe the nature of impact of credit insurance on working capital management

(3) To describe the nature of impact of credit insurance on firm's value

(4) To find out the advantages of credit insured companies over non credit insured.

## Limitation of the Study

(1) Time available for survey was limited, around a month packed with tight academic schedules.

(2) The study is limited only to Bangalore. A sample of 20 manufacturers exporting engineering products may not represent the population of around 100 exporters in Bangalore.

(3) Considered only the database consisting of around 1000 manufacturers exporting engineering products from all over India was obtained for the study from Engineering export Promotion Council of India.

## Research Methodology

The approach begins with an initial survey, primary data collected by detailed interviews and structured questionnaire. The *secondary data* includes the profiles and contact details of the exporters from the database obtained from Engineering Export Promotion Council, and internet websites. The sampling methods include simple random and convenient sampling. The sample consists of 20 exporters manufacturing engineering exporters, most of them located in Peenya Industrial Estate, Asia's largest Industrial estate.

## Findings

(1) Out of 20 manufacturing exporters contacted, only 35% of them have obtained credit insurance for exports.

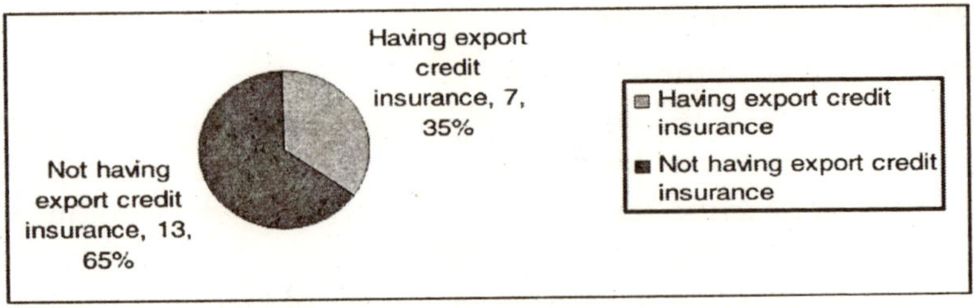


**Figure 1: Percentage of Companies Having/ Not Having Credit Insurance**

(2) 6 out of 7 exporters have preferred credit insurance as they consider 'hedging of accounts receivables' more reasonable, 1 firm just considered.

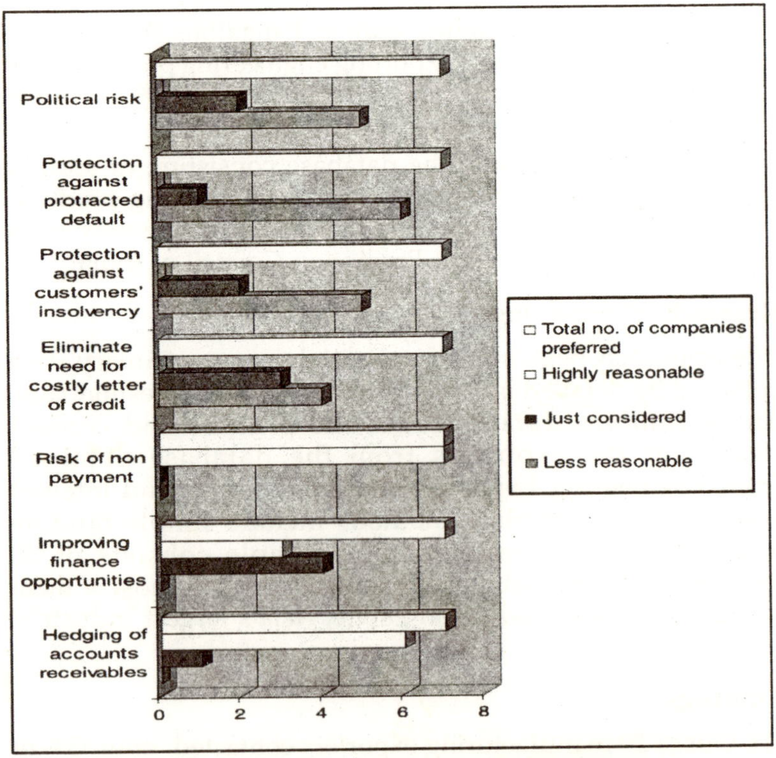


**Figure 2: Reasons for Preferring Credit Insurance**

Only 3 considered 'improving finance opportunities' as highly reasonable for obtaining credit insurance and 4 others just considered.

All the credit insured companies consider 'risk of non payment as highly reasonable.

More than 50% of them do not consider that credit insurance eliminate need for costly letter of credit. As most of the credit insured companies export to well known, creditworthy buyers, they are not at all bothered about customers' insolvency, their protracted default. The buyers are located in countries namely America, Germany, Italy, France and few other European countries and hence they feel political risk to be relatively very low.

(3) Around 9 out of 20 exporters do not prefer to have credit insurance as they do business with their principals, collaborators and some of them have credit

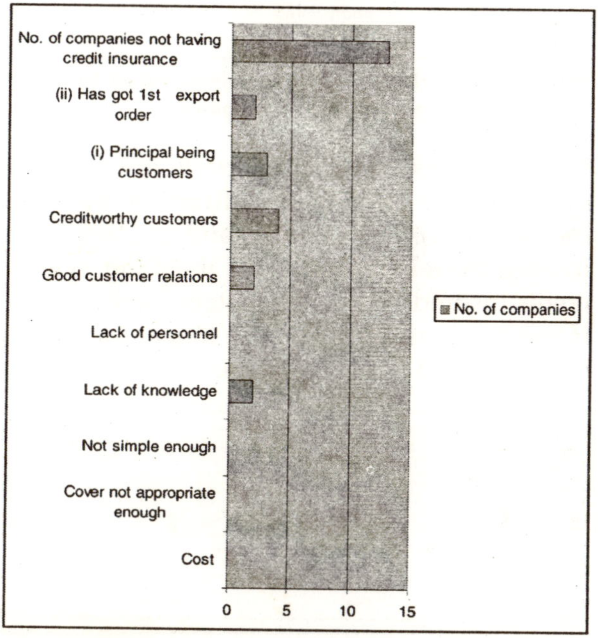


**Figure 3: Reasons for Not Prefering Credit Insurance**

worthy customers and few have good customer relationships. Other than these, 2 exporters have got 1st export order and 2 more do not have any knowledge of credit insurance.

(4) 9 out of 13 companies say they may face working capital problems by not having credit insurance for their exporters in case the buyer defaults.

(5) Out of 9, 2 firms had non payment by buyer and had to go in for high interest short term borrowings to meet working capital requirement.

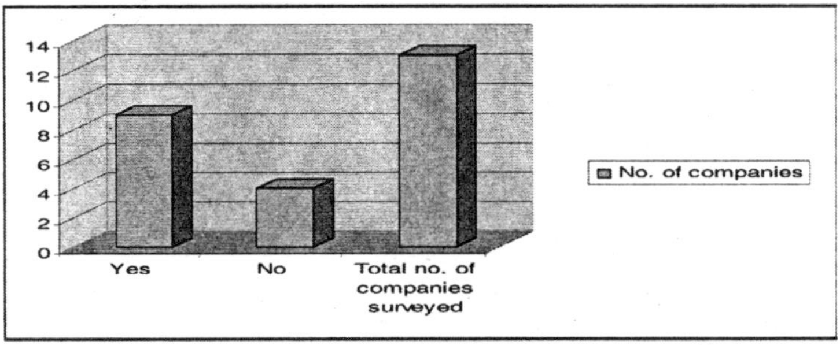


**Figure 4: If Working Capital Problems Faced by Non Credit Insured Companies**

(6) Both credit insured and non credit insured companies *agree* that the credit insured firms are more customer focused, have repeat sales, and get better access to finance from banks. Most of them are *neutral* if the credit insured companies obtain bank loan at lower interest rate and if they have longer payment period with discount from suppliers.

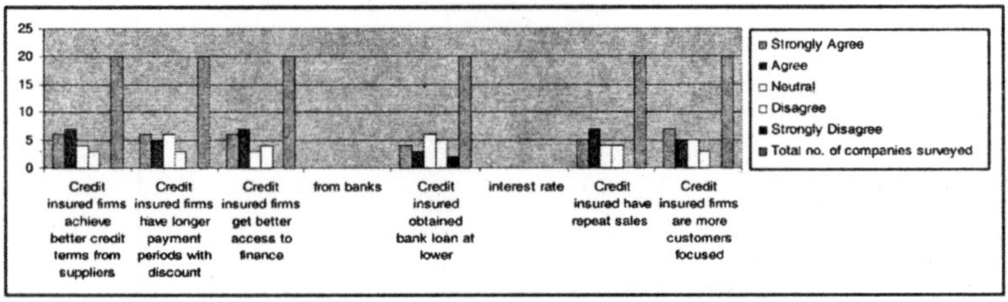


**Figure 5: Companies' Attitude Towards Credit Insurance**

(7) Credit insured companies find that they have got their cash flows *easily* stabilized, thus *easily* reducing unexpected bad debt losses and boots their borrowing power providing the lender with the security of insured accounts. It is evident that they have repeat sales and hence increased customer loyalty. So *very easily* they have obtained more professional credit management in place.

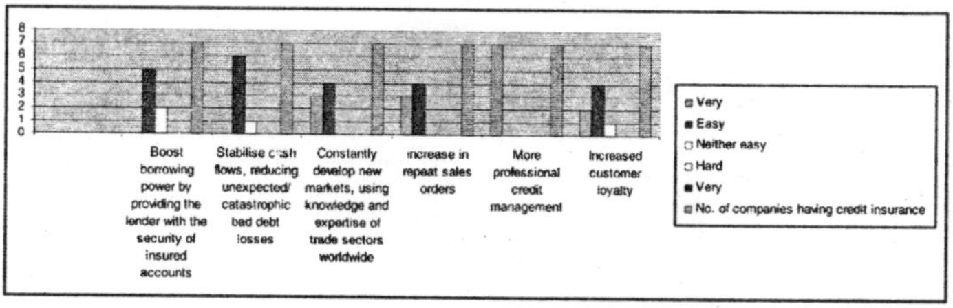


**Figure 6: Benefits Achieved by Credit Insured Exporters with Ease**

(8) All the credit insured companies have substantially increasing turnover in subsequent years of getting insurance.

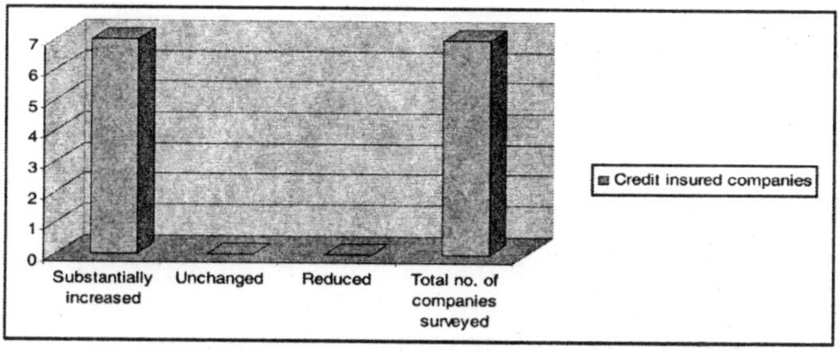


**Figure 7: Turnover of Credit Insured Companies**

(9) Only 3 of 20 companies know about domestic insurance for exports, but at present they do not prefer to obtain it as they deal with trustworthy buyers.

(10) All the credit insured companies are satisfied about the insurance covers they have obtained.

(11) The pre-insurance problems faced by exporters are (i) more time involved and (ii) lengthy documentation procedure involved

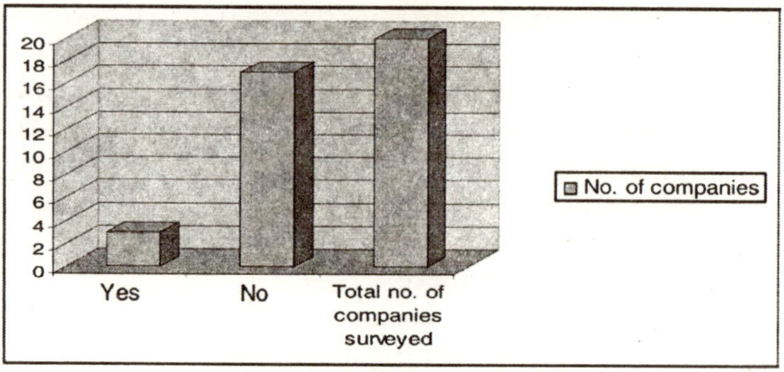


**Figure 8: Awareness of Domestic Credit Insurance**

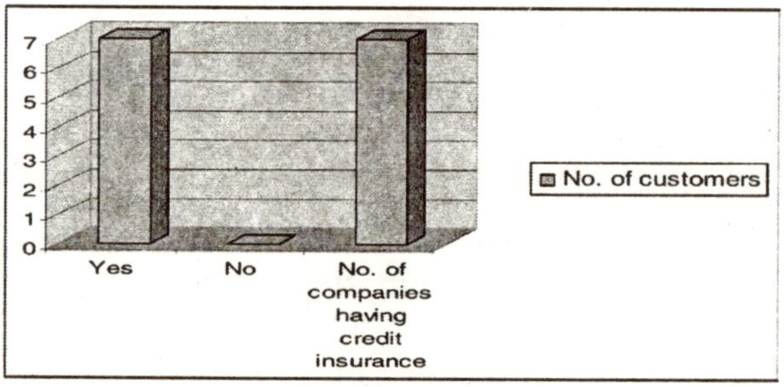


**Fig. 9: Satisfaction of Insurance Covers Obtained**

(12) Exporters do not face any considerable post insurance problems.

(13) Except 3 firms, every exporter understand the importance of credit insurance to working capital management.

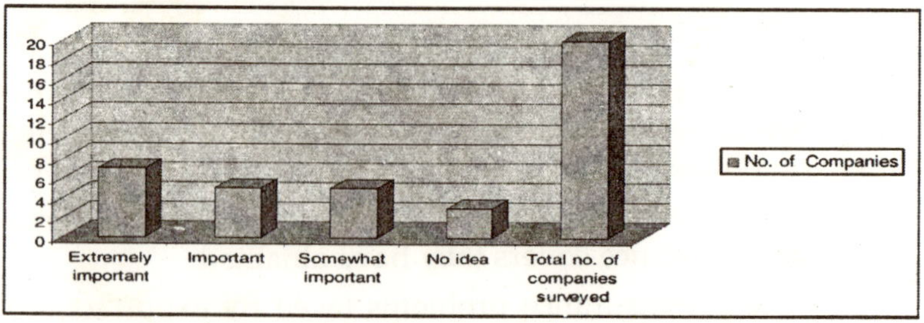


**Figure 10: Importance of Credit Insurance to Working Capital Management**

(14) The impact of credit insurance on the financial health of the company can be seen from the point of liquidity, profitability, working capital financing and firm's value. All the 7 firms find that credit insurance have high impact on liquidity and firm's value.

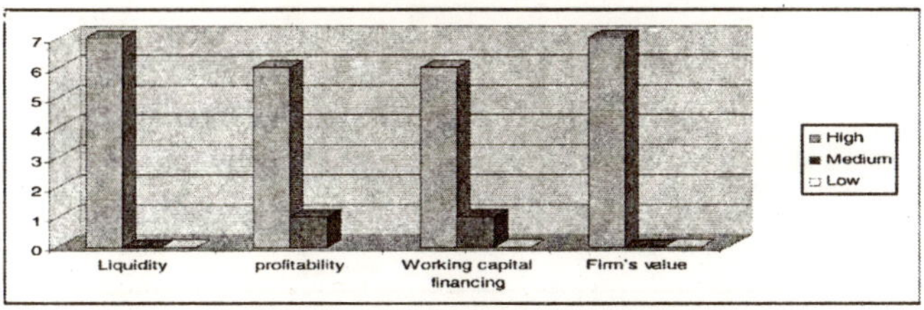


**Figure 11: Financial Impact of Credit Insurance**

(15) All credit insured companies have achieved financial benefits in terms of reduced bad debts, reduced operating costs, reduced frauds, reduced amount for obtaining credit information, reduced interest on bank loans

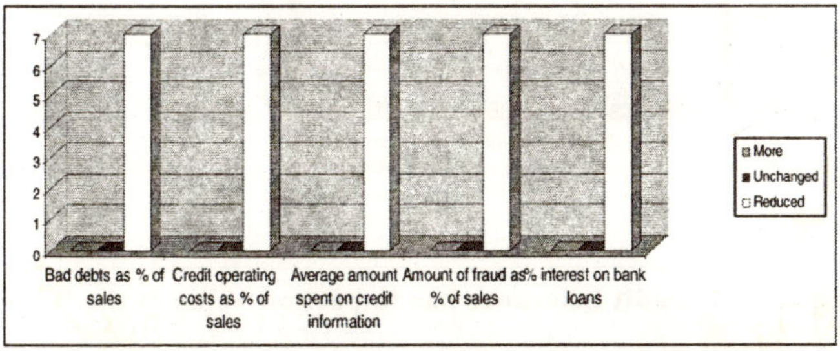


**Figure 12: Financial Benefits on Obtaining Credit Insurance**

(16) More than 50% of the credit insured firms strongly agree that increase in their sales is due to credit insurance.

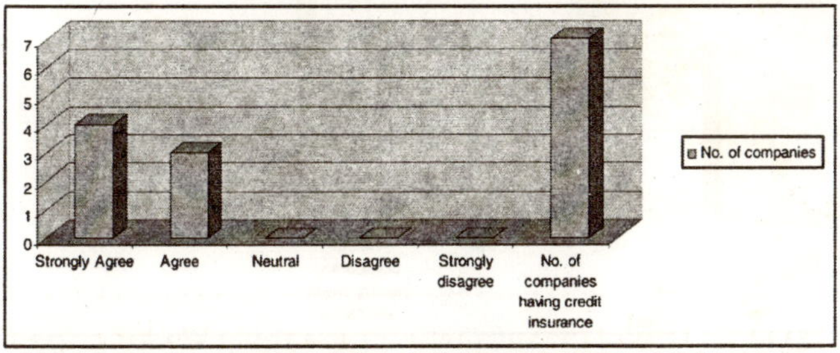


**Figure 13: Increase in Sales Attributed to Credit Insurance**

(17) 5 out of 7 firms use Return on Investment (ROI) to value their firm.

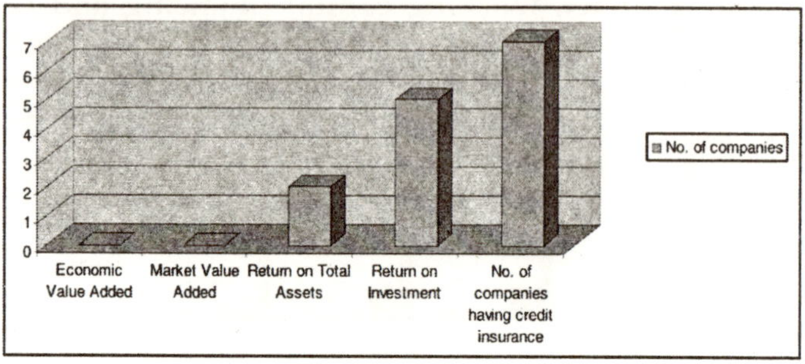


**Figure 14: Methods Adopted to Determine Value of the Firm**

(18) All the 7 firms strongly agree that credit insurance has impact on the value of the firm.

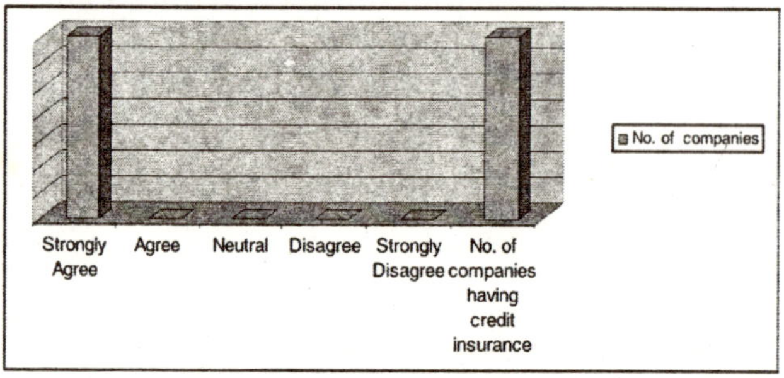


**Figure 15: Credit Insurance has Impact on Value of the Firm**

(19) 5 out of 7 exporters find high impact of credit insurance, 2 firms find medium impact on the firm's value.

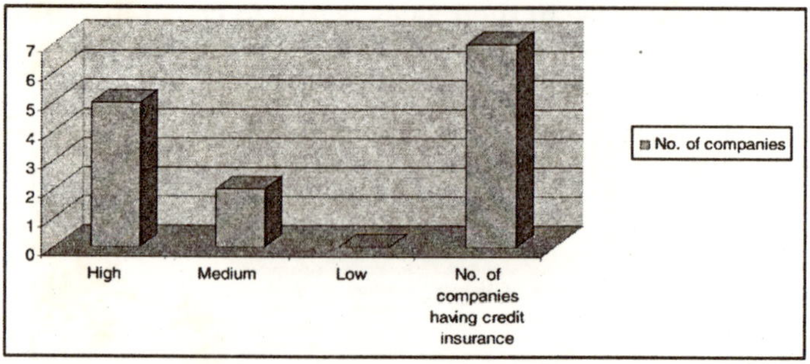


**Figure 16: Impact of Credit Insurance on the Value of the Firm**

By interviewing the key personnel of credit insured firms, it is found that they have following advantages over non credit insured firms who deal with strange buyers.

- Risk Mitigation.
- Enables development of new markets against protection provided
- Expert advice since buyers are analyzed for credit worthiness
- Allows conversion of other recourse terms like L/C to open account sales thus allowing seller better leverage in pricing
- Enhances financing since the policies can be assigned
- Efficient collection of debts
- Complements credit management of the seller

Credit insured companies agree strongly that credit insurance

(i) works as a receivable management and recovery tool

(ii) works as a marketing tool as it helps in increasing the sales and in expanding customer base.

(iii) increases the competitiveness of the insured as the exporting firm can give the credit to the customers thereby reducing the cost for the customer

(iv) reduces the bad debts to almost zero.

(v) also works as financing tool in the sense that it reduces the cost of borrowing and increases the banking limit as banks feels more comfortable and secured.

Thus Credit Insurance offers one of efficient and cost effective ways of managing credit risk for any enterprise.

The credit insured firms have experienced the following benefits:

(i) Ability of exporters to offer buyers competitive payment terms

(ii) Protection against risks and financial costs of non-payment

(iii) Access to working capital

(iv) Protection against losses from foreign exchange fluctuations

(v) Reduction of need for tangible security when borrowing from banks

**Credit Insurance Policy Reduces Exporter's Liquidity Risk**

Outstanding receivables are usually the largest or second largest item on a trading company's balance sheet. Bad debt losses can affect liquidity and profits. Even worse, they can spell a company's mean financial ruin. Late payments or non-payments therefore pose a considerable threat to the future liquidity of that company if no measures are taken. By insuring these receivables against non-payment or late payment, the exporting firms ensures its cash flow.

## INSURANCE COVERS THAT PROTECT THE WORKING CAPITAL FINANCE GRANTED BY BANKS AGAINST RECEIVABLES

Financial *guarantees issued to banks* in India to protect them from risks of loss involved in their extending financial support to exporters at the pre-shipment as well as post-shipment stages.

- *Packing Credit Guarantee:* Timely and adequate credit facilities at the pre-shipment stage are essential for exporters to realize their full export potential. The Packing Credit Guarantee of ECGC helps the exporter to obtain better and adequate facilities from their bankers. The Guarantees assure the banks that, in the event of an exporter failing to discharge his liabilities to the bank, ECGC would make good a major portion of the bank's loss.
- *Export Production Finance Guarantee:* The purpose of this Guarantee is to enable banks to sanction advances at the pre-shipment stage to the full extent of cost of production when it exceeds the f.o.b. value of the contract/order, the differences representing incentive/duty drawback receivable
- *Post-Shipment Export Credit Guarantee:* If the exporter intends to continue the credit facilities till the

value of shipment is realised from the foreign buyer, he has to avail of post-shipment credit. It provides protection to banks against non-realisation of export proceeds and the resultant failure of the exporter to repay the advances availed.

- *Export Finance Guarantee:* This guarantee covers post-shipment advances granted by banks to exporters against export incentives receivable in the form of cash assistance, duty drawback, etc.
- *Export Performance Guarantee:* An exporter who desires to quote for a foreign tender may have to furnish a bank guarantee in the form of a bid bond. If he wins the contract, he may have to furnish bank guarantees to foreign buyers to ensure due performance or against advance payment or in lieu of retention money or to a foreign bank in case he has to raise overseas finance for his contract. Further, for obtaining import licenses for raw materials or capital goods, exporters may have to execute an undertaking to export goods of a specified value within a stipulated time, duly supported by bank guarantee.
- *Export Finance (Overseas Lending) Guarantee:* If a bank financing an overseas project provides a foreign currency loan to the contractor, it can protect itself from the risk of non-payment by the contractor by obtaining Export Finance (Overseas Lending) Guarantee.

*Special Schemes*

- **Exchange Fluctuation Risk Cover:** It is intended to provide a measure of protection to exporters of capital goods, civil engineering contractors and consultants who have often to receive payments over a period of years for their exports, construction works or services. Under it cover is available for payments scheduled over a period of 12 months or more, upto a maximum of 15 years.
- **Transfer Guarantee:** When a bank in India adds its confirmation to a foreign Letter of Credit, it binds itself to

honour the drafts drawn by the beneficiary of the Letter of Credit without any recourse to him provided such drafts are drawn strictly in accordance with the terms of the Letter of Credit. The confirming bank will suffer a loss if the foreign bank fails to reimburse it with the amount paid to the exporter. The Transfer Guarantee seeks to safeguard banks in India against losses arising out of such risks.

- *Overseas Investment Guarantee:* Export Credit Guarantee Corporation of India Limited has evolved a scheme known as the 'Overseas Investment Guarantee' or 'Overseas Investment Insurance' scheme in order to provide protection for Indian investments abroad. It provides insurance cover for the investments made by Indian corporates in Government of India approved joint ventures (JVs) or their wholly owned subsidiaries (WOSs) abroad either in the form of equity or loan.

## CONCLUSION

From the study, it is evident that a few exporters, who are techno entrepreneurs, are unaware of credit insurance for exports. Around 85 per cent of exporters do not know about domestic credit insurance. All insured companies have considered the risk of non payment as primary reason for preference Therefore ECGC need to motivate the credit insurance agents, provide them required training and make them to reach non-credit insured exporters. These firms have certain constraints namely time and knowledge to relate such financing tools to the value of the firm. It shows that credit insurance agents play a significant role, to identify the budding and growing exporters, educate them the importance of export and domestic credit insurance and make them understand its impact on working capital financing, liquidity and profitability and hence on the value of the firm.

## REFERENCE

*http://business.gov.in/doing_business/overseas_insurance.php*

*http://www.ecgc.in/Portal/pdf/ecicb.pdf*

*http://www.financialexpress.com/news/ECGC-to-venture-in-domestic-credit-insurance/344956/*

Paper on 'Credit Support Companies' Profitable Growth-An Independent Research Study of 2000 Businesses in 10 European Economies by Euler Hermes, accompany of Allianz *(studybrochurecreditmanagment.pdf)*

Paper on 'Export and Trade Credit Insurance' by Paul Delbridge FIA and Bryan Joseph FIA (export.pdf)

*www.insurance4india.com/business%20credit%20insurance.html-33k*

# 12

# "PROBLEMS OF INDIAN EXPORTERS IN GETTING THE EXPORT INCENTIVES"

**K. Jeyachandran & N. Sundaram**

## INTRODUCTION

India has been well–known to the world for international trade. "In spite of geographical, linguistic and racial isolation, India always maintained its contact with the outside world. The ports and the passes of our country were used by indigenous and foreign traders from very early times of its history. She formed an integral part of the ancient commercial world which extended from the Mediterranean Sea to the Indian Ocean".

The Government of India earns foreign exchange through exports. Exports should be increased to increase the foreign exchange reserve. The Government of India provides different types of export incentives to exporters in order to motivate them to increase their exports. Some of the exporters are not even aware of the export incentives offered by the Government of India. Exporters have to follow an elaborate documentary procedure to utilise the incentives. The documents are to be routed through the various offices regulating export trade. Unless the exporters complete all the documentary formalities, they cannot get the incentives in time. Export incentive schemes should motivate the exporters to come forward and take the initiative for increasing exports.

Export incentives should motivate exporters to utilise such incentives extensively for increasing their exports. Motivation and the utilisation of export incentives should go hand in hand. The real objective of export incentives can be achieved only when the exporters utilise them. If the incentives fail to motivate, exporters do not come forward to utilise incentives. Hence, a study of the motivational value of the export incentive schemes and their exploitation by the exporters is essential. The researcher has made a modest attempt to study the motivational value and the utilisation of important export incentive scheme such as the Export Finance. The motivational value of export incentives and their utilisation are core aspects of foreign trade. These core aspects of foreign trade should be given importance by the Government of India. So than expected growth in foreign trade can be achieved within the stipulated time. A study of the motivational value and the utilisation of the export incentives will throw light on the issues and problems associated with the process.

## STATEMENT OF THE PROBLEM

The Government of India earns foreign exchange through exports. Exports should be increased to increase the foreign exchange reserve. The Government of India provides different types of export incentives to exporters in order to motivate them to increase their exports. Some of the exporters are not even aware of the export incentives offered by the Government of India. Even if they are aware of them, they are not utilising them due to so many reasons. Exporters have to follow and elaborate documentary procedure to utilise the incentives. The documents are to be routed through the various offices regulating export trade. Unless the exporters complete all the documentary formalities, they cannot get the incentives in time. Export incentive schemes should motivate the exporters to come forward and take the initiative for increasing exports.

Export incentives should motivate exporters to utilise such incentives extensively for increasing their exports. Motivation and the utilisation of export incentives should go hand in hand. The real objective of export incentives can be achieved only when the exporters utilise them. If the incentive fail to motivate, exporters do not come forward to utilise incentives. Hence, a study of the motivational value of the export incentive schemes and their exploitation by the exporters is essential. The researcher has made a modest attempt to study the motivation value and the utilisation of important export incentive schemes such as the export finance, Duty Drawback, Market Development Assistance, Export Promotion Capital Goods scheme and the problems of exporters in utilising these. The motivational value and the utilisation of important export incentive schemes such as the Export Finance, Duty Drawback, Market Development Assistance, Export Promotion Capital Goods Scheme and the problems of exporters in utilising these. The motivational value of export incentives and their utilisation are core aspects of foreign trade. These core aspects of foreign trade should be given importance by the Government of India. So that expected growth in foreign trade can be achieved within the stipulated time. A study of the motivational value and the utilisation of the export incentives will throw light on the issues and problems associated with the process.

## OBJECTIVES OF THE STUDY

The Objectives of the Study are given below:

(1) To study the motivational value of the export incentive schemes to the exporters.

(2) To study the utilisation of the export incentive schemes by the exporters.

(3) To study the opinions of the exporters regarding the procedural aspects of the utilisation of the export incentives, and

(4) To summarise the findings of the study and to provide suggestions for increasing the level of motivation and utilisation of export incentives.

## METHODOLOGY

The present study is descriptive and analytical. The study is basen on both secondary and primary data. A comprehensive and duly pre-tested questionnaire has been designed to collect primary data. The sample selection is based on the judgement sampling technique. Statistical tools such as Mean, Co-efficient of Variation, Correlation, Chi-square test and Z test are used to interpet the processed data. Likert's Five point Scale is used in Questionnaire to collect primary data. The Five Point Scale is used for analysis also. Z test is used to find out whether the sample mean is significant to the Grand Mean. Grand Mean is assumed as population mean.

## DATA SOURCE

Both primary data and secondary data were used for fulfilling the objectives of the present study.

## PRIMARY DATA

For collecting primary data, the researcher designed a questionnaire with due care and attention. Questions relating to various aspects of the export incentive schemes were incorporated in the questionnaire. The researcher designed a questionnaire with the assistance of executives of the Export Promotion Councils and selected exporters. Questions relating to various aspects of export incentive schemes Viz., Export Finance, Duty Drawback, Market Development Assistance, Export Promotion Capital Goods were incorporated in the questionnaire. The questionnaire was duly pre-tested and pilot study was undertaken. The researcher collected the primary data through questionnaire in person and met all 170 sample exporters. Out of 170 sample exporters 75 are garment exporters, 32 are leather exporters, 33 are engineering exporters and 30 are plastic exporters. The researcher selected value-added products for this research.

## SECONDARY DATA

The researcher utilised the offices of the apex bodies of foreign trade in India such as Export promotion Councils, Indian

Institute of Foreign Trade, Federation of Indian Chamber of Commerce, Federation of Indian Export Organisation, Confederation of Indian Industry, the Union Ministry of Commerce, and Reserve Bank of India to collect relevant secondary data required for the study. The researcher approached the embassies of the various countries to gather the data regarding export incentives offered by them. Library services available in Indian Institute of Technology, Chennai, Institute of Financial Management and Research, Chennai, University of Madras, Chennai, Sri Venkateshwara University, Andra Pradesh and other universities were utilised by the researcher for collected secondary data.

## PRE-TESTING AND PILOT STUDY

Researcher distributed the questionnaire to a selected twenty exporters at a random for the purpose of pilot study. The exporter's suggestions relating to the construction of questionnaire are carefully assessed and incorporated suitable to make the questionnaire a comprehensive data collection tool.

## SAMPLING

The identification of products and sample exporters of the products for the purpose of this study is based on Judgement Sampling. The entire sample selection process regarding products and exporters is based on the value judgement of the officials involved in the Export Promotion Councils and Federation of Indian Export Organisation. The suggestions of the officials were carefully considered in the process of sample selection. The researcher had discussions with the officials of the Federation of Indian Export Organisations, Tamilnadu, for the identification of the products. The FIEO officials suggested the four value added products gaining exports in the world market. They are garment, engineering, leather and plastic. The first two products i.e. garment and engineering are at the top of the Indian export basket and the other two products, i.e., leather and plastic, are at the bottom. The share of garment, engineering, leather and plastic in the total of the export of the Government of India are 11.9%, 14%, 5.4% and 1.5%

respectively. This is the average of the period from 1992-93 to 1998-99.

Later, the researcher had discussions with the officials of the Apparel Export Promotion Council, Tirupur, the Engineering Export Promotion Council, Chennai, the Council for Leather Exports, Chennai, and the Plastic Export Promotion Council, Chennai, for identifying the sample exporters. The above Export Promotion Councils maintain detailed records relating to export performance of the exporters. They publish the Directory of Exporters periodically.

Officials of the Apparel Export Promotion Council suggested 75 exporters, the Leather Export Promotion Council 32 exporters, the Engineering Export Promotion Council 33 exporters, and the Plastic Export Promotion Council 30 exporters for the purpose of the present research study. The total sample respondents of this study thus amounted to 170. The exporters suggested by the Export Promotion Councils have been actively involved in export business for the past ten years. Their export units are located in Chennai, Coimbatore, Tirupur, Dindigul, Madurai and other towns of Tamilnadu. The researcher met all the 170 sample exporters in person for collecting relevant primary data.

Export incentives contribute to price competitiveness in the world market for the exportable commodities. The Government of India provides export incentives such as Export Finance, Duty Drawback, Market Development Assistance, Export Promotion Capital Goods, Duty Entitlement Pass Book Scheme, Special Import Licence, Quantity Based Advance Licence, Value Based Advance Licence, etc., for the benefit of exporters for increasing exports. Of the above export incentives, export finance, duty drawback, market development assistance and export promotion capital goods are popular and are highly utilised export incentives. The researcher analysed the export finance in this study.

## EXPORT FINANCE

"Finance is the life blood of any business activity". Exporters approach bankers and private financial institutions to get finance in order to meet different types of expenses for their business activity. Generally exporters approach commercial banks for export credit, because they provide export credit at lower rate of interest. To promote exports and to motivate exporters Government of India provider export credit a concessional rate of interest. This is one of the incentives provided to exporters. Exporters approach commercial banks and the Export–Import Bank of India in order to get export credit. They utilise this incentive for the promotion of exports. "For promoting the country's exports the banks play a key role by providing timely, and adequate assistance to the exporter community."

Finance in the most significant aspect in export trade. Once the export order is received, production of exportable commodities should take in time. It requires adequate finance for procuring the needed raw materials and other components. In some cases, materials are to be imported from foreign countries. It requires foreign currency unless the financial requirements for exports are fulfilled, an export order cannot be met in the scheduled time. Further getting payment for the export cargo will take some time. Adequate credit facilities are extended to exporters till they receive their export proceeds from foreign countries. Realising the significance of export finance and to encourage exports, the R.B.I has come forward to extend export finance to Indian exporters at a concessional rate.

It is equally important that finance should be available at relatively attractive terms. "Cost of finance is one of the important constituents of cost that enter into the price of the product. If the exporter has to been a high cost in the form of a high rate of interest he cannot reasonably be expected to be competitive in the market, and therefore, there is a need to provide him cheap finance so as to ensure his competitive ability in the market." Those firms or companies, which are efficient, from the financial markets also. "Exporting firms with a proven record in fiercely competitive international markets are treated favourably capital markets. They face lesser finance constraints than firms that aperate mainly in domestic markets that have been largely protected. Thus the financial markets have successfully offered an enabling environment for exporting firms to grow". The key to success in the international market place seems to be the attitude 'I will make what you need' and not 'I will sell that I make.' To meet the needs of the customers in the international market, finance is required by all businessmen, specifically exporters.

## TYPES OF EXPORT FINANCE

There are two types of export finance. They are:

(1) Pre-shipment credit or Packing credit.

(2) Post-shipment credit.

## PRE-SHIPMENT CREDIT

The reserve bank of India has defined pre-shipment credit as "any loan to an exporter for financing the purchase, processing, manufacturing or packing of goods".

"A pre-shipment credit is any loan or advance granted to an exporter for financing the purchase, processing, manufacturing or packing of goods meant for export".

Pre-shipment credit is granted by commercial banks for purchasing and processing of materials, manufacturing of exportable commodities and packing of such commodities.

Packing credit granted by the commercial banks for a period of 180 days from the date of sanctioning the credit. Further extension will be given for a period of 90 days, provided adequate reasons are given by the exporters for such extension.

## POST-SHIPMENT FINANCE

"The exporters require post-shipment finance as there is a time gap between the selling of goods and receiving payment from their buyers abroad. This period of waiting depends upon the pay terms. The period of waiting is longer when the payment term is open account consignment of DA (Documents against Acceptance) as against letter of credit."

The post-shipment finance is the financial facility extended by the banks after the goods have been shipped and against the submission of export documents evidencing the despatch of goods.

The post-shipment finance in India is met by banks by.

(1) Negotiating documents under letter of credit.

(2) Purchasing DP (Document against payment) and DA bills.

(3) Lending against export bills tendered for collection abroad, and

(4) Financing against the security of claims for export incentives.

## FINDINGS OF THE STUDY

(1) 90 per cent of the sample exporters utilised pre-shipment finance. Among them, 127 are small scale exporters and 26 large scale exporters. The chi-square test results revealed that there in a significant relationship between the size of exporters and the utilisation of pre-shipment finance. It is concluded that the size of exporters and the utilisation of pre-shipment finance are dependent.

(2) The majority of the merchant exporters (84%) and manufacturer exporter (94%) utilised pre-shipment finance.

(3) The average amount of pre-shipment finance utilised by the majority of the (80%) exporters in below Rs. 200 lakhs during the review period. It is revealed in this study that 76% of the garment exporters, 67% of the leather exporters, 69% of the engineering exporters and 96% of the plastic exporters utilised an average amount of pre-shipment finance, below Rs. 100 laksh, during the review period.

(4) A majority of the merchant exporter (75%) and a majority of the manufacturer exporters (77%) have utilised, an average amount of pre-shipment finance below Rs. 100 Lakhs during the review period.

(5) A majority of the large scale exporter (96%) and a majority of the small scale exporter (98%) obtained export finance from public sector banks.

(6) It is shown in this study that 76% as the garment exporters, 67% of the leather exporters, 69% of the engineering exporters and 96% of the plastic exporters utilised below Rs. 100 Lakhs as the average amount of Post-shipment finance during the review period.

(7) The sample exporters are highly motivated by the export finance and the percentage of motivation is 95. The percentage of utilisation of export finance is 86%. The level of motivation of the sample exporters in high. The level as utilisation of export finance is bring to the sample exporters.

(8) There is a perfect positive correlation (+.8102) between motivation and utilsation of export finance.

(9) The sample exporters are satisfied with the amount of export finance provided by banks and the percentage of agreement with the sample exporters with the statement "Export finance provided by banks is sufficient" is 77. Z test result shows that the sample mean of this statement significant to the grand mean and it is found that the opinions of the sample exporters reflect the opinions of the population about the statement "Bank provides pre-shipment credit which is sufficient."

(10) A majority of the exporters do not support the suggestion that the pre-shipment finance period should be extended from 180 days to 270 days and the percentage of agreement of sample exporters to the statement 'Pre-shipment' finance period should be extended to 270 days' is 73.

(11) The sample exporters are not fully satisfied with the present interest rate charged on pre-shipment finance. The percentage of agreement of the sample exporters with the statement 'Rate of interest charged on export finance is reasonable is 71. Z test result shows that the sample mean of this statement is significant to the grand mean and it is found that the opinions of the sample exporters reflect the opinion of the population about the statement 'Rate of Interest charged to Export Finance is reasonable.

(12) The percentage of agreement of the sample exporters with the statement 'Delay in sanctioning pre-shipment credit makes exporters borrow from other financial institution at high rate of interest is 71. They are of the opinion that they borrow from other financial institutions at a high rate of Interest.

(13) The percentage of agreement of the sample exporters to the statement 'ECGC Guarantee is essential for pre-shipment credit is 71. Z test result shows that the sample mean of the statement is significant to the grand mean and it is found that the opinion of the sample exporters reflect the opinion of the population about the statement 'ECGC Guarantee is essential for pre-shipment credit."

## SUGGESTIONS

The following suggestions are made based on the findings of the presently study.

(1) The bankers should provide pre-shipment credit under studies and standard norms irrespective of the size of exporters (large scale or Small Scale) because there is a relationship between the size of exporters and the utilisation of pre-shipment finance. Banks should make small scale and large scale exporters to utilise pre-shipment credit in an equitable manner. So with the various categories of exporters.

(2) Bankers should ensure equitable utilisation of packing credit by all types of exporters (merchant exporters and manufacturer exporters.)

(3) Bankers should charge less than the normal rate of interest to those exporters applying for export credit below to those exporters applying for export credit below Rs. 100 lakhs, as a majority of the exporters utilised pre-shipment finance below Rs. 100 lakhs.

(4) The study shows that there is a significant relationship between experience in export business and the average amount of pre-shipment finance. So bankers should encourage less experiented exporters to utilise export credit.

(5) The present study shows that there is a positive correlation between motivation and utilisation of export incentives. Procedures relating to utilisation of export incentives should be simplified. Delay in sanctioning incentives should be minimised and the rate of interest charged on export credit should be at par with the prevailing interest rate in the global financial market.

(6) The sample exporters are not fully satisfied with the present interest charged on pre-shipment finance. The Z test result shows that the sample mean is significant to the grand mean. The Opinions of the sample exporters reflect the Opinions of the population. Therefore the Reserve Bank of India should take steps to reduce the rate of interest charged on export finance.

Exporters felt that the delay in sanctioning pre-shipment credit makes them borrow from other financial institutions at higher rates of interest. The process of sanctioning pre-shipment credit should be speeded up and packing credit should be sanctioned within a week. A separate bank branch should be established in selected export centers exclusively for providing export credit.

Bankers should not insist on ECGC guarantee for sanctioning pre-shipment credit. The sample exporters opined that the ECGC guarantee is got essential for pre-shipment credit.

## CONCLUSION

The present research study analyses export finance and their utilisation by exporters in Tamilnadu State.The research studies in detail the procedural aspects involved in the utilisation of the selected export incentive schemes.In this research study the researcher finds the level of agreement of the exporters on the various procedural aspects of export incentive schemes.

# 13

# THE MPEDA'S SUBSIDY ASSISTANCE SCHEMES AND ITS IMPACT ON INDIAN MARINE EXPORT– A CRITICAL ANALYSIS

**K. Mohan, M. Suresh & T. I. Prabhu**

## INTRODUCTION

India is the one of the fastest developing nation in the world. India is an Agri-based country. It has a rich potential in land, water and human resources. The easiest way to do a successful manufacturing or production is by utilizing the locally available resources. In the present world, all the developing countries are concentrating on the export and trying to bring surplus position. Export is one of the powerful tools to attract foreign exchange to every nation. As per Indian Business Directory (INBD), there are 78,160 manufacturing, exporters and suppliers units companies are working in India. From the total companies, 23,643 of them were Apparel. This has been followed by 11,352 of Automobiles companies, 9715 of handicrafts, handmade and gifts companies and 9,680 of Agro, Marine and food products and Beverages companies and remaining are occupied by others. India has a long coastline of 8,129 Kms, Exclusive Economic Zone of 2.02 million sq. Kms, Brackish water area of 1.2 million hectors and fresh water of 5.4 million hectors. At present there are six major harbors, 33 minor fishing harbors, more than 2000 fishing landing centres and more than 4000 village are in fishing business India. Fish is one of the high quality food, it contain an average of 15 to 25 per cent of protein. Fish is one of the best proteins sources available to the human body in quality and quantity. The fish is highly perishable goods, it needs careful handling process till it has been consumed. In India government has appointed a number of export promotion councils and development authorities to watch closely and to provide effective services for improving and strengthening every industry.

The Marine Product Export Development Authority (MPEDA) is the statuary body, functioning under Ministry of Commerce, Government of India. The Marine Product Export Development Authority (MPEDA) was constituted in 1972 under the MPEDA act 1972 (No.13. of 1972). It is a coordinating agent different central and state government to establish and engage in fishery production and in its allied actives. Also it has cover all activities in fisheries, increasing the export, specifying standards, processing, marketing, extension and training in various aspects of the industry.

## OBJECTIVES OF THE STUDY

(1) To study the objective and subsidy schemes of MPEDA.

(2) To study the fish export trend of India and forecast for 2012.

(3) To analyse the performance of exports in terms of volume and growth using index numbers.

## RESEARCH METHODOLOGY

This study shall be based on the data collected mainly from secondary sources. The data are purely collected form internet, journal, magazines, etc.

## STATISTICAL TOOLS USED

The researcher has used modern and sophisticated statistical tools like Least Square Method to forecast value and volume in 2012 and Index Number is used for analyse the growth percentage from 1997-98 to 2006-07, on country wise and product wise from 2005-06 to 2006-07.

## LIMITATIONS OF THE STUDY

The study is only deals with subsidy schemes of Marine Product Export Development Authority (MPEDA) and Indian Marine Products Export. The period of study is ten years from 1997-08 to 2006-07. the earlier periods has not been considered for analysis due to time and resource constraint.

## THE MPEDA'S OBJECTIVES

(1) Conservation and management of fishery resources and development of offshore fishing.

(2) Registration of exporters and processing plants.

(3) Regulations of marine products export.

(4) Laying down standards and specifications.

(5) Acting as an agency for extension of relief as per directions from Government.

(6) Helping the industry in relation to market intelligence, export promotion, and import of essential items.

(7) Imparting training in different aspects of the marine products industry, with special reference to quality control, processing and marketing.

(8) Promotion of commercial shrimp farming.

(9) Promotion of joint ventures in aquaculture, production, processing and marketing of value added seafood.

## SUBSIDY ASSISTANCE SCHEMES

The financial subsidiaries are classified in four heads by MPEDA. They are follows:

### Export Production by Capture Fisheries

(a) Turtle Excluder Devises (TED) provided at free of cost to mechanized trawlers to protect Turtles during fishing as a conservation measure.

(b) To encourage mechanized fishing vessel owners two types of financial assistance are provided:

   (i) For installation of Fish Finders, GPS, RT and installation of insulated/refrigerated Fish Hold, Refrigerated Sea

Water system (RSW) and Ice making machine on board mechanized fishing vessels upto a subsidy of 30% of the cost (or) a maximum of Rs.5 lakhs per owner.

(ii) For the conversion of existing fishing vessels to Tuna long liners and for harvesting deep sea tuna by diversified fishing using mono filament long line, the subsidy is provided upto 50% of the cost.

(c) Grant from Ministry of Food Processing Industries for setting up new processing plant/pre-processing plant or modernization of existing processing/pre-processing plant. The subsidy is to the extend upto 25% (or) Rs. 50 lakhs to the Technical, civil work and machinery, in the case of units in general area and 30% of the cost (or) upto Rs. 75 lakhs in the case of difficult areas.

**Export Production by Culture Fisheries**

(a) The financial assistance the shrimp scampi farmers for setting up of new farms for augmenting production in undeveloped area at a subsidy of 25% on the capital cost or Rs.50, 000/ha Water Spread Area. A farmer is eligible to avail maximum subsidy of Rs.2.50 lakhs for developing shrimp/scampi farms in 5.00 ha. Water spread area.

(b) Promotion of commercial hatcheries for seed production of exportable species. The assistance is provided for setting up hatcheries for production of healthy and quality seeds for aquaculture and the quantum of subsidy schemes are upto:

(i) 25% of capital cost to the maximum of Rs. 3.00 lakhs/ hatchery/ for a small-scale hatchery of 10 to 30 million post larvae production capacity and

(ii) 25% of capital cost to the maximum of Rs. 6.00 lakhs/ hatchery/for a medium scale hatchery of 30 million and above post larvae production capacity.

(c) There are two types of financial assistance for establishment of Effluent Treatment System (ETS). First one for shrimp farms and other is for shrimp hatchery. The objective are:

(i) For shrimp farms is mandatory for shrimp farms above 5 ha water area, the subsidy is upto 25% of the capital cost (or) Rs. 1.5 lakhs whichever is less per unit of 5 ha area, subject to Rs. 6.00 lakhs per beneficiary.

(ii) For shrimp hatchery setting up, the subsidy is 25% of the capital cost subject to maximum of Rs.1.5 lakhs per unit (One unit per hatchery).

(d) Development assistance for setting up of PCR labs in private hatcheries/Pvt. Lab. The subsidy is provided upto 50% of capital cost (or) a maximum of Rs. 5.00 lakhs per unit.

(e) Financial assistance to set up chill room facilities in shrimp farming areas, the subsidy is provided upto 25% of the cost of establishment (or) a maximum of Rs. 3.00 lakhs per beneficiary.

(f) For purchase of water quality testing equipment, the subsidy is provided upto 25% of the cost of the water testing kits/ equipment (or) a maximum of Rs. 30, 000/- per beneficiary.

(g) for setting up of office, ware house/auction hall, common facility etc., Laboratory facilities, Hiring technicians, training farmers/technical personnel and methodology for promoting environmentally sound farming, the subsidy is provided upto 50% of the estimated cost (or) a maximum of Rs. 5.00 lakhs

(h) There are two new schemes were introduced by MPEDA in this year. They are–

(i) For establishment of Ornamental Fish Breeding Units, the quantum of subsidy is upto 50% of the cost of eligible expenditure (or) a maximum of Rs. 75,000 for Grade I unit, Rs. 2 lakhs for Grade II unit and Rs 7.5 lakhs for Grade III unit.

(ii) For establishment of Ornamental Fish Marketing Societies (OFMS), the quantum of subsidy is upto Rs. 5 lakhs per unit.

**Induction of New Technology, Modernization of Processing Facilities and Development of Infrastructure Facilities**

(a) Technology Upgradation Scheme for Marine Products (TUSMP) is to promotion of value addition in seafood processing, the quantum of subsidy is upto 25% of the expenditure incurred (or) a maximum of Rs.100 lakhs for new units and Rs.85 lakhs for the existing units.

(b) To assist seafood processors to set up tuna cannery/ processing facilities for value added tuna products and the quantum of subsidy is upto 25% of the cost of machinery & equipment (or) a maximum of Rs.65.25 lakhs.

(c) To encourage seafood processors to acquire Refrigerated Trucks/containers for transportation of raw material/ finished products, the quantum of subsidy is upto 25% of the cost of Refrigerated Truck/container (or) a maximum of Rs. 3.50 lakhs.

(d) To encourage individuals to establish Cold Storages for keep the surplus seafood and the quantum of subsidy is upto 25% of the cost of cold storage (or) a maximum of Rs. 60 lakhs.

(e) Assistance for the setting up of new/ modern ice plants/ renovation of existing ice plants, finance provide at a subsidy maximum of Rs. 22 lakhs for new units and Rs. 12 lakhs for renovation.

(f) Insulated fish boxes are distributed at 50% subsidy.

(g) Subsidy for setting up Mini Laboratory, the quantum of subsidy is upto 25% of the cost (or) a maximum of Rs. 1, 50,000/- per unit.

(h) Assistance to seafood processors for construction/ renovation of Captive Pre-processing Centres, the quantum of subsidy is upto 50% of the cost of eligible expenditure (or) a maximum of Rs.15 lakhs.

(i) Financial assistance to pre-processors for construction/ renovation of independent pre-processing centres, the quantum of subsidy is upto 50% of the cost of eligible expenditure (or) a maximum of Rs. 22 lakhs for new construction.

(j) Financial assistance for procurement of quick testing kit at a subsidy 33.3% of the cost (or) a maximum of Rs.1 lakh per unit.

(k) Assistance for setting up of Ornamental fish Breeding units, the quantum of subsidy is upto 50% of the capital cost for the infrastructure specified, subject to a maximum of Rs. 75000/- per unit linked to export.

(l) Developmental assistance for Export of Ornamental/ Aquarium fishes, the quantum of subsidy is upto 10% of F.O.B. value of export subject to the ceiling of Rs. 3 lakhs per exporter per year.

*Maximum amount of subsidy (in rupees) per unit:*

(i) Small mechanized boat/country craft (less than 32 ft. OAL) is Rs. 4500.

(ii) Mechanized boat owners (Above32 ft. OAL) is Rs. 15000

(iii) Peeling shed/pre-processing plant is Rs. 50000

(iv) Processing plant Rs. 100000

(v) Shrimp farmers 5 ha. & less is Rs. 35000

(vi) Shrimp farmers above 5 ha. is Rs. 50000

(vii) Fresh/Chilled Fish Handling Centres is Rs. 100000

**Market Promotion**

(a) Financial Assistance for extending Insurance Coverage to Workers Employed in the Fish Processing Units. The objective is the Insurance scheme for envisaged workers employed in the Seafood Processing Units with a terminal benefit of Rs. 50, 000 for the insured, medical expenses (hospitalization) reimbursement upto Rs. 10, 000/- for the insured or his/her parents or dependants and also to insure house hold articles against calamities either natural or man made upto Rs. 20, 000/- and for emergency medical evacuation, Rs. 2, 000/- (maximum) and the quantum of subsidy is upto The premium of the insurance will be paid by the employer, employee and MPEDA in a ratio of 50%, 25% and 25% and the annual premium works out to Rs. 200/- per worker.

**Provision for Marine Exports and Imports in Foreign Trade Policy (2004-09)**

*The Products are permitted follows:*

(a) There are no restrictions on export quantities.

(b) Licence is not require for import of 125 species/groups of fish, crustaceans, molluscus and other aquatic invertiberates, except five groups of live. *Eg*: Importing Whale Shark and its parts and products of the species.

*Promotional Measures:*

(a) State Governments are getting financial assistance from central for development of critical infrastructure for export such as roads, inland container depots, container freight stations, Export Promotion Industrial Parks and for equity participation in infrastructure projects.

(b) State Governments are permitted to encourage to setting up Export Zones.

(c) Declaration of Towns of Export Excellence to encourage setting up of critical infrastructure for export production, encourage common service providers and facilitate availability of better technological services and integrate benefits under the other schemes of EXIM Policy for the units in such towns.

(d) To increase marketing efforts by exporters/Brand promotion, Market Access Initiative Schemes (MAIS) has been introduced.

(e) To promote the Concept of Total Quality Management.

*Import for Export Production*

(a) Advance authorization for duty free import of inputs for export production.

(b) Duty free import authorization (DFIA) Scheme:-

This scheme allow duty free import of inputs, fuel, oil, energy sources, catalyst which are required for production of export product. DGFT, by means of Public Notice, may exclude any product(s) from purview of DFIA. This scheme is in force from 1st May, 2006.

(c) Entitlement Provisions of paragraph 4.1.3 (FTP) shall be applicable in case of DFIA. However, these Authorizations shall be issued only for products for which Standard Input and Output Norms (SION) have been notified. Pre-export Authorization shall be issued with actual user condition and shall be exempted from payment of basic custom duty, additional customs duty, education cuss, anti-dumping duty and safeguard duty, if any. A minimum 20% value addition shall be required for issuance of such authorization.

(d) Manufacturer exporters, merchant exporters tied to supporting manufacturers and service providers eligible for import of capital goods at 5% Customs duty linked to fulfillment of export obligation in 8 to12 years under EPCG Scheme.

*EOU/ EPZ/ SEZ*

(a) Scheme of 100% EOU/Export Processing Zone/Special Economic Zone for export production continues. No trading units permitted under the scheme.

*Package for Marine Sector*

(a) Duty free import of specified specialized inputs/chemicals and flavoring oils as per a defined list shall be allowed to the extent of 1% of FOB value of preceding financial years export. Use of these special ingredients for seafood processing will enable us to achieve a higher value addition and enter new export markets.

(b) To encourage the existing mechanized vessels and deep sea trawlers to adopt modern technology for scientific exploitation of our marine resources in an eco-friendly manner and boost marine sector exports, it is proposed to allow import of monofilament long line system for tuna fishing at a concessional rate of duty.

(c) The present system of disposal of waste of perishable commodities like seafood after inspection by a customs official is very cumbersome and leads to development of unhygienic conditions. To overcome this, a self removal procedure for clearance of waste shall be applicable, subject to prescribed wastage norms (announced on 1.4.2007).

**Focus Market Scheme (FMS)**

Objective is to offset high freight cost and other externalities to selected international markets with a view to enhance India's export competitiveness in these countries.

Entitlement Exporters of all products through EDI enabled ports to notified countries shall be entitled for Duty Credit scrip equivalent to 2.5% of FOB value of exports for each licensing year commencing from 1st April, 2006. However additional Markets notified in Appendix 37C of HBP v1 shall be entitled for Duty Credit scrip on exports w.e.f 1.4.2007.

**Focus Product Scheme (FPS)**

Objective is to incentives export of such products, which have high employment intensity in rural and semi urban areas, so as to offset infrastructure inefficiencies and other associated costs involved in marketing of these products. Entitlement Exports of notified through EDI enabled ports to all countries shall be entitled for Duty Credit scrip equivalent to 1.25% of FOB value of exports for each licensing year commencing from 1st April, 2006.

**Calculation of Index Percentage**

| *Year* | *Value (in Cr)* | *Growth Percentage* | *Volume (in MT)* | *Growth Percentage* |
|---|---|---|---|---|
| 1997-98 | 4697.47 | Base year | 385818 | Base year |
| 1998-99 | 4626.87 | -1.5 | 302935 | 21.48 |
| 1999-00 | 5116.67 | 10.59 | 343031 | 13.24 |
| 2000-01 | 6443.89 | 25.94 | 440473 | 28.41 |
| 2001-02 | 5957.05 | -7.56 | 424470 | -3.63 |
| 2002-03 | 6881.31 | 15.52 | 467297 | 10.09 |
| 2003-04 | 6091.95 | -11.47 | 412017 | -11.83 |
| 2004-05 | 6646.69 | 9.11 | 461329 | 11.97 |
| 2005-06 | 7245.30 | 9.05 | 512164 | 11.02 |
| 2006-07 | 8363.53 | 15.43 | 612641 | 19.62 |
| Total | 62070.74 | 65.11 | 4362175 | 100.37 |

*Source: www.mpeda.com*

The above table shows that, in 2000-01 there was a high export Index growth percentage in value and volume, 25.94% and 28.41% respectively. As per the Index percent total, the average growth rate on value is 6.51% and for the volume is 10.04% per year.

**Indian Marine Export in Value (Rs.)**
Calculation in Least Square Method

| *Year* | *Value (in Cr)* | *X* | *XY* | *X²* | $Y_c$ |
|---|---|---|---|---|---|
| 1997-98 | 4697.47 | -4 | -18789.92 | 16 | 4525.2357 |
| 1998-99 | 4626.87 | -3 | -13880.61 | 9 | 4945.6955 |
| 1999-00 | 5116.67 | -2 | -10233.34 | 4 | 5366.1553 |
| 2000-01 | 6443.89 | -1 | -6443.89 | 1 | 5786.6152 |
| 2001-02 | 5957.05 | 0 | 0 | 0 | 6207.075 |
| 2002-03 | 6881.31 | 0 | 0 | 0 | 6207.075 |
| 2003-04 | 6091.95 | -1 | 6091.95 | 1 | 6627.5348 |
| 2004-05 | 6646.69 | -2 | 13293.38 | 4 | 7047.9947 |
| 2005-06 | 7245.30 | -3 | 21735.90 | 9 | 7468.4545 |
| 2006-07 | 8363.53 | -4 | 33454.12 | 16 | 7888.9143 |
| Total | 62070.74 | 0 | 25227.59 | 60 | 62070.75 |

*Source: www.mpeda.com*

The equation of the straight line is Yc = a + bx

$\Sigma x = 0$;

$$a = \frac{\Sigma Y}{N} = \frac{62070.74}{10} = 6207.074$$

$$b = \frac{\Sigma XY}{\Sigma x^2} = \frac{25227.59}{60} = 420.45983$$

Yc = 6207.074 + 420.45983 x

The expected value of export in the year 2011-12 is:-

Yc = 6207.074 + 420.45983 (9)

= Rs. 9991.2135 crores.

To forecast the value of export to the year 2012, the least square calculation is used. As per the forecasting, in the year 2012 the estimated export value shall be Rs. 9991.2135/- crores.

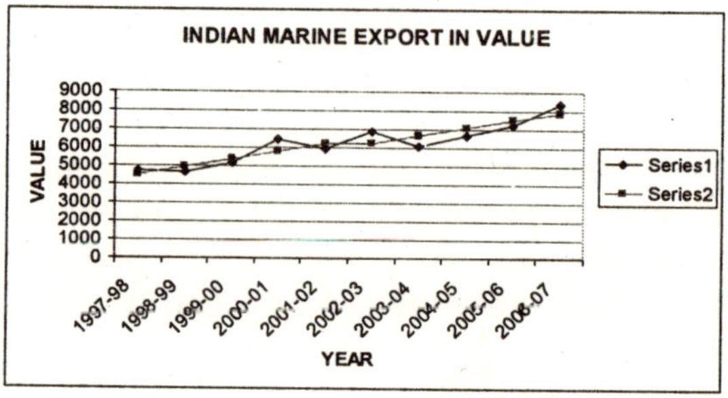

**Indian Marine Export in Volume (MT)**

| *Year* | *Volume (in MT)* | *X* | *XY* | *X²* | $Y_c$ |
|---|---|---|---|---|---|
| 1997-08 | 385818 | -4 | -1543272 | 16 | 320009.598 |
| 1998-99 | 302935 | -3 | -908805 | 9 | 349061.551 |
| 1999-00 | 343031 | -2 | -686062 | 4 | 378113.534 |
| 2000-01 | 440473 | -1 | -440473 | 1 | 407165.517 |
| 2001-02 | 424470 | 0 | 0 | 0 | 436217.5 |
| 2002-03 | 467297 | 0 | 0 | 0 | 436217.5 |
| 2003-04 | 412017 | 1 | 412017 | 1 | 465269.483 |
| 2004-05 | 461329 | 2 | 922658 | 4 | 494321.466 |
| 2005-06 | 512164 | 3 | 1536492 | 9 | 523373.449 |
| 2006-07 | 612641 | 4 | 2450564 | 16 | 552425.432 |
| Total | 4362175 | 0 | 1743119 | 60 | 4362175 |

*Source: www.mpeda.com*

The equation of the straight line is Yc = a + bx

$\Sigma x = 0;$

$$a = \frac{\Sigma Y}{N} = \frac{4362175}{10} = 436217.5$$

$$a = \frac{\Sigma XY}{\Sigma X^2} = \frac{1743119}{60} = 29051.983$$

Yc = 436217.5 + 29051.983x

The expected volume of export in the year 2011-12 is:-

Yc = 436217.5 + 29051.983x

$Y_{2011\text{-}12}$ = 436217.5 + 29051.983(9) = 784841.296 MT

To forecast the volume of export to the year 2012, the least square calculation is used. As per the forecasting, in the year 2012 the estimated export volume shall be 784841.296 MT.

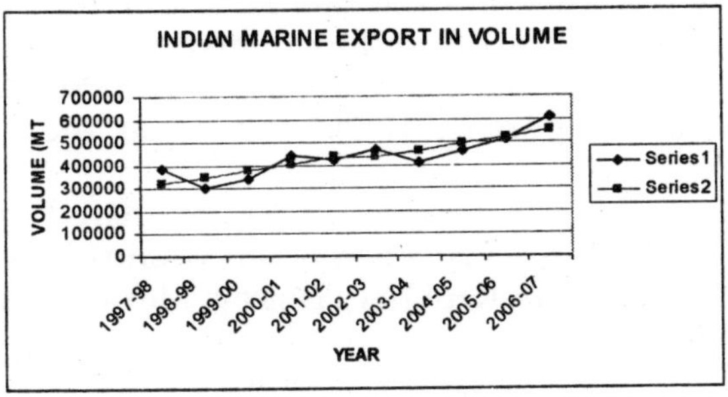

**Country wise Export of Marine Products**

Q: Quantity in M T, V: Value in Rs. Crore, $: US Dollar Million

| *Country* | *% Share in 2006-07* | | *Apr-Mar 2006-07 (Rs in Cr)* | *Apr-Mar 2005-06 (Rs in Cr)* | *Variation* | *Index Growth %* |
|---|---|---|---|---|---|---|
| Japan | 11 | Q | 67437 | 59785 | 7652 | 12.80 |
| | 16.18 | V | 1353.38 | 1155.97 | 197.42 | 17.08 |
| USA | 7.00 | Q | 43758 | 55817 | -12059 | -21.60 |
| | 16.12 | V | 1347.80 | 1639.24 | -291.44 | -17.78 |
| European Union | 24.00 | Q | 149760 | 136842 | 12918 | 9.44 |
| | 33.00 | V | 2759.92 | 2134.25 | 625.67 | 29.32 |
| China | 33.00 | Q | 203513 | 137076 | 66437 | 48.47 |
| | 13.83 | V | 1156.96 | 849.45 | 307.52 | 36.20 |
| South East Asia | 11.00 | Q | 67650 | 60140 | 7510 | 12.49 |
| | 7.37 | V | 616.70 | 585.85 | 30.85 | 5.27 |
| Middle East | 4.00 | Q | 23599 | 22270 | 1329 | 5.97 |
| | 4.44 | V | 371.47 | 307.65 | 63.82 | 20.74 |
| Others | 9.00 | Q | 56924 | 40234 | 16691 | 41.48 |
| | 9.06 | V | 757.30 | 572.90 | 184.40 | 32.19 |
| Total | 100.00 | Q | 612641 | 512164 | 100478 | 19.62 |
| | 100.00 | V | 8363.53 | 7245.30 | 1118.23 | 15.43 |

*Source: www.mpeda.com.*

The European Union has emerged as the largest market for Indian marine products. From the total marine products is export 33% on the value and 24% on the volume are exported to European Union and the index growth percentage is 29.32% on value and 9.44% on the volume.

China becomes the 2nd largest market in terms of value and holds first position on volume. Its percentage of import is 13.83% in value and 33% on volume and the index growth percentage is 36.20% on value and 48.47% on the volume.

The position is followed by Japan, it share 16.18% on value and 11% on volume of Indian marine export. The index growth percentage is 17.08% on value and 12.80% on the volume.

The 4th largest market for Indian marine products is USA. While comparing to the past year 2005-06, in 2006-07 USA has reduced their import by 17.78% on value and 21.60% on volume.

The remaining 36.99% on value are shared by SOUTH EAST ASIA, MIDDLE EAST and others countries like Canada, Australia, Dominican Republic, Turkey, Mexico, Maldives Is., Norway etc.

**Item wise Export of Marine Products**
Q: Quantiy in MT, V: in Rs. Crore

| *Items* | *% Share to Total* | | *Apr-Mar 2006-07* | *Apr-Mar 2005-06* | *Variation* | *(%)* |
|---|---|---|---|---|---|---|
| Frozen Shrimp | 22 | Q | 137396 | 145180 | -7784 | -5.36 |
| | 53.88 | V | 4506.08 | 4271.51 | 234.57 | 5.49 |
| Frozen Fin Fish | 44 | Q | 270751 | 182344 | 88407 | 48.48 |
| | 17.37 | V | 1452.88 | 998.70 | 454.18 | 45.48 |
| Frozen Cuttle Fish | 9 | Q | 55701 | 49651 | 6050 | 12.19 |
| | 9.53 | V | 797.37 | 549.15 | 248.22 | 45.20 |
| Frozen Squid | 8 | Q | 47251 | 52352 | -5101 | -9.74 |
| | 6.80 | V | 568.32 | 575.52 | -7.20 | -1.25 |
| Dried items | 4 | Q | 24293 | 14167 | 10125 | 71.47 |
| | 2.19 | V | 183.16 | 132.56 | 50.60 | 38.17 |
| Live items | 0 | Q | 2478 | 2568 | -90 | -3.50 |
| | 0.77 | V | 64.06 | 61.71 | 2.35 | 3.80 |
| Chilled items | 1 | Q | 7200 | 5060 | 2140 | 42.29 |
| | 1.40 | V | 117.30 | 81.56 | 35.74 | 43.82 |
| Others | 11 | Q | 67571 | 60841 | 6730 | 11.06 |
| | 8.06 | V | 674.35 | 574.58 | 99.76 | 17.36 |
| TOTAL | 100 | Q | 612641 | 512164 | 100478 | 19.62 |
| | 100 | V | 8363.53 | 7245.30 | 1118.23 | 15.43 |

*Source: www.mpeda.com*

The Frozen Shrimp holds the first position on the terms of value. Its share on the total is 53.88 % in terms of value and 22% in volume. Comparing to the previous year, it rose by 5.49% on valve and decreased by 5.36% on the volume.

Frozen Fin Fish is the 2nd largest item exported from in terms of value and it hold first position in terms of volume.

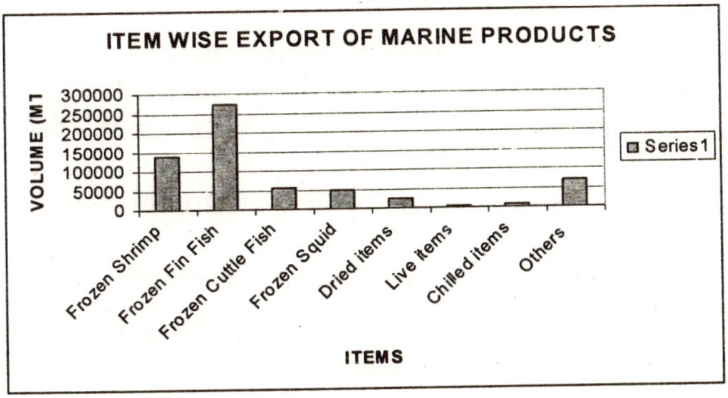

Its share on the total is 17.37 % in terms of value and 44% in volume. Comparing to the previous year, it produced a good result on the both. It has been rose by 45.48% on valve and 48.48% on the volume.

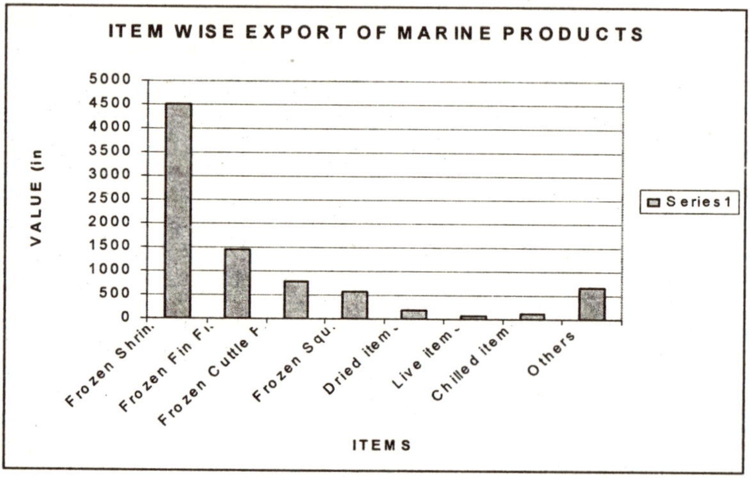


The following position was occupied by Frozen Cuttle Fish in terms of both value and volume. It shows excellent growth on value i.e. 45.20% and 12.19% on volume. The remaining positions are occupied by Frozen Squid, Dried items, Live items, Chilled items, etc.

## FINDINGS

(1) A unit can get subsidy upto Rs. 3,54,500/- for starting (or) setting-up a fish culture firm in India.

(2) India has good export potential on marine products. The estimated value of export in the year 2012 is Rs. 9991.2135/- crores.

(3) The estimated volume of export in the year 2012 is 784841.296 MT.

(4) The average growth ratio on value is 6.51% per year.

(5) The average growth ratio on volume is 10.04% per year.

(6) India has increased its export both (on value and volume) in 2006-07 to all of its markets expect USA market.

(7) Frozen Shrimp export value continuing its first position in 2006-07, but comparing to its volume on the pervious year, it has been 5.36% decreased.

(8) Frozen Fin Fish export capture first position on volume and second position on value in 2006-07. It has been rose by 45.48% on valve and 48.48% on the volume from the pervious year.

## CONCLUSION

The above analysis clearly portrays the excellent potential that India has got for exporting marine products thereby there is a good scope for earning enormous forex earnings which in turn can strengthen India's forex reserves. Similarly, the forecast for the year 2012 clearly indicates growth potential both in terms of value of exports and volume of exports. However, a methodical, systematic and planned approach is the need of the hour to fully tap the resources and channelising them in an organized manner to achieve total success as far as augmenting India's export potential of marine products. The Researchers, Government, Policy makers, Bureaucrats, and the Administrators need to have a deep look at the issues and prompt and timely steps taken by them will, no doubt, yield good results.

## REFERENCE

*www.Mpeda.Com*

Facts for You–Market Survey–By–G.P. GANDHI–Page no-26-33, June-2005.

Focus: India–Fisheries Sector–Modernising to Gain–Global Market Access, P. No. 33-37, INFOFISH *International* 2/2006.

Live Fish Trade in Asia: Update–By–SUDARI PAWIRO– P. No. 56-59, INFOFISH *International* 1/2006.

*www. India fisheries profile, FAO India fisheries profile, India fisheries country profile.com*

Fisheries Institution–Development of Marine Fisheries in India–Role of the Fishery Survey of India–Page No. 24-27, Bay of Bengal News, December 2006–March 2007.

Statistic–S. P. Gupta.

14

# PROBLEMS FACED BY RURAL AGRICULTURAL EXPORTERS IN DOING BUSINESS INTERNATIONALLY

**Rizwana M. & A. Kumudha**

## INTRODUCTION

Agriculture continues to be the most crucial sector of the Indian economy. With 26.8 percent contribution to the Gross Domestic Product (GDP) at current prices and providing employment to nearly 2/3rd of the work force, agriculture is so much at the center stage in the Indian economy that any situational change in this sector, positive or negative, has a multiplier effect on the entire economy. The largest industries of the country like sugar, jute, textiles, food processing, milk, etc. are dependent on agriculture for their raw materials. Besides, the agriculture sector and rural areas are the biggest markets for low priced and middle priced consumer goods, including durable use items.

## NATURE OF INDIAN AGRICULTURE

Though more than five decades have passed since independence and agricultural production has increased several folds.

The following Table & Graph below depicts the growth of agriculture sector in decade wise break-up from 1950 to 2002 but certain features of Indian agriculture hamper the balanced growth and development.

**Agriculture Growth Rate in India**

| *1950-1960* | *1961-1970* | *1971-1980* | *1981-1990* | *1991-2002* |
|---|---|---|---|---|
| 3.1% | 2.5% | 1.9% | 3.8% | 2.8% |

Finance is the major constraint here. Despite the introduction of rural banking, credit societies, kisan credit cards, the small and marginal farmers still go to the same old pawn broker or money lender and become their victims. Low wages for agricultural labour due to excessive population is another major issue, which is ailing this sector. Lack of opportunities, low skills of agriculture laborers denies them to think something else other than agriculture and cheapness of labour leads to adoption of labour-intensive methods of production instead of modern technology. Added to all these, the Indian agriculture depend heavily on monsoon. Nearly 70% of the areas continue to depend on monsoon rather than irrigation. Agricultural inputs, seeds, irrigation, electricity, plant protection, fertilizers and agricultural investment are seen as other major problems characterizing Indian agriculture.

## WHY EXPORT?

Expanding world population and higher per capita incomes abroad should lead to greater export marketing opportunities, outpacing growth in the domestic market. Among all developing countries India represent future markets for agricultural exports. For some Indian agricultural products, export markets already are crucial and for many others increased production will not be absorbed domestically and must be exported. So increased exports represent an opportunity for some and a necessity for others. Yet exporting has much common with domestic marketing. Foreign customers expect to buy from a reliable supplier who provides quality products at competitive prices and has a commitment to good service.

However, exporting does pose some additional challenges. Language and cultural differences must be overcome in communications and business dealings. Foreign exchange rates; import regulations, requirements and restrictions; transportation; and payment are other differences to contend with. To be successful, an exporter must make a firm, long-term commitment to export markets and must possess or be willing to acquire the necessary management skills and knowledge. In return for meeting these challenges, exporters have an opportunity to increase profits because of increased volumes produced and to reduce their dependence on a single market.

## PROBLEMS FACED BY RURAL AGRICULTURAL EXPORTERS

India is facing stiff competition in the world markets for export of agricultural produce. Besides, there are many domestic problems for agricultural exporters. If these internal problems are relaxed to the extent possible, the exporters may find easy way to boost agricultural export and such measures will go a long way to sustain the exports. Some of the major problems are discussed in this chapter below:

- ¾ Decline in investments in rural electrification, and in its availability. This has vastly affected production in eastern India, where huge groundwater potential remains untapped.
- Low public investment in irrigation and poor maintenance of rural infrastructure, specially canals and roads.
- ¾ Rising level of subsidies for power, water, fertilizers and food are eating into public sector investments in agriculture, besides inducing inefficient use of scarce resources, such as water.

  This further aggravates environmental problems leading to loss of soil fertility and groundwater, which intern reduces returns on capital. Farmers then demand further subsidies to maintain the same level of production.

- Inadequate credit support.
- Continuing imbalanced use of N, P, K fertilizers, (which was 8.5:3.1:1 in 1998-99 as against the desirable norm of 4:2:1) and increasing deficiency of micro nutrients.
- As per the state Govt. policy, various taxes are imposed on agricultural exports, such as the states are imposing Purchase Tax (on indirect export), Market Fees, Rural Development Fund, Administrative Charges etc. These taxes are rendering the pricing of agricultural produce internationally in competitive. Thus, Indian rice becomes costlier in the international market as compared to other competing countries in the world and Indian rice exports get setback many times. Infact, in Pakistan rice meant for exports specially the branded ones; duties are extremely low or duty free.
- There is lack of proper infrastructural facilities. Many times exporters, when they carry their stock to sea port and if the stock is not loaded due to some reason or the other, exporters do not find godown or proper place to store their stocks properly and safely at sea port, exporters have to face lot of difficulties, besides, it adds additional expenditure to the exporters.
- Due to increase in the cost of inputs used for cultivation the production cost goes up and the Minimum Support Price (MSP) for the agricultural produce is enhanced every year by the govt. of India to safeguard the interest of the growers.
- Mills have not been fully modernized to ensure high milling recovery and reduce the percentage of broken agricultural produce. The conventional mills are having Rubber Roll Sheller in which percentage of broken cereals is more than the modern mills that are having under Runner Sheller. Hence, head rice obtained from milling of conventional mills becomes costly due to recovery of higher percentage of broken rice. Therefore, conventional mills are required to be

modernized to get recovery of higher percentage of head rice suitable for export.

- Lack of proper arrangements for production of sufficient quantity of quality seeds needed for cultivation of agricultural produce for export purposes.
- The export is also suffering much due to the competition from other exporting countries like Thailand, Vietnam and Pakistan because the cost of production in these competing countries is low as compared to the cost of production in India. In fact, trade segment believes that Indian rice can face the global competition if subsidy is provided.
- Post harvest handling of produce is another important aspect. Generally, farmers are harvesting the crop at different moisture levels and keeping the produce at higher moisture level for a longer period will impair the intensity of aroma.
- Poor knowledge about the packaging materials put down the quality in International market. Packing is essential to protect the agricultural produce during marketing. It is generally packed in polythene bags of 250 gm-400 gms for local markets. For long distance transport, pulp board punnets wrapped with PVC films should be used instead of polythene bags.
- The high costs of getting agricultural produce from farm to market erode any advantage the Indian farmer enjoys by virtue of being a cheap producer. For example, it costs three times more to transport grapes from India to the Netherlands than it does from Chile to the Netherlands, although Chile is twice as far from the destination as India is. India's transportation costs are, on average, 20-30 percent higher than those of other countries mainly due to a fragmented supply chain. This fragmentation is itself the result of policies that have inhibited investment, integration and competition in transport, storage and distribution. Not surprisingly, the biggest markets for Indian horticultural

exports are the neighboring countries of South Asia and the Middle East

- There is a huge gap between the stringent health, safety, and quality standards required by foreign governments and buyers, especially in the richer countries, and the weak standards and assessment mechanisms in India. Crucially, some of the most demanding standards today are not imposed by foreign governments but by foreign buyers because of greater consumer preference for quality in all its dimensions. The concerns voiced by foreign consumers today will be the concerns raised by domestic consumers tomorrow. And Indian products may then not even be able to compete at home.
- Foreign trade regimes are opaque and complex and adopt deceptive forms of protection. Among the most pernicious forms of trade protection in horticulture are those that discriminate against efficient delivery, quotas that impose harsh tariffs on imports above certain low levels, and a system of special safeguards that is a source of considerable uncertainty for successful exporters. Preferential access schemes such as from Turkey to the EU and Mexico to the US discriminate against imports from other countries. And. tariff escalation clauses discourage the export of processed fruit by imposing higher tariffs on products that have been through more advanced stages of processing.
- Poor logistics lead to delays and wastage, and weaken farmers' incentives to improve quality. Limited standardization makes physical inspection a must before any transaction, further adding to costs. A protected domestic market can increase transport costs for exporters because low imports mean that exporters must not only bear the cost of the outward journey, but also the unutilized capacity on the way into the country. High delivery costs increase the burden of

foreign tariffs because they are imposed on the final product price.

## STRATEGIES & ACTION PLAN

Wheat being a major commodity of agricultural exports from developed countries, India will have to face a tough competition from them. Future projections suggest continued upsurge in domestic wheat consumption and relatively small surpluses. While continuing the export of *basmati* rice targeted mostly to Middle East and to NRIs in Europe and USA, the limited scope for accelerating the export of *basmati* and other scented varieties will have to be kept in mind.

The potential market for rice lies in the Southeast Asian countries like Indonesia, Malaysia and the Philippines and in East Asian countries like Japan and South Korea and also in Sub-Saharan countries. Rice exports to these countries from Thailand have reached a plateau and India has the potential to enter these markets provided we succeed in developing and growing varieties preferred by consumers in these countries and make vigorous efforts to capture the market. Crops like barley and maize hold export potential either as cattle feed or as industrial raw material. The competitive edge can be further improved if the productivity of these crops is raised.

### Horticultural Produce

Opportunities of extended production of various fruits, vegetables and floriculture crops and exporting them to newer markets in Central and South Asian countries and Japan in addition to the traditional markets of Europe, USA, Russia and some countries in Africa, need to be tapped on a priority basis. Several spices, condiments and medicinal crops can be marketed abroad at a fancied price. Efforts are needed for identification of potential markets, choice of cost effective, eco-friendly and sustainable technologies for product development, value addition and for devising innovative trade practices with emphasis on quality, transparency and timely delivery. Policy interventions and incentive packages leading to regional specialization in production and processing of tradable horticultural products, foreign participation in investment, transfer of technology and buy-back arrangements are also advocated. *Commercial Crops* The dynamic demand for coffee in the world market opens up splendid Opportunities for our country to emerge as a major player. Despite stagnation in international market of tea both in terms of prices and quantities and the stiff competition that Indian tea faces, India should continue to work and aspire for leadership in this crop. The inter-year instability in production coupled with low yields of cotton stand as major constraints for cotton to emerge as a stable exportable commodity. The possibility to keep our presence in international cotton market lies in the increased productivity and enhanced stability in production. India holds a great potential to take advantage of the surge in export of tobacco, especially by improving its productivity.

**Oilseeds**

The mission mode approach implemented through Technology Mission on Oilseeds (TMO) not only narrowed down the large, domestic demand-supply gap for vegetable oil but also paved the way for devising separate strategies for import substitution and export of oilseeds. Exportable oilseeds include the production of HPS groundnut free from aflatoxin content, developing varieties of mustard with low glucosinilate, organising production of white sesame without pesticide residues and rice bran extraction with low silica content.Castor oil has also emerged as an important export item. The strategy for export of oilseeds must include enhanced productivity, development of needed infrastructure, pre- and post-harvest measures to upgrade the quality and popularisation of quality oilseeds production through contract farming in potential places. Improving production efficiency would be most critical in the oilseeds sector.

**Dairy Products**

The growth rate of 4.5 per cent per annum in milk production in the country against the world average growth of 1.48 per cent, and its static growth in most milk producing countries indicates the potential of India to emerge as a major player in the export of milk products like whole milk powder, skimmed milk powder, butter, cheese etc., in the rising markets for these products in Southeast Asian countries and the Middle East. The emergence of the country from a net importer to an exporter of milk products since early nineties is an indication of pushing the sector from an occasional exporter to a regular exporter in the years to come.

The immediate need is to push up the production of milk to a level of making adequate surplus for export after meeting the steadily rising internal demand. To develop dairy products of international standard for export, adequate thrust on quality and clean milk production is required.

There is a need to segmentise the milk production systems for catering to different market segments including export market which in turn will demand investment on mechanized milking; chilling systems, quality packaging etc., with strict adherence to Codex Alimentarius Standards and developing branded market for consumers

## AGRICULTUTRAL MARKET REFORMS

(1) The APMC Act in different States/Union Territories needs to be amended on the lines of the draft of the amended. APMC Act circulated by the Government of India. It would encourage private sector investment in development of agricultural marketing.

(2) Need for review of the Essential Commodity Act and other Acts/Orders concerning storing, marketing and processing etc of the agricultural commodities.

(3) Improve the marketing infrastructure and bring about more transparency in auction and other marketing related matters in the regulated matters.

(4) The role of the Agricultural Produce Marketing Committees and the State Agricultural Marketing Boards to change from regulation to development and promotion of markets for the local products and better marketing practices.

(5) Restructure the Land Use Boards and provide technical

support to then to give pro-active advice to the farmers based on meteorological, marketing and managerial information on matters concerning choice of crops/ varieties/timing/marketing etc.

(6) Establish commodity based farmer's organisation to develop market orientation among the farmers and articulate farmer's issues on commodity basis.

(7) Develop a farmer centric 'Code of Conduct' for contract faming and encourage farmer's groups/organizations to deal with the purchaser/processor.

(8) Reduce the post harvest losses by training, development of appropriate equipments, facilities and also tightening of the supply chain. Encourage farmer's groups/ cooperative societies to involve in marketing of agricultural produce.

## CONCLUSION

Despite the significant progress in industry and services, which grabs all the headlines as far as India's economic progress is concerned, the Indian economy's mainstay has always been, and still is to a large extent, agriculture. Agriculture and related sectors contribute between two-fifth to one-third of India's gross domestic product (GDP), and employs more than 60 per cent of its population. Indian agriculture has made great progress since Independence, becoming close to a food self-sufficient nation in just about 40 years. There are various factors that have been responsible for this growth. It also greater research in biotechnology; Improvements in seed varieties and development of high-yielding seeds; Better irrigation and water management; Sensible cropping practices and judicious use of fertilizers

If the Government and farmers follow the above strategies for problems sure they can overcome the exporting problems of the Indian agricultural produce.

## REFFERENCES

Agriculture Marketing: Interventions & Innovations by K.H. Vedini,

Economic Reforms and Rural Development in India by G. Parthasarathy.

*www.economywatch.com/database/agriproductsexport.html-23k*

*www.icar.org.in*

*www.apeda.com*

15

# EMERGING DIMENSIONS OF CREDIT RISK MANAGEMENT IN CROSS BORDER TRADE

**R. K. Saxena**

Growing interest in cross border trade can be justified by changing competitive structures coupled with shifts in demand characteristics in markets throughout the globe. With the increasing globalization of markets, companies find they are unavoidably enmeshed with foreign customers, competitors and suppliers even from within their own borders. The role of cross border trade in the developing economies has been increasing due to vast opportunities, mass markets, rapid development and encouragement of competition. Exports play very crucial role and are given utmost priority in the foreign trade policy of developing countries. Indian economy being one such, is attaching great importance to promote exports. The subject of risks in cross border trade, particularly the nature and dimensions of the risks associated with export credit operations has assumed increased importance. All commercial transactions carry risk. Finances as the process of financial intermediation are confronted with various kinds of financial and non-financial risks. Risk is exposure to uncertainty. There are two components of risk viz. uncertainty and exposure to that uncertainty. Credit risk management has become very important for healthy and steady growth of exports.

## CREDIT RISK

Credit risk is the likelihood of a borrower's failure to perform an obligation for full value either when due or at any time thereafter. It can arise due to internal factors related to a particular exporter or certain external factors related to any exporting company or industrial sector or economy of a nation as a whole. This is a major risk faced by lender on account of their business activity of granting credit/lending or investment operations or off-balance sheet operations which may be extended to corporates, individuals, other banks, financial institutions and other countries. In cross border trade, credit risk assumes a greater significance when the exporters are operating in different countries with different political set up, different currencies and different level of risks. A foreign exchange transaction is confirmed by a contract which stipulates defined commitments on the part of beneficiary. The risk here is that one counterparty may not be able to execute his side of the contract on or before the due date. It may arise because of inability of payment by the defaulting party. Proper selection of borrowers through sound credit granting process, adoption of sound credit granting policies and risk assessment systems, limiting credit concentrations through adoption of prudential limits for industries, sectors or geographical areas. Controlling risks through effective loan review mechanism process, adoption of scientific risk rating and risk based pricing systems, evolving adequate framework for managing exposure in off-balance sheet products, fixing inter-bank and country exposure limits and monitoring portfolio quality and changes, migration therein etc. are some of the important tools for management of credit risk. The financial conditions of the exporter as well as the values of the available collateral are some of the tools for financing bodies and bankers to limit the level of export credit risk.

## EXPORT PROMOTION AND EXPORT CREDIT

By way of incentives for stepping up exports, the government of India, through the Reserve bank, has arranged to provide to the exporter's cash compensatory assistance for price differentials, duty drawbacks etc. in certain exports. Besides, there are also a number of autonomous organizations functioning as Export Promotion council for the purpose of export promotion. With the same object, the Reserve bank of India in order to stimulate bank financing of exports introduced the pre-shipment credit scheme, the Export bills credit scheme and the Export credit (Interest subsidy) scheme. It has also arranged, through the export credit guarantee corporation Ltd; to provide guarantee to the bankers for the pre-shipment or post-shipment finance they grant to exporters and for insurance cover for export to exporters. For purpose of export promotion, the EXIM bank provides term credit facilities for Indian exports of machinery and engineering goods an deferred payments basis. The facilities take the form of direct loans to exporters, refinance facilities to commercial banks in respect of such loans extended by them and overseas buyers and suppliers credits. Exim banks also provides bank guarantees on behalf of Indian contractors undertaking construction and turnkey project abroad. In addition, it provides merchant-banking and counseling services to Indian Exporters, particularly to exporters of machinery and engineering goods. Commercial banks also play an important part in promoting exports. This role consists primarily in providing export credits to exporters and furnishing guarantees on behalf of exporters. Exports bills, supported by shipping documents cannot be sent directly to the foreign buyers but have under the exchange control regulations, to be negotiated or lodged for collected with a banker authorized to deal in foreign exchange. The banker may provide post shipment finance to the exporters by negotiating such bills drawn under a letter of credit or by purchasing/discounting bills covering exports under a firm order or on consignment basis. Where exports are covered by a letter of credit or a firm order, the banker may, if required by the exporter, provide packing credit i.e., pre-shipment finance to him for the purpose of manufacturing, processing, purchasing and packing the goods for export. Bankers may also establish credits for the Indian importers in favour of foreign suppliers of capital goods; raw materials for export goods etc.

## INITIATIVES BY THE GOVERNMENT

For purposes of export promotion the incentives offered to the Indian exporters by the Government of India are as follows:

### Cash Assistance

The export prices of Indian products are not always at par with the domestic prices thereof. Therefore, to offset the disparities in prices faced by the Indian products in the international competitive markets, compensatory support in the form of payment of a certain percentage of the value of the exports is extended by the Government of India to the exporters of selected products.

On offering the export, the exporter is required to submit his application to the Director General of Foreign Trade to claim the assistance due to him. Cash assistance varies from 5% to 20% of EO.S.

Banks may, if an approached by exporters, grant to them advances free of interest against their incentives receivable pending payment thereof by the concerned disbursing Authority.

These advances are eligible for interest-free full finance from the Reserve Bank.

A duty drawback is rebate allowed to an exporter on the Customs (i.e. import) duty and or the central Excise duty paid by him on raw materials and components, imported or Indigenous which are used in the manufacture of products for export or on the products themselves, on the exportation such products.

The drawbacks are paid out of the Market Development Fund. A claim for a drawback should be filed on the shipment of goods or dispatch thereof by post with the Controller of Customs (Drawbacks) or the Central Excise (Refunds) as the case may be, and should be supported by documents as in the case of cash assistance.

### Import Entitlement

To the above two categories of incentives may be added another one which goes by the name of Import Entitlement is in import entitlement is an import license issued to an exporter as an incentive only for the export of specified engineering product, chemicals, sport-goods, carpets which are non-traditional manufactured exports. The import entitlement is available up to 70-75% of the F.O.B .value of exports or export value at international prices.

This entitlement is transferable to another manufacturer but not to a merchant trader.

Exporters of same specified products such as engineering goods, garments etc., have been given what is called "Green form Allotment". This allotment refers to the guaranteed supply of indigenous raw-materials needed by registered exporters in the manufacture of their export products.

**Export Incentives by the RBI**

***Duty Drawback Credit Scheme***

As it usually takes a long time for exporters to receive the cash against their duty drawback entitlements from the concerned disbursing authority, the Reserve Bank introduced with effect from February, 1976 its Duty Drawback Credit Scheme. Under the scheme, scheduled banks authorized to deal in foreign exchange can grant to exporters interest-free advances for 90 days against their duty drawback entitlement as previously certified by the Customs authorities, pending final sanction and payment. Interest may however be charged at 13 per cent for 90 days on cash incentives, etc. when covered by ECGC guarantee. For the purpose the banks may sanction suitable limits to individual exporters, taking into account their export performance, eligibility for the entitlement, credit-worthiness, etc.

The exporter should in each case apply for the finance, and the application should contain his endorsement authorizing the disabusing authority to make payment to the bank. The bank in its turn is required to issue a certificate of export on the copy of the invoice.

Though the advance should be interest-free, the lending bank may charge a reasonable amount towards administrative expenses and cost of transmission of funds by way of refinance and repayment thereof from and to the Reserve Bank.

### *Pre-Shipment Credit Scheme*

*(a)* This scheme was introduced by the Reserve Bank in February 1969 under Section 17(3A) of the Reserve Bank of India Act, 1934. Under the Scheme, the Reserve Bank allows advances to scheduled commercial banks up to 100 per cent of the pre-shipment credits granted by them to bonfire exporters, subject to minimum of Rs. 1lakh, on the strength of letters of credit or firm export orders in favor of the exporters lodged with them, or in the absence of an *l/ C* or a firm export order, on the_strength of letters, cables, etc. provided that the exporter undertakes to produce the *l/ C* or the export order with in a reasonable time.

The advance is available from the Reserve Bank against an application from the borrowing bank, indicating the amount required and supported by a declaration in writing that the bank has granted a pre-shipment loan or advance to an exporter or any other person in India to enable him to export goods from India. The amount of loan or advance drawn and out standing at any time must not be less than the outstanding amount of the loan or advance obtained from the Reserve Bank.

The export credit which is granted by the bank should bear interest at a rate not exceeding the ceiling rate fixed by the Reserve Bank for the time being.

### *Export Bills Credit Scheme*

The Scheme was introduced by the Reserve Bank in March 1963 under Section t7(3A)of the Reserve Bank of India Act, 1934 Under the scheme, any licensed scheduled Bank authorized to deal in foreign exchange is eligible for this credit from the Reserve Bank against:

it is promissory note repayable on demand or on the expiry of a fixed period not exceeding 180 days; and a declaration in writing that it holds and will, as long as any such loan or advance remains unpaid, continue to hold export bills of a value not less than the amount of such loan or advance outstanding for the time being.

The loan or advance is available against a written request to the Reserve Bank, indicating the amount required and supported by a declaration in prescribed form. The declaration should be made separately in respect of usance export bills drawn in Indian rupees and bills drawn in other currencies.

The loan or advance may be granted up to 100% of the total value of outstanding eligible bills, subject to a minimum of Rs.1lakh. The borrowing banker should make sure that the total outstanding borrowings from the Reserve Bank at any time are fully covered by the amount of export bills reported in the declaration.

All export bills including those having a usance not exceeding 180 days and purchased/negotiated/discounted by the borrowing bank under letters of credit or otherwise, and drawn in India on any place in any country outside India which is a member of the IMF, or in any other country notified in this behalf by the Reserve Bank in the Gazette of India, will be eligible for the purpose of the loan or advance.

**Export Assistance by the Exim Bank**

*Long-term Finance Guarantees:* The International Finance Wing of the Exim Bank looks after the Export loans granted by it. It provides long-term finance and guarantees for the export of capital and engineering goods and services on deferred payment basis in participation with scheduled commercial banks which are authorized dealers in foreign exchange.

*Refinancing of Export Credits:* The Exim Bank provides refinance to eligible banks, i.e. scheduled banks authorized to deal in foreign exchange, against medium or long-term export credits granted by them on deferred payment terms. The credits should be granted against export of capital and/or engineering goods or for the export of capital/engineering goods, equipment materials, services, etc, of Indian origin under construction projects abroad, and should be for periods exceeding six months but not exceeding five years in the case of a medium-term project and 10 years in the case of a long-term project. Refinance is also available to banks against packing credits granted by them for the manufacture and processing of export goods.

The refinance could be up to 100% of the export credit, without a prescribed minimum or maximum limit, at confessional rates of interest which are fixed from time to time by the Exam Bank.

## CREDIT RISK INSURANCE

The primary goal of the E.C.G.C. is to support and strengthen the Export Promotion drive in India:

(i) By providing a range of credit risk insurance covers to exporters against loss in export of goods and services and also,

(ii) By providing guarantee to banks and financial institutions to enable exporters to obtain better facilities from them.

*Export credit insurance is designed to protect the exporters from–*

Political risks, such as coups, insurrections, civil disturbances etc.

Economic hurdles, such as balance of payment problems, and

Commercial risks, such as the buyer's insolvency, protracted default and failure to accept the goods by the buyers etc.

Export credit insurance also creates a favorable climate in which exporter may get timely and liberal facilities from banks by providing guarantees to banks, protecting them from loss inherent in granting various kinds of financial facilities to exporters.

### Policies Issued by ECGC

#### *Standard Policies Shipments (Comprehensive Risks Policies)*

The Shipment (Comprehensive Risks) Policy, commonly known as the Standard policy. This is ideally suited to cover risks up to 90% of commercial and political risks in respect of goods exported on short term credit, i.e. credit not exceeding 180 days. This is a whole turnover policy which covers both commercial and political risks from the date of shipment. It is issued to exporters whose anticipated export turnover for the next 12 months is more than Rs. 25lakhs.

***The Commercial Risks Covered Under this Policy by the E.C.G.C. are***

Insolvency of the buyer, the buyer's protracted default to pay within a specified period from the due date usually 4 months, and the buyer's failure to accept goods subject to certain conditions.

***Political Risks Covered are***

Restriction on remittances in the buyer's country or any Government action blocking or delaying payment;

War, civil war, revolution or civil disturbances in the buyer's country;

New import licensing restrictions or cancellation of a valid import license in the buyer's country after the date of shipment/ contract;

Additional handling, transport or insurance charges due to an interruption in, or diversion of, a voyage not recoverable from the buyers, and Any other cause of loss occurring outside India, not normally insured by commercial insurers and beyond the control of the exporter or buyer.

***Shipments Covered***

The Standard Policy covers all shipments made by an exporter on credit terms, *i.e.* on DP, DA or Open Delivery terms, to all buyers other than his own associates, during a period 2 months ahead. No policy is obtainable for selected shipments, selected buyers or selected markets.

***Contract Cover:***

The Standard Policy provides cover only for the post-shipment stage, *i.e.*, from the date of shipment. Cover for pre-shipment losses, *i.e.*, losses sustained by an exporter due to impossibility of exporting goods already manufactured or purchased for reasons like ban on export of the items, restriction on import of the item(s) into the buyer's country or war, civil war etc., is not a available. Where, however the export involves an item which has been manufactured to some non-standard specification of the buyer, cover can be provided for the pre-shipment risks as well by an endorsement to the Standard Policy.

### *Maximum Liability*

The maximum liability under a Standard Policy, i.e. the limit up to which ECGC would accept liability for shipment made in each of the policy years for both commercial and political risks, is fixed by it in each case, on the basis of the exporter's estimate of the maximum outstanding payments due from his overseas buyers at any time during the policy period. This limit may, where necessary, be enhanced subsequently.

*Percentage of Cover:* The corporation normally pays 90% of the loss whether its arises due to commercial or political risks. The remaining 10% has to be borne by the export.

*Minimum Premium:* A policy will be issued on payment of a minimum premium of Rs. 7500 which will be adjusted against premiums payable on shipments declared. Additional premium will have to be paid on the shipment(s) declared after the minimum premium gets fully adjusted. No part of the minimum premium will be refunded to the exporter even if the premium payable on actual shipments falls below the minimum premium paid.

### *Time for Payment of Claim*

A claim arises when any of the risks covered materializes, and the exporter becomes eligible for the claim one month after his loss is admitted or after four months from the due date, whichever is earlier.

In the case of protracted default the claim is payable after four months from the due date .

A claim in respect of additional handling; transport or insurance charged incurred by the exporter because of interruption or diversion of voyage outside India is payable after proof of the loss is furnished.

In all other cases claim is payable after four months from the date of the event causing the loss. in the case of exports to countries where long transfer delays are experienced, The ECGC may extend the waiting period and claims for such shipments will be payable after the expiry of the extended period.

Where the buyer does not accept the goods or pay for them because of disputes over the fulfillment of the terms of contract by the exporter, counter-claims or set- of the ECGC will consider the claim after the dispute is settled and the amount payable is established under a decree of a court a law in the buyer's country. This condition is waived where the ECGC is satisfied that the exporter is not at fault and that no useful purpose will be served by proceeding against the buyer.

## Debt Recovery

Payment of claims by the ECGC does not relieve the exporter of his responsibility for taking recovery action and realizing whatever amount can be recovered. The exporter should, after consultation with the ECGC, take prompt and effective steps for recovery of the debt. The ECGC will on its part help the exporter by providing the name of a reliable lawyer or debt collecting agency and by enlisting the help of India's commercial representative in the buyer's country. Nor does the payment of claim by the ECGC relieve the exporter from his obligation to the Exchange Control authorities for recovery of the amount from the overseas buyer. All amounts recovered, net of recovery expenses, has to be shared with the ECGC in the ratio in which the loss was originally shared.

### *Specific Policies*

The standard Policy, as indicated above, is a whole turnover policy designed to provide a confirming insurance for a regular flow of an exporter's shipments of raw materials consumer goods and consumer durables for which the credit period does not exceed 180 days he other hand, for exports involving medium and long-term credits.

Specific Policies have been designed to protect Indian firms against the risk of not receiving payment in respect of Export on deferred payment forms Services rendered to foreign parties construction works including turnkey projects undertaken overseas

### *Insurance Cover for Buyer's Credit and Line of Credit*

Byers Credit is a credit extended by a bank in India to an overseas buyer for the propose of enabling him to pay for machinery and equipment that he may be importing from India for a specified project. A Line of Credit is a credit extended by a Bank in India to an overseas bank, institution or government for the purpose of a facilitating import of some listed goods from India into the overseas country. A number of importers in the overseas country may import the goods from India Under a Line of Credit.

The ECGC cover is designed to protect the lending banks from certain risks, political or comprehensive, of non-payment. The cover takes the form of an agreement between the lending bank and the ECGC decided on a case-to-case basis.

The comprehensive risk includes protracted default of the borrower to pay the amounts due under the loan agreement and insolvency of the borrower where applicable, in addition to the political risks mentioned above. The premium rates applicable to comprehensive risks cover will be higher than those for the political cover.

At least 20% of the total premium payable for the cover should be paid in advance, and the balance may be paid on a quarterly basis in proportion to the amount of credit disbursed.

### Policies Under Special Scheme

To protect the financial institutions in India which extend buyer's credit or line of credit overseas buyers, or the Indian entrepreneurs who take up industrial projects abroad, and the Indian exporters and the bankers financing exports from exchange risks, the E.C.G.C. has evolved, besides the Transfer Guarantee, the following types of insurance cover under special schemes:

Overseas Investment Insurance
Exchange Fluctuation Risk Cover
Exchange Fluctuation Risk (Bid) Cover
Exchange Fluctuation Risk (Contract) Cover, and
Buyer's Credit and Line of Credit Cover.

# 16

# PRESENT SCENARIO OF INDIAN MOTOR CYCLE EXPORTERS

**S. Senthilkumar & N. Priya**

## EXPORT PERFORMANCE OF THE TWO-WHEELER INDUSTRY IN INDIA

India is emerging as one of the top two-wheeler exporters of the world. In 2006-07 around 619,318 two-wheelers were exported, which was around 21% more than the quantity exported in the previous year. The issues faced by Indian two-wheeler exporters include pricing as Chinese motorcycles are cheaper. Some markets like Indonesia only require step-thrust which are currently not manufactured in India. Also Indian two-wheeler exports are targeted at motorcycles whose capacity is 100-125 cc and there is no export in the 250 cc and above segment. But in order to get better realizations, Indian motorcycle manufacturers have to export motorcycles with capacity above 250 cc.

In India there are 100 people per vehicle, while this figure is 82 in China. It is expected that Indian automobile industry will achieve mass motorization status by 2014. Since the first car rolled out on the streets of Mumbai (then Bombay) in 1898, the Automobile Industry of India has come a long way. During its early stages the auto industry was overlooked by the then

Government and the policies were also not favorable. The liberalization policy and various tax reliefs by the Govt. of India in recent years have made remarkable impacts on Indian Automobile Industry. Indian auto industry, which is currently growing at the pace of around 18 % per annum, has become a hot destination for global auto players like Volvo, General Motors and Ford. A well developed transportation system plays a key role in the development of an economy, and India is no exception to it. With the growth of transportation system the Automotive Industry of India is also growing at rapid speed, occupying an important place on the 'canvas' of Indian economy. Today Indian automotive industry is fully capable of producing various kinds of vehicles and can be divided into 03 broad categories: Cars, two-wheelers and heavy vehicles. The following are the key points which are mentioned below on India's performance on motor cycle exports–

- India is being recognized as potential emerging auto market.
- Foreign players are adding to their investments in Indian auto industry.
- Within two-wheelers, motorcycles contribute 80% of the segment size.
- Unlike the USA, the Indian passenger vehicle market is dominated by cars (79%).
- Tata Motors dominates over 60% of the Indian commercial vehicle market.
- 2/3rd of auto component production is consumed directly by OEMs.
- India is the largest three-wheeler market in the world.
- India is the largest two-wheeler manufacturer in the world.
- India is the second largest tractor manufacturer in the world.
- India is the fifth largest commercial vehicle manufacturer in the world.
- The number one global motorcycle manufacturer is in India.

- India is the fourth largest car market in Asia-recently crossed the 1 million mark

## GLOBAL DEMAND TO RISE 5.4% ANNUALLY THROUGH 2011

Demand for motorcycles worldwide will rise 5.4 per cent annually to 55.7 million units in 2011, with growth emanating from a mix of developed market incremental improvements and emerging market expansions. Demand for all categories of motorcycles is expected to remain healthy, despite the anticipated slowdown in key markets. China, for example, the largest motorcycle market and producer in unit terms, is rapidly transitioning away from motorcycles toward cars, and in the process flooding the world market with motorcycle exports. In contrast, rising fuel prices and increasing restrictions on car use are favoring motorcycles in developed markets. The market for large and expensive high displacement motorcycles will remain strong through 2011, but concerns regarding demand have emerged due to the aging of the customer base and rising insurance costs, especially in the US and Western Europe.

The Indian two-wheeler industry has attracted worldwide attention over the last ten years. Probably, for the first time Indian industry was seen as competitive when Hero Honda became the world's largest two-wheeler manufacturer. This was further reinforced when Hero Honda's motorcycle 'Splendor' became the largest selling model in the world. However, Hero Honda is not the only Indian two-wheeler manufacturer of international class. Both Bajaj Auto and TVS Motors are not lagging far behind. In fact, some of Bajaj Auto's products are superior to that of Hero Honda. There are also a number of other smaller two-wheeler manufacturers. These include Honda Motorcycles and Scooters India, Suzuki, Yamaha, Eicher and Kinetic Motorcycles.

## GOING GLOBAL' BUILDING COMPETITIVENESS THROUGH INTERNATIONALIZATION

The Indo-Japanese joint ventures—Hero Honda, TVS Suzuki, Bajaj Kawasaki—adopted different strategies to become competitive. TVS Motors used cost reduction (value engineering, global sourcing, lean manufacturing, waste elimination and continuous reduction in cost) and securing product leadership (good brands, innovative package, IT, developing energy efficient technologies and market/product expansion) to become competitive. Bajaj Auto's strategy was to customize its products as per market needs. Hero Honda's plan for the domestic market was to manufacture fuel-efficient vehicles. Its global plan was to give the best product to customers by upgrading technologies and to view the world as one market.

## GLOBAL DEMAND TO RISE 5.4% ANNUALLY THROUGH 2011

Demand for motorcycles worldwide will rise 5.4 per cent annually to 55.7 million units in 2011, with growth emanating from a mix of developed market incremental improvements and emerging market expansions. Demand for all categories of motorcycles is expected to remain healthy, despite the anticipated slowdown in key markets. China, for example, the largest motorcycle market and producer in unit terms, is rapidly transitioning away from motorcycles toward cars, and in the process flooding the world market with motorcycle exports. In contrast, rising fuel prices and increasing restrictions

**World Motorcycle Demand, 2008 (43.11 Million Units)**

on car use are favoring motorcycles in developed markets. The market for large and expensive high displacement motorcycles will remain strong through 2011, but concerns regarding demand have emerged due to the aging of the customer base and rising insurance costs, especially in the US and Western Europe.

## THE INDIA ADVANTAGE

India has the potential to become one of the top 5 automotive economies by 2025 based on its present growth potential. Steered here by the country's high engineering skills, established production lines, a thriving domestic Motor cycle industry and competitive costs, global auto majors are rapidly ramping up the value of components they source from India. The industry is poised to jump from exports of US$ 1.8 billion in 2004-05 to US$ 5.9 billion in 2008-09. According to the Automotive Component Manufacturers Association of India, more than a third (36 per cent) of Indian auto component exports head for Europe, with North America a close second at 26 per cent. In 2006, components worth US$ 2 billion were exported by Indian companies, 75 per cent of which were bought directly by car companies. The original equipment manufacturers (OEMs) include firms like Hero Honda, Bajaj, Yamaha, Suzuki, and Enfield.. Over 20 OEMs have set up their International Purchase Offices (IPOs) in India to the components. This number is expected to double by the year 2010. India enjoys a cost advantage with regard to castings and forgings. The manufacturing costs in India are 25 to 30 per cent lower than its western counterparts. India's competitive advantage does not come from costs alone, but from its full service supply capability. The below points gives Weightage to India's advantage on exports-

- Low cost Manufacturing
- Politically and Economically stable market.
- Exponentially growing automotive industry.
- Manufacturing and imports free from Licensing and approvals.

- 100% foreign investment allowed in Automobile sector.
- No Local content regulation in Automobile industry.
- Foreign Exchange convertible on capital account.

**Vehicle Production Vs. Export Trend Over 5 Years**

| | *2002-03* | *2003-04* | *2004-05* | *2005-06* | *2006-07* |
|---|---|---|---|---|---|
| Production | 5,316,302 | 6,279,967 | 7,243,564 | 8,467,853 | 9,735,216 |
| Domestic | 5,225,788 | 5,941,535 | 6,810,537 | 7,897,629 | 8,910,224 |
| Exports | 184,680 | 307,308 | 479,919 | 629,544 | 806,494 |

## INDUSTRY STRUCTURE

The two-wheeler manufacturing business is capital-intensive, and requires facilities for making engines, body fabrication and assembly. Huge investments are required to increase capacity or set up new manufacturing facilities. The cost of setting up a full-fledged motorcycle manufacturing line with a capacity of 0.4 million units, is estimated at Rs. 2.5-3.0 billion. A motorcycle assembly line of the same capacity costs around Rs. 750 million. A scooter manufacturing line of 0.1 million units costs around Rs. 2 billion. Hero Honda, Bajaj Auto, TVS Motor have been the main players of the two wheeler industry. While Hero Honda operates dominantly in the motorcycle segment, a modest entry has been made in the scooterette segment by launching Hero Honda Pleasure. Bajaj Auto and TVS Motor ride in all the three segments–motorcycle, scooter and moped. The other players in the industry have been LML, Kinetic Motor, Kinetic Engineering, Yamaha and Royal Enfield. Hero Honda's overall sales raced much above industry growth and registered a CAGR of 28% between 1999-00 and 2004-05. Bajaj Auto and TVS Motor followed with CAGR growth of 10.5% and 8.4% respectively. Other than Royal Enfield Motors, who registered a CAGR growth of 3% during the said period, all other players registered a negative growth in the period under review. Thus if overall two wheeler market is considered, Hero Honda commands a 40% share in the market, followed by Bajaj Auto at 24% and TVS Motor at 17.8%. Honda Motorcycle & Scooters entered the Indian scooter market during 2001-02 and made its foray into the motorcycle market in 2004-05. In a span of 4 years, the company today has 8.4% share in the overall Indian two wheeler market.

**Two-wheeler: Player-wise Market Share**

| *(%)* | *1999-00* | *2000-01* | *2001-02* | *2002-03* | *2003-04* | *2004-05* |
|---|---|---|---|---|---|---|
| Hero Honda | 22.0 | 28.8 | 33.1 | 33.2 | 36.8 | 39.9 |
| Bajaj Auto | 28.0 | 24.9 | 27.8 | 24.8 | 22.9 | 24.4 |
| TVS Motor | 22.5 | 24.2 | 20.1 | 22.1 | 20.4 | 17.8 |
| Honda Motorcycle & Scooters | 0.0 | 0.0 | 1.3 | 3.3 | 6.1 | 8.4 |
| Yamaha Motors | 7.3 | 4.8 | 5.4 | 6.0 | 4.7 | 3.8 |
| LML | 8.2 | 5.8 | 4.0 | 3.8 | 3.7 | 1.6 |
| Kinetic Motor | 3.5 | 3.6 | 2.9 | 2.6 | 2.2 | 1.6 |
| Kinetic Engineering | 4.7 | 4.3 | 2.9 | 2.0 | 1.4 | 1.1 |
| Majestic Auto | 3.2 | 3.1 | 1.9 | 1.6 | 1.3 | 1.0 |
| Royal Enfield Motors | 0.7 | 0.6 | 0.6 | 0.6 | 0.5 | 0.4 |
| Total | 100.0 | 100.0 | 100.0 | 100.0 | 100.0 | 100.0 |

*Source*: Sector Outlook: Two-wheeler Industry, CAPITALINE-Corporate Database on Capital Market Publishers India Pvt. Ltd.)

**Two-wheelers Exports Trend**

| Category | 2001-02 | 2002-03 | 2003-04 | 2004-05 | 2005-06 |
|---|---|---|---|---|---|
| Scooters | 28332 | 32566 | 53687 | 60699 | 83873 |
| Motorcycles | 56880 | 123725 | 187287 | 277123 | 386202 |
| Mopeds | 18971 | 23391 | 24078 | 28585 | 43181 |
| Grand Total | 104183 | 179682 | 265052 | 366407 | 513256 |

## MOTORCYCLE

Consumer demand in India has moved in line with the demand pattern followed in other countries by switching over to motorcycle from the traditional geared scooters preferred in the past. Motorcycle sales have witnessed an astounding CAGR growth of 24.7% during 1999-2000 to 2004-05. The growth in sales picked up strongly in 2001-02 as motorcycles became affordable since April 01 following the decline in excise duty levels on the >75 cc motorcycles. A large influx of new models in the past few years at various price points, power, performance attributes and aesthetic levels led to increased consumer interest in the motorcycle segment. The motorcycle segment can be further subdivided into economy, executive and premium segments on the basis of price range, fuel efficiency, target income groups and margins.

**Motorcycles: Economy VS Executive VS Premium**

| | *Target Income Groups* | *Price Range* (Rs '000) | *Fuel Efficiency* | *Margins* |
|---|---|---|---|---|
| Economy | Low | Upto 38 | High | Low |
| Executive | Medium | 38.50 | High | Moderate |
| Premium | High | 50-60 | Moderate | High |

The price sensitive economy segment caters largely to the lower middle class common man and low-income buyers from rural areas, which are highly dependent on monsoons and overall economic performance of the economy. Increasing competition has narrowed down the price differential between the economy and executive segments. While CT-100's success has proved that the price-conscious economy segment customers are ready to pay a few thousands more for better styling and mileage and hence pulled in some executive customers, aggressive pricing of 125 cc Discover effectively reduced the prices in executive segment. This triggered price cuts, mainly in the form of discounts by select players (as direct price cuts can dilute the brand value of a model). The premium segment witnessed the entry of HMSI in motorcycles segment through the launch of Honda Unicorn. Though the product was well received, it was not able to fuel high growth in the segment. The premium segment was estimated to account for around 10.5% in 2004-05 as against 11.5% in 2003-04. Hero Honda remains the undisputed leader in the motorcycle market. Though in 2002-03, it lost some of its market share to TVS Motors and LML, it regained back soon and today has a 50% share in the motorcycle market as against 43.7% during 1999-2000. Bajaj Auto has a commendable 28% market share (2004-05) as against 24% (2002-03) and TVS Motor has a share of 13% (2004-05) as against 18.8% (2002-03). Yamaha stands at a distant fourth with a share of 4.8% as against 7.9% three years back.

## EXPORTS

Motorcycles, scooters and even mopeds have been doing well on the export front- mainly to neighboring countries in Asia like Sri Lanka, Thailand, and Indonesia. Many of the Indian players have also set up plants in those countries. Bajaj Auto leads in exports with a 49.6% growth in units over 2003-04 (see table 'Motorcycle exports'). In scooters, it's Honda Scooters all the way (see table 'scooters exports'). Scooter exports overall grew 13% in 2004-05 over the previous year.

**Motorcycle Exports**

| *Company* | *2006-07* | *Growth %* | *2005-06* | *Growth %* | *2004-05* |
|---|---|---|---|---|---|
| Bajaj Auto | 123,950 | 49.6 | 82.828 | 80.9 | 45.777 |
| Hero Honda Motors | 64,015 | 63.1 | 39.254 | 71.7 | 22.859 |
| Yamaha Motors | 39,211 | 19.2 | 32,906 | -28.3 | 45,876 |
| TVS Motors | 38,828 | 62.4 | 23,912 | 215.9 | 7.570 |
| LML Ltd. | 5,974 | 75.2 | 3,410 | 342.9 | 770 |
| Kinetic Engg | 3,220 | -10.5 | 3,596 | 69.1 | 2,126 |
| Royal Enfield | 1,577 | 16.6 | 1,352 | -5.1 | 1,425 |
| Majestic Auto | 300 | 934.5 | 29 | NA | – |
| Honda Motorcycles & Scooters | 25 | NA | – | NA | – |
| Total Export | 277,100 | 48.0% | 187,287 | 48,2% | 126,403 |

%

*Source*: SIAM and ETIG analysis

## TVS EXPORTS

The company's exports have also picked up well and it plans to strengthen its presence in the key overseas markets. TVS also plans to invest Rs 2.3bn towards setting up a manufacturing plant in Indonesia for two wheelers with an initial capacity of 120,000 vehicles. Indonesia is the third largest market for two wheelers globally and TVS expects to generate its volumes in the ASEAN region through this facility in Indonesia. TVS expects to achieve cash break-even in the first year of operations itself in its Indonesian venture.

**Global Two Wheeler Market -2007**
**Size of the Total Market in 2007: 35 Million Numbers**

*Figure in %*

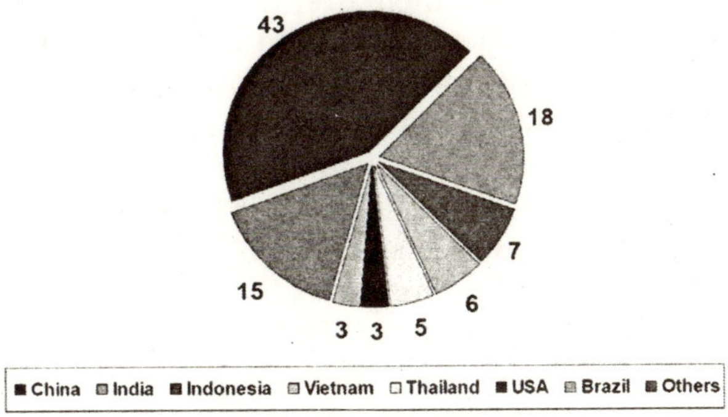


TVS MOTOR COMPANY

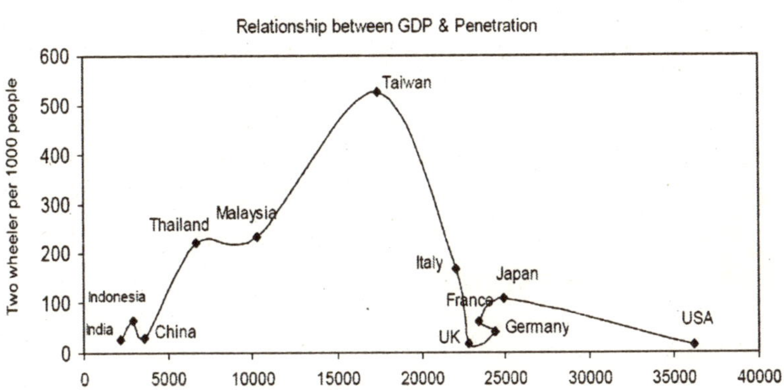


GDP per capita in $ at PPP, 2007

## HERO HONDA'S EXPORT

Between April and December 2007, the company exported only about 60,000 units, around one-sixth of what its nearest rival Bajaj Auto Ltd sold in the overseas markets. Vehicle sales are usually a proxy for economic growth and while India's bike makers enjoyed a robust run for several years as the economy expanded, they have had a bumpy ride in the past few months. With interest rates at a five-year high—most two-wheeler buyers fund their purchases through bank loans—sales of motorcycles registered their first decline in a decade. Hero Honda's Haridwar factory, its third overall, will increase its total installed capacity to 4.4 million units a year. Between April and December 2007, customers bought only 5.57 million motorcycles. Analysts, however, aren't sure how the move to making components could help Hero Honda's margins. "Auto components is a much more tough business compared to vehicle manufacturing and sales," said Ashutosh Goel, an analyst with Edelweiss Capital. There is "pricing pressure from both directions—from raw material suppliers and from OEMs (original equipment makers, or vehicle companies that buy components)." The Hero group, which owns a 26% stake in Hero Honda, is already present in the component business through some of its units such as Hero Motors Ltd and Munjal Auto Industries Ltd. Total two-wheeler sales between April and December fell 7.7% from a year ago, according to data provided by the Society of Indian Automobile Manufacturers. This has forced all two-wheeler manufacturers to scale back production; Hero Honda, which makes one of every two motorcycles and scooters sold in India, cut production by 1.3% to 2.45 million units last year.

## HERO GROUP'S EXPORT

### Activities

Manufacturers & Exporters of Bicycles, Bicycle Components, Auto Parts, Tractor Parts and Light Engineering Items, Aluminium Castings, Plastic Extrusions & Components, Metals/Minerals such as Iron Ore, Ferro Manganese, Agriculture Implements, Pre Fabricated Housing and Galvanised steel coils.Exporters of Pistons, Piston rings, Starters, Starter motors, Alternators, Armature, Starter drives, Solonoid Switches, Rotors, Startos, Rack and Pinion steering units, Tie rod ends, Ball joints, Bearings, Taper rolls bearings, Springs and Wiring harnesses.

**Export**

Afghanistan, Argentina, Bahrain, Bangladesh, Belgium, Brazil, China, Congo, Egypt, France, Germany, Greece, Hungary, Iraq, Iran, Italy, Ireland, Jordan, Kenya, Kuwait, Kirgyzstan, Malawi, Mexico, Mozambique, Myanmar, Nigeria, Peru, Poland, Portugal, Russian Federation, Saudi Arabia, Slovakia, South Africa, Africa, Europe, Asia

**Import**

Indonesia, China, Turkey, Asia

## YAMAHA MOTOR'S EXPORT

YAMAHA IS to start exporting to Europe from India as it seeks to end losses at its south Asian unit. The Indian unit has posted losses since 2001, including an operating loss of 8.8 billion yen (£45 million) last year. The company's sales in India plunged 48 per cent last year as it lost customers to Hero Honda Motors' Splendor and Hunk models. The Iwata City-Japan based company is only using 33 per cent of its manufacturing capacity in India. Yamaha is bleeding in India and its losses will just expand, if it does nothing," said Koji Endo, a senior analyst at Credit Suisse Group, in Tokyo. "It has to increase operation rates and to do so, exports make sense." Yamaha Motor India Pvt's motorcycle sales fell to 120,000 units last year from 230,000 in 2006, the company said. For help, Yamaha has turned to Mitsui & Co., Japan's second-largest trading company, to use its sales network in India. The company will export motorcycles specifically developed for the Indian market with engine capacity of more than 125cc, Kajikawa said. Yamaha's export strategy contrasts with that of Honda Motor Co. which is expanding capacity in the country to meet local demand. Yamaha said last month it will invest 7 billion rupees (£80 million) over the next three years to increase sales more than five-fold to 650,000 units in 2010. On March 5, the company said Mitsui & Co. will buy a 30 per cent stake in a new joint venture in the country. Yamaha will use the investment to develop higher-end models in a country where entry-level 100cc motorcycles are the most popular, Kajikawa said. Yamaha will sell more powerful motorcycles, a shift from its current low-priced line-up.

## INTERNATIONAL SCENARIO

The Japanese dominate world motorbike sales, led by Honda, Yamaha, Kawasaki and Suzuki. *(See table 'Global 2-wheeler sales').*

| *Year* | *Honda* | *Yamaha* | *Suzuki* | *Total'000* |
|---|---|---|---|---|
| 2004 | 5118 | 1920 | 1539 | 8,5 77 |
| 2005 | 6095 | 2041 | 1625 | 9,761 |
| 2006 | 8080 | 2335 | 1660 | 12,075 |
| 2007 | 9206 | 2681 | 2165 | 14,052 |

*Source*: Company Annual Reports.

The total of just these three Japanese majors is 14 million units worldwide, against total motorcycle sales of 4.9 million in the whole of India. However, India is already one of the world's largest markets and certainly with one of the highest growth rates anywhere.

## INDIAN AUTOMOBILE INDUSTRY: PATTERNS OF EXPANSION, ENTRY AND PERFORMANCE

In order to enter in international business and promote export many companies had alliance. The following table details the alliances of some major two-wheeler manufacturers in India. Besides the below mentioned technology alliances, Suzuki Motor Corporation has also followed the strategy of joint ventures (SMC reportedly acquired equity stake in Integra Overseas Limited for manufacturing and marketing Suzuki motorcycles in India). With the two-wheeler market, especially the motorcycle market, becoming extremely competitive and the life cycle of products getting shorter, the ability to offer new models to meet fast changing customer preferences has become imperative. In this context, the ability to deliver newer products calls for sound technological backing and this has become one of the critical differentiating factor among companies in the domestic market.

| | *Nature of Alliance* | *Company* | *Product* |
|---|---|---|---|
| Bajaj Auto | Technological tie-up | Kawasaki Heavy Industries Ltd, Japan | Motorcycles |
| | Technological tie-up | Tokya R&D Co Ltd, Japan | Two -wheelers |
| | Technological tie-up | Kubota Corp, Japan | Diesel Engines |
| HHML | Joint Venture | Honda Motor Co, Japan | Motorcycles |
| KEL | Technological tie-up | Hyosung Motors & Machinery Inc | Motorcycles |
| KEL | Tie up for manufacturing and distribution | Italjet, Italy | Scooters |
| LML | Technological tie-up | Daelim Motor Co Ltd | Motorcycles |
| Hero Motors | Technological tie-up | Aprilia of Italy | Scooters |

*Source: http://www.fadaweb.com/two_wheeler_industry.htm, accessed January 1, 2008.*

## FUTURE PLAN ON EXPORTS OF INDIAN MOTOR CYCLE

- Increase distribution in Asian, African and Latin American countries
- Intensive sales and marketing efforts in Srilanka and Bangladesh to establish leadership
- Market entry into South East Asia.
- Entry into three wheeler business by next year
- Investment in phase 1 of Rs. 500 million
- To cater to both passenger and cargo segments
- Capacity expansion
- New projects
- R & D infrastructure
- Over seas projects

## CONCLUSION

To sum up, Indian Motor cycle Market is at a stage of take-off. The business and economic environment is favourable for any company planning to set up a manufacturing base in India and manufacture products suited for India and global market. The market is dynamic and is becoming more and more customer-centric. The customer is open to novel products, services and concepts. Apart from plant and machinery, the new entrant should invest a significant effort and resources for understanding the customer and building the brand. Careful planning, prudent investment decisions, professional management and meticulous implementation of the recommended strategies is the right cocktail for making a "zooming" entry, creating a mark in the market and achieving profitability in the medium term.

17

# INITIATIVES OF EXPORT PROMOTION COUNCILS (EPCS) IN PROMOTING INDIA'S EXPORTS

**J. Srinivasan**

The world market place and the entire global economic environment are at one of the most profound points of change. The rapid pace of technological development, the shifting markets with the changes in global consumer tastes and preferences, emergence of global corporations and their conduct of worldwide operations, and the process of restructuring of the industrial economies and the liberalisation policies pursued by the developing nations are among the forces which are reshaping the world economy and its trading patterns.

The internationalization of the world economy has been rapid during the last two decades. Besides, there is now a greater flow of capital, labour, information, technology and organisation of the production process itself across borders. The major forces influencing the globalisation of markets:

- The integrating role of Technology
- Dynamics of Capital Flows
- Production Sharing and Globalisation
- Strategic Alliances and Global Competition.

Globalisation of business has been rapid during the last two decades. In addition to the factors mentioned above, the efforts undertaken by the industrial countries to restructure their economies, and the economic reforms carried out by the developing countries will further intensify the globalisation process in the coming years.

Globalisation of world economy offers both, challenges as well as opportunities, to the developing countries. Already they have lost a lot of time in preparing for global competitiveness. A higher level of world prices, continuing devaluation of their currencies and increase in the quantum of their imports, is adding new complexities to their international marketing efforts. The opportunities that are opening for global marketing are further dampened by rising protectionism, discriminatory government procurement policies, offset requirements, forced technology transfers, local content requirements and other mechanisms used, and the growing trend towards bilateralism instead of multilateral trade agreements.

## EXPORT PROMOTION COUNCILS (EPCS)

In the framework of Globalisation and Economic Liberalisation, to boost exports and facilitate Indian exporters better, the Government of India manages various Export Promotion Councils (EPCs). The basic purpose of EPCs is to promote and develop exports of the country. Each council is responsible for the promotion of a particular group of products, projects and services.

There are at present 22 EPCs in India, out of which *twelve* are functioning under the administrative control of the Ministry of Commerce, *nine* in the textile sector working under the administrative control of the Ministry of Textiles and *one* under the Department of Information Technology, Ministry of Communication and Information Technology. In addition, there are *five* Commodity Boards and *two* Export Development Authorities working under the Ministry of Commerce, *two* boards under the Textiles Ministry and *one* board under the Ministry of Agro and Rural Industries. (List enclosed).

EPCs are registered as non-profit organizations under the Companies Act/Societies Registration Act. These councils perform both advisory and executive functions. EPCs encourage and monitor the compliance of international standards and specifications by their exporter member. The EPCs keep track of trends and opportunities in international markets for goods and services.

The main focus of the export promotion is to project India's image abroad as a reliable supplier of high quality goods and services. Towards this end, Export Promotion Councils encourage and monitor the compliance of international standards and specifications by their exporter members. The EPCs keep track of trends and opportunities in international markets for goods and services. They also assist their member in taking advantage of such opportunities, in order to expand and diversify exports. The EPCs are professional bodies and therefore, executives with a professional background in commerce, management and international marketing are chosen to manage them, as they have are wide-ranging experience in government and industry and are involved in their running.

## MAJOR FUNCTIONS OF EXPORT PROMOTION COUNCILS (EPCS)

- Providing commercially useful information and assistance to their members in developing and in increasing their exports.
- Offering professional advice to members in areas such as technology upgradation, quality and design improvement, standards and specifications, product development, innovation, etc.
- Organising visits of delegations of members abroad to explore overseas market opportunities.
- Organising participation in trade fairs, exhibitions and buyer-seller meets in India.
- Promoting interaction between the exporting community and the government, both at the central and state levels.

- Building a statistical base and providing data on exports and imports of the country, of their members and other relevant international trade data.

Exporters must apply to the concerned EPC for membership in the prescribed application form with the requisite fee amount. They will then be enrolled as members and granted a Registration-cum-Membership Certificate (RCMS) of the EPC concerned, subject to such terms and conditions as may be in force at that time. This RCMS entitles the exporter to avail the various facilities provided by the EPC. It is also required to claim export incentives like drawback.

## ROLE OF EXPORT PROMOTION COUNCILS (EPCS)

- To carry out market surveys for the items with export potential in the Latin American countries and disseminate information to their members through their publications.
- To encourage members to participate in specialized International Fairs.
- To bring out promotional literature in Spanish/Portuguese.
- To hold commodity specific seminars in selected industrial centres.
- To prepare compendia of main importers/associations in the Latin American countries and disseminate this information to their members.
- The Councils will have separate Chapters on LAC on their websites and will add separate sections in their newsletters.
- The Department of Commerce will sponsor one or two officials from each Council for courses in Spanish/ Portuguese at Indian Institute of Foreign Trade.
- Every Buyer Seller Meet (BSM) in India/LAC will be followed by a press conference by the Council/Missions in the respective countries for projecting the capabilities of Indian Exporters.
- A "Made in India" show should be preceded by BSMs and catalogue shows in the countries adjoining the country where such an exhibition is being organised.

- The services of the ITPO office at Sao Paulo will be utilized for trade information in LAC.
- Each EPC may fix an indicative export target for the LAC region.
- The LAC region is to be explored as a centre for investments for export promotion.
- EPCs may source trade analysis from NCTI.

## ASSISTANCE TO EXPORT PROMOTION COUNCILS (EPCS)

- Export Promotion Councils (EPCs) are autonomous in administrative matters and no financial assistance is provided to them from MDA for administrative expenditure (non-code). The EPCs can, however, be considered for assistance from MDA in modernization, computerization for data collection, analysis, dissemination and to reduce recurring administrative expenses by cutting down identified surplus manpower through Voluntary Retirement Scheme so that they can provide efficient, online and cost effective better services to the trade etc.,
- EPCs are required to send their detailed annual action plan to F&MDA Division six months in advance. The activities approved in the annual meetings with each EPC well before the start of the financial year shall only be financed from MDA funds. EPCs shall have to utilise the MDA funds in a financial year for purposes for which these are sanctioned. Earmarked grant for the financial year but not claimed within the year or wherein complete information has not been provided to facilitate its release, would lapse and shall not be carried over to the next financial year.
- EPCs shall have to furnish detailed accounts activity -wise for each approved code activity certified by a Chartered Accountant and the utilization certificate for the funds released in a financial year by 30th September of the succeeding financial year positively.
- The EPCs shall plan development and export promotion activities in overseas markets for export promotion of

particular products, based on the market surveys/the findings of the desktop studies/findings of the strategy papers etc., to penetrate into new potential markets and to consolidate in the already explored export markets. Eligible activities shall be marketing studies; trade delegations to potential markets, organizing participation in the important trade fairs/exhibitions in the focus markets associated with BSMs, focused publicity for the event etc.

- Role of the EPCs shall be to diversify the export promotion activities to new emerging potential markets wherein the participation by the Indian companies is yet to be established. The trade fairs/exhibitions organized and participated by the EPCs on three or more occasions shall be left to the exporters for participation individually. For such established trade fairs, EPC shall organize booking of the space/stalls for its members based on the pre-accessed requirement, construction/furnishing of stalls, publicity for the event etc. Member exporters of the council shall participate individually in the space/stall allotted to them by the EPC or booked by them directly with the event organizers. MDA assistance to the EPC shall be available for a particular fair upto a maximum of three participations and thereafter, participation in such established fairs shall be on self-financing basis.
- Export Promotion Councils with the prior approval of the E&MDA Division, based on the recommendations of the concerned Commodity Division(s) of the Department of Commerce/Ministry of Textiles can undertake promotional & export development activities abroad and within India with assistance from MDA to stimulate and diversify the exports of Indian products and commodities as follows.

**PROMOTIONAL ACTIVITIES OUTSIDE INDIA**

- Market Studies/Survey(s)-EPCs as part of their annual MDA allocation can take up market studies/surveys as promotional activity on 60% funding from MDA and the remaining 40% shall be met by the councils from contributions by its members, trade etc.

- The exporters participating in EPC sponsored trade delegations and fairs/exhibitions/buyer cum seller meets etc. abroad shall receive the MDA assistance on reimbursement basis on scales as applicable while participating as individual exporters in sale cum study tour and participation in fair/exhibition respectively. However, recognized export/trading house(s) participating in such activities can claim MDA assistance through the concerned Export Promotion Council for a combined participation and effective presentation to promote brand image of the country.
- One official of the EPC (subject to an upper ceiling of two visits in one financial year by individual official) can accompany EPC sponsored trade delegation/organized participation in trade fair/exhibition followed by BSM. His air travel cost in economy excursion class, per diem allowance as notified by MEA for Government officials on duty abroad, hotel stay in mission approved hotels etc. on scales as applicable to equivalent Government officials on duty abroad and incidental/contingent expenses @ Rs.100 per night stay, would only be permissible on 100% basis from MDA. This would, however, be subject to the condition that a minimum of five exporters participate in such events. In rare circumstances, the Joint Secretary of the concerned commodity division can relax the condition of a maximum of two visits by an individual official in a financial year.
- Per Diem allowance, hotel charges etc. would not be permissible from MDA funds to exporters/elected office bearers of the EPCs etc. travelling abroad.
- Regarding other common promotional expenditure in EPC sponsored export promotion activities abroad like Council's central stall, entertainment, interpreter's expenses, expenses of conducting buyer seller meet, seminar, audio-visual presentation, publicity etc., 60% of the total approved cost would be met from MDA and the remaining 40% shall be met by the EPC etc. through contributions from the participants, members, trade etc.

Total expenses on entertainment upto a maximum of US$ 500 per EPC sponsored activity would be eligible for MDA assistance in events where the trade delegation/participation is led by the Chairman of the concerned EPC and US$ 250 wherein it is led by the Vice chairman, Executive Director and Additional Executive Director of the concerned EPC.

## DEVELOPMENT AND PROMOTIONAL ACTIVITIES WITHIN INDIA

The following type of development and export promotional activities can be undertaken by the EPCs within India with the prior approval of the E&MDA Division on the recommendations of the concerned commodity division(s) of the Department of Commerce/Ministry of Textiles:

- Organising seminars, workshops etc. (common expenditure only), on quality upgradation, awareness creation etc., with focus on export promotion.
- Publicity material and common expenses in organizing important fairs, exhibitions with main thrust on export promotion in the initial stages of organizing particular fair.
- Research and product development for diversification and stimulating export growth.
- Publications for issue within the country/abroad including journals, directories, pamphlets, product catalogue etc. subject to the condition to make the regular publications self-financing to the extent possible and assistance shall be calculated on the net expenditure after taking into account the revenue from sales and advertisements.
- Films, CD Rom etc., for collective publicity etc.

MDA assistance shall be limited to 60% of the total approved cost and the remaining has to be met by the EPCs from the contributions from participants, members, trade etc:

**Salient Promotional Initiatives under the Foreign Trade Policy 2004-09**

The Foreign Trade Policy 2004-09 and the subsequent Annual Supplements in 2005 and 2006 have all re-emphasized the significance of exports and have suggested concrete *measures to promote exports* as an integral part of the country's economic growth strategy. The policy aims to double India's share of global merchandise trade by 2009 and to make exports an effective instrument of economic growth and employment generation. The *key strategies adopted in the policy to boost exports* include:

- Simplification of procedures.
- Reduction in transaction cost.
- Neutralization of incidence of all levies and duties on inputs used for export.
- Facilitating development of India as a global hub for manufacturing, trading and services.
- Identifying and nurturing special focus areas like agriculture, handlooms, handicraft, gems and jewellery and leather, footwear etc.
- Export promotion schemes like "Vishesh Krishi Upaj Yojna' and 'Served from India' scheme to accelerate the growth of agriculture and the introduction of service exports.

There are strong indications of further smoothening of the road for exporters from India. One can safely say that the policy-makers of the nation are quite alert to respond to the challenges thrown by globalisation under the WTO regime.

The new and modified promotional initiatives aim at realizing the full potential of India as a centre of excellence for the global customer. The *new initiatives under the policy* are:

- Vishesh Krishi and Gram Udyog Yojana
- Assistance to States for Infrastructure Development of Exports
- Market Access Initiative
- Marketing Development Assistance

- Towns of Export Excellence
- Brand Promotion and Quality
- Upgradation of Test Houses
- Star Export Houses
- Services Exports
- Served from India Scheme

## VISHESH KRISHI AND GRAM UDYOG YOJANA

Vishesh Krishi Upaj Yojana (Special Agricultural Produce Scheme) has been renamed as Vishesh Krishi and Gram Udyog Yojana to induce the export of village and cottage industry products by awarding duty free scrip @ 5% of FOB value of exports under the expanded version. The new scheme covers export of fruits, vegetables, flowers, minor forest produce, dairy/poultry and their value added products, and Gram Udyog products.

A built-in incentive has been introduced under this scheme for exporters utilising domestic raw material for export production. Such exports would now get additional benefits under the Vishesh Krishi and Gram Udyog Yojana @ 1.5% of FOB value of exports, compared to those who use imported agricultural inputs that avail of benefits at a reduced rate of 3.5%. This has been done with the aim of encouraging the use of indigenous inputs for agricultural exports and to help the farming community.

The objective of the scheme is to promote export of fruits, vegetables, flowers, minor forest produce, and their value added products, by incentivising exporters of such products.

## ASSISTANCE TO STATES FOR INFRASTRUCTURE DEVELOPMENT OF EXPORTS (ASIDE)

To encourage state governments to participate in promoting exports from their respective states the Department of Commerce has formulated a scheme called ASIDE. Department of Commerce has made suitable provision in its annual plan for allocation of funds to the states on the twin criteria of gross exports and the rate of growth of exports.

The states shall utilize this amount for the following purpose(s):

- Developing infrastructure such as roads connecting production centres with ports
- Setting up of Inland Container Deports and Container Freight Stations
- Creation of new state level export promotion industrial parks/zones
- Augmenting common facilities in existing zones
- Equity participation in infrastructure projects.
- Development of minor ports and jetties
- Assistance in setting up of common effluent treatment facilities
- Stabilizing power supply
- Any other activity as may be notified by Department of Commerce from time to time.

## MARKET ACCESS INITIATIVE (MAI)

The Market Access Initiative (MAI) scheme provides financial assistance for medium-term export promotion efforts with a sharp focus on a country and product. The financial assistance is available for Export Promotion Councils, Industry and Trade associations, Agencies of state governments, Indian Commercial Missions abroad and other eligible entities as may be notified from time to time.

Activities that can be funded under the scheme include:

- Market studies
- Setting up of showrooms/warehousing facilities
- Sales promotion campaigns
- International departmental stores
- Publicity campaigns
- Participation in international trade fairs
- Brand promotions
- Registration charges for pharmaceuticals and testing charges for engineering products.

## MARKETING DEVELOPMENT ASSISTANCE (MDA)

The Marketing Development Assistance (MDA) Scheme provides financial assistance for a range of export promotion activities implemented by export promotion councils, industry and trade associations on a regular basis every year. The financial assistance under MDA is available for exports with annual export turnover of upto Rs.5 crores.

## TOWNS OF EXPORT EXCELLENCE

A number of towns in specific geographical locations have emerged as dynamic industrial clusters contributing handsomely to India's exports. It has been decided to recognize these industrial clusters to maximizing their potential and enabling them to move higher in the value chain as they tap new markets.

Selected towns producing goods of Rs. 1000 crores or more have been notified as Towns of Exports Excellence on the basis of their potential for growth in exports. However, for the Towns of Export Excellence in the Handloom, Handicraft, Agriculture and Fisheries sectors, the threshold limit would be Rs. 250 crores.

These recognized units wili be able to access funds under the Market Access Initiative scheme for creating focused technological services. Further, such areas will be accorded priority for assistance for rectifying identified critical infrastructure gaps from the ASIDE scheme.

## BRAND PROMOTION AND QUALITY

The policy is committed to encourage manufacturers and exporters to attain internationally accepted standards of quality for their products. Towards this end, the Central Government will extend support and assistance to trade and industry to launch a nationwide programme on quality awareness and to promote the concept of total quality management.

## UPGRADATION OF TEST HOUSES

The Central Government will assist in the modernization and upgradation of test houses and laboratories in order to bring them at par with international standards.

## STAR EXPORT HOUSES

Under the current foreign trade policy, Merchant as well as Manufacturer Exporters, Service Providers, Export Oriented Units (EOUs) and Units located in Special Economic Zones (SEZs) Agri Export Zones (AEZs), Electronic Hardware Technology Parks (EHTPs), Software Technology Parks (STPs) and Bio Technology Parks (BTPs) are eligible for applying for status as Star Export Houses.

The categorization of applicants is based on his total FOB/ FOR export performance during the current plus the previous three years as follows:

| *Category* | *Performance (in Rupees)* |
|---|---|
| One Star Export House | 15 crores |
| Two Star Export House | 100 crores |
| Three Star Export House | 500 crores |
| Four Star Export House | 1500 crores |
| Five Star Export House | 5000 crores |

The following special privileges are available to Star Export Houses:

- They are allowed licence/certificate/permissions and Customs clearances for both imports and exports on self-declaration basis.
- Fixation of Input-Output norms on priority within 60 days.
- They are allowed exemption from compulsory negotiation of documents through banks.
- 100% retention of foreign exchange in EEFC account.
- They are permitted enhancement in normal repatriation period from 180 days to 360 days.
- They are entitled for consideration under the Target plus Scheme.
- They enjoy exemption from furnishing of Bank Guarantee in Schemes under the foreign trade policy.

## SERVICES EXPORT

Service exporters must register themselves with the Federation of Indian Exporters Organisation. However, software exporters shall register themselves with Electronic and Software Export Promotion Council. Services include all the 161 tradable services covered under the General Agreement on Trade in Service (GATS), where payment for such services is received in free foreign exchange.

With a view to offer proper direction, guidance and encouragement to the services sector, an exclusive Export Promotion Council for Services shall be set up. The Council will offer the following facilities:

- Map opportunities for key services in key markets and develop strategic market access programmes for each component of the matrix.
- Co-ordinate with sectoral players in undertaking intensive brand building and marketing programmes in target markets.
- Make necessary interventions with regard to policies, procedures and bilateral/multilateral issues, in co-ordination with recognized nodal bodies of the services industry.

## SERVED FROM INDIA SCHEME

Service export to be given acceleration such that a formidable 'Served from India' brand gets recognized and respected across the globe. All service providers having a total foreign exchange earning of at least Rs.10lakhs in the preceding or current financial year shall be eligible to qualify for a duty credit entitlement. For individual service exporters, the eligibility will be total foreign exchange earning of Rs.5 lakhs in the preceding financial year.

Service exports in Indian rupees, which are otherwise considered as having been paid for in free foreign exchange by RBI, have now been allowed to qualify for benefits under the Served from India Scheme. In addition, the foreign exchange earned through International Credit Cards and other instruments as permitted by the RBI for rendering of service by the service providers shall be taken into account for the purposes of computation of entitlement under the scheme.

## WTO COMPATIBILITY OF INDIA'S EXPORT PROMOTION MEASURES

The various export promotion and incentive schemes of the Government of India are under the WTO scanner as these falls under the purview of the WTO Agreement on Subsidies and Countervailing Measures (ASCM). Countervailing measures mean duties imposed to offset subsidies offered. The WTO Agreement on Subsidies and Countervailing Measures disciplines the use of subsidies, and regulates the actions that countries can take to counter the effects of subsidies. The table presented below summarises the position on all the export incentives available in India with respect to the ASCM.

As is evident, a majority of the schemes are countervailable. The need of the hour therefore, is to work on bringing out non-countervailable export incentive schemes. India needs to prepare itself much better to take on the impending challenges of the WTO.

**Status of Incentives Under WTO**

| *Export-Incentive Schemes* | *Status within the SCM Agreement* |
|---|---|
| Advance licence | Non-countervailable |
| Duty-free replenishment certificate | May be countervailable |
| EOUs/EPZs/EHTPs/STPs | Countervailable |
| SEZs | Can be made non-countervailable |
| Export promotion capital goods scheme | Countervailable |
| Duty-entitlement passbook scheme | Countervailable |
| Duty-drawback schemes· | |
| • All industry rates· | Countervailable |
| • Branded rates | Non-countervailable |
| Income-tax exemptions (80HHC, 10A, 10B) | Countervailable |
| Loan guarantees | Countervailable |
| Export Credit· | |
| • Below benchmark rates· | Countervailable |
| • Above benchmark rates | Non-countervailable |
| Export credit guarantee and insurance | Can be make non-countervailable |

## SPECIAL FOCUS INITIATIVES TO PROMOTE EXPORTS

### Special Focus

With a view to doubling our percentage share of global trade within 5 years and expanding employment opportunities, especially in semi urban and rural areas, certain special focus initiatives have been identified for the agriculture, handlooms, handicraft, gems & jewellery, leather and marine sectors. Government of India shall make concerted efforts to promote exports in these sectors by specific sectoral strategies that shall be notified from time to time.

### New Sectoral Initiatives

Further Sectoral Initiatives in other sectors will also be announced from time to time. For the present, the thrust sectors indicated below shall be extended the following facilities:

*Agriculture and Village Industry*

- A new scheme called the Vishesh Krishi and Gram Udyog Yojana (Special Agricultural and Village Industry Scheme) for promoting export of fruits, Vegetables, Flowers, Minor Forest produce, Dairy, Poultry and their value added products and Gram Udyog products has been introduced.
- Funds shall be earmarked under ASIDE for development of Agri Export Zones (AEZ)
- Capital goods imported under EPCG shall be permitted to be installed anywhere in the AEZ.
- Import of restricted items, such as panels, shall be allowed under the various export promotion schemes.
- Import of inputs such as pesticides shall be permitted under the Advance Authorization for agro exports.
- New towns of export excellence with a threshold limit of Rs. 250 crores shall be notified.

*Handlooms*

- Specific funds would be earmarked under MAI/ MDA Scheme for promoting handloom exports.

- Duty free import entitlement of specified trimmings and embellishments shall be 5% of FOB value of exports during the previous financial year.
- Duty free import entitlement of hand knotted carpet samples shall be 1% of FOB value of exports during the previous financial year.
- Duty free import of old pieces of hand knotted carpets on consignment basis for re-export after repair shall be permitted.
- New towns of export excellence with a threshold limit of Rs. 250 crores shall be notified.
- Government has decided to develop a trade mark for Handloom on lines similar to 'Woolmark' and 'Silkmark'. This will enable handloom products to develop a niche market with a distinct identity.

*Handicrafts*

- New Handicraft SEZs shall be established which would procure products from the cottage sector and do the finishing for exports.
- Duty free import entitlement of trimmings and embellishments shall be 5% of the FOB value of exports during the previous financial year.
- The Handicraft Export Promotion Council shall be authorized to import trimmings, embellishments and consumables on behalf of those exporters for whom directly importing may not be viable.
- Specific funds would be earmarked under MAI & MDA Schemes for promoting Handicraft exports.
- CVD is exempted on duty free import of trimmings, embellishments and consumables.
- New towns of export excellence with a reduced threshold limit of Rs. 250 crores shall be notified.

*Gems & Jewellery*

- Import of gold of 8kg and above shall be allowed under the replenishment scheme subject to the import being accompanied by an Assay Certificate specifying the purity, weight and alloy content.

- Duty free import entitlement of consumables for metals other than Gold, Platinum shall be 2% of FOB value of exports during the previous financial year.
- Duty free import entitlement of commercial samples shall be Rs. 300,000.
- Duty free re-import entitlement for rejected jewellery shall be 2% of the FOB value of exports
- Cutting and polishing of gems and jewellery, shall be treated as manufacturing for the purposes of exemption under Section 10A of the Income Tax Act.

*Leather and Footwear*

- Duty free import entitlement of specified items shall be 5% of FOB value of exports during the preceding financial year.
- The duty free entitlement for the import of trimmings, embellishments and footwear
- Components for footwear (leather as well as synthetic), gloves, travel bags and handbags shall be 3% of FOB value of exports of the previous financial year. The entitlement shall also cover packing material, such as printed and non printed shoeboxes, small cartons made of wood, tin or plastic materials for packing footwear.
- Machinery and equipment for Effluent Treatment Plants shall be exempt from basic customs duty.
- Re-export of unsuitable imported materials such as raw hides & skins and wet blue leathers is permitted.
- CVD is exempted on lining and interlining material notified at S.No 168 of Customs Notification No 21/2002 dated 01.03.2002.
- CVD is exempted on raw, tanned and dressed fur skins falling under Chapter 43 of ITC (HS).

## CONCLUSION

This paper focused on the role and functions of Export Promotion Councils in India. There are more than 20 such agencies working in different areas for promotion of exports in India. Each council/agency is responsible for the promotion of a particular group of products, projects and services.

This paper also covered the various special export promotion incentives under the Foreign Trade Policy, 2004-09 including the latest changes announced in the Annual Supplement 2006-07 to the FTP. All these schemes aim to double India's share of global merchandise trade by 2009 and to make exports an effective instrument of economic growth and employment generation. WTO compatibility of various export promotion schemes was analysed. The analysis revealed that a majority of the Indian export promotion schemes are counterv ailable. The need of the hour, therefore, is to work on bringing out non-countervailable export incentive schemes. India needs to prepare itself much better to take on the impending challenges of the WTO.

## REFERENCES

Agrawal, Raj (2005), *International Trade*, Excel Books, New Delhi.

Arvind (2008), *India: The Emerging Giant*, Oxford University Press.

*http://commerce.nic.in/aboutus/aboutus_autonomousbodies.asp#b1*

*http://commerce.nic.in/flac/flac10.htm*

*http://cyberjournalist.org.in/linkst.html*

*http://dgft.gov.in*

*http://inhome.rediff.com/money/2007/may/29export.htm*

*http://www.eepcindia.com/export-statistics.asp*

*http://www.eximpolicy.info/chapters/general-provisions-regarding-imports.html*

*http://www.eximpolicy.info/chapters/promotional-measures.html*

*http://www.indiacatalog.com/web_directory/exim/1111.html*

*http://www.mumbaispace.com/business/exportpromotioncouncils.html*

*http://www.tata.com/tata_sons/articles 20020924 wto(1).html.*

Jeevanandam C. (2004), *Foreign Exchange-Practice, Concepts & Control*, Sultan Chand & Sons, New Delhi.

Kumar, Aseem (2007), *Export and Import Management*, Excel Books, New Delhi.

Kumar, Rajesh, & Anand Sethi (2005), *Doing Business in India*, Palgrave Macmillan, New Delhi.

Kumar, Rajiv (2008), s*India's Liberalisation Experience: Hostage to the WTO?* Sage Publications Pvt. Ltd, New Delhi.

Sankaran S. (2007), *International Trade*, Margham Publications, Chennai.

*www.apeda.com*

*www.commin.nic.in*

*www.eepc.gov.in*

*www.indiacoffee.org*

*www.indianexportregister.com*

*www.mpeda.com*

*www.wto.org*

# APPENDICES

## LIST OF EXPORT PROMOTION COUNCILS AND COMMODITY BOARDS

***Export Promotion Councils under Department of Commerce***

1. **ENGINEERING EXPORT PROMOTION COUNCIL**
   Address :Vanijya Bhawan, 1st Floor
   International Trade Facilitation Centre
   1/1, Wood Street, Kolkata – 700 016
   Tel.: 91-33-22890651/52, Fax: 91-33-22890654
   E-mail: eepcho@eth.net
   *Website: http://www.eepcindia.org or http://www.eepcindia.com*

2. **PROJECT EXPORTS PROMOTION COUNCIL OF INDIA**
   Address : H-118,Himalaya House,11th Floor,23,Kasturba Gandhi Marg, New Delhi-110 001
   Tel. : (91)11-23722425/23350367, Fax : (91)11-23312936
   *E-Mail : info@projectexports.com*
   *Website : - http://www.projectexports.com/*

3. **BASIC CHEMICALS, PHARMACEUTICALS AND COSMETICS EXPORT PROMOTION COUNCIL**
   Address : Jhansi Castle, 4th floor, 7-Cooperage Road, Mumbai-400 039
   Tel. : (91)22-2021288/2021330/2026549, Fax : (91)22-2026684
   *Website: http://www.chemexcil.gov.in*

4. **CHEMICALS & ALLIED PRODUCTS EXPORT PROMOTION COUNCIL**
   Address: World Trade Centre, 14/IB, Ezra Street, Kolkata-700 001.
   Tel. : (91)33-22215652/22358217/8219, Fax : (91)33-22215657
   *Website: http://www.capexil.com*

5. **COUNCIL FOR LEATHER EXPORTS**
   Address : 3rd floor, CMDA Tower-2 Gandhi Irwin Bridge Road, Egmore,Chennai-600 008
   Tel. : (91)44-28594367-71(5 lines)
   Fax : (91)44-28594363/64, E-Mail : cle@vsnl.com
   *Website : http://www.leatherindia.org*

6. **SPORTS GOODS EXPORT PROMOTION COUNCIL**
   Address: 1-E/6, Swami Ram Tirth Nagar, Jhandewalan Extn. New Delhi-100 055
   Tel. : (91)11-23525695-23516183
   Fax : (91)11-23632147
   *E-Mail : sgepc@vsnl.com*
   *Website http://www.sportsgoodsindia.org*

7. **GEM & JEWELLERY EXPOR PROMOTION COUNCIL**
   Address: Diamond Bazar, 5th floor,
   391-A, Dr.D.Bhadkamkar Marg, Mumbai-400 004
   Tel. : (91)22-23821801/23821806
   Fax : (91)22-23808752/23804958
   *Website: http://gjepc.org*

8. **SHELLAC & FOREST PRODUCTS EXPORT PROMOTION COUNCIL**
   Address: "Vanijya Bhawan" International Trade Facilitation Centre,1/1 Wood Street, 2nd Floor, Kolkata-700016
   Tel. : (91)33-22834417,22834697, 22834698
   Fax : (91)33-22834699
   *Website: http://www.shellacepc.com*

9. **CASHEW EXPORT PROMOTION COUNCIL**
   Address : Post Box No.1709,Chittor Road, Ernakulam South., Cochin-682 016
   Tel. : (91)484-351973/361459
   Fax : (91)484-370973
   *Website: http://www.cashewindia.org*

10. **PLASTICS EXPORT PROMOTION COUNCIL**
    Address : Crystal Tower, Crystal Co-operative Housing Society(Ltd.), Gundwali Road No. 3, Offsin M.V.Road, Andheri (East) Mumbai-400 005
    Tel. : (91)22-26833951/52, Fax : (91)22-26833953/4057
    *E-Mail : plexcouncil@vsnl.com*
    *Website: http://www.plexcon.org*

11. **EXPORT PROMOTION COUNCIL FOR EOUS & SEZ UNITS**
    705, Bhikaji Cama Bhawan,
    Bhikaji Cama Place, New Delhi- 11 0066
    Tel. : (91)11-26167042/5805/6185 Fax : (91)11-26165538
    *E-Mail : epces@vsnl.net*
    *Website: http://eouindia.com*

12. **PHARMACEUTICAL EXPORT PROMOTION COUNCIL**
101, Aditya Trade Center Ameerpet,
Hyderabad - 500038
Tel : (91)40-23735462/66
Fax: (91)40-23735464
*E-Mail : info@pharmexcil.com*
*Website : www.pharmexcil.com*

***Export Promotion Councils under Ministry of Textiles***

1. **APPAREL EXPORT PROMOTION COUNCIL**
Address: NBCC Towers,15 Bhikaji Cama Place,
New Delhi-110 066.
Tel. : (91) 11-26183351/26169393/94/56/57
Fax : (91) 11-26188584/26188300
E-Mail : *hochrm@nda.vsnl.net.in*
*Website* : http://www.aepc.com

2. **CARPET EXPORT PROMOTION COUNCIL**
Address : 101-A/1, Krishna Nagar, (Behind Govt. Sr. Sec. School),
Safdarjung Enclave, New Delhi 110029.
Tel. : (91) 11-26102742/26101024
Fax : (91) 11-26165299
*E-Mail : cepc@nda.vsnl.net.in.*
*Website: http://www.indiancarpets.com*

3. **COTTON TEXTILE EXPORT PROMOTION COUNCIL**
Engineering Centre, 5th Floor, Mumbai - 400 004.
Tel. : (91) 22-23632910/11/12/13
Fax : (91) 22-23932914
*E-Mail : exprocil@bom3.vsnl.net.in*
*Website : http://www.texprocil.com*

4. **EXPORT PROMOTION COUNCIL FOR HANDICRAFTS**
Address: Plot No.1,Pocket 6&7,Sector-C,Local Shopping Centre,Vasant Kunj,New Delhi - 110 070.
Tel. : (91) 11-6875377/60087
Fax : (91) 11-606144
*E-Mail : epch@vsnl.com*
*Website : http://www.epcd.com*

5. **HANDLOOM EXPORT PROMOTION COUNCIL**
Address: 18, Cathedral Garden Road, Nunagambakkam, Madras 600 034.
Tel. : (91) 44-8278879/8276043
Fax : (91) 44-8271761
*E-Mail : hepccatp@vsnl.com*
*Website: http://www.hepcindia.com*

6. **INDIAN SILK EXPORT PROMOTION COUNCIL**
Address : 62, Mittal Chambers, 6th Floor, Nariman Point, Mumbai - 400 021.
Tel. : (91) 22-202049113/2027662/2025866,
Fax : (91) 22-2874606
*E-Mail : isepc@bom2.vsnl.net.in*
*Website: http://www.silkepc.com*

7. **POWERLOOM DEVELOPMENT & EXPORT PROMOTION COUNCIL**
Address : 16, Ist Floor, Mittal Chambers, Nariman Point, Mumbai -400 021.
Tel. : (91) 22-2846518/19
Fax : (91) 22-2846517
*E-Mail: pdexcil.pdepc@gems.vsnl.net.in*
*Website: http://www.pdexcil.org*

8. **SYNTHETIC & RAYON TEXTILE EXPORT PROMOTION COUNCIL**
Address : Resham Bhavan,
78, Veer Nariman Point Road, Mumbai - 400 020.
Tel. : (91) 22-22048797/22048690
Fax : (91) 22-22048358
*E-Mail srtepc@vsnl.com*
*Website: http://www.synthetictextiles.org*

9. **WOOL & WOOLENS EXPORT PROMOTION COUNCIL**
Address : 906, New Delhi House,
27, Barakhamnba Road, New Delhi - 110 001.
Tel. : (91) 11-23315512/23315205
Fax : (91) 11-23730182
*E-Mail : wwepc@bol.net.in*
*Website : http://www.wwepcindia.com*

***Commodity Boards under Department of Commerce***

1. **RUBBER BOARD**
   Contact Person: Chairman
   Address : Sub-Jail Road, P.B.No.1122,
   Kottayam, Kerala 686002
   Tel. : (91) 481-571231, 571232, 571235, 571236, 571361
   Fax : (91) 481-571380
   *E-mail : rbktm@ker.nic.in, rrii@vsnl.com*
   *Website : http:/ / rubberboard.org.in/*

2. **COFFEE BOARD**
   Contact Person : Chairman
   Address : 1- Dr.Ambedkar Veedhi, Bangalore - 560001
   Tel. : (91) 80-257890
   *Fax : (91) 80-2255557*
   *Website : http:/ / www.indiacoffee.org/*

3. **TEA BOARD**
   Contact Person : Chairman
   Address : 14, BTM Sarani, Brabourne Road,
   P.B.No.2172, Kolkata - 700001
   Tel. : (91)33-2251411
   Fax : (91)33-2251417
   *Website : http:/ / www.indiateaportal.com*

4. **TOBACCO BOARD**
   Contact Person : Chairman
   Address : P.B.No.322, G.T.Road, Guntur - 522004
   Tel. : (91) 0863-2358399, 2358499, 2327550, 2358531, 2358532, 2327555, 2327554, 2327556
   Fax : (91) 0863-2354232
   *E-mail : info@indiantobacco.com*
   *Website : http:/ / www.indiantobacco.com/*

5. **SPICES BOARD**
   Contact Person : Chairman
   Address: Sugandha Bhavan,
   P.B.No.2277, Palarivattom.P.O., Cochin - 682025
   Tel. : (91) 484-2333610 to 2333616 (7 Lines) & 2348417, (91) 484-2331429/ 2334429
   *E-mail : spicesboard@vsnl.com, mail@indianspices.com*
   *Website : http:/ / www.indianspices.com*

**Marine Products Export Development Authority, Cochin**
Address : MPEDA House, Panampilly Avenue,
COCHIN-682016.
Telephone : (91)484-311971
Fax : (91)484-313361.
*Web Site : http://www.mpeda.com*

**Agricultural and processed Food Products Export Development Authority, New Delhi**
Address : 3rd Floor, NCUI Building,
3 Siri Institutional Area, August Kranti Marg,
Hauz Khas, NEW DELHI-110016.
Telephone : (91)11- 26513204, 26514572, 26513219
Fax : (91)11- 26534870
*Email : headq@apeda.com*
*Web Site : http://www.apeda.com*

and other continue to suffer because of the quality problems. Poor quality/inadequacy of inputs, technology and facilities affect the quality. Carelessness or lacks of commitment on the part of the exporters are also responsible. Adulteration and duping are also not uncommon. There is a general impression that a proper export culture is lacking in India.

**Unreliability**

Besides quality, Indian exporters have been regarded as unreliable on certain other factors. As the Tan don Committee has observed, a very important black mark on the Indian exporters is reneging–a term used in the U.S.A to refer to going back on a contract and refusing to fulfill it on its original terms.

Indian exporters have been regarded as unreliable also because of their inability to provide prompt after-sale-service.

**Supply Problems**

A serious drawback of the Indian export sector is its inability to provide continuous and smooth supply in adequate quantities in respect of several products. The problem is that 'much of the exporting is the result of the residual approach rather than conscious effort of producing for export. The tendency for exporting what we produce rather than producing for export still continues to characterise the export behavior.

**Faceless Presence**

Although India is an important supplier of several commodities in foreign markets, her presence in these markets is faceless in the sense that the consumers do not know that these commodities are Indian.

**Infrastructure Bottlenecks**

The following observation made by the national convention on exports organized by the federation of Indian chamber of commerce and industry is indeed a recapitulation of the indisputably held view of the infrastructure situation of India. infrastructural shortages such as energy shortages, inadequate and unreliable transport and communication facilities hinder the growth in exports .power shortages and breakdown s disrupt production schedules, increase cost and adversely affect timely shipments .the conventional size of the country necessitates that the inland haulage of exports cargo as also its shipments. The conventional size of the country necessitates at reasonable cost. exports also suffer for want of efficient and economic communication facilities .indeed ,with advancement in communication and computer technologies, the very complexion of international trading has changed with more and more of cargo documentation and banking transaction getting into the electronic media .the Indian exporter ,however has to communicate through inefficient and relatively outdated telecommunication network.

Improving the transportation system, including the expansion and modernization of the port facilities, rationalization of the charges, improving the procedural system etc. Are very much essential for the Indian scenario causing heavy damages to export development.

**Structural weakness**

A major handicap of the Indian export sector is its structural weakness .two of the important factors responsible for this ,viz., low efficiency and productivity in resources use and poor technology have already been described .another very important factor is the absence of a system approach to the process of management ,marketing ,information ,planning and decision making.

It is important to note that "India's exports do not pick up in periods of boom conditions .on the other hand, India is quick to pick up sluggishness in exports in the response to sluggishness in world trade much more quickly than other exporters. This asymmetry in the response of the export sector as a whole.

**Uncertainties, procedural complexities and institutional rigidities**

One of the defects of our trade policy regime has been the uncertainty about future policies, incentive scheme etc. there is a general feeling that there are too many controls and overlapping of policies but also "the principle of Indian policy is to elaborate rules to them, which are not only detailed and specific, but also subject to wide discretion." These are indicative of the structural weakness of the institutional system in India.

**Inadequacy of Trade Information System**

An efficient trade information system is essential for success in the dynamic global market but ,"our marketing infrastructure as well as marketing techniques are neither effective nor efficient .we do not have any machinery to keep prompt track of business information overseas, as done by JETRO in Japan, KOTRA in Korea, CETDC in Hong Kong and STDB in Singapore with wide network of offices abroad these organisation have evolved an efficient system which help them to get information pertaining to tenders and the like much before these are released officially in India, we get these information, at times, after the expiry date. India has, no doubt a plethora of organisation– governmental, semi–governmental as also non-governmental– engaged in this task in one way or other.

**Export License**

The exports of some items are banned and of some items controlled by means of licences, through many items are permitted to be exported freely. Needless to say that exporter should make sure that the item sought to be exported is not one which falls in the banned list. If the item to be exported requires a licence, it is necessary to obtain it before finalizing the contract.

**Packing and marking**

Once the goods are ready, they are packed and marked properly. If the buyer has given instruction about packing and marking, they should be followed accordingly if there are no such instructions, it should be ensured that the packing and marking are of the standards recommended or specified the bureau of Indian standards has prescribed packing standards for certain items. The British standard packing code published by the British standard institution, and the exporter's encyclopedia published in the USA, give detailed packing instruction shipping companies also give certain packing instruction, especially for highly dangerous goods.

The exporter should take meticulous case in respect of marking also. The marking should include the shipping marks of the consignee, the port of destination, measurements, the country of origin and any other matter the buyer specified. the international cargo handling co-ordination association has, for the use of exporters and carriers, made a number of recommendation for the marking of goods carried by ocean-going vessels. The international trade forum has set out important rules of goods marking procedures which should be followed by exporters.

**Customs formalities**

Goods may be shipped out of India after customs clearance has been obtained. For this purpose, the exporter (or the clearing and forwarding agent of the exporters) should present the following documents to the customs authorities:

(i) Shipping bill.

(ii) Declaration regarding truth of statement made in the shipping bill.

(iii) Invoice.

(iv) GR form

(v) Export licence (wherever required).

(vi) Quality control inspection certificates (wherever required).

(vii) Original contract contract wherever available or correspondence, leading to contract.

(viii) Contract registration certificate (wherever applicable).

(ix) Letter of credit (wherever applicable).

(x) Packing list.

(xi) AR-4 form.

(xii) Any other documents.

The customs authorized scrutinize the shipping bill and other requisite documents, and if, prima facia, satisfied, they pass it for export, subject to a physical examination by the dock or air transit staff of the custom .the shipping bill passed by the export department has to be presented to the cargo supervisor or the or the steamship company or the shed manager, who is the port official, for permission to bring the cargo for export.

A facility is available for customs checking of the goods at the factory. Applications for this purpose should be made to the Assistant Collector of Customs. The Customs Appraiser will go to the factory to check the consignment: and after checking it, he seals the packages. However, the preventive officer on board the ship has also the right to inspect the sealed packages before they are actually loaded on the ship: but when he is satisfied about the bonafides of the party, he does not open the sealed packages nor check them again. This process of obtaining custom clearance is a big problem to the exporters.

## CONCLUSION

Problems in accessing funds for the purpose of day-to-day business operations (working capital) were the leading issue facing the export sector. High transaction costs, high interest rate, and lack of security were also identified as problems currently faced by the exporters. In addition to these financial issues, exporters identified high ports, freights and utility charges, lack of information on export markets/products and lack of investment incentives as important issues that they face. To confirm that most exporters were unaware of the Export Finance Facility. Apart from the lack of public awareness, the high level of domestic liquidity has been a major hurdle to the success of the EFF. Some exporters had also indicated that there is no need for this facility as they are able to obtain finance from alternative means (such as self finance or bank overdraft facility). Moreover, there is a demand for an export credit insurance facility. However, it is uncertain whether the exporters have a clear understanding of how such a facility would work. Suggestions by exporters on ways to boost exports include increasing tax and duty concessions, introduction of an export credit insurance facility and subsidizing freight and port charges may be a solution to address the problems.

19

# INITIATIVES OF EPC IN PROMOTING INDIA'S EXPORT

**M. Divya & K. M. Chinnadorai**

## INTRODUCTION

Export Promotion Councils (EPC) promotes and develops the exports of the country. Each Council is responsible for the promotion of a particular group of products, projects and services. The main role of the EPCs is to project India's image abroad as a reliable supplier of high quality goods and services. In particular, the EPCs shall encourage and monitor the observance of international standards and specifications by exporters. The EPCs shall keep abreast of the trends and opportunities in international markets for goods and services and assist their members in taking advantage of such opportunities in order to expand and diversify exports.

## FUNCTIONS OF THE EPC

- To provide commercially useful information and assistance to their members in developing and increasing their exports;
- To offer professional advice to their members in areas such as technology upgradation, quality and design improvement,

standards and specifications, product development, innovation, etc.;

- To organise visits of delegations of its members abroad to explore overseas market opportunities;
- To organise participation in trade fairs, exhibitions and buyer-seller meets in India and abroad;
- To promote interaction between the exporting community and the Government both at the Central and State levels; and
- To build a statistical base and provide data on the exports and imports of the country, exports and imports of their members, as well as other relevant international trade data.
- To attend to Child Labour issues on monitoring & registration of looms and issuance of Kaleen Labels.
- To execute the marketing assignments of UNDP Carpet Project.
- To handle management of Welfare Projects under the Child Welfare Activities.
- To make projection for future development of the industry.

## NON-PROFIT, AUTONOMOUS AND PROFESSIONAL BODIES

The EPCs are non-profit organisations registered under the Companies Act or the Societies Registration Act, as the case may be.The EPCs shall be autonomous and regulate their own affairs. However, if the Central Government frames uniform bylaws for the constitution and/or for the transaction of business for EPCs, they shall adopt the same with such modifications as Central Government may approve having regard to the special nature or functioning of such EPC. The EPCs shall be required to obtain the approval of the Central Government for participation in trade fairs, exhibitions etc and for sending sales teams/delegations abroad. The Ministry of Commerce and Industry/Ministry of Textiles of the Government of India, as the case may be, would interact with the Managing Committee of the Council concerned, twice a year, once for approving their annual plans and budget and again for a mid-year appraisal and review of their performance.

In order to give a boost and impetus to exports, it is imperative that the EPCs function as professional bodies. For this purpose, executives with a professional background in commerce, management and international marketing and having experience in government and industry should be brought into the EPCs.

## GOVERNMENT SUPPORT AND REGISTRATION CUM-MEMBERSHIP

The EPCs may be provided financial assistance by the Central Government.

An exporter may, on application, register and become a member of an Export Promotion Council. On being admitted to membership, the applicant shall be granted forthwith Registration-cum- Membership Certificate (RCMC) of the EPC concerned, subject to such terms and conditions as may be specified in this behalf.

*Some of the Export Promotion Councils are listed below*

### Handloom Export Promotion Council (HEPC)

Handloom Export Promotion Council (HEPC) functions as a non-profit making company under section 25 of the Companies Act. The Memorandum and Articles of Association framed by the Council govern the company. It is a statutory body constituted under The Ministry of Textiles, Government of India to promote the exports of all handloom products like fabrics, home furnishings, carpets and floor coverings, etc. Constituted in the year of 1965 with 65 members and today it has a membership around 2000 spreading all over the country. The Handloom industry mainly exports fabrics, bed linen, table linen, toilet and kitchen linen, towels, curtains, cushions and pads, tapestries and upholstery's, carpets and floor coverings, etc. The HEPC functions with the main objective to provide all kind of support and guidance to the Indian Handloom exporters and the International buyers for trade promotion and international marketing. With its headquarter at Chennai and regional offices at Mumbai and New Delhi, it is administered by an Executive Committee consisting of elected representatives from the export trade, ex-officio members and nominated Government officials. Primary objectives of HEPC: Organizing participation in the fairs, exhibitions and buyer-seller meets in India and Abroad. It aims to provide guidance, consultation and support to the handloom exporters in view to promote handloom exports. Laying down standards of quality and packaging in respect of Indian Handlooms for export. It approves agents, representatives or correspondence in foreign markets for continuous reporting of prices, market preferences and reception accorded to Indian Handloom products.

### Coir Board of India

Coir Board is a statutory body established by the Government of India under a legislation enacted by the Parliament namely Coir Industry Act 1953 (45 of 1953) to promote Coir Industry in India as a whole.

*The main functions are*

(a) Promoting exports of coir yarn and coir products and carrying on propaganda for that purpose

(b) Regulating the production of husks, coir yarn and coir products under the supervision of the Central Government by registering coir spindles and looms for manufacturing coir products.

(c) Undertaking, assisting or encouraging scientific, technological and economic researches to maintain one or more research institutes

(d) Collecting statistics from manufacturers of and dealers in coir products. It can also obtain such information from the other persons related to the coir industry. The publication of statistics so collected or portions thereof or extracts therefrom

(e) Fixing grade standards and necessary inspection of coir fibre, coir yarn and coir products

(f) Improving the marketing of coconut husk, coir fibre, coir yarn and coir products in India, preventing unfair competition

(g) Setting up or assisting in the setting up of factories for the producers of coir products with the aid of power;

(h) Promoting cooperative organisation among producers of husks, coir fibre and coir yarn and manufacturers of coir products

(i) Ensuring remunerative returns to producers of husks, coir fibre and coir yarn and manufacturers of coir products

(j) Licensing of retting places and warehouses and otherwise regulating the stocking and sale of coir fibre, coir yarn and coir products both for the internal market and for exports k) Advising on all matters relating to the development of the coir industry

**The Carpet Export Promotion Council of India**

The Carpet Export Promotion Council of India (CEPC) was set up by the Government Of India in 1982 with a view to promote the exports of hand knotted carpets and other floor coverings. The council advises the government onxports promotion measures and helps the exporter's community in bringing their problems and requirements to the notice of the government. It provides expertise in many spheres both for the Indian exporters and foreign buyers. The council is a high profile body consisting of senior Trade Representatives and Government officials. It provides the necessary assistance to the Indian exporters. It identifies the markets, provides financial assistance, sponsors participation in fairs and exhibitions and also conducts publicity abroad. Regarding overseas buyers/importers, the CEPC locates the estimate suppliers and provides credibility reports on Indian exporters. It also arranges buyer-seller meets and assists in trade disputes. To eradicate the incidence of child labour from the carpet industry CEPC has adopted a label "KALEEN" This KALEEN label on carpets ensures that no child labour has been used for the production of the carpet. The exporters are required to fulfill certain prerequisites to obtain this label. They have to contribute % of the FOB value of their exports to the child welfare fund. The main objectives of adopting this label are: n Total eradication of child labour. n Welfare of the weaver community n Education for the children with mid- day meal n Medicare of the weaver families n Vocational training for the children with assured stipend.

### Apparel Export Promotion Council (AEPC)

The Apparel Export Promotion Council (AEPC) was incorporated under section 25 of the Companies Act, 1956 on 22nd February 1978. The council carries out its function as a nodal agency sponsored by the Ministry of Textiles, Govt. of India. It holds the dual responsibility of monitoring garment exports quotas and promotion of exports of readymade garments from India. AEPC acts as a catalyst for the Indian Garment Exports. It organizes the Buyer Seller Meets, garment shows with sponsoring of the Trade Delegations and offers technical advice and market briefs etc. It also provides service to its more than 35,000 registered exporter members in a specialized manner through its committees and various sub-committees. AEPC's Executive Committee functioned through its various Sub-Committees including, Quota Advisory Committee, Export Promotion Committee, Exhibition Advisory Committee, and Finance and Budget Sub Committee. It organises variety of fairs including India and International Garment Fair twice a yearat Delhi, India Knit Fair at Tripur, the knitwear capital of India, Men's Fashion Fair at Mumbai, the commercial capital of India. AEPC runs Apparel Training and Design Centres at places like Delhi, Mumbai, Tirupur, Bangalore, Chennai, Jaipur and Hyderabad. These centres impart training and thereafter even help the trained to get placed in various industries at shop-floor level to improve the efficiency and productivity of the Garment Industry. AEPC also provides rich library to its members as well as research scholars. Its grandiose project of a world class Trade Mart cum Exhibition Complex in Delhi is in the anvil. It will house exclusive showrooms of exporters as much as hundred and an auditorium plus a permanent "Exhibition Complex". The council administers the Export Entitlement Policy of the Government of India. It has also been authorized to allot quotas to exporters and issue Certificate.

**Export Promotion Council for Handicrafts**

Export Promotion Council for Handicrafts (EPCH) has been established under the Exim Policy of Govt. of India in 1986-87 and is a non-profit organisation. The organisation works under the administrative control of O/o Development Commissioner (Handicrafts), Ministry of Textiles, Govt. of India and governed by Policies of Ministry of Textiles. It is an apex body which projects India's image abroad as a reliable supplier of high quality of handicraft goods & services. It also insures various measures keeping in view of observance of international standards and specifications. The Council has created necessary infrastructure as well as marketing and information facilities, which are availed both by the member exporters and importers. The membership of the council rose from 35 in year 1985-86 to 6873 in 2002-03 EPCH Council The Council is run and managed by team of professionals headed by Executive Director. The Committee of Administration consist of eminent exporters, professionals and senior Govt. officials. The Export Promotion Council for Handicrafts has a rarest distinction of being considered as MODEL COUNCIL which is self sustaining and where all the promotional activities are self financed Indian Handicrafts & Gifts Fair Indian Handicrafts and Gifts Fair, today has become a show window of Indian handicrafts among all the leading overseas buyers need no introduction.

EPCH's are one of the leading organizations who work for the development of handicrafts industry. They are managed by govt. bodies to make it more responsible and positive. Their various objectives aims at creating positive and healthy environment for handicraft community and products in the international arena. In our EPCH section we have listed few of these bodies and provided detailed information on their functioning and role.

**Export Performance of Carpets**

| *Year* | *Value of Exports* |
|---|---|
| 2000-01 | 2315.15 (512.03) |
| 2001-02 | 2436.13 (514.07) |
| 2002-03 | 2590.26 (532.96) |
| 2003-04 | 2779.79 (614.44) |
| 2004-05 | 2583.62 (591.62) |
| 2005-06 | 3082.06 (696.53) |
| 2006-07 | 3674.86 (807.94) |

## The Gem & Jewellery Export Promotion Council

Set-up in 1966, the *GJEPC* has over the years effectively molded the scattered efforts of individual exporters to make the gem and jewellery sector a powerful engine driving India's export-led growth. This apex body of the gem & jewellery industry has played a significant role in the evolution of the Indian gem and jewellery industry to its present stature. *GJEPC* is continuously working towards creating a pool of artisans and designers trained to international standards so as to consolidate the Indian jewellery industry and establish it as a prominent global player in the jewellery segment.

With strength of 6,500 members' spread all over the country, the Council is primarily involved in introducing the Indian gem & jewellery products to the international market and promotes their exports. To achieve this, the Council provides market information to its members regarding foreign trade inquiries, trade and tariff regulations, rates of import duties, and information about jewellery fairs and exhibitions.

The role of *GJEPC* can be broadly classified under the following categories:

### *Trade Facilitator*

The Council undertakes direct promotional activities like organising joint participation in international jewellery shows, sending and hosting trade delegations, and sustained image building exercises through advertisements abroad, publications and audio-visuals.

*GJEPC* also invites countries to explore areas of co-operation in supply of rough diamonds and rough colored stones as well as offers co-operation in jewellery manufacturing. The Council regularly communicates with Indian Embassies, trade bodies and associations in various countries. And finally, *GJEPC* also organizes seminars, buyer-seller meets, symposiums.

### *Advisory Role*

A crucial area of activity of the Council has also been aiding better interaction and understanding between the trade and the government. The Council takes up relevant issues with government and agencies connected with exports and submit documents for consideration and inclusion in the Exim Policy. The Council also grants membership, registration certificates and performs other roles as per the Exim Policy.

### *Nodal Agency for Kimberly Process Certification Scheme*

*GJEPC* works closely with the Government of India and the trade to implement and oversee the Kimberly Process Certification Scheme. To that effect, the Council has been appointed as the Nodal Agency in India under the Kimberly Process Certification Scheme.

### *Training and Research*

The *Gems & Jewellery Export Promotion Council* runs a number of institutes that provide training in all aspects of manufacture and design in Mumbai, Delhi, Surat and Jaipur. These training programs are being conducted to ensure that the Indian industry achieves the highest levels of technical excellence.

### *Varied Interests*

The Council also publishes a number of brochures, statistical booklets, trade directories and a bi-monthly magazine-Solitaire International, which is distributed internationally as well as to its members. Finally, the Council has also developed its own promotional audiovisual film-'India-Your First Choice', which is dubbed in various international languages as well as screened at various trade shows.

## Analysis of Export Performance

### *Europe (including Germany & Scandinavian Countries)*

According to the statistics compiled for country wise exports from India in the year 2000-01, the share of our exports to Europe is 43.07% (Germany accounts for 24.53%, Scandinavian 4% and Rest of Europe 14.59%). Germany registered a decline of 8.3% in value term whereas the decline in Europe was only 2.9%. The reasons for decline in German Market is because of piling of stocks with German Importers. Germany is importing carpets of different quality. The share of India in terms of volume for carpets less than 350 knots is around 49% whereas it is having the share in value of only 33%. The German Market for medium and low knottage carpets (less than 350 knots) is dominated by Nepal and India. The Nepal is getting more price for similar products from India. The competitive edge is because of the status of poor country given to Nepal without payment of any duty. For Carpets above 350 knots in the German Market is being supplied mainly by Iran and India. India is having 38% share in volume whereas 21% in value. The Iran which is having 22% share in volume having 40% share in value.

The German Market for Silk Carpets is again dominated by India and China. China is having 52.3% share in volume and 42% share in value whereas India is having 33.7% share in volume but only 19% share in value. The analysis above in German Market clearly reveals that although we are having a strong grip in the market in various qualities of carpets but we are not having grip on unit value realisation. We are not getting the right price for our products because of our lack of marketing skill of the exporters. The under cutting by exporters and too much supply to one buyer without assessing the capacity of the buyer to sell is placing us in an disadvantageous position.

The Bhadohi and Mirzapur are the main supply area of carpets and floor coverings in wool to Germany and other European countries. Lack of resources to keep stock and pressure of banks for payment of interest on export credit is forcing them to sell on lower unit value realisation.

*The Suggestions for arresting the declining trend and improving the unit value realisation are:*

- Liberalized export credit both for pre-shipment and post-shipment to be made available to the manufacturers/exporters on concessional rate of interest. Govt. may also like to write to RBJ not to insist for repatriation of export proceeds within 180 days and grant extension upto 360 days in hard pressed cases.
- The rate of interest on Export Credit is very high as compared to China where the interest rate for export is only 3% to 4% and repayment is relaxable upto 12 Years.
- The Indian Exporters should also look for alternate buyer and offer products in new design stressing more on quality.
- Stress on use of Kaleen Label for restoring the confidence of the importers.
- A ware house facility to be provided to the exporters for temporary storing their consignments on refusal of payment by the buyers to avoid auctioning by the customs.
- Extensive participation in fairs & exhibition to be suggested for increasing demands particularly in Scandinavian Countries.
- Regular publicity for image building

### *USA & Canada*

According to the statistics compiled for country wise exports from India in the year 2000-01, the share of our exports to USA & Canada is 45.33% (USA accounts for 43.55% whereas Canada accounts for only 1.78%). There is an increase of 19.03% in exports to USA & Canada during the year 2000-01 compared with the figures of 1999- 2000. USA consumes around 28% of the world import of carpets & floor coverings. The major portion of import of carpets and floor coverings into USA is of knotted carpets accounting for 38% whereas other woven carpets accounts for 29.8% and tufted accounts for 27%. There is an overall increase of 19.73% in import of carpets and floor coverings into the USA. The major competitor of India in carpets & floor coverings is China followed by Pakistan, Nepal and Turkey. The imports of carpets and floor coverings is largely controlled by a group of importers based in New York. The market in the USA for carpets and floor coverings is unevenly distributed. Most of the parts in the USA are almost nonexistence markets for carpets and floor coverings. The American consumers are choose about colours and fashion dominate the sale of carpets and floor coverings into the USA. The position of Indian Carpets till 2000 was very comfortable because of embargo on import of carpets from Iran which has lifted since February, 2000.

Canada is relatively small market for carpets and floor coverings. Iran is dominating the market because of embargo in USA. India is No. 2 but the market has not grown much over the last 3 years.

*Suggestion for promoting the exports and increasing share*

Although India has a sizable portion of US Market but still there is tremendous scope for expansion of the market by exposing the products to the consumers.

Since participation in fairs & exhibition by the suppliers in US Market is not relished by the importers, it is proposed that specialized Indian Exhibition either directly or in collaboration with Importers or Departmental Stores be arranged extensively especially in South of America around Dallas and Houston and West of USA i.e. San Francisco and Seattle.

- Extensive publicity is required for generating consumer awareness.
- Ware House facility for temporary storing of goods by individual or by group of exporters.

***South East Asian Countries (including Japan and Australia)***

The South East Asian Region because of climatic conditions and economy have not developed for carpets and floor coverings. Although Japan has grown small market for carpets and floor coverings but Indian exporters have not been able to penetrate much in this market because of dominance of China and Pakistan. These countries account for only 4.2 1% of the total exports of carpets and floor coverings from India. The main competitors in these markets are China and Pakistan.

*The reasons for our exporters not penetrating much in the markets are:*

(1) Distant location and edge of competitors because of proximity in the markets;

(2) Slow moving of economy in the region;

(3) Climatic conditions.

*Suggestions*

- Freight subsidy to be provided for exports to South East Asian Countries;
- Storage facility to be provided for exporters to sell product to alternate buyers in case of refusal;
- Special emphasis to be made for promotion of carpets & floor coverings in the Region.

***Rest of the World including LAC***

The share of exports of Indian Carpets and Floor coverings to rest of the world including LAC accounts for only 7.3 9% which clearly shows that these markets remained un-explored.

Since Government of India is paying special emphasis for promotion of exports to LAC and Carpets & Floor coverings from India have huge potential for expansion the following suggestions are being made:

- To Lower down the Tariff Structure be taken up in Bilateral Trade Agreement;
- Fashion Oriented and less expensive products to be promoted i.e., Woven Durries, Chain Stitched Rugs, Woven Carpets, Tufted Carpets & Art Silk Carpets.

## CONCLUSION

Export growth depends upon competitiveness, technology and marketing, there is a large constituency of exporters who have grown up only on incentives.The Indian Industry has potential for expansion since adequate skilled manpower & raw-material is available, requirement for capital is almost negligible, Indian Products are acceptable all over the World and are at par on quality and competitive in prices. India has tremendous flexibility and adaptability. It has large range of products to offer. India can supply coverings strictly in accordance with the requirement of consumers. The only weakness is marketing and fore-sightedness of the exporters besides resources. Generally the exporters are small in comparison with our competitors thus having limited resources. Indian exporters have so far been making carpets as per orders of Buyers and have not paid much attention or priority on keeping inventory for spot sales. The trend in buying has undergone a radical change switching over to stock buying rather than placing orders.

20

# INITIATIVES OF ELECTRONICS AND COMPUTER SOFTWARE EXPORT PROMOTION COUNCIL IN INDIA'S ICT TRADE

**N. Thangavel, R. Akila & R. Mahaprabhu**

Electronics is now a matured industry sector in the country at least as far as various application segments is concerned. Production of electronics instruments registered a growth of 24 per cent (27 per cent in US$ terms) during the year 2006-07 over the year 2005-06. In value terms, production of electronics instruments during the year 2006-07 is estimated to be Rs. 14900 crore (US$ 3445 million) up from Rs. 12000 crore (US$ 2711 million) estimated in the year 2005-06. Production of Electronics instruments during the past five years has been growing at an annual average growth of 19 per cent (21 per cent in US$ terms). State-Of-art and reliable SCADA, PLC/ Data Acquisition systems are being applied across various sections of the process Industry. Latest AC drive systems from smaller to very high power levels also find application in large engineering industries like steel plants and/or metal industries.

Manufacturing of related hardware in technology areas like PLC, Distributed Control Systems, UPS, various Power Electronic equipment and Systems has been increasing in the country. Newer technologies involving wireless sensors and sensor networking are rapidly emerging as potential application in the field of industry automation technologies because these are inexpensive and easy to install.

About 20 per cent of total production of electronic instruments was exported during the year 2006-07 in comparison to 19 per cent in the year 2005-06. Export of electronics instruments registered a high growth of 30.43 per cent (33.51 per cent in US$ terms) during the year 2006-07 over the year 2005-06. In value terms, export of electronics equipments during the year 2006-07 is estimated to be Rs. 3000 crore (US$ 694 million) up from Rs. 2300 crore (US$ 520 million) estimated in the year 2005-06. Export of Electronics instruments from India has been growing at an annual average growth rate of 25.85 per cent (28.38 per cent in US$ terms) during the past five years. Electronics instruments exports constitute 24 per cent of India's total electronics hardware exports.

## TOP ITEMS OF EXPORTS

UPS has been maintaining its top position under electronics instruments exports since 2000-01. Exports of UPS during the year 2006-07 registered a very high growth of 35 per cent (38 per cent in US$ terms) over the year 2005-06. In value terms, export of UPS increased from Rs. 1260 crore (US$ 285 million) estimated in 2005-06 to Rs. 1702 crore (US$ 393 million) in the year 2006-07. Export of medical instruments has maintained its 2$^{nd}$ position during the year 2006-07. The other major items under electronics instruments export which registered growth during the year 2006-07 are inverters, Induction heating furnaces, control equipments and ATMs. Export of Solar lamps and automatic test equipments registered a decline during the year 2006-07.

## MAJOR DESTINATIONS FOR ELECTRONICS INSTRUMENTS EXPORTS

Despite of decline in export of instruments to North America, it remains top destination for export of electronics instruments during 2006-07 as well. Export to this region registered a decline of 32 per cent (30 per cent in US$ terms) during 2006-

07 over 2005-06. In value terms, export to North America during 2006-07 is estimated to Rs. 960 crore (US$ 222 million) falling form Rs. 1413 crore (US$ 319 million) estimated in the year 2005-06. With a high growth of 67 per cent (71 per cent in US$ terms), South Asian companies remains at the 2$^{nd}$ top destination of export in this sector during 2006-07. Export to EU countries, Middle East, Far East, Africa, Oceanic Countries have registered a good growth during 2006-07.

## ELECTRONICS AND COMPUTER SOFTWARE EXPORT PROMOTION COUNCIL (ESC)

Electronics and Computer Software Export Promotion Council (ESC) is India's largest electronics and IT trade facilitation organization sponsored by Government of India. It is responsible for the promotion of exports of Electronics, Computer/Services and ITES. It has over 2300 member companies across the length and breadth of the country in several ICT sub sectors including:

- Computer Software/Services.
- Electronics Hardware

The World looks for outsourcing to India for competitiveness and value for the clients and to ESC for ICT. With India proving to be the Knowledge Capital of the World, the whole world is looking towards ESC for international cooperation in the ICT sector to make their foothold strong and enhance their market share in global markets. Today, ESC has linkages with counterpart organizations across the world including US, Canada, Denmark, The Netherlands, Germany, Japan, Vietnam, Indonesia, Italy, Israel, Brazil, China, Venezuela, Sri Lanka, Egypt, Republic of Korea, Oman, Bangladesh, Ethiopia, Russia, Hungary, Bulgaria, Croatia, Kenya, Dominican Republic, and many more.

## ESC'S INTERNATIONAL COOPERATION ACTIVITIES INCLUDE

- Arranging and participating in international conferences, expositions, fairs and industry-level talks,
- Arranging delegation visits.

- Implementing joint activities to exchange information,
- Provide technological support and Exchanging trade missions.

## MEMBERSHIP IN THE COUNCIL

All the companies exporting or planning to export items/ services in the following sectors are required to register themselves with ESC.

## ELECTRONICS HARDWARE

(i) Consumer Electronics Products

(ii) Electronics Instruments/Appliances, industrial Electronics products, Electronic Laboratory Equipments, Medical Equipments.

(iii) Electronic Component/Sub assemblies.

(iv) Computer Hardware and peripherals.

(v) Computer Software and Related Services IT Enabled Services.

(vi) Telecommunication Services.

## ASSISTANCE PROVIDED BY THE COUNCIL

ESC makes contacts with foreign missions in India as well as Indian missions abroad to collect necessary information to be disseminated among the member exporters. It provides market exposure to member exporters by participating in various expositions and trade delegations. The council organizes interactive meetings for the member delegations and invites various delegations from all over the world. It also organizes Buyer Seller Meets (BSMs) of member companies with global buyers in India and abroad.

## ESC CREDENTIALS

- Awarded FIEO's Prestigious Niryat Bandhu Award For Outstanding Export Supporting Activities for the last consecutive 7 years.
- ESC has been adjudged as the Best Trade Supporting Organisation by Japan External Trade Organisation

(JETRO). ESC was the only organisation among Developing Countries to receive this honour. Other recipients were USA & Italy .

## ESC PRODUCT PROFILE

### Consumer Electronics

Video Software, Magnetic Cassette Tape, Wall Clocks, Television, Recorded Compact Diskette, Electric Sound Amplifier, Analog Watches, Recorded Audio Cassettes, Blank Video Cassettes, Two in one (Radio cum Cassette Player), Electronic Calculators, Radio Communication Receivers, Musical System, Video Compact Disc, Recorded Video Cassettes, Alarm Clocks, Audio Software, Blank Audio Cassettes, Microphones etc.

### Telecommunication

Pagers, Telecom Software, Transmission apparatus, Push Button Type Telephone, Rural Automatic Exchange, Telecom Modules, Telecom Cards, Cordless Telephone, EPAB/EPAX/ Intercom, Television cameras, Telephone Activity Monitor, Telephony or Telegraphy apparatus, Transmission apparatus, Communication Connector Box, Duplexers, Optical Fibre Cable, Modems, Direction measuring equipment etc.

### Instrumentation

Automatic Test Equipments, Electronic Automatic Regulators, Linear ultrasound scanner, Uninterrupted power supply, Automatic typewriter, Battery Chargers, Industrial Machines & Instruments, Electric Inverters, Process control equipments, Induction heating furnaces, Geophysical instruments, Component Tester, Cable Fault Locators, Timer, Voltage Stabilizer, Frequency meter, Sensors, etc.

### Electronic Components

Unpopulated Printed Circuit Board, Soft Ferrite, Colour Picture Tube, Connectors,Parts of Transformers, Dip bridge rectifiers, B/W Picture Tube, Hard Ferrites, X-Ray Tubes, Floppy diskettes, Erasing Heads, Printed Circuits, Static converters,

Mica Capacitors, Resistors, Multicrystalline silicon ingots, Multi-crystalline Silicon Wafers, Mono and Multi Silicon Solar Cell, Solar Photolvoltaic Modules, Solar Photovoltaic Systems, Solar LED lights, Solar Water Heating Systems, Solar Cooling Systems, Single Glazed Flat Plate Collectors, Double Glazed Flat Plate Collectors etc.

**Computer Hardware:**

Computer Hardware and Peripherals Winchester/Hard disc drives, Head Stack, CGA monitor, Computer Parts, Switching Mode Power Supply, Data-entry Terminal, Dot Matrix Printer, Personal Computer, Add on cards, etc.

**ESC SERVICES**

ESC is a helping hand to members for participation in

(1) International trade fairs

(2) Exhibitions

(3) Buyer-Seller meets

(4) Catalogue shows

(5) Business delegations abroad

(6) Foreign delegations visiting India.

ESC acts as a platform between the industry and the government to help members in

(1) Policy and procedural related matters

(2) Fixation of DEPB rates

(3) Raising issues of Bilateral and WTO negotiations

(4) EU anti-dumping and anti-subsidy cases

As per para 3.6.2 of Foreign Trade Policy of India and para 3.12 of Hand Book of Procedures Volume I all the IT, software/ services including ITES exporters are required to get registered with ESC. ESC membership is required for various benefits under the Foreign Trade Policy of India as mentioned below :-

(1) DEPB Benefits

(2) Advanced Licence

(3) EPCG Scheme

(4) Duty Draw Back Scheme

(5) Any other licence to import/export

(6) Deemed Export Benefit

ESC keeps its members abreast of the latest developments in the world economic scenario and inform members about

(1) Latest happenings

(2) Trade enquiries

(3) Threats

(4) Global tenders:

ESC has initiated a new and unique service of providing information relating to Electronics Hardware and Telecommunication Computer Software/Services Global-tenders and procurement opportunities. The tender information will include :

(1) Tenders

(2) Bid Notices & Corrigendum's (if any).

(3) Request for Quotes

(4) Procurement forecast

(5) Expression of Interest

(6) GPN (General Procurement Notices)

ESC acts as a facilitator to facilitate Joint Ventures, Collaborations, Sub-Contracting tie-ups, technology transfer etc.

ESC maintains a comprehensive database of the industry, companies, products and capabilities of all the major players and SMEs.

ESC has initiated several programmes to help the Indian SME's in the field of Electronics and IT. The major ones include:

*INDIASOFT Series of Events:* To cater to the needs of the small and medium IT companies, ESC organises INDIASOFT – IT Exhibition and Conferences in February each year at New Delhi. Indian IT companies exhibit their capabilities during the event and buyers are invited from around the world to visit the exhibition. Conferences on contemporary themes are also organised simultaneously during the event. Thus, INDIASOFT provides an excellent opportunity the Indian IT companies to interact with delegates from over 40 companies and the foreign delegates are able to know about the capabilities of the Indian small and medium IT companies. To give a new impetus to Indian exporters for overcoming the language barrier for diversification of their export into the Japanese and German IT market, ESC has initiated a scheme namely Language Related Market Access Facilitation. Under the scheme, 75% of the expenditure on the tuition fee is reimbursed.

*ESC is the implementation agency for the promotional programme assisted by the Government such as:*

1. MDA : Marketing Development Assistance
2. MAI : Market Access Initiative
3. LRMAFI : Language Related

**ESC OFFERS**

- The largest pool of Indian companies in the industry as its members;
- A comprehensive database on the industry, companies, products, capabilities of all major players in electronics, computer hardware, software and telecom products;
- Access and arrangements to facilitate import/export, collaborations, joint ventures, subcontracting, tie-ups;
- Access to published reports on markets, products, trade statistics, business opportunities; and

Facilitation in establishing joint ventures and strategic alliances-for contract manufacturing, captive production, design and test facilities.

## MARKETING DEVELOPMENT ASSISTANCE (MDA)

Export promotion continues to be a major thrust area for the Government. In view of the prevailing macro economic situation with emphasis on exports and to facilitate various measures being undertaken to stimulate and diversify the country's export trade, Marketing Development Assistance (MDA) Scheme is under operation through the Department of Commerce to support the under mentioned activities:

- Assist exporters for export promotion activities abroad
- Assist Export Promotion Councils (EPCs) to undertake export promotion activities for their product(s) and commodities
- Assist Focus export promotion programmes in specific regions abroad like FOCUS (LAC), Focus (Africa), Focus
- (CIS) and Focus (ASEAN +2) programmes

## MARKET ACCESS INITIATIVE (MAI) SCHEME

Market Access Initiative (MAl) Scheme is an Export Promotion Scheme envisaged to act as catalyst to promote India's exports on a sustained basis, during the 10th five year Plan. The scheme is devised on focus product- focus country approach basis to evolve specific strategy for specific market and specific product through market studies/survey Assistance would be provided to Export Promotion Organizations/Trade Promotion Organizations/Exporters etc for enhancement of export through accessing new markets or through increasing the share in the existing markets Under the Scheme the level of assistance for each eligible activities has been fixed.

Participation in Trade Fairs. BSMs etc. : - Under the Scheme the assistance would be provided for participation in trade fairs/exhibitions at identified potential places abroad on Focus Country-Product basis. Participation in such fairs/exhibitions will normally be part of a comprehensive strategy. To maximize the benefits such efforts should be linked with effective publicity campaign, seminars, buyer-seller meets etc. These activities will be coordinated by the Export Promotion Councils.

## CONCLUSION

ESC is a catalyst for Indian ICT industry. It is one stop window to assist overseas buyers of ICT products, electronics hardware and services, solar power equipment, modules, systems etc for discussion on business cooperation, strategic alliances etc. ESC also helps foreign firms seeking investment opportunities in the ICT product and services sector, solar power equipment, other solar power products and devices sector etc. in India.

## REFERENCES

Justin Paul, Rajeev Aserkar, "Export & Import Management" Himalaya Publications

Trade Policy 2004 -2009 supplement.

Francis Cheruniliam, "Export Management", Himalaya Publications.

*The Hindu*

*www.escindia.in*

*www.telecommunication.indiabizclub.com*

A Report on Indian Electronics Hardware Exports-A Study by the Electronics and Computer Software Export Promotion Council New Delhi, 25th July, 2005.

# 21

# ROLE OF EXIM BANK AND COMMERCIAL BANKS IN PROMOTING INDIA'S EXPORTS IN THE PRESENT COMPLEX NATURE OF WORLD TRADE

**Arati Basu**

In the globalize world, business decisions taken with respect to opportunities occurring in international dimensions. With removal of barriers for movements of goods and services, companies now have opportunities to enter into export- import business. Yet international trade can operate with its full potential, only when there is supporting international financial structure. International movements of goods and services across the boarder involve time, country risks, transportation risks, moral hazard of not keeping up commitments by concern parties arising out of transactions across boarder. International movements of goods and services across the boarder involve time, country risks, transportation risks, moral hazard of not keeping up commitments by concern parties arising out of transactions across boarder. Some big business houses may use their own funds or can afford to keep their fund illiquid for some time , but most of the business cannot afford to enter into the investment of highly illiquid and risky financing of exports and imports. These discourage companies even when they are competent in technology and production, to enter into international markets. International financial intermediations are a specialize function and require international intermediation with special skills Countries which are performing well in international trade, have been following well-structured policies for development of their own international financial agencies. Newly developed countries such as India, China, Indonesia, South Korea and Japan have their Exim banks playing crucial roles for financing exports from their respective countries. US and European economies have well established Exim Banks to facilitate financial transactions parallel to international flows of goods and services all over the world. In order to hedge against country risks, imperfect flows of information and uncertainties of market and export financing these banks have evolved specialize operational system and networks through participations of Govts, Development Finance Organizations, and domestic financial institutions of the respective countries. Though procedures are complex, countries which are able to develop efficient systems of international finance through Exim banks or specialized institutions in this field are able to support their respective export sectors and create dynamism there. Worldwide export financing agencies are supporting $800 billion exports each year. One out of eight dollar of world trade is financed by Export Credit Agencies (ECAs). There are two hundred ECAs in 100 countries. Their contribution to trade and development is massive. Their activities exceed that of all Multinational Development Banks. Financial support of exports is the highest among Asian Countries as they are financing on an average $15 billion of exports in1996.

In recent years as economic development is taking place, consumer's tastes are being standardized all over the world, trade barriers have fallen. Developing countries are in great need of increasing their share in world trade for faster economic growth. As a result, countries face growing pressure to improve their competitiveness in the export market. In the developing countries such as India and China which are aspiring to develop dynamic export sector, operate on various constraints visa vie the world market. For example, it is necessary for each country to develop their own financing systems tailored to fulfill and create efficient, low cost and low risk international financial intermediation for trading requirements.

Export Credit Agencies (comprising of Exim banks and providers of financial and other services) which are recognized for their contributions to financial support and consequent expansion of exports, in general are private financial agencies operating in various countries. They are supported by their respective Govt and have networks with international financial agencies. They offer loans/guarantees, insurance, technical assistance to exporters, so that they are protected against commercial and political risks and flows of funds are simultaneous along with commodity flows across the boarder. They operate in co-operation with other reputed national financial institutes with the approval of national govt. These institutes are dedicated to support their respective national exports. Export credit agencies of different countries have been developing networks with other development banks or agencies dealing with Asian, African, Latin American trade blocks in order to develop efficient and quick financial flows parallel to the flows of commodities across the boarders. They have been performing double role by supporting domestic enterprises in their globalization effort and providing opportunities for the importing counties not having international banking system to be able to import from these sources. ECAs have made credit available to many countries where commercial banks and other private banks are not willing to make trans boarder loans and making credit available at lower rates of interest. This has been helping growth of world trade.

## INDIA'S EXPORT PERFORMANCE AND NEED FOR EXPORT FINANCING AGENCY

Indian exports have been stagnant till the decades of eighties due the policy of import substituting autarkic growth. With changing economic scenario as a consequence of massive globalization, Indian Economy could not grow in autarky.

Now India introduced economic reforms from early nineties with an aim to have growth through export orientation thus integrating with word economy. GOI has been creating infrastructure for all round support for the export sector.

At present Indian export is growing a the rate of 20-25 per cent. Export/GDP ratio was 14 per cent in 2004. Share of Indian export in the world trade is only 0.9 per cent (2005). GOI proclaims to increase the share of Indian exports to 1.5 in coming years. Along with other promotional measures, dynamism in the export sector can be introduced only through penetration to new markets, introducing new products to the existing markets, supporting new entrepreneur to enter into export markets. All these have been changing direction and patterns of trade and India is able to have a break through in export performance. Emerging economies in Asia, such as China, Malaysia, Thailand and Philippines have achieved phenomenal growth of exports which helped them experienced faster economic growth India has taken steps for building financial infrastructure to support development of exports by establishing Export Import Bank of India in 1982.

## EXPORT-IMPORT BANK OF INDIA(EXIM BANK OF INDIA)

Export-Import (Exim) aims to facilitate and promote India's exports through development of channels of financial flows between Indian exporters and importers world wide. This has also been coordinating functioning of institutions/ commercial banks operating in financing exports and imports domestically and in the regional trading blocks engaged The bank has been helping a target set of externally oriented companies by offering them a comprehensive range of products and services for enhancing their exports. The bank has been specially proactive to promote export of projects, products and services from India to other developing countries in Asia, Africa, Latin America and CIS.

Categories of services offered by the Exim Bank is listed the box below:

Exim bank's services offered to various export houses for carrying out trans boarder business transaction such as :

- Export Marketing
- Pre-shipment
- Post-shipment
- Export production
- Import financing

The Bank's services covers following promotional activities such as:

- Export Product Development in accordance to foreign demands
- Financing Investment abroad for Indian Companies
- Advisory services :dissemination of information to potential exporters through market research

*Source*: Venkat Subramanian T. C., (Chairman & Managing Director) (July 21, 2006), "Indian Banking: Shaping an Economic Powerhouse Presentation on Exim Bank Exim Bank of India through export linkage"- FICCI Banking Conclave, Kolkata.

## METHODS OF FINANCING BY EXIM BANK

In product base financing Exim bank offers Line of credit (LOC) pre-shipment credit and post shipment credit. For service exports, the bank offers suppliers credit and buyers credit while for projects it offers seller's & buyer' credit, pre-shipment credit and credit guarantees.

The Exim bank offers different categories of loan such as term loan, working capital, product development funds and funds for investment on overseas projects. The Exim bank also provides value addition services such as export marketing services, participates in multilateral funding. joint Venture and consultancy support services. It provides funds for seminars and workshops for disseminations of information and educate the exporters about international financial contracts, risks and opportunities of export business. It also offers rediscounting and refinancing facilities to commercial banks involved in export financing. The Exim Bank extends non-founded facility to Indian exporters in the form of guarantees of loans. (Venkat Subramanian T. C., July 21, 2006).

*Line of Credit (LOC):* This has been a successful instrument for both exporters and importers to develop their business internationally. Line of credit enables import of Indian commodities, equipments and technology on deferred credit terms particularly relevant for small and medium sectors. LOCs are extended to Overseas Governments, Government agencies overseas, national or regional development banks as well as commercial banks abroad. For this, a letter of Credit is written by the importer to the exporter singed by a bank acting on behalf of the buyer promising that it would honour the draft on itself if the seller confirms to the specific conditions set forth in the letter . Thus this is a financial contract between a bank and the importer involved in international transaction. LOC provides several benefits both to the exporters as well as importers in reducing risks and uncertainties in international transactions. For example, it is impossible for an exporter from another land to have information regarding credit worthiness of the importers but the exporters can find out the reputation of the bank issuing LOC on behalf of the importer This also reduces risk and uncertainty of the importers about timely delivery of the consignment as well as quality assurance as the exporter can receive payment against LOC only after the shipment documents are submitted. Also the letter of credit provides assured market for the exporters thus hedge against uncertainty of cancellation of order by the importers. LOC is needed for development of export markets in those countries where financial systems are still in nascent stage and not able to deal with the complexities of international financial transactions. Flows of goods and services across the boarder are only possible only when there is corresponding flows of financial service. When financial market is limited in operation, govts of trading partners are involved in the mechanism of LOC

## PROCEDURE OF ISSUING LOCS

Of late Exim bank of India requires that LOCs should pass through processes presented in the flow diagram

Thus the process of financing international transaction proceeds through following steps as described by the flow diagram.

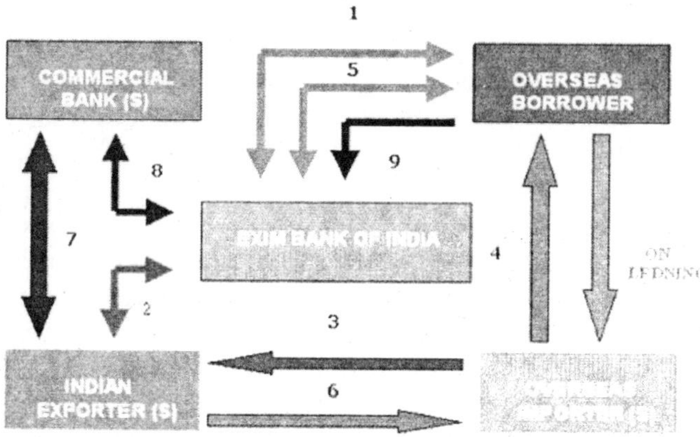


(1) *Exim Bank* signs agreement with Borrower and announces when effective.

(2) *Exporter* checks procedures and Service fee with *Exim Bank* and negotiates contract with *Importer*.

(3) *Importer* consults *borrower* and signs contract with *exporter*.

(4) *Borrower* approves contract.

(5) *Exim Bank* approves contract and advises *borrower* and also *exporter* and *commercial bank*.

(6) *Exporter* ships goods.

(7) *Commercial bank* negotiates shipping documents and pays *exporter*.

(8) *Exim Bank* reimburses *Commercial bank* on receipt of claim by debit to *borrower*.

(9) *Borrower* repays *Exim Bank* on due date

General Guidelines on Government of India-Approve Export Lines of Credit Routed Through Export-Import (Exim) Bank of India (Under team-9 and NEPARD initiatives) *www.eximbankindia.in*

First, overseas borrowing agency on behalf of the importer approaches the Indian Exim bank for funds for importing specific consignment of products in transit. Interested exporters checks procedure and fees that Exim Bank would charge for intermediation of funds to the exporters when the product is being shipped and then start negotiating the contract with importers. The importer after consulting his borrowing agency signs the contract. The Borrower approves the contract which is sent to the EXIM bank for further approval. After approval EXIM bank forwards the contract to the exporter and the commercial bank examines the contract. Then as the exporter submitting shipment document , the commercial bank pays the exporter the value of his international consignment. On receipt of claim by debit to borrower, EXIm Bank reimburses the amount. The borrower repays the amount to the EXIM bank on due date. This is a proactive instrument to promote export of products and services from India to other developing countries in Asia, Africa, Latin America and CIS. Regional Dispersion of LOC shows that Exim bank has high penetration in African Countries.( Africa–64%; South & Southeast Asia–13%; West Asia– 12%; LAC–5%; CIS – 3% in 2006) (General Guidelines on Government of India-Approve Export Lines of Credit Routed Through Export-Import (Exim) Bank of India.

Exim Bank has now (2008) 100 LOCs, covering 91 countries in Africa, Asia, Latin America, Europe and the Commonwealth of Independent States (CIS) with credit commitments amounting to $ 3.28-billion, available for utilization for financing exports from India.

Recently following LOCs are being reimbursed to CIS and African Countries.

Exim Bank has extended a line of (LOC) of $10 million to Uzbekistan's National Bank for Foreign economic activity. In order to boast India's exports to Uzbekistan. Exim Bank promises to reimburse 90 per cent of contract value to Indian exporters upfront upon the shipment of goods. Indian exports to Uzbekistanin in FY 08 was $79 million which is an increase of 37 per cent over the previous year. India exports mainly manufacturing goods to this country.

Export-Import Bank of India (Exim Bank) has extended a third Line of Credit (LOC in 2005) to support India's exports to Russia. The LOC was granted to Absolut Bank for $ 10 million. Exim Bank has also extended two LOCs, one for $ 10 million to Bank for Foreign Economic Affairs (Vnesheconombank)

**Table 1**

| *Year* | *Country* | *LOC (Amount($)* | *Bank in the Importing Counties* | *Type of Goods Exported* | *Volume of Regional Exports in 2007-08 ( million $)* |
|---|---|---|---|---|---|
| 2008 | Uzbekistan | 10 million | Uzbekistan's National Bank for Foreign economic activity. | Manufacturing goods | CIS & Baltic region1,313.39 |
| 2005 | Russia. | 10 million | Absolut Bank | Drugs, pharmaceuticals &fine chemicals, readymade garments of cotton, tea, coffee, un-manufactured tobacco and processed minerals. | Largest Trading Partner among CIS |
| | Russia. | 25 million | Vneshtorgbank | | |
| | Russia. | 10 million | Vneshtorgbank | | |
| | Kazakhstan | 10 million | Bank TuranAlem, | | |
| 2004 | Mozambique, | 20 million | Through Govt. | water drilling and drip irrigation equipment. | Indian Exports to African Countries7,334.63 |
| 2007 | Nigerian | 5 million | Neximbank. | capital and engineering goods, industrial manufactures, consumer durables, commodities and services | |
| | Gambia, | 10 million | Govt of Gambia, | construction of the government of Gambia's National Assembly building complex. | |

*Source*: General Guidelines on Government of India-Approve Export Lines of Credit Routed Through Export-Import (Exim) Bank of India eximloc@eximbankindia.com

and $ 25 million to Bank for Foreign Trade (Vneshtorgbank) of Russia. Absolut Bank is the first Russian commercial bank to be provided with Credit Facility by Exim Bank.

Under the LOC to Absolut Bank, importers based in Russia will make advance payment of 10% of contract value and Exim Bank sanctioned credit for 90% of contract value to Absolut Bank. Exim Bank is to reimburse Indian exporters upon the shipment of goods and services. Credit period is up to 5 years.

Russia is India's largest trading partner in the Commonwealth of Independent States (CIS). India's main exports to Russia are drugs, pharmaceuticals & fine chemicals, readymade garments of cotton, tea, coffee, un-manufactured tobacco and processed minerals. Exim Bank's LOC to Absolut Bank will help strengthen India's trade relations with Russia and facilitate exports from India.

The Mozambican government signed a financing agreement with the Export-Import (Exim) Bank of India, at the behest of Government of India, for a Line of Credit (LOC) of US$ 20 million to finance the transfer of water drilling technology and equipment from India to Mozambique.This is the third LOC extended by Exim Bank to Mozambique, at the behest of Government of India. The first LOC of US$ 20 million, which was extended in September 2004, was used to finance export of items including water drilling and drip irrigation equipment.

Exim Bank of India (2008) signed a memorandum of understanding (MOU) with African Export-Import Bank (Afreximbank) to extend a US$30 million line of credit (LOC) to finance Indian exports to Africa.

Under the LOCs, Exim Bank reimburses 100% of contract value to the Indian exporter, upfront upon the shipment of goods/provision of services.

## PROJECT FINANCING BY EXIM BANK

Exim Bank plays a pivotal role in promoting and financing Indian companies in the execution of projects in North Africa, Sub Saharan Africa, West Asia, South & South East Asia, CIS and Latin America. Project financing mutually benefits both recipient and the investing countries. The recipient country is able to get technology as well as human resources for constructing the investment projects while the investing country is able to build up connectivity with the destination economy. This enables them to develop cultural break through as well as entry into new markets. Thus this operates for mutually beneficial trade relations.

Exim bank's project exports comprise Civil engineering construction projects, Turnkey projects and services Currently, 190 project export contracts valued at US$ 6.4 bn are under execution in 38 countries by 42 exporters West Asia accounts for a bulk of these exports (49%); North Africa–20%; South Asia 14%; Sub Saharan Africa–8%; Southeast Asia–6%. Sectoral composition of projects are the following : Civil construction–22%; Power generation–33%; Power transmission–16%; Consultancy service–4%; Others–26%.

EXIM Bank has arrangements with International Finance Corporation, Washington, to provide Indian consultancy needed for private sector development in Africa. Indian consultants offer technical and managerial services in assignments under Business Advisory Services for the Caribbean & Central America, South Pacific Project Development Facility, Polish Business Advisory Services and the Technical Assistance Trust Funds Programme. EXIM Bank has concluded similar arrangements with Eastern & Southern African Trade and Development Bank and African Management Services Company (AMSCO), Netherlands, for providing Indian consultants for African Countries. Most recently, the EXIM- IFC arrangement has been extended to help entrepreneurs in the Mekong region to identify and implement investment projects.

**EXIM BANK AND ASIA PROJECT FUNDING**

Exim has invested US$ 10 mn in the Pan-Asia Project Development Fund (PPDF) sponsored by IL&FS and Orix Corporation, Japan. This projects relate to infrastructural development across Asian countries and operational in

Cambodia, Indonesia, Malaysia, Philippines, Sri Lanka, Thailand and Vietnam. The bank has been providing both funded and non-funded financial support. Exim bank's objective is to involve Indian companies across Asia by providing seed capital so that trade connections are established and foundations for the growth of exports by Indian companies are laid (Exim Bank Extends US$ 2 Million Credit Line to Philippines) eximloc@eximbankindia.com.

**EXIM BANK AND AFRICAN MISSION**

African countries were the poorest in the world having lowest per capta income till recently. They have barely experienced positive rate of growth for decades. Present liberalisaon and globalisaion process has not helped to alleviate poverty in Africa. Only recently( 2007) these countries are attracting FDI in large amount and there has been some sign of improvement of growth conditions there (5 per cent in 2007). India has much to offer in terms of technology, manpower development and building up potential for trade. African Economic relations with India has been proving to be beneficial for both. These countries are able to achieve 5 per cent rate of growth in 2007 mainly through export expansion. African development bank and other Development Finance organisation operating in Africa in collaboration with Exim bank of India, have been financing developmental projects in variour African countries For example Government of India and the eight (8) countries in West Africa, viz. Governments of Burkina Faso, Chad, Cote d'Ivoire, Equatorial Guinea, Ghana, Guinea Bissau, Mali and Senegal have set up a regional cooperation mechanism called Techno-Economic Approach for Africa-India Movement, known as Team-9. Under the Team-9 initiative, GOI provides LOCs through Exim Bank to these countries, to finance setting up of various projects by Indian companies there. Also, GOI provides LOCs through Exim Bank, under the NEPAD (New Partnership for Africa's Development) initiative of Africa, to finance setting up various projects by Indian companies, across Africa. These projects are in operation in following fields.

- Turnkey contract for Gas Based Power Project in Tanzania funded by World Bank.
- Transmission System Rehabilitation and Maintenance Project in Zambia.
- Turnkey contract for Multi-Product Pipeline Project in Sudan
- Consultancy assignment in Small Town water supply project in Nigeria.
- Supplies for Urban Power Rehabilitation Project in Uganda.
- Transmission Line Projects in Algeria, Tunisia
- Construction of Cyber Towers in Mauritius.

Table 2 describes the projects financed by Exim Bank to the Indian companies to undertake projects in various African countries. India has been playing a significant role in building of Africa with cooperation of other development agencies. Indian has an advantage due to the fact that technological gap between India and African nations are narrow compared to that of developed nations. Table 2 shows that Indian companies with the help of finance of Exim bank are constructing some of the basic industries such as bicycle , cotton yarn plans rural electrification, railway locomotives, pump sets for irrigations, buses, tractors etc.

**Table 2**

| *LOC Recipient Government* | *Amount ofCredit (US$ mn.)* | *Project* |
|---|---|---|
| Government of Chad | 50.00 | A cotton yarn plant<br>A bicycle plant<br>A steel billet plant and rolling plant mill (Under Modification)<br>A plant for assembly of agricultural equipment (Under Modification) |
| Governmentof Ghana. | 60.00 | Design & build the seat of Govt &presidency, Ghana<br>Electrical Equipment and for Rural Electrification |

*Contd...*

| *LOC Recipient Government* | *Amount of Credit (US$ mn.)* | *Project* |
|---|---|---|
| Governments of Mali and Senegal | 27.70 | Supply of 38 New Meter Gauge Railway Coaches with maintenance spares.<br>Supply of 3 Newly Manufactured 2300 hp diesel locomotive with maintenance spare.<br>Supply of 1 Locomotive & 12 Coaches. |
| Government Of Mali | 27.00 | Rural electrification.<br>Tractor Assembly Plant<br>Machinery & Tractor Assembly Plant. |
| Government of Côte d'Ivoire | 26.80 | Vegetable Oil processing Unit.<br>Cashew Nut<br>Export of Tata Buses.<br>processing Unit.Plants for<br>i) Chips-making &Packing<br>ii) Liquid sugar.<br>iii) Starch Making.(Cassava) |
| Government of Senegal | 27.00 | Pump sets for Irrigation |
| Government of DR Congo | 33.50 | Buses, spare parts, Tools |
| Government ofGambia. | 6.70 | 500 Tractors with spares and assembly |

*Source*: Report of the Working Group to Review Export Credit (2005), Department of Banking Operations and Development, Reserve Bank of India.

**Table 3**
**Growth of Indian Exports ( 2005-07) by Destination**

| *Name of Countries* | *% Growth Values (INR in Crores)* | *% Growth Values (US$ in Millions)* | *% Share Values (INR in Crores)* | *% Share Values (US$ in Millions)* |
|---|---|---|---|---|
| India Export To Europe | 18.25 | 15.27 | 22.88 | 22.88 |
| India Export To Africa | 56.37 | 52.42 | 6.52 | 6.52 |
| Southern Africa | 44.26 | 40.62 | 2.17 | 2.17 |
| West Africa | 27.98 | 24.74 | 1.85 | 1.85 |
| Central Africa | 29.45 | 26.18 | 0.16 | 0.16 |
| East Africa | 113.58 | 108.18 | 2.34 | 2.34 |
| India Export To America | 15.29 | 12.38 | 19.24 | 19.24 |

*Contd...*

| *Name of Countries* | *% Growth Values (INR in Crores)* | *% Growth Values (US$ in Millions)* | *% Share Values (INR in Crores)* | *% Share Values (US$ in Millions)* |
|---|---|---|---|---|
| North America | 11.55 | 8.73 | 15.94 | 15.94 |
| Latin America | 37.53 | 34.05 | 3.3 | 3.3 |
| India Export To Asia & ASEAN | 31.7 | 28.37 | 49.97 | 49.97 |
| East Asia | 53.22 | 49.35 | 1.21 | 1.21 |
| ASEAN | 27.73 | 24.5 | 10.07 | 10.07 |
| WANA | 43.7 | 40.06 | 18.38 | 18.38 |
| NE Asia | 24.22 | 21.08 | 15.13 | 15.13 |
| South Asia | 20.47 | 17.42 | 5.17 | 5.17 |
| India Export To CIS & Baltics | 22.32 | 19.23 | 1.17 | 1.17 |
| CARs Countries | 16.82 | 13.87 | 0.15 | 0.15 |
| Other CIS Countries | 23.19 | 20.08 | 1.02 | 1.02 |
| India Export To Unspecified Region | 25.34 | 22.17 | 0.22 | 0.22 |
| Total | 26.13 | 2.95 | 100 | 100 |

*Sources*: Ministry of Commerce, Government of India (taken from InfodriveIndia 1999-2008).

The Table 3, gives the picture of regional growth of Indian exports. Due to development of financial infrastructure in African and Asian countries, they are able increase imports from India at a faser rate. Indian exports to African region has increased 52 per cent during 2005-06 which the highest for all the regions of the African countries, East Africa registered the highest rare of growth of exports.

## SMES AND EXPORTS PROMOTION- ROLE OF EXIM BANK

Worldwide SME sector is well-recognized for its significant contribution to exports, fostering new entrepreneurship and providing depth to the industrial base for the economy. India's SME sector has been playing an important role in expansion of international trade. The capacity of Indian SME products to compete in international markets is reflected in its share as high as 34 per cent of national exports. SSI sector in India has been exhibiting a striking export performance. Barring few years, exports have grown double digit in the last 10 years. Exports at current prices in 2002-03, the latest year for which data is available, stood at Rs. 86000 crores. This works out to about 34% of total exports in India in the same year. Major sectors contributing to SSI exports include readymade garments (27%.), engineering goods (14.5%), chemicals & pharmaceuticals, electronics & computers, and processed foods (11% each) In terms of export orientation sports goods have 100 per cent followed by readymade garment 90 per cent leather 70 per cent, marine 47 per cent and chemicals & pharmaceuticals 44 per cent .(2005) EXIM BANK: Research Brief, Export performance of Small and Medium Enterprises In India ) (www. Eximbank.com)

International activities expose SMEs to more complex and risky business environment for which they are relatively unprepared Trade among countries needs logistic supports and development of supply chains which small enterprises do not understand neither they are capable of developing these on their own. As it has been mentioned, international transactions have different kind of complexities for which SMES need to educate themselves even to take help from specialsed agencies Yet many SMEs can help realize the potential and prospects of high growth if they are able to gain access to global markets. At present many SMEs are working as the outsourcing units of MNCS catering to international market. Direct entry of SMEs in trade can offer a host of business opportunities for them. Exports and foraying into international markets can also pose challenges and threats by exposing them to heightened international competition from foreign firms of standard and international compatibilities.

The SMEs find the services of reputed national and international consultants as not cost effective and often, not adequately focused on their specific problems. Recognizing this knowledge gap, Exim Bank of India has been endeavoring to provide a range of services to its SME clients. These include providing business leads, handholding during the process of winning an export contract and thus assisting the generation of export business on success fee basis, countries/sector information dissemination, capacity building in niche areas such as quality, safety, export marketing, etc. and financial advisory services such as loan syndication, etc. Exim Bank has been supporting capability creation and skill development for SMEs in the following fields - Pharmaceuticals, Textiles & garments, Light engineering, Chemicals, Auto components.

Exim Bank has programmes to support SMEs as an industrial cluster. SMEs are often weak economic actors if considered individually, but they can reach high levels of competitiveness if they work in a cluster environment ensuring complementarities, common activities, collective goods and institutional stability. It has joined hands with IIFT, UNIDO & DCSSI to implement the Business Development Services programme to train consultants in developing a sectoral approach for identified clusters. This approach includes financing cluster units & SPVs, providing information & advisory services, supporting capacity building of cluster units. Enterprise Management Development Services (EMDS) programme of ITC, Geneva developed financing and evaluation tools to suit the requirements of SMEs . Separate resources are earmarked for extending loans under this programme

Export Marketing Services programme helps Indian SMEs to establish their products overseas and enter new markets.

Exim Bank initiatives for supporting SMEs are summarised in the project document.

(Building Competencies for SME Financing-IND/A1/01B, ( 2006) ITC International Trade Center, UNO/WTO PROJECT DOCUMENTASIA TRUST FUND Financed by the European Commission and International Trade Centre).

(a) The special SME fund of USD$11 million is set up and ready for the project activities;

(b) Offices and communication facilities when required;

(c) Organization of the training events, preparation of training materials;

(d) Appointment of a coordinator within Exim Bank to act as contact person and local project coordinator;

(e) Training facilities, including PCs (at least one PC for 2 participants) and Internet access, during information sharing events;

(f) Identification and selection of potential SMEs using the ITC methodology;

(g) Identification and selection of local consultant(s) and qualified and experienced translators/interpreters when required;

(h) Stationery and office supplies;

(i) Support in providing and collecting information and documents to carry out the activities;

(j) Arrange for feedback on questions, draft reports, etc.

In its US$ 11 million project under aegis of International Trade Centre to be funded by Asia Trust Fund , Exim bank has introduces SME specific loan schemes in which their earning capacities would be given priorities rather than their past record, a special Technical assistance fund would be created. Bank offers would be fully trained to understand the SME sector This methodology would be provided to other FI to improve their lending facilities to SMEs.

## EXIM BANK AND INDIA'S SERVICE EXPORTS

In 2004, while India's share in world merchandise exports was 0.8 per cent, the corresponding share in world commercial services was 1.9 per cent. Services, accounting for 54.1 per cent of GDP in 2005-06, is a sector of critical interest in India.

According to NASSCOM Sources, there is a sharp rise in services exports due to software exports. Software exports rose from US$ 0.7 bn in FY 1996 to US$ 17.2 bn in FY 2005. Exim Bank was associated with development of Indian software industry since 1986. The bank undertook Comprehensive financing/service package for software industry such as providing working capital for project equipments, helping the companies in acquiring product and process certification. The bank has been helping export marketing and product development.

Besides software in which India has already made an impact, there is good potential for export of many other professional services, like super-speciality hospital; satellite mapping; printing and publishing; accounting, auditing and book-keeping services. Engg services exports jump 25.6% in FY08 (Ministry of Commerce and Industry, Government of India, 2006).

## CONSULTANCY SERVICE SECTOR IN INDIA AND EXPORT GROWTH

It is estimated that the consultancy business in India engages about 100,000 persons in about 5000 consulting firms. According to estimates, the current sizeof the consulting industry in India is about Rs. 10,000 crores including exports and is expected to grow at a CAGR of approximate 25% in the next few years. An analysis of the consultancy contracts secured by Indian project overseas has been carried out by Exim Bank of India. As per the analysis, the geographical dispersion of contracts secured during 1995–96 to 2000–01 indicates that consultancy contracts were secured largely in West Asia which accounted for 39% number wise and 46% value wise followed by South East Asia and Pacific & South Asia. South East Asia constituted 22% both by number and by value whereas South Asia was 18% number wise and 16% value wise. According to the 2002 data of the Federation of Indian Export Organizations (FIEO), India's share in global trade in services was about 1.3% while India's share of consultancy exports is about 0.5% of global trade in services. Initiatives in development of consultancy service will improve India's export performance considerably.

Though Competitiveness of Indian Consultancy Exports is still at a lower level compared to large international firms already operating in the field, yet Indian consultancy organizations are making their presence in the niche market and are able to cope up with competitive environment. It needs large expenditure for business development. Indian firms are operating on those areas in which business development cost is low.

Some of the key initiatives of the government in promoting exports of consultancy services are coming through Exim bank's initiative as Market Development Assistance (MDA), Market Access Initiative (MAI) schemes.

## CONCLUSION

In the globalize world, backbone of promotion of export is to develop specialised financial infrastructure for financial intermediation in different courtiers. Exim bank's operations in various developing areas have been successful in terms of improving India's export performance as well as helping these countries constructing infrastructure for economic development. In this venture Exim bank has been providing Indian exporters in expanding their market in various developing and newly emerging countries such as Africa, Latin America, CIS and Russia as well as Asian countries. Exim bank has been offering various methods of financing such as LOC, project financing. The bank provides short and long term fiancé for both promotional and research and development. Exim bank's initiates have helped expansion of service exports to developing countries in a big way. Exim bank is also helping SMES to enter into export markets through special methods developed with the help of International Trade Centre. Exim bank has tailored a financing programme for exporters of Soft wares from India which is helping them to make their presence in both developed developing countries. Indian service sector and the consultancy services though are growing fast, this can perform better with sector specific financial and market development assistance- Exim bank has an important role to play there.

## REFERENCES

Following web pages are consulted:

*www.eximbankindia.in*

*www.eimbankindia.in/ sme.asp*

*www.eximbankindia. Com*

*eximloc@eximbankindia.com*

### Articles

Abhishaik, (2007), *Functions of Exim Bank* –MBACLUBINDIA An interactive platform for anagement Professionals of India *www.MBAclubindia.com*

Gianturco,Delio E. (2001), Export Credit Agencies, Greenwood Publishing Group.

Sampath Divya (2006), Dissertation on *How Indian SMEs can become Export Competitive* –CRISIL Young Thought Leader Series.

**Internet Posting**

Exim Bank of India signs MoU with Afreximbank for $30mn LOC *March 2008 par* Magazine Finance ( Internet Posting).

EXIM Bank Extends $10 mn Credit to Senegal ( 2007) *Economic Times* (Internet Posting).

Infrastructure projects in Africa/Financial Mail Infrastructure Project Finance Conference/An Investment with Long Term Returns ( 2008) Database press release related to Africa (Internet Posting)

Building Competencies for SME Financing-IND/A1/01B, ( 2006) ITC International Trade Center, UNO/WTO PROJECT DOCUMENTASIA TRUST FUND Financed by the European Commission and International trade Centre.

**Government of India Source**

Trade Promotion Programme-Focus: CIS Finances, Department of Commerce (2oo8), Govt of India ( available in internet posting)

General Guidelines on Government of India-Approve Export Lines of Credit Routed Through Export-Import (Exim) Bank of India (Under team-9 and NEPARD initiatives) *www.eximbankindia.in*

Export promotion of Consultancy and Management Services from India, (2006 )Ministry of Commerce and Industry, Government of India, New Delhi.

Exim Bank Extends US$ 2 Million Credit Line to Philippines *eximloc@eximbankindia.com*

Exim Bank annual Report. Doc.

*eximbankindia.com.*

Exim Bank's Operative Lines of Credit

*eximloc@eximbankindia.com*

Exim Bank- Research Brief: *Export Performance of Small and Medium Enterprises in India (2005), Visit at www.eximbankindia.com.*

## Presentations by Exim Bank

Venkat Subramanian T. C., (Chairman & Managing Director) (July 21, 2006), "Indian Banking: Shaping an Economic Powerhouse Presentation on Exim Bank Exim Bank of India through export linkage"- FICCI Banking Conclave, Kolkata.

Rikesh ChandResident Representative, Ahmedabad Regional Office.

"Exim Bank Initiatives in facilitating International TradeBy Export-Impørt Bank of India", Project Finance India.

Rao S.R. Chief General Manager (2006)"Exim Bank of India–An Overview & Initiatives in Africa's Development" Paris, March 16-17.

Tarun Sharma, Export-Import Bank of India, 2002, "India-Latin America Health Summit –Exim Bank's Credit Programmes and Latin America", September 18, New Delhi.

# 22

# EXIM BANK: HELPING HANDS FOR EXPORTERS

**Gajendra Singh & Charu Singhal**

## INTRODUCTION

In the developing country like India, the real barometer of sustained economic growth is the growth index of exports. Though India is a self-sufficient country but for the overall development, growth and survival in today's global scenario the process of import and export is necessary for the country. To support the exporter, Government of India established ECGC and Exim Bank, which offers a diverse range of information, advisory and support services, which enable exporters to evaluate international risks, exploit export opportunities and improve competitiveness. The purpose of Exim bank is to financing, facilitating and promoting India's foreign trade. Exim Bank offers a range of fund and non-fund based support to enhance the export competitiveness of Indian companies. The main function of ECGC is to protect exporters from the risk of non payment from the buyers.

In a scenario of cut-throat competition, selling the goods on cash doesn't remain as attractive as selling on terms of credit to the buyers. Like any other seller, exporters too generally use to sell their goods on secured terms of credit. To safeguard the exporters from the loss incurred from selling goods on credit, government of India has setup export credit insurance in 1957 and tries to cover the payment risk for Indian exporters. Not only the developed countries are utilizing export credit insurance to improve their competitiveness, but the developing countries are also providing export credit insurance through their government institutions. Time to time improvements in export credit insurance policies and Exim bank policies has been done by the government for the appropriate result and outcomes.

## EXPORT CREDIT INSURANCE (NEED OF TIME)

When exporters does trade on terms of credit payments from importers are open to risks even at the time of shiny skies. The reason for non payment could be any as commercial, economical, social or political risk. The fast and far changing conditions of the importer and its country affect not only the exporters but also effect the whole world. An outbreak of war or civil war may block or delay payment for goods exported. A coup or an insurrection may also bring about the same result. Economic difficulties or balance of payment problems may lead a country to impose restrictions on either import of certain goods or on transfer of payments for goods imported. In addition, the exporters have to face commercial risks of insolvency or protracted default of buyers. The commercial risks of a foreign buyer going bankrupt or losing his capacity to pay are aggravated due to the political and economic uncertainties. Export credit insurance is therefore designed to protect exporters from the consequences of the payment risks, and to enable them to expand their overseas business without fear of loss.

## EXPORT CREDIT GUARANTEE CORPORATION (ECGC) OF INDIA

In order to provide export credit insurance support to Indian exporters, the Government of India set up the Export Risks Insurance Corporation (ERIC) in 1957. The name of the Corporation was changed in 1964 as "Export Credit & Guarantee Corporation Limited" (ECGC) in 1964. To bring the

Indian identity into the name, the Corporation's name was changed as the present Export Credit Guarantee Corporation of India limited in 1983. Being essentially an export promotion organization, it functions under the administrative control of the Ministry of Commerce and is managed by a Board of Directors representing Government, Banking, Insurance, Trade and Industry. The vision of ECGC is to excel in providing export credit insurance and trade related services. The mission of ECGC is to support the Indian Export Industry by providing cost effective insurance and trade related services to meet the growing needs of Indian export market through the optimal utilization of available resources. It creates a favorable climate for exporters under which they can hope to get timely and liberal credit facilities from the banks at home. With a clear vision and mission, corporation has further set before itself the following objectives:

(1) To encourage and facilitate globalization of India's trade.

(2) To assist Indian exporters in managing their credit risks by providing timely information on worthiness of the buyers, bankers and the countries.

(3) To protect the Indian exporters against unforeseen losses, which may arise due to failure of the buyer, bank or problems faced by the country of the buyer by providing cost effective credit insurance, covers in the form of Policy.

(4) Factoring and Investment Insurance services comparable to similar covers available to exporters in other countries.

(5) To facilitate availability of adequate bank finance to the Indian exporters by providing export credit insurance to bankers at competitive rates.

(6) To achieve improved performance in terms of profitability, financial and operational efficiency indicators and achieve optimum return on investment.

(7) To develop world class expertise in credit insurance among employees and ensure continuous innovation

and achieve highest customer satisfaction by delivering top quality service.

ECGC is the fifth largest credit insurer of the world in terms of coverage of national exports and has completed fifty years of operations. With the establishment of National Export Insurance Account (NEIA), ECGC now provides credit risk insurance cover even to high risk countries where such insurance cover was not earlier provided. NEIA has already provided Rs.396 crores to ECGC and a balance amount of Rs.1704 crores will be provided during the current Plan Period to enhance ECGC's under-writing capability. ECGC has also reduced its premium by more than 10% to provide relief to exporters affected by rupee appreciation. The present paid-up capital of the company is Rs.800 crores and authorized capital Rs.1000 crores.

Export Credit Guarantee Corporation (ECGC) of India Ltd. ranks countries in seven categories (A1, A2, B1, B2, C1, C2 and D) in ascending order of risk. It has placed India in Group A1 of countries in the risk ratings of December 2007. As banks move over to internal rating systems, banks may use the seven category classification given by Export Credit Guarantee Corporation of India Ltd. for the purpose of classification and making provisions for country risk exposures. ECGC shall provide to banks, on request, quarterly updates of their country classifications and shall also inform all banks in case of any sudden major changes in country classification in the interim period. The seven categories classification is given in Table 1 below:

**Table 1**

| *Risk Category* | *ECGC Classification* | *Provisioning Requirement (per cent)* |
|---|---|---|
| Insignificant | A1 | 0.25 |
| Low | A2 | 0.25 |
| Moderate | B1 | 5.00 |
| High | B2 | 20.00 |
| Very high | C1 | 25.00 |
| Restricted | C2 | 100.00 |
| Off-credit | D | 100.00 |

## ROLE OF ECGC IN INDIAN EXPORT

ECGC provides a range of credit risk insurance covers to exporters against loss in export of goods and services. It offers guarantees to banks and financial institutions to enable exporters to obtain better facilities from them and provides overseas investment insurance to Indian companies investing in joint ventures abroad in the form of equity or loan. ECGC help exporters by offering insurance protection to exporters against payment risks, provides guidance in export-related activities, makes available information on different countries with its own credit ratings, makes it easy to obtain export finance from banks/financial institutions, assists exporters in recovering bad debts and provides information on credit-worthiness of overseas buyers.

It offers 4 main role/services to the exporters of the nation:

### SCR or Standard Policy

Shipments Comprehensive Risks Policy, commonly known as the Standard Policy, is the one ideally suited to cover risks in respect of goods exported on short-term credit, i.e. credit not exceeding 180 days. This policy covers both commercial and political risks from the date of shipment. It is issued to exporters whose anticipated export turnover for the next 12 months is more than Rs.50 lacs. Small Exporters Policy is the appropriate policy for exporters with an anticipated turnover of Rs.50 lacs or less. Specific Shipment Policy, Exports (Specific Buyer) Policy, Exports Turnover Policy, Buyer Exposure Policy, Multi-Buyer Exposure Policy, Consignment Exports Policy (Stockholding Agent) and Consignment Exports Policy (Global Entity), Services Policy, IT-Enabled Services Policy, Software Projects Policy, Full Fledged Factoring Scheme to protect them against payment risks involved in exports on short term credit. Under the Standard Policy, ECGC covers, from the date of shipment, the following risks:

*Commercial Risks:* It includes the risk of insolvency of the buyer/buyers, failure of the buyer to make the payment due within a specified period, normally four months from the due date and buyer's failure to accept the goods, subject to certain conditions.

*Political Risks:* Includes imposition of restriction by the Government of the buyer's country or any Government action, which may block or delay the transfer of payment made by the buyer, War, civil war, revolution or civil disturbances in the buyer's country. New import restrictions or cancellation of a valid import license in the buyer's country, interruption or diversion of voyage outside India resulting in payment of additional freight or insurance charges which can not be recovered from the buyer, any other cause of loss occurring outside India not normally insured by general insurers, and beyond the control of both the exporter and the buyer.

**Specific Policies**

This policies are designed to protect Indian firms against payment risks involved in (a) exports on deferred terms of payment (b) services rendered to foreign parties and (c) construction works and turnkey projects undertaken abroad. Specific Shipment Policies-Short Term (SSP-ST) provide cover to Indian exporters against commercial and political risks involved in export of goods on short-term credit not exceeding 180 days. Exporters can take cover under these policies for either a shipment or a few shipments to a buyer under a contract. These policies can be availed of by (i) exporters who do not hold SCR or standard policy and (ii) by exporters having SCR or standard policy, in respect of shipments permitted to be excluded from the preview of the SCR Policy.

**Financial Guarantees**

Financial guarantees issued to banks in India to protect them from risks of loss involved in their extending financial support to exporters at the pre-shipments well as post-shipment stages; and

**Special Schemes**

Special schemes in other words known as transfer guarantee meant to protect banks which add confirmation to letters of credit opened by foreign banks, insurance cover for buyer's credit; Line of Credit, overseas investment insurance and exchange fluctuation risk insurance. In addition to the policy covers, which are issued to exporters, ECGC also extends its guarantee support to banks in India against both funded and non-funded facilities extended to project exporters.

## EXPORT-IMPORT BANK OF INDIA (EXIM BANK)

Exim Bank was established as a wholly Government-owned financial institution, under an Act of Parliament in 1982, by relocating IDBI's International Finance Division, for the purpose of financing, facilitating and promoting India's foreign trade. Exim Bank is managed by total 16 Board of Directors, which has representatives from the Government, Reserve Bank of India, Export Credit Guarantee Corporation of India (ECGC), a financial institution, public sector banks, and the business community. It has one Chairman and Managing Director, 5 Directors from Government of India, 3 Directors from Scheduled Banks, 4 Directors who are professionals/experts in this field. These 13 directors are appointed by Government of India. Beside these directors there are 3 more Directors, each nominated by RBI, IDBI and ECGC. The vision of Exim bank, since the time of its establishment has changed from product centric approach to customer centric approach. As per the customer centric approach, the vision of the bank it to develop commercially viable relationships with a target set of externally oriented companies by offering them a comprehensive range of products and services, aimed at enhancing their internationalization efforts. The major objectives of Export Import Bank of India are to provide economic assistance to importers and exporters and to function as the apex financial institution. The head office of Export Import Bank of India is located in Mumbai and its regional offices are located at Pune, Kolkata, Hyderabad, New Delhi, Bangalore, Chennai and Ahmedabad. The Bank's overseas offices are located at London, Washington D.C., Dakar, Dubai, Singapore and Johannesburg.

Exim bank of India launched the Asian Exim Banks Forum in 1996 and brought together 8 Exim Banks operating in Asia to promote intra-regional trade and reduce transaction cost among them. Exim Bank was awarded in 2002 by the World

Trade Centre's Association (WTCA) Award, instituted by the US-based WTCA, in recognition of its contribution to world stability through trade. The bank also receives the "Export Development Award" by Association of Development Financing Institutions of Asia & Pacific (ADFIAP) in 2002, 2004, 2005 and 2006. In the latest trend where entertainment industry has a potential to grow at the fast pace, Exim Bank made an entry into financing of the entertainment industry and also forayed into financing of the healthcare service sector. According to the Commerce Minister exports in 2004 stood at a little over US $ 63 billion which have exceeded US$ 155 billion in year 2007-08. We have managed an average cumulative annual growth rate (CAGR) of 23%, year on year, way ahead of the average growth rate of international trade. The total merchandise trade–exports and imports together–will be almost US $ 400 billion this past year, accounting for 1.2% of world trade. If the trade in services is added to this, commercial engagement with the world would be in the region of US $ 525 billion. On the basis of the total trade in goods and services is equivalent to almost 50% of GDP.

## ROLE OF EXIM BANK IN PROMOTING INDIAN EXPORT

The function of Exim bank comprises of financing projects, products and services exports, building export competitiveness, promotional programmes and financing research and development activities of exporting companies. Like ECGC, Exim bank too provides long range of product and services to their exporters. Exim Bank provides financial, information, advisory and support services to enable exporters to evaluate international risks, exploit export opportunities and improve their competitiveness. It provides the funded and non-funded based support to improve the export competitiveness of Indian companies. It helps Indian industries in identifying technology suppliers, partners with regard to domestic and overseas joint ventures. Small and medium sized exporters are also helped by the Exim bank, as it provide market driven export financing solution to them. the various product offered by the Exim bank are shown in the given Figure 1.

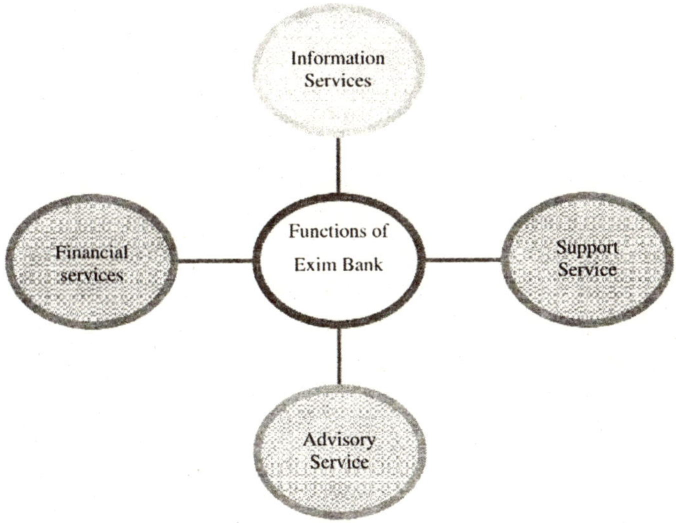


**Figure 1**

The product and services offered by the bank are supported by the financial programmes run by the bank for their clients. These programmes not only include financial services for exporters but provide facility to the importers of the country. Further on according to the Exim bank these programmes are classified as export credit, import credit and loans for exporting units. Moreover the institutional link of the bank is world-wide. It is linked by multilateral agencies like WTO, UNCTAD etc. it is also linked by trade & investment promotion agencies and export credit agencies of various nations. Its services include export credit, overseas investment finance, agri & SME finance, film finance and finance for units that are export oriented. The Bank's functions are segmented into several operating groups including: Corporate Banking Group which handles a variety of financing programmes for Export Oriented Units (EOUs), Importers, and overseas investment by Indian companies. Project Finance/Trade Finance Group handles the entire range of export credit services such as supplier's credit, pre-shipment credit, buyer's credit, finance for export of projects & consultancy services, guarantees, forfeiting etc. Lines of Credit

Group Lines of Credit (LOC) is a financing mechanism and export transactions in the agricultural sector for financing. Small and Medium Enterprises Group to the specific financing requirements of export oriented SMEs. The group handles credit proposals from SMEs under various lending programmes of the Bank. Export Services Group offers variety of advisory and value-added information services aimed at investment promotion. Fee based Export Marketing Services Bank offers assistance to corporate Affairs.

## CONCLUSION

From the above discussion, it become very clear that the services/functions performed by the ECGC and Exim bank in promoting/supporting exporters swing Indian exports to reach new heights of achievement. Exports during July, 2008 were valued at US $ 16345 million which was 31.2 per cent higher than the level of US $ 12454 million during July, 2007. In rupee terms, exports touched Rs. 70018 crore, which was 39.1 per cent higher than the value of exports during July, 2007. Cumulative value of exports for the period April- July, 2008 was US$ 59191 million (Rs. 248498 crore) as against US$ 47487 million (Rs. 194689 crore) registering a growth of 24.6 per cent in Dollar terms and 27.6 per cent in Rupee terms over the same period last year.

ECGC is currently in its 51st year of operations and is the only insurance company in India operating exclusively in the export credit insurance sector under 'non-life' category, has earned a gross premium income of Rs 668.36 Crores during 2007-08 as compared to Rs 617.66 Crores of previous year. ECGC achieved recoveries of Rs 161.50 Crores during the year. The net profit after tax for the year was Rs. 479.43 Crores as against the previous year's profit of Rs. 369.70 Crores. ECGC has provided covers aggregating Rs. 437882 crores to exports & export finance in the year 2007-08. The Government of India has continued to extend support to the Corporation. Rs 100 Crores was added to the equity base of the Corporation in the year 2007-08 which has resulted in augmenting the paid up capital to Rs. 900 Crores.

## REFERENCES

B.K. Chaudhuri & O. PAggarwal (2006.), "A Text Book of Foreign Trade and Foreign Exchange", Himalayan Publishing House.

C. Rama Gopal (2006), "Export Import Procedures, Documentation and Logistics", New Age International Publishers.

Dr. Khushpat S. Jain (2007), Export Import Procedures and Documentation, Himalayan Publishing House.

Francis Cherunilam (2007), International Trade and Export Management, Himalayan Publishing House.

Weekly Economic Bulletin Date: February 26–March 3, 2008 Issue No. 253.

Dr. G. Satyanaryana W. Export Credit Insurance in India.

India: Brief Profile, Exim Bank: Research & Planning, March 2008.

Kevin Shah & Kevin Enterprises Pvt. Ltd. The Right Export Strategy for Young Indian Technology Companies, Technology Exports, Vol. 8 No. 1, May-June 2008.

*www.exportersindia.net*

*www.eximbankindia.in*

*www.eximbankagro.in*

# 23

# ENVIRONMENT OF VOLATILITY AND UNCERTAINTY IN EXPORTS

**K. Krishnakumar & B. Nirmala Devi**

## INTRODUCTION

The industrial policy proposal undertaken by the government since July 1991 have been designed to build on the past industrial achievements and it step up the process of making Indian industry internationally competitive. It also recognizes the strength and maturity of the industry and attempts to provide the competitive stimulus for higher growth. These initiatives have been to increase the domestic and external competitions which encourage dynamic relationship with foreign investors and suppliers of technology. There are some major industries that competitively entered the global market among which textiles industries is one of the major sector. It plays a vital role in the nation's economy, both in regard with employment generation and earning of foreign exchange. Recently, inflation surge a far above the ground 13 year high and the expectation of its rate is driven up by unrelenting pressures that originated from international commodity prices particularly in the price of crude oil, edible oil and metals. It affects all the sectors directly or indirectly without leaving any one to respire freely and textile industries are one among them.

The present study is focused on the environment of volatility and uncertainty in exports of textile industry located at Salem in Tamilnadu.

## STATEMENT OF THE PROBLEM

Textile industries are one of the major sectors in India. Textile exports presently account for more than $1/3^{rd}$ of the country's total export earnings. It is one of the single largest earners of foreign exchange. The marvelous feature of the textile and clothing exports is its low import intensity as compared to other major export products. Inflation is a necessary evil for economic growth representing a state where the value of money falls considerably with the prices on persistent rise. Most of the industrial sector both private and public, household, are get affected due to inflation met by India which was not at all gone through before. The fluctuations and uncertainty-in the market environment, decline in production, decelerated growth-lead instability among the textile exporters and others problems (at micro level). The present study highlights the current scenario of the Salem exporters. The study took a span of period of 30 days commencing from $13^{th}$ August 2008-$13^{th}$ September 2008.

## OBJECTIVES

(1) To study the effect of currency fluctuations faced by the textile exporters in Salem city.

(2) To study the market risks undertaken by the textile exporters in Salem city.

(3) To give suggestions for restructuring the existing market environment.

## MEASUREMENT OF TOOLS

Statistical tools like correlation and chi-square tests were employed along with bar chart and line chart to arrive at conclusion. Sources of data were collected from export garments situated at Salem city. The sample consists of 50 export garments in Salem. The nature of work of these organizations varied in three aspects namely (i) Production process: The weaving clothing, stitching or sewing process are held outside the industry (ii) Source of capital investment and (iii) Nature of exports (varied according to the capability of capturing export orders globally or from foreign countries).

**REVIEW OF LITERATURE**

In view of inflation many theoreticians and empirical research have come forward to propose or explain inflation in indifferent methods or strategies for managing its consequences. On a closer scrutiny of these perspectives, only few research findings were highlighted in the following section

*Feldman and Gang (1990)* study suggests that the simplest indictor was the money/GDP ratio, which measures the degree of monetization in the economy. Financial development was generally identified with the growth of the real size of the financial sector and in relation to GDP that supports textiles.

*Liu and Woo (1994)* recommended that a proxy for the degree of financial sophistication was the ratio of the long term to short term financial assets value. Money Supply (M1) is used as the short term financial assets value. The ratio of broad money to narrow money (M2/M1) should be positively related to a country's level of financial development.

*King and Levine (1993)* study found that the ratio M2/GDP measures the overall size of the financial intermediary sector and were strongly correlated with both the level and the rate of change of the real GDP per capita. On the other hand, M1/GDP is not strongly associated with the level of economic development.

*JF Outreville (2005)* study views that human resources development can be promoted only at the expense of economic growth poses false trade off. The measures of financial development are positively correlated with real GDP per capita and with measures of human capital development and negatively correlated in most cases but not significantly with measures of political instability. Measures in regard with inflation, the real interest rate and monopoly power in the financial sector are all insignificant determinants of financial development.

## INDIAN TEXTILES AN OVER VIEW

Industry group's jute and other vegetable fibre textiles recorded a decline in production. Wool, Silk, manmade fibre textiles, textiles products, cotton textiles recorded decelerated growth in 2008 Global cotton prices, represented by the "Cotlook A Index", declined by almost 4% over march 2008. Cotton prices were higher by account 27%, year on year, in June 2008. According to the international Cotton Advisory Committee (ICAC), world cotton production is expected to decline by about 3% in 2008-2009 and therefore, world cotton stocks are expected to fall further by almost 9% to 11% million Tonnes. According to ICAC report, prices are expected to go up by 12% in 2008-2009. Sources taken from RBI Bulletin 2007.

Indian textile exports had exports had shot up from 14.03$ billion in 2004-2005 to 20.25$ billion in 2007-2008. This hype built shows potential improvement in performance since 2004. Due to adverse effect in price and quality, combination brings the competitiveness' of Indian textiles with China, Pakistan and Bangladesh. This leads steady inroads into India's major market in the US.

The see-saw on interest subvention of 2% for pre-shipment and post-shipment credit for textiles readymade garments in the 1st fiscal part and additional subvention of 2% from Nov 1, 2007 shows a steady appreciation of the rupee till end-march 31-2008. But 4% interest subvention announced by RBI tantalized the textile industry to face a higher draw back rate source from Mr. Rakesh Vaid-Apparel Export Promotion council Chairman.

In order to support textile exports, fashion designers help them to compete in the international market. In addition to the existing National Institute of Fashion Technology (NIFT) centre at New Delhi, the major NIFT centres at Mumbai, Hyderabad, Calcutta, Chennai, Ghandhinagar also provide its substantial effort to increase export in the international market in an effective manner. Other than these, Universities and University Colleges' also showed their innovativeness in their creation of export designs. To promote research and other scientific work, Ahmedabad Textile Industry's Research

Association, Bombay, South India Research Association, Coimbatore and Northern Indian Textiles Research Association, Ghaziabad are the four textile research associations registered under Societies Registration Act 1860 and functioning under the administrative control of the Ministry of Textile. The total employment in textile sector in estimated about 64.20 million more.

## REASONS FOR CURRENCY FLUCTUATIONS

Current situation shows that the rupee depreciation vis-sa-vis US dollar had fluctuation in the current fiscal leads to a salutary trend in Indian exports. A definite slow down in the US market where out of Rs. 100 of exports, Rs 20 came from the US and this would down to Rs 15. This has been made good by diversifying export destination to Latin Ameirca, South East Asia and Asean region by India exporters in recent period.

The hurricane Gustav could be the first major threat to the US Gulf of Mexico oil fields and ports, since hurricanes Katrina and Rita in 2005. The hurricane which was developed from a Storm has its trail of destruction in Jamaica, Haiti and The Dominican Republic was headed towards the US after sweeping through Cuba. The Gulf is the source of 25% domestic oil and 15% of the natural gas. Due to it threat, the support of crude oil's barrel price worth 10$ facing its resistance up to 125-132$ a barrel. This leads a great deal of currency fluctuations in the world market. In the mean time, the exchange rate of the rupee has exhibited appropriate flexibility in response to market conditions. Furthermore, the international currency markets also saw large changes in cross-currency rates. Due to this, the domestic Wholesale Price Indices (WPI) for most commodities had risen by a much lower extent than world level.

## ANALYSIS

The sample of the present study consisted of 50 exporters. They were selected randomly using random number table method. An open-ended question was asked to identify most important causes as perceived by the exporters that often lead them to take market risk and finding uncertainty while distribution of sales. The wide distribution of sales covered by Salem city exporters are USA, Europe, UK, Middle East, Australia and Others. The following table was used to identify how investment influences on sales by using chi-square table.

## HYPOTHESIS: HO: HIGH INVESTMENT INFLUENCE HIGH MARKET RISK ON SALES AMONG THE EXPORTERS

**Table 1**
**Global Sales**

| *Investment* | *USA* | *Europe* | *UK* | *Sales Mid.East* | *Australia* | *Others* |
|---|---|---|---|---|---|---|
| < 5 crores | 4 | 4 | 0 | 3 | 2 | 3 |
| 5Crores-10 Crores | 5 | 3 | 4 | 3 | 2 | 2 |
| 10Crores-50 Crores | 3 | 2 | 2 | 1 | 0 | 1 |
| > 50 Crores | 3 | 2 | 1 | 0 | 0 | 0 |
| Total | 15 | 11 | 7 | 7 | 4 | 6 |

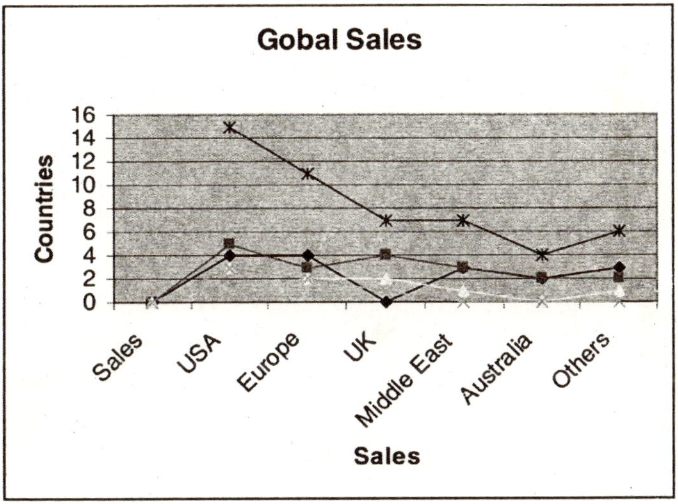


| *Factor* | *Chi–Square Value* | *D.O.F* | *Table Value* | *Remarks* |
|---|---|---|---|---|
| Global Sales | .998 | 15 | 7.61 | Not Significant at 5% level |

From the above table it is noted that the calculated Chi-Square value is less than the table value and hence the null hypothesis is rejected. Hence, it is inferred that "high investment did not influence high market risk on sales among the exporters".

The investment made by the Salem city exporters and the type of industry are given in the following table. The industry types are categorized into four types of viz., Partnership, Proprietorship, Private Limited and Others and their investments are categorized into below five crores, 5-10 crores, 10-50 crores, and above 50 crores.

**Table 2**
**Investments**

| | *Investments* | | | | |
|---|---|---|---|---|---|
| *Industry* | *< 5 Crores* | *5-10 Crores* | *10-50 Crores* | *>50 Crores* | |
| Partnership | 9 | 8 | 0 | 0 | 17 |
| Proprietorship | 4 | 5 | 1 | 0 | 10 |
| Private Limited | 5 | 6 | 2 | 0 | 13 |
| Others | 3 | 6 | 1 | 0 | 10 |
| | 21 | 25 | 4 | 0 | 50 |

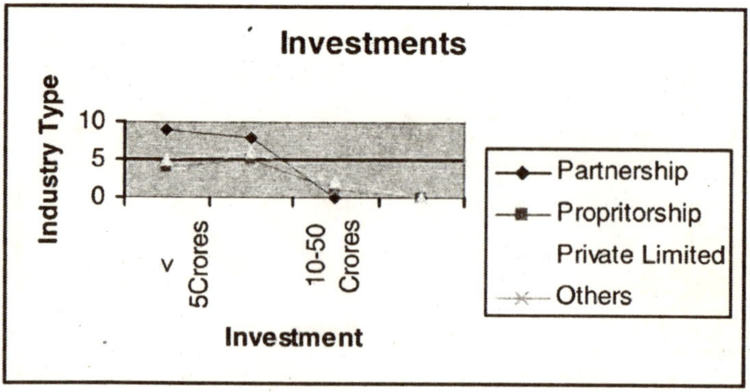


## SCOPE FOR DEVELOPMENT

Going for accredition of ISO 17020 certification solves the problems in the parameters like length, width etc. According to this certification, the buyers can assess the quality of products pertaining to count of warp and weft, dimension of the piece (length and width), weight/sq.m and fastness properties to washing, rubbing and exposure to sunlight etc. This certification will solve the problems of exports of quality level.

Penetration in foreign countries is another aspect of development in textile industries. If India's engagement with Asean market took place, then it is possible for tetile exports to Japan, China, Korea, Newzealand and Australa. The remarkable thing is that the country enjoying FTA with Asean would pay zero duty. This is one of the golden opportunities for Indian textiles to global market widely.

Recently, China is facing tougher times with currency rise and closure of many units of textiles to reduce pollution levels in Beijing. Chinese textile exports saw a 2.4% fall from September 2007 to may 2008, while during the same perod, Inda way about 25 growths. Because Indian exporters push towards the markets in South Africa, Kenya and other African countries and also to South-East Asean nations like Thailand, Malaysia and Singapore.

Further, world cotton production is expected to decrease by 5% to 24.9 million tones in 2008-2009 due to declines in both area and yield. The US output projected to fall by more than one metric tonnes to 3.1 metric tones. Indian market will not remain insulated from overseas influences. In 2007-2208, domestic prices escalated by 30-35% with a shadow cast on the production prospect in India, The world may be starved of much needed cotton and India is expected to being supplying in recent years.

## ARGUMENTS

### Do all the Items in the WPI List get Affected Due to International Market Volatility?

The domestic Wholesale Price Indices (WPI) for most commodities had risen by a much lower extent than world level. Deglobalization results in price rise in rubber and cotton at domestic price than world price. This benefit is realized by the Indian farmers at the expense of tire manufacturers and textile millers. The basic chemical and chemical products and transport equipments and parts in relation with manufacturing tobacco, beverages and related products are shown double-digit growth. Mining industry picked up by 5.6% as compared with 3.2% a year ago.

## Who is the Benefactor of International Market Volatility?

Textile millers, mining industry, manufacturing of beverages industry, the farmers of rubber, cotton are the benefactors of market volatility.

## Do the Salem Textile Exporters get Befitted Due to International Market Volatility?

Yes, but all the exporters are not. By taking the market risk, the Salem exporters who are in the member of exporters association slowly start their penetration towards the markets in South Africa, Kenya and other African countries. On the other hand, few of the individual exporters, tries to get orders from Thailand, Malaysia and Singapore.

Their major risk is the rupee depreciation vis-sa-vis US dollar/Euro currency variations during the supply order cost, shipment cost and full settlement.

## CONCLUSION

The rise in price of crude oil, deorecuation of rupee value vis-visa-vis dollar/ Euro are the major cause for affecting domestic as well as international market. But the fall in price is not merely considered in the domestic market. So, textile industries also get affected due to this. The imbalance of supply and demand in market wizards figures out the possible idea of future shortage in cotton and textile products. Government policy makers should take some measures to mitigate the existing condition to support the exporters to widening their distribution of sales.

## REFERENCE

Indian Economic General View, Finance India, March 2005.

RBI Bulletin 2008, www.statistics of Indian Finance.com

Feld Man and Gang (1990), "Financial Development and Price of Services", *Economic Development and cultural Change*, Vol. 38, 2, pp. 341-352

King and Levin (1993), "Finance, Entrepreneurship and Growth: Theory and Evidence", *Journal of Monetary Economics*, Vol. 32, pp. 341-352

Liu and Woo (1994), "Saving Behaviour under Imperfect Financial Markets and the Current Account Consequences", *The Economic Journal*, Vol. 104, pp. 512-527.

Outreville (2005), 'Finance Development, Human Capital and Political Instability", *Finance India*, Vol. XIX, 2, pp. 481-492.

# 24

# EXPERIENCE OF EXPORTERS IN MANAGING CURRENCY RISKS BY DERIVATIVES

**S. Muruganandan & E. P. Sengottuvel**

## INTRODUCTION

Foreign exchange risk is the possibility of a gain or loss to a firm that occurs due to unanticipated changes in exchange rate. In export transaction, if the value of foreign currency depreciates exporter will get less domestic currency. So, the primary aim of the exporter is to protect export profit from the negative impact of exchange rate fluctuations.

In the present state of economy, there is a need for the exporters to protect their profit by shifting of the uncontrollable fluctuation in foreign exchange rate to those who are able to bear and manage them. Thus, risk management becomes a must for survival since there is a high volatility in current fluctuation.

In this context, derivatives occupy important place as a risk reducing machinery. Derivatives can ensure that the currency fluctuation risks hedged by using derivatives like forward, futures, options, swaps etc., this really protect the exporter from s exchange fluctuation risks.

Derivatives are based upon all the major financial instruments which are explicitly traded like equities, debt equities, debt instruments, forex instruments and commodity based contracts. Thus we talk about derivatives, we usually mean only financial derivatives, namely forwards futures, options, swaps etc.

Derivatives can be defined as "derivatives involves payments/receipts of income generated by the underlying assets on a notional principal"

We can also define the derivatives as instruments which make payments calculated using price of interest rates derived from a balance sheet or cash instrument but do not actually employ those cash instruments to fund payments".

Above definition point out the fact that transactions are carried out on a notional principal, transferring only the income generated by the underlying assets.

The important financial derivatives are the following:

(i) Forwards

(ii) Futures

(iii) Options and

(iv) Swaps

**Forwards**

Forwards are the oldest of all the derivatives. A forwards contract refers to an agreement between two parties to exchange an agreed quantity of an asset for cash at a certain data in future at a predetermined price specified in that agreement. The promised assets may be currency, commodity, instruments etc.,

***Forward Rate Currency Contracts***

It is a contract where exchange of currencies is promised at an agreed exchange rate at a specified future date. The important feature of this contract is that the pay off is proportional to the different between the rate specified in the forward rate contract and the price of the currency prevailing in the market at the time of settlement.

It is similar to a spot transaction but the settlement date is deferred much further into the future. No currency is exchanged until that settlement date. Therefore, a forward contract invloues contracting today for the futures purchase of sale of foreign currency

**Future**

A future contract is very similar to a forwards contract in all respect expecting the fact that it is completely a standardized one. Hence, it is rightly said that a future contracts is nothing but a standardized forward contract. It is legally enforceable and it is always traded an organized exchange.

***Currency Future***

Currency future refers to a future contract in foreign exchange currency future are very popular in western countries as hedging instruments to protest against exchange rate fluctuation. Just like forwards exchange rate currency contract we have futures contract on currency fluctuation. Risks due to exchange rate fluctuation are very common. This risk cannot be eliminated but transferred to counterparty. This counterparty may have a hedging motive with opposite requirement.

**Options**

In the volatile environment risk heavy fluctuations in exchange rate very heavy. Option is yet another tool to manage such risks.

As the very name implies, an option contract gives the buyer an option to buy or sell an underlying assets (e.g.: currency) at a predetermined price on or before a specified date in future. The price so predetermined is called the "Strike price" or "exercise price".

***Currency Option***

Suppose an option contract is entered into between parties to purchase. Sell foreign exchange, it is called "currency option". A forex option gives to buyer the right, but not the obligation to buy from the seller or to sell to the writer (seller) a specific quantity of one currency in exchange rate, known as the strike price, on a given future date.

### Swap

Swap is yet another exciting trading instrument. Infact, it is a combination of forwards by two counterparties. It is arranged to reap the benefits arising from the fluctuation in the market either currency market or internet rate market, or any other market for that matter.

A currency swap is a contract between two parties to deliver one sum of money against another sum of money at regular intervals and the periodic exchange rate prevailing at the time of originating of the Swap.

## NECESSARY STEPS TO MANAGE CURRENCY RISK MORE EFFICIENTLY

The following points should consider to manage the currency risk. Such points are.

### Select your Currency

It is desirable to hedge but all part of it, as the favorable side may generate great benefits. We may put different currencies in order of our requirement and hedge in order of our requirement and hedge in order preference. Suppose an exporter is exposed from receivable in dollar and euro, one may kind dollar to be less strong than euro for specific period so while hedging the currency, it may hedge dollar first.

### Seek more Quotations

Different banks or dealers may different rates, so it is always better to get two or more quotations from different dealers. Even quotation from same dealer at different times also differs.

### Knowing the Spread

It is the different between the prices we buy at (also known as ask) and the price we sell at (also known as the bid). The exporter should develop the ability to sell the buy price (ask) and the sell price (bid) at all times. Spread has historically been a "hidden" cost. An exporter can see the spread and thus can know exactly what the cost of the trade is prior to entering a position.

### Try to Minimize Dependence on One Currency Hedge

An exporter should try to expose to different currency and hedge accordingly exporters exposed to dollar in early nineties suffered a lot buy using risk profiting, the method of worst case and best case through scenario management on performance measure of individual currency.

### Shift

Exporter should shift from one 'instruments' to another or one currency to another depending upon the changing market conditions or changing economy indicators.

### Exchange Rate Predictions

Based on economic forecasting models (PPP – relative purchasing power parity, balance of payment, interest rate parity) exchange rate may be predicted and acted accordingly.

Rate expected = spot rate (1+different inflation rate)year

Suppose inflation in 'A' currency is 6% and 'B' currency 3%, and the spot rate is 48.25 after 5 years, the predicted rate would be:

$$\text{Rate expected} = 48.25\,(1+ (0.06-0.03)^5$$
$$= 48.25\,(1+0.03)^5$$
$$\text{Rate expected} = \text{Rs. } 55.93$$

## HEDGING AGAINST FOREIGN EXCHANGE RISK

### Forward Market Hedge

Generally, forward market hedge would take the following form.

Suppose an Indian exporter sells merchandise to an American importer for USD 1, 00,000 payable in 90 days. Ending up with fewer rupee. To hedge forward against the potential risk caused by the dollar depreciation, the Indian exporter can take the following action.

(a) Assuming that the Indian exporter wants rupee payment of Rs. 4500000 for the goods. Supplied he will calculate the dollar value of that amount at 90 days rate on forward dollar which based at Rs. 45 would be us $ 100000 {450000/45}.

(b) When the sales contract with the American importer is signed, the exporter immediately sells USD 100000 forwards for 90 days at Rs. 45. If at the end of 90 day the spot dollar rate falls below Rs. 45 the exporter is fully protected because the exporter can sell the USD 100000 received from the importer for Rs. 4500000 under the forwards contract which is the rupee amount demanded by the exporter.

## SPOT AND MONEY MARKET HEDGE

In the earlier example about the India exporter sending goods worth US $ 100000 to an American importer, the exporter can resort to money market. The exporter can borrow the USD 100000 in New York for 90 days and immediately convert the dollar into rupee at the spot rate and either lend such funds or them in his business. At the end of 90 days the exporter would then repay the dollar loan including interest with the dollar received from the American importer. Depending upon the prevailing rate of interest in both countries, the exporter can come out better off.

*Using the following formula*

$$FA= [A/ (1+USDi] \times S \times [1+INRi]$$

Where

FA = the amount of received from forward hedging.

A = the dollar amount due to the exporter in 90 days.($ 100000in the example}

S = the rupee/dollar spot exchange rate.

USDi = the New York annual interest rate adjusted to the 90 days period.

Suppose USD = Rs. 45, the annual USDi = 0.08 and the annual INRi = 0.09, the exporter would end up with the following rupee amount at the end of 90 days.

$$= \frac{100000}{\frac{(1+0.08)}{4}} * 45 * \frac{1+0.09}{4}$$

$$= \frac{100000}{0.27} * 12.2625$$

$$= \text{Rs. } 4541666.67$$

Comparing this result with the outcome of forward hedging {i.e. Rs. 4500000} it would appear more advantages for the exporter {i.e., Rs. 41666.67} to hedge through the spot and money markets.

From the above argument when the exporter hedges through the spot and money market he is behaving as an interest arbitrager. In such a case if,

$$FA > [A/\ (1+USDi] \times S \times [1+INRi]$$

Exporter will hedge in forward market and conversely if

$$FA < [A/\ (1+USDi] \times S \times [1+INRi]$$

Then the exporter borrows in New York.

**CASE-I**

TCS Ltd., in accordance with its risk management polices and procedure enters into foreign currency forward contract to manage its exposure in foreign currency. The counter party is generally banker.

During the three month period ended June 30, 2008 TCS Ltd has re-evaluated its risk management program and hedging strategies in respect of forested transmission.

Net loss on derivatives instruments of $ 53.2 million recognized in accumulated other comprehensive income as of June 30, 2009.

The movement in accumulated other comprehensive income during the period ended June 30, 2008 for derivative designated as cash flow hedge is as follows:

In addition to the above cash flow hedges, the company has outstanding foreign exchange forward contract and currency option contract aggregating $540.5 million and $593.3 million , whose fair value showed a loss of $1.1 million and $loss of $1.2 million as on march30, 2008and june30, 2008 respectively.

| | *Period Ended March31, 2008* | *Period Ended June30, 2008* |
|---|---|---|
| | | In million of US$ |
| Balance @ beginning | $18.4 | $(3.8) |
| Gain/(loss) transferred to income statement on accordance of forecasted hedge transaction | (16.2) | 2.5 |
| Change in the fair value of effective portion of outstanding cash flow derivative | (43.6) | (85.1) |
| Net derivative gain/(loss) related to a discontinued cash flow hedge | 37.6 | (8.9) |
| Balance @ the end | $ (3.8) | $(95.3) |

*Source:* TCS Ltd, Notes to unaudited condensed consolidated financial statement.

Although, these contracts are effective as hedge from an economic perspective, they do not quality for hedge accounting and accordingly these are accounted as derivative instrument at fair value with changes in fair value recorded into earning. Exchange gain of $46.4 million and exchange loss of $67.4 million of foreign currency forward exchange contracts have been recognized during the period ended june30, 2007 and 2008 respectively.

## CASE –II

*India Axis Bank: Clients' Notional Derivative Loss $169mln*

India's Axis Bank said derivative contract had helped structure for its corporate clients to hedge risk had caused notional loss of $169 million to the clients. The private sector bank which posted a 62 percent jump in earnings for the financial year ended 31.3.2008, said it had helped for mark-to-market loss of 720 million rupees of two clients who had the deals and filed lawsuits. It did not name the clients.

Several Indian firms have taken the help of banks to cover over foreign exchange derivatives trade that have gone sour. About five to six small firms have filed lawsuits against private sector bank with alleging mis-selling of derivative products.

*Source*: www.reuters.com

## CASE-III

*Exporters meet Finance Minister, demand settlement of derivative loss issue*

A group of medium and small exporters on September 02, 2008 met finance minister P Chidambaram and pleaded for amicable settlement of the issue concerning derivatives losses with the banks on "no profit and no loss" basis. "The minister is aware of the problem and has promised to forward the memorandum to the Reserve Bank of India to look into the grievances of the exporters," president of the forex derivative consumers' forum Raja M Shanmugam said after meeting Chidambaram. Many exporters, who tried to hedge their currency risk by executing forex derivatives contracts with banks, suffered huge losses on fluctuation in the value of rupee and now want that the issue to be settled with banks amicably. "Members of the forum are prepared to refund the profit earned, if any, from these exotic derivative products and the banks are requested not to claim the losses incurred", said the memorandum submitted to the minister.

Chidambaram, who gave a patient hearing to exporters, told them as the matter involves private and foreign banks, government cannot interfere directly but will refer the matter to the central bank. Exporters' claim that they were lured into entering derivatives contracts to hedge foreign currency losses by banks and were not informed that "these contracts are purely speculative and...has the inherent potential to result in enormous loss"

*Source:* Business Line, September 02, 2008

## GROUNDS FOR DERIVATIVE LOSS

One of the important characteristics features of derivative is that they lend themselves to leveraging. That is, they are 'high risk- high reward vehicle'. There is a prospect of either high return or huge loss in all derivative instruments. So, only a few can play with this. Derivatives needs high experienced person to handle it. Hence it is not suitable to all exporters.

To achieve the desired result, derivative should supported by proper accounting system efficient internal control and strict supervision. Unfortunately, they are all at infancy level as far as derivative concern.

In fact all the derivative contracts are structured basically on the basis of future price movement over which the speculators have an upper hand. Thus, derivatives possess an inbuilt speculative mechanism.

An important requirement for using derivative instruments is the existence of proper infrastructure. But it is not exists.

## OTHER METHODS FOR EXCHANGE RISK MANAGEMENT

### Denomination in Local Currency

The exchange risk can be totally avoided if the transaction is denominated in local currency. In such a case the exchange risk will be borne by the other party to the transaction. For instance, if exporter from India are invoiced in Indian rupee, the obligation of the importer id to pay a fixed sum of rupees. The exporter will not affected by any movement in exchanges rate. The importer will be bearing the exchange fluctuation risk entirely.

### Exchange Fluctuation Risk Cover

The Exchange Fluctuation Risk Cover is intended to provide a measure of protection to exporters of capital goods, civil engineering contractors and consultants who have often to receive payments over a period of years for their exports, construction works or services. Where such payments are to be received in are foreign currency, they open to exchange fluctuation risk as the forward exchange market does not provide cover for such deferred payments.

## THE TERMS OF THE EXCHANGE FLUCTUATION RISK COVER

Exchange Fluctuation Risk Cover is available for payments scheduled over a period of 12 months or more, upto a maximum of 15 years. Cover can be obtained from the date of bidding right up to the final installment. At the stage of bidding, an exporter/contractor can obtain Exchange

Fluctuation Risk (Bid) Cover. The basis for cover will be a reference rate agreed upon. The reference rate can be the rate prevailing on the date of bid or rate approximating it. The cover will be provided initially for a period of twelve months and can be extended if necessary. If the bid is successful, the exporter/contractor is required to obtain Exchange Fluctuation (Contract) cover for all payments due under the contract. The reference rate for the contract cover will be either the reference rate used for the Bid Cover or the rate prevailing on the date of contract, at the option of the exporter/contractor. If the bid is unsuccessful 75 percent of the premium paid by the exporter/contractor is refunded to him.

## THE CURRENCIES COVERED UNDER EXCHANGE FLUCTUATION RISK COVER

Cover under the schemes is available for payments specified in US Dollar, Pound Sterling, Deustche Mark, Japanese Yen, French Franc, Swiss Franc, UAE Dirham and Australian Dollar. However, cover can be extended for payment specified in other convertible currencies at the discretion of ECGC

## BEARER/ RECEIVER OF LOSS OR GAIN IN EXCHANGE RATE

The loss or gain within a range of 2 percent of the reference rate will go to the exporter's account. If the loss exceeds 2 percent, ECGC will make good the portion of loss in excess of 2 percent but not exceeding 35 per cent of the reference rate. In other words, loss/gain upto 2 per cent and beyond 35 percent of the reference rate will be to the exporter's account. If there is gain in excess of 2 percent and upto 35 percent it will be turned over to ECGC.

## PREMIUM RATES

The rate of premium is 40 paise per Rs.100/- per year or 10 paise per Rs.100/- per quarter for the bid cover. The total premium is payable at the time of issue of the Policy. Premium for contract cover is also payable at the rate of 40 paise per Rs.100/- per annum. Ten percent of the total premium payable and premium for the first two years should be paid at the time of issue of the Policy.

Thereafter, the annual premium will have to be paid in such a manner that premium for two years ahead is always kept paid to the Corporation. Exchange Fluctuation Risk Cover will normally be provided along with suitable credit insurance cover. There is, however, provision to grant the cover independently also in which case premium will be loaded by 20%.

## CONCLUSION

When the exporter know well that they have to face risk of volatility in currency fluctuation, it is better to transfer this risk to those who are ready to bear them. So, they have necessarily to go for exchange fluctuation risk cover, because derivative instruments are very risky even it has high gain. Hence, derivative instruments are not suitable to all exporters. Denomination in the currency of exporter puts the other party (i.e., importer) at risk, due to this, importer may not like this. From the above argument it may be said that exchange fluctuation risk cover, like the one offered by ECGC, is better to mitigating the currency fluctuation risk.

## REFERENCE

Pradeep Tipbrewal (2004), "Managing Currency Risk by Derivatives, "The Chartered Accountant, 593-598.

Ekpenyoung D. B. (1987), "Hedging Against Foreign Exchange Risk," *Journal of Financial Management and Analysis*, 64-66.

S.S.S. Kumar (2007), Financial Derivatives, Pentice Hall of India Pvt. Ltd, New Delhi, p. 10-27.

E. Gorden & K. Nataragan (2005), Financial Markets and Services, Himalaya Publication House, p. 354-375.

Madhu vil (2003), International Financial Management, Excel Book, New Delhi, p. 97.

### Website

*www.tcs.com*
*www.icicidirect.com*

25

# ROLE OF EXIM BANK AND COMMERCIAL BANKS IN PROMOTING INDIA'S EXPORTS IN THE PRESENT COMPLEX NATURE OF WORLD TRADE

**P. Velmurugan & N. Chakkaravarthy**

## INTRODUCTION

In the present complex nature of world trade export from the perspective of Indian companies is not easily achievable and trouble-free. Though there are several capable companies who are highly flourishing in the domestic market they do not participate in overseas projects, possibly due to lack of self confidence in operating in an unfamiliar environment. There is a definite necessity for the government to take them to the world by promoting them, coordinating them and provide a source of finance & consultants. All these expectations are duly fulfilled by the Export Import Bank of India, which is the principal financial institution for promoting Indian Project Export. The Projects are funded by multilateral funding agencies offers strong payment assurance (MFAs) with which several contracts have been won by the Indian companies against stiff international competition with the help of EXIM. As the funds for such projects are fully tied up, the contractors are ensured timely payment during contract execution moreover the selection processes are very transparent and fair. Recent trends indicate that there is an increasing focus and funding of projects in the social sector and poverty reduction programs. Increasingly, projects on BOT (Build, Operate and Transfer) basis are becoming popular. Long term deferred credit will play a major role in securing project export contracts. India could take membership, through equity participation, in other MFAs such as the European Bank for Reconstruction & Development and Inter-American Development Bank (currently nonmembers\can't participate in projects funded by IDB), which will enable India to effectively participate in projects funded by such institutions. Role of credit in export facilitation is now well recognized. With export facilitation regime being regulated by the provisions of WTO, credit has become the single most external factor, which can inhibit growth of exports from countries.

For providing such credit, export credit agencies (ECAs- also referred to as EXIM Banks) around the world have become an important component of the export promotion strategy of a country. To conclude in order enable Indian companies to take advantage of the current opportunities, EXIM Bank of India will need to play an effective role, with a strengthened institutional framework, in terms of offering internationally competitive financing packages with longer tenors.

## BACKGROUND

Project Exports from India have been increasing steadily over the years (see chart), indicating the growing stature of Indian expertise overseas in a wide range of activities, and upward movement in the value chain of its export performance. From a modest beginning in the early seventies, Indian companies have made impressive progress in a number of areas like civil construction projects (road, railways, dams, airports, etc.), turnkey projects (power generator, transmission and distribution, industrial plants, etc.), technical services (engineering design, project engineering, operation and maintenance of industrial plants, etc.) and earned a niche for themselves in the developing country markets. Major policy initiatives since the past decade have been instrumental in preparing India for a period of rapid export growth as also becoming a major player in an increasingly inter-dependent world economy. Project Exports reflect the technological maturity and industrial capability of a country. The nature of Project Exports being undertaken now, reflects the technological maturity and industrial capabilities in the country. They indicate growing sophistication of Indian exports giving visibility to the Indian technical expertise and project execution capability in overseas markets and boost the economy in manifold ways including generating project revenues, creation of secured markets for goods and services, import of new technology and training of personnel, employment creation during construction and operation phases and saving of foreign exchange.

**CURRENT STATUS**

At present, there are 140 project export contracts valued at over Rs. 17,800 crore (approx. US$ 4 bn) under execution in 39 countries across Asia, Africa and Europe by 31 Indian companies. The projects range from building hydro electric power stations in Bhutan, transmission line projects in Tunisia to operations and maintenance of cement plant in Saudi Arabia. Many of these projects are funded by MFAs and the contracts have been won by the Indian companies against stiff international competition.

Though the current level of Project Exports at US$ 4 bn appears impressive, the potential is much greater. More companies will need to be encouraged to participate in the overseas project opportunities. There are many capable companies who are highly successful in the domestic market, but do not participate in overseas projects, possibly due to diffidence in operating in an unfamiliar environment. Such companies can be encouraged to go either as subcontractors or consortium members with successful Indian companies already operating in export markets.

## GROWING OPPORTUNITIES

Projects funded by multilateral funding agencies (MFAs) are characterized by professional appraisal for technical feasibility and economic viability. As the funds for such projects are fully tied up, the contractors are ensured timely payment during contract execution. Also, host country payment risks do not exist and bid evaluation and selection process are very transparent and fair. Such projects cover most of the major sectors of economy such as agriculture, energy, transport and communication, industry, water supply and sanitation, education, health and urban development. Recent trends indicate an increasing focus and funding of projects in the social sector and poverty reduction programmes. These projects represent a sizeable and promising business opportunity for Indian project exporters in areas where they possess significant competitive advantage and domain expertise, while simultaneously minimizing the risk of non-payment. Projects in the developmental field conducted by developing nations are those where the level of technology is high with difficult operating conditions and the skills and expertise required to execute such projects are well within the capabilities of Indian project exporters. At the same time, the fact that funding is being provided by MFAs, offers strong payment assurance. However, the level and extent of competition are much higher as many firms from developed countries prefer to participate in these project opportunities.

Though Indian companies' share in projects funded by MFAs in India is impressive, the share in overseas projects is marginal. For instance, as per prior review contracts under World Bank funded projects in 2003, Indian companies secured contracts valued at US$ 324.5 mn, out of which, 96% contracts by value were for projects in India and only 4% for overseas projects. WB data related to payments to India for local and foreign procurement shows that India's share in foreign procurement is marginal in comparison to local procurement (see table). For instance, in 2003, World Bank payments to India for local and foreign procurement amounted to US$ 1.2 bn (of which US$ 67 mn is for foreign procurement), which accounted for 6.76% of World Bank's total disbursements. While the total disbursements to India for foreign procurement has almost doubled, growing from 1.21 per cent (of World Bank's total project disbursements) in FY 2001 to 1.27 per cent in FY 2002 and further to 2.34 per cent in FY 2003, there is scope for Indian companies to enhance their prospects of securing more contracts in World Bank funded projects. Even a modest increase in India's share, would translate into significant additional export earnings. In addition to projects funded by MFAs in various countries, many developing countries offer scope for project exports, if suitable credit packages are offered by the bidders. Increasingly, projects on BOT (Build, Operate and Transfer) basis are becoming popular. Long term deferred credit will play a major role in securing project export contracts.

## NEED FOR STRATEGIC APPROACH

Clearly, Indian companies have demonstrated capabilities to secure contracts in India under international competitive bidding conditions. This, however, does not get reflected into contracts overseas although the nature of such projects, the sectors to which these pertain and the skills and expertise required are well within the capabilities of Indian project exporters. Thus, increased overseas bid participation is essential. Indian project exporters must seriously consider the possibility of developing strategic partnerships as also securing sub-contracts from major European/American/Japanese companies. A conscious effort must be made by Indian companies to make structured marketing efforts through presentations on their skills, expertise and cost competitiveness to the overseas project companies. Also, Indian consultancy firms can also do well in exports markets, if they can establish strategic alliances with major international consultancy firms for joint bidding. Indian consultancy costs in specialized fields like design engineering, project management, etc. is approximately one-eighth of European cost and one-third of the cost in ASEAN region. As a member of MFAs viz. World Bank, Asian Development Bank and African Development Bank, India should be able to leverage its position for increased overseas business. Also, India could take membership, through equity participation, in other MFAs such as the European Bank for Reconstruction & Development and Inter-American Development Bank (currently nonmembers can't participate in projects funded by IDB), which will enable India to effectively participate in projects funded by such institutions. Also, India's membership by way of equity participation in regional development banks will strengthen efforts to expand the trade canvas. Early identification of a project opportunity at the initial stage of the project cycle can endow advantages in terms of gaining valuable lead-time for prefacing activities and preparation of competitive bids for such projects by Indian companies. Role of credit in export facilitation is now well recognized. This is so not only for the developing countries, but equally if not more, for developed countries as well. With export facilitation regime being regulated by the provisions of WTO, credit has become the single most external factor, which can inhibit growth of exports from countries. For providing such credit, export credit agencies (ECAs - also referred to as Exim Banks) around the world have become an important component of the export promotion strategy of a country. The correlation coefficient between export credit and exports in India during the period 1991-92 and 2002-03 is significant, at 0.97. Funds flow to the export sector would enable Project Exports to be generated, which would otherwise be lost by the country due to uncompetitive financial packages for Project Export contracts. As capacity utilization in many industries in India is currently low due to lack of domestic demand, availability of additional export credit would drive growth in exports, thus enhancing capacity utilization with attendant multiplier benefits for the economy. Recognizing the importance of availability of adequate export credit, most countries around the world maintain official systems for supporting national exports through a national ECA. A typical ECA acts as an export financing institution, a commercial export insurer, a foreign investment catalyst and a project finance expert. Exim Banks, though differing in role and function (depending upon the country's economic status) and resources, are mostly government owned. However, supporting exports on medium/long term credit basis. With the backing of their governments, Exim Banks in other countries are able to take on longer terms and higher risks than commercial banks can do. For instance, large projects that have substantial credit requirements and carry high investment risk are simply not be viable without the involvement of Exim Banks. In this way, the official export credit that Exim Banks provide, increases the opportunities for enhanced project exports. Recently, the Prime Minister's Office set up a high level Task Force on Project Exports to explore ways and means to register a quantum jump in India's project exports. The Task Force observed that Exim Bank of India must be strengthened through regular infusion of share capital and resources support, in order to evolve and expand as an institution and strengthen its reach, coverage as a major international financial institution to support India's international trade and investment. Exim Bank of India has been playing a significant role in catalyzing India's exports by assisting companies with export orientation through developing commercially viable relationships with such companies by offering them a comprehensive range of products and services directed at enhancing their internationalization efforts. To enable Indian companies to take advantage of the current opportunities, Exim Bank of India will need to play an effective role, with a strengthened institutional framework (see picture), in terms of offering internationally competitive financing packages with longer tenors. Against this backdrop, this book is an attempt to capture the evolution and growth of Project Exports from India over the past three decades, based on data available with the Bank, primary research on activities and policies of MFAs and their current focus, and interaction with leading Indian project exporters. The book giving an overall perspective of the past, present and future of 'Project Exports' will throw more light on the issues involved in this area as it explores the positive instrumental role that Project Exports is capable of playing in India's quest for a sustainable rapid economic growth. It is beyond doubt that the time is opportune for giving an impetus to India's Project Exports and to take advantage of the emerging opportunities around the world.

## CONCLUSION

To conclude in order enable Indian companies to take advantage of the current opportunities, EXIM Bank of India will need to play an effective role, with a strengthened institutional framework, in terms of offering internationally competitive financing packages with longer tenors. There is a definite necessity for the government to take them to the world by promoting them, coordinating them and provide a source of finance & consultants. All these expectations are duly fulfilled by the Export Import Bank of India, which is the principal financial institution for promoting Indian Project Export. The Projects are funded by multilateral funding agencies offers strong payment assurance (MFAs) with which several contracts have been won by the Indian companies against stiff international competition with the help of EXIM.

## REFERENCES

Alis, O.F., Karakurt, E. & Melli, P. (2000), *Data Mining for Database Marketing at Garanti Bank, Proceeding of the International Seminar "Data Mining 2000"*, WIT Publications.

Beckett-Camarata, E.J., Camarata, M.R., Barker, R.T., (1998), *Integrating Internal and External Customer Relationships Through Relationship Management: A Strategic Response to a Changing Global Environment, Journal of Business Research*, 41, 71-81.

Berry, M.J.A. & Linoff G.S. (2000), Mastering Data Mining: The Art and Science of Customer Relationship Management, John Wiley & Sons, Inc.

Cabena, P., Choi H.H., Kim I.S., Otsuka S., Reinschmidt J. & Saarenvirta G. (1999), Intelligent Miner for Data Applications Guide, IBM Redbooks, SG24-5252-00.

Cook, W.D., & Hababou, M., (2001), *Sales Performance Measurement in Bank Branches*, Omega, 29, 299 –307.

Couldwell, C., (1998), *A Data Day Battle, Computing*, 21 May, 64–66.

Hosking, J.R.M., Pednault, E. P. D. & Sudan, M. (1997), *A Statistical Perspective on Data Minin, Future Generation Computer Systems*, 13, 17-134.

Mihelis, G., Grigoroudis, E., Siskos, Y., Politis, Y. & Malandrakis, Y. (2001), *Customer Satisfaction Measurement in the Private Bank Sector, European Journal of Operational Research*, 347-360.

Peppard, J. (2000), *Customer Relationship Management (CRM) in Financial Services, European Management Journal*, Vol. 18, No. 3, pp. 312–327,

Peppers, D. & Rogers, M. (1995), *A New Marketing Paradigm, Planning Review*, 23(2), 14–18.

Ryals, L., & Knox, S. (2001), *Cross-Functional Issues in the Implementation of Relationship Marketing Through Customer Relationship Management, European Management Journal*, Vol. 19, No. 5, pp. 534–542.

Yli-Renko, H., Sapienza, H. J., Hay, M. (2001), *The Role of Contractual Governance Flexibility in Realizing the Outcomes of Key Customer Relationships, Journal of Business Venturing*, 16, 529–555.

Yuan, S.T., & Chang, W.L. (2001), *Mixed-Initiative Synthesized Learning Approach For Web-Based CRM, Expert Systems with Applications*, 20, 187-200.